PENGUIN BOOKS

LUTYENS AND THE EDWARDI

Jane Brown's first two books for Penguin were *Gardens of a Golden After-noon* (1982), the story of the partnership between Gertrude Jekyll and Edwin Lutyens, and *Vita's Other World* (1985), a gardening biography of V. Sackville-West. *Lutyens and the Edwardians: An English Architect and His Clients* completes this 'trilogy'. Her other books include *The English Garden in Our Time* (1986), *Lanning Roper and His Gardens* (1987), *Eminent Gardeners* (1989) and *Beatrix: The Gardening Life of Beatrix Jones Farrand, 1872–1959* (Viking, New York, 1995).

Jane Brown moved from south-east England to north Cambridgeshire in the summer of 1996, and she has lectured extensively in Britain and the United States.

JANE BROWN

LUTYENS AND THE EDWARDIANS

An English Architect and his Clients

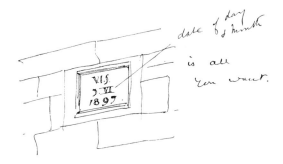

PENGUIN BOOKS

PENGUIN BOOKS

Published by the Penguin Group
Penguin Books Ltd, 27 Wrights Lane, London W8 5TZ, England
Penguin Books USA Inc., 375 Hudson Street, New York, New York 10014, USA
Penguin Books Australia Ltd, Ringwood, Victoria, Australia
Penguin Books Canada Ltd, 10 Alcorn Avenue, Toronto, Ontario, Canada M4V 3B2
Penguin Books (NZ) Ltd, 182–190 Wairau Road, Auckland 10, New Zealand

Penguin Books Ltd, Registered Offices: Harmondsworth, Middlesex, England

First published by Viking 1996
Published in Penguin Books 1997
1 3 5 7 9 10 8 6 4 2

The map on p. 18 was drawn by Reg and Marjorie Piggott
Frontispiece: Sir Edwin Lutyens and Lady Horner in the garden at Mells Manor, *c.*1939

Set in Monotype Van Dijck
Typeset by Selwood Systems, Midsomer Norton
Printed in Great Britain by Butler & Tanner Ltd, Frome, Somerset

Contents

List of Colour Illustrations

1. Edward Burne-Jones, *The Golden Stairs*, commissioned by Cyril Flower and painted in 1880 (*Trustees of the Tate Gallery*).
2–4. Milford House, the home of the Webb family, three of a series of watercolours painted by Augusta Webb in the 1920s (*Guildford Muniment Room*).
5. *A Bloomsbury Family* by William Orpen, 1907 (*Scottish National Gallery*).
6. The 'castle in the air' that Lutyens drew to entertain Barbara Webb (*RIBA Drawings Collection*).
7. Design for the drawing-room set for J. M. Barrie's *Quality Street*, produced at the Vaudeville Theatre, 1902 (*RIBAD*).
8. Title page from the Orchards Workbook, 1897 (*Geoffrey Robinson*); William and Julia Chance (*Sir Jeremy Chance*).
9. Lutyens's design for an entrance gate at Munstead Wood, 1892–3 (*RIBAD*).
10. Lutyens's design for the memorial to Edward Horner, Mells Church (*RIBAD*).
11. Reginald McKenna, as chairman of the Midland Bank, by James Gunn (*Midland Bank plc archives*).
12. Mrs Florence Phillips by Jean Boldini (*Municipal Gallery of Modern Art, Dublin*).
13. Lindisfarne Castle, which Lutyens renovated for Edward Hudson (*Photograph by author*).
14. Lindisfarne, the East Bedroom (*The National Trust*).
15. Jonathan and David Fenwick by Annie Swynnerton (*The Medici Society*).
16. (*Left*) Mrs Antonie Rosalie Merton, painted as a young woman by her first husband, Hermann Schmiechen (*Private collection*).
17. (*Right*) Zackary Merton, by an unknown artist (*Private collection*).
18. Folly Farm in recent years (*Photograph by author*).
19. The partners of Barings Bank by Ambrose McEvoy (*Baring Bros & Co Ltd*).
20. Archery at Lambay, detail from a fresco painted by Cecil and Maude Baring's daughter Daphne (*Mrs Philip Jebb*).
21. Alice, Viscountess Wimborne by Sir John Lavery, 1937 (*Colnaghi, London and New York*).
22. Lutyens's designs for Captain Day's house, 1919. (*RIBAD*)
23. Lutyens's memorial tablet to William Congreve VC (*Photograph by author*).
24. Doorway from Papillon Hall, Leicestershire (*Photograph by author*).
25. A rare surviving example of Lutyens's barns, Marsh Court, Stockbridge (*Photograph by author*).
26. Watercolour plan and elevation by Harold Stevens of Lutyens's cottages, Ashby St Ledgers, Northamptonshire (*The Modern Home*, ed. W. S. Sparrow).

Acknowledgements

Everything that Sir Edwin Lutyens built has developed a history of its own, and the families of his clients and the criss-crossing of their relationships offer an endlessly fascinating saga (confirming fact to be much more amazing than fiction) to a curious author. I have discovered stories enough to fill ten volumes and I am very sorry that so much could not be included in one. I am grateful to all the authors I have quoted and for the use of the illustrations; both are credited in detail on other pages. Here I extend my gratitude to those who have helped me with *Lutyens and the Edwardians*: my first thanks, for permission to use family papers and for constant help, are to Mary Lutyens, Clayre Percy, Jane Ridley and Charles Lutyens. Second, my thanks for indispensable guidance go to Margaret Richardson, to Jill Lever, then Curator, Neil Bingham and the staff of the RIBA Drawings Collection, to the RIBA Library and to the Librarian and staff of the London Library. My remaining thanks are grouped according to the text:

For help with the Surrey clients, Douglas Q. Watson and other Thursley residents, John Flower, Marion May and the Shamley Green Local History Society, Douglas Moeller at Chinthurst Hill, David Coombs, Michael and Frances Edwards, the Hon. Mrs Lavinia Fleming, Mrs E. M. Goschen, Mrs Handa Bray, Michael Hanson, Mrs Anthea Gilmore, the late Ronald Chapman, Godalming Museum, Roderick Gradidge, Faith Robinson, Mary Mackey and the staff at Guildford Muniment Room, Mathew Alexander of Guildford Museum, Guildford Public Library, Mrs Edna M. Thompson and Joan Esch, the author of a biography of Mary Watts.

For help with more Surrey clients and others, my thanks to Lady Adam Gordon, Michael and Caroline Mitchell of the Libanus Press, Mr John Chuter and Frensham Local History Society, the present owners of Hazlehatch, Harry Spencer ARIBA, Miss Rosemary Rendel, Mrs R. B. Curteis, Russell Morris, Margaret and Julian Hastings, Lynne Amidon and the Royal Free Hospital Archives, Bruce A. Bailey, Archivist to the Althorp Estate, and Richard Jackson, the present owner of Beatrice Webb House (Pasturewood). Here I must also record formal thanks to my fellow trustees of the Lutyens Trust for allowing me to use material I gathered about Goddards while I was acting administrator there, 1992–3.

For material about the Fenwick families, my thanks to Benedict Fenwick,

Sebastian Fenwick, Lavinia Orde, Cynthia Carnegie and my friends at Princess Helena College (Temple Dinsley).

For the Blackburn connections – Richard Pennington, Clare Topley, Hilary Richardson (née Blackburn) and Tim and Pauline Ractliff at Little Thakeham.

In Hertfordshire I am grateful to Barbara Oakley, Hermione, Lady Cobbold and Clare Fleck, Keeper of the Knebworth Archive. For my visits to Cambridge and East Anglia, my thanks to Diane Haigh and William Fawcett, to the present owners of Middlefield, John Rollo, Sir Francis Pemberton, Charles Morris and his family, and to Jack Whitehead for his research on Woolverstone.

In Ireland my very special thanks to all who made my visit so wonderful – Mrs Ida Grehan Dover, Harold Clarke, Barbara Dawson, Terry Trench, Nicola Gordon Bowe and Father Seamus Cummins SDB, who has looked after Heywood garden for many years and has now handed it into the care of the Board of Works.

I am deeply grateful to the following people for help with their particular client connections: Dr John Orbell and Mrs Philip Jebb (Barings), Mr and Mrs David McKenna and Edwin Green, Archivist to the Midland Bank, the Earl of Oxford and Asquith (Mells), Mrs Ursula Weaver and Giles Weaver (Grey Walls), Mrs Shirley Corke and Mr H. Robertson (Farrers), Mrs Bea Broad (The Dormy House) and Robbie James (Walton Heath Golf Club) and Robin Marsh (the Golf Club and Walton on the Hill and District Local History Society). English history made on the greens and fairways at Walton Heath is certainly worth a book in itself!

If one trail has been more fascinating than all the rest it is because moments of real contact with this vanished era have come from my meetings with Liza Banks, the daughter of Sir William Nicholson and Edith Stuart-Wortley (née Phillips) and thus the grand-daughter of the remarkable Florrie Phillips. For these moments and for lending me Thelma Gutsche's marvellous book on her grandmother, my very special gratitude to Mrs Banks. But also to Andrew Nicholson, Tim Nicholson, the William Nicholson Trust, and to Patricia Reed, whose research on her Nicholson *catalogue raisonné* coincided with mine and led us to Professor Patrick Merton (via Mary Lutyens and Mr Colin Merton) and to Mrs I. C. Kelly and Mrs H. Gething of the Theosophical Society and the unravelling of some of the mystery of Folly Farm.

And then, of course, there is the other Nicolson connection (without the *h*): at the outset Nigel Nicolson agreed that *his* grandmother would need a whole chapter – well, here it is (though it could have been twice as long), and my thanks to him for all his generosity and help. Also to Peter Miall, for arranging explorations in Sussex and Kent.

For the later chapters my thanks to Hugh Meller and Patrick Harris (Castle Drogo), to Hugh Petter and Robert Adam (Rome), to Jillian Carman (Johannesburg Art Gallery), to Alexander Hoare, Bertram Hoare and Dan Marrows of RMJM (Daneshill Brickworks Office, now Lutyens House, Kingsland Business Park, Basingstoke), to Dan and Anthea O'Neill (whose material on the National Theatre I never had time to see!), to the Grange and Rottingdean Preservation Society, to Philip Endean SJ and Father Vincent Bywaters SJ at Campion Hall, to Patrick and Caroline Taylor in Wells and to Michael McGarvie for his history of Mells Park, to Stephen Green, Librarian of the MCC at Lords, to J. P. Marix-Evans for his researches on the Flowers at Great Tangley, to Sunita Kohli (for the copy of *Rashtrapati Bhavan*) and to Jill O'Grady and the Friends of Ashby St Ledgers' Church of St Leodegarius for an inspiring patronal festival service on 1 October 1994.

My final thanks go to all those associated with the production of *Lutyens and the Edwardians* but particularly to Annie Lee, my copy-editor, and to my editor, Eleo Gordon, whose enthusiasm and hard work have kept me going.

Jane Brown,
Dogmersfield, 1996

ILLUSTRATION ACKNOWLEDGEMENTS

The author and publishers are grateful to the following for permission to reproduce illustrations: Mary Lutyens, 4 (left), 10, 31, 85, 181; C. B. Lutyens, 4 (right); David McKenna, 134, 215; The Earl of Oxford and Asquith, ii, xii, 108, 173, 174, 218, 221, 226, 227; Mrs Philip Jebb, 101, 102; Mrs Lavinia Orde, 72, 75 (top), 76; Nigel Nicolson, 193, 195, 198, 200, 201, 205, 210; Mrs Hugh Astor, 181; Colin Smythe, 56; Christopher Lloyd, 139; Sebastian Nohl, 27; Mrs O. Robinson, 39, 40, 43; Geoffrey Robinson, 33 (top left), 33 (bottom), 34, 36 (top); Giles Weaver, 112, 124; Mrs Elizabeth Curteis, 49 (bottom); Dr Jane Ridley, 171 (right); Mrs Bea Broad, 122 (top); The Hon. Mrs Lavinia Fleming, 49 (top); Mrs Desmond Banks and the Sir William Nicholson Trust, 170, 177 (right), 183, 185, 186, 187; Richard Pennington (Blackburn Family Albums), 82 (top), 119; Lady Adam Gordon/The Lutyens Trust, 64 (bottom), 70; Knebworth Estate Archives, 89, 91, 92, 94, 127; The Grange/Rottingdean Preservation Society, 179 (right); Museum of Eton Life, Eton College, 188; National Portrait Gallery, Scotland, 177 (left); RIBA Drawings Collection, 16 (top), 23, 24, 57, 142, 178; Johannesburg Art Gallery, 152; Hugh Lane Municipal Gallery of Modern Art, Dublin, 147, 156, 157; Surrey Local Studies Library, Guildford, 20; Surrey County Council Archives, Guildford Muniment Room, 14, 51, 52, 53; Illustrated London News, 141; The National Trust, 116, 234, 236; National Portrait Gallery, London, 96, 111; Commonwealth War Graves Commission, 165, 169; Imperial War Museum, 168, 229; Documents Collection, College of Environmental Design, University of California, Berkeley, 35 (bottom); British School at Rome/Hugh Petter, 161; Northamptonshire County Council, 179 (left); Mail Newspapers Plc, 171 (left); Gertrude Jekyll and Christopher Hussey, *Garden Ornament* 33 (top right), 75, 82 (bottom), 117, 128; Randolph Caldicott's *Picture Book No. 1*, 6; Stephen Calloway, *Twentieth Century Decoration*, 182; Jane Brown/Libanus Press, *Fulbrook*, iii, 64 (top), 66, 68, 71, 87; Jane Brown, 16 (centre and bottom), 19, 41, 47, 90, 122, (bottom) 182, 198, 199, 209, 219, 242, 254.

Foreword

In *Country Life* of 8 May 1915 there appeared a half-page tribute to mark the death of the architect Philip Webb by 'E.L.Lutyens RA'. It was extremely rare for Edwin Lutyens to venture into print, for he deeply distrusted words and those who wielded them, but Webb was one of his heroes, so he made a special effort. After some memories and mild analysis of Webb's architectural thoroughness, comes an inconsequentially ringing outburst: 'There will never be great architects or architecture without great patrons.'

It came from Lutyens's own heart; for a moment he sensed the power of despised words, and thrust onwards on the subject of patrons: 'Webb was fortunate in these, and to their honour they gave him scope for his genius. He had the courage to refuse work which he felt to be incompatible with his ideals, and withstood what he must have considered ignoble in the modern world.'[1]

It was a secret of Edwin Lutyens's heart that he coveted Philip Webb's unworldliness. Webb, the 'consistently retiring and self-contained', of whose work little was written, wrote to one of his patrons, Percy Wyndham: 'I do not lay myself out to do work for people who do not in any degree want what I could honestly do for them.'[2] He was about to build 'the house of the age', Clouds in Wiltshire, for the Wyndhams, but otherwise, in forty years he accomplished some sixty buildings, living and working in modest harmony with his socialist principles.

Edwin Lutyens could not have been more different. From his earliest beginnings as an architect, before he was twenty, he never refused work; he was always chasing 'jobs' and invariably compromising with the influences of the world he seemed forced to inhabit. In his working life, from 1889 until 1943 (he died on New Year's Day 1944), he amassed something like 550 commissions, which are almost impossible to quantify because they range from cottages and tombs to the former Viceroy's House (now Rashtrapati Bhavan) in New Delhi. Edwin Lutyens paid for his genius with a soft heart and weak spirit, and his lot was to be seemingly buffeted by fate. His career still has meaning because he inhabited a very real world of vexations and terrors, as opposed to Philip Webb's ascetic earthly paradise.

In that spring of 1915, when Lutyens wrote of Webb's courage and the honour of his patrons, the circumstances might suggest ulterior motives. Lutyens was forty-six, and undoubtedly the most fashionable country house architect of his day, yet he knew that his own 'great patrons' were slipping away and he was to be mired in the tribulations of building commissions and committees. His fame, polished by the publication of Lawrence Weaver's monograph *Houses and Gardens by E. L. Lutyens* in 1913, and acknowledged by the commission for New Delhi and his election to the Royal Academy, was miserably tainted. He hated the prospect of spending one-third of every year far from home, as a kind of part-time Indian Civil Servant, yet he needed the money, and had little of a home life of his own. His family, Lady Emily and their five children, of whom Barbara, the eldest, was sixteen, occupied a large and expensive house in Bedford Square, which they all disliked (except for the six-year-old Mary); Lady Emily, acknowledging her own unworldliness and socialism, was immersed in theosophy, and Lutyens's children regarded him alternately as ogre or clown.

In that spring of 1915, too, the casualty lists from Gallipoli and Ypres had finally convinced the English at home that the war was no chivalric skirmish. Lutyens had known from the very start that for him, and for architecture, the war would be an unmitigated disaster: he could not have known that in after years his cry that 'there will never be great architects or architecture without great patrons' would seem to echo from that May of 1915 as from the rim of the abyss.

For at the same moment as those words were being read, as the pages of that issue of *Country Life* were turned in the drawing-rooms of England, one particular casualty, the seriously wounded Lieutenant Edward Horner, was being carried up the line to hospital in Boulogne. Edward Horner was the son and heir of Sir John and Lady Horner at Mells, and Lady Horner was one of Lutyens's most influential patrons and friends. The privileged treatment that his family and friends demanded for Edward (soon to be out of the question) allowed him to recover from his wounds and return to the fray. Just two and a half years later Edward Horner was killed, on 21 November 1917, in the Battle of Cambrai.

In that brief interlude of borrowed time, the Horners' ancestral home, Mells Park, was gutted by fire. For Edward, 'so ancestral' himself, with 'a great inborn sense of beauty', an extravagant vitality and 'intense natural gusto', the fire was a disaster, to be overcome on his return home.[3] In a letter to Lady Diana Manners, who might have been the new chatelaine of Mells, Patrick Shaw Stewart imagined the Horner family's impending financial ruin as Edward rebuilt, 'seizing the opportunity to put in a pink marble staircase on the Dorchester House scale with platignum fittings'.[4] It may not have been *pink* marble, nor platignum, but the architect would have been Edwin Lutyens. Except that now Edward would never come home to rebuild.

Edward Horner symbolizes all the great patrons that Lutyens was never to

Edward Horner

find. After the war it was his architect's lot to work for endless, patient hours, comforting so many of his patrons, who were also his friends, and memorializing their losses. Once started, the memorials became a stream; they mingled into tombstones for clients and contemporaries, and the elemental quality of sadness enshrined in stone tinged all his other buildings, though this was not really desirable in the post-war world. There was no brave new beginning in the 1920s for Edwin Lutyens. He felt that his profession had failed him, that patronage as he wished it had died, and his income evaporated; there were occasional lavish consultancy fees, but more often an overdraft in excess of £200,000 in today's equivalent value.[5] Half his commissions were for memorials and tombs, including the Cenotaph and the Thiepval Arch on the Somme, in addition to 126 war cemeteries. Of his other buildings, city edifices and a few houses, almost all were built for patrons he had known before the war. His only building in Oxford, Campion Hall, was directly connected with the sadness at Mells, and the memorials inspired the commission for his Cathedral in Liverpool, the work which dominated the last decade of his life, but which was never to be built.

Though Lutyens was a child during the reign of Queen Victoria, and he outlived George V, whom he served so well, into the reign of George VI, he was, as Osbert Sitwell defined him, 'in the same way that I should classify Elgar, as essentially an Edwardian; that decade of freedom and prosperity was most surely his home'.[6] His patrons belong there too; this book is devoted to them, who they were, why they built, what they built and what they paid for their buildings, for they allowed Edwin Lutyens his dearest dream.

I

DREAMS OF PALACES
ETCETERA

I am still charged with the old complaint of singing in the early hours
when I can prove that I was in bed (asleep). Perhaps I dream of palaces
etc. and trumpet in my joy . . .

(EDWIN LUTYENS, aged sixteen, to his mother, 1885)[1]

It is impossible to teach an architect how to meet his patrons; it has always been a matter of chance and a favourable wind. Christopher Wren, 'that miracle of a youth', was thirty-one and a professor of astronomy before his Oxford colleagues presented him with a constructional problem on the Sheldonian Theatre. Sir John Vanbrugh, the dramatist, found lordly builders among his fellows at the Kit-cat Club. Victorians passed the flame through nepotistic dynasties, the Waterhouses, Scotts, Barrys, Pugins and Wyatts. Pure chance sent a local doctor's son, Philip Webb, into George Edmund Street's temporary Oxford office, with a fellow pupil, William Morris, who was to be his first patron. Richard Norman Shaw, in Street's office after Webb, so brilliantly marketed 'Old English' (by mixing Streetian Gothic with farmhouse vernacular'[2] and 'Queen Anne' (from builders' classical of Georgian country towns) that he was overwhelmed with newly-rich, artistically inclined middle-class clients. The floodgates thus opened still left a gulf between the young architect and would-be patrons. It was crossed in many ways. Detmar Blow flourished after a romantic friendship with Pamela Wyndham, who married Edward Tennant. Herbert Baker had only to meet one man, Cecil Rhodes, at his first dinner party on arriving in South Africa, for his future to be assured. M. H. Baillie Scott was meant by his father to manage a sheep farm in Australia, but persevered in the Isle of Man, making his name and graduating southwards to London. Halsey Ricardo married Lord Rendel's daughter and through the Rendel engineering contracts in India he built Calcutta station. Charles Holden came from obscure beginnings and took a job with H. Percy Adams's hospital practice, which led him to his greatest patron, the London Underground's Frank Pick.

Edwin Lutyens, who came from further back in education and opportunity than most of these, forged his way towards his chosen profession with the instinct of a baby turtle making for the sea. He seemed to discard most of his birthright in the process.

Edwin Landseer Lutyens was born on a Monday, 29 March 1869, at 16 Onslow Square, South Kensington. He was the tenth child and ninth boy of Mary Theresa, née Gallwey, and Charles Henry Augustus Lutyens, a portrait painter. Their eldest child, Charles Benjamin, was sixteen, a schoolboy at Winchester, and seven other sons had tumbled and laughed their way through life (the Lutyens genes are persistently cheerful ones) until a beloved first daughter, Molly, had preceded Edwin by a year. Another, Aileen, was to follow him.[3]

The baby's first asset might seem to have been his name. It is such an unusual surname that it is always noticed, though easily stumbled over: it is pronounced with the *Lut* rhyming with *hut*. It comes from the Dutch Lütkens, actually a Dutch barber who came to England via Hamburg in the early eighteenth century and begat a vigorous clan, predominantly soldiers.[4] Charles Henry Augustus Lutyens had an adventurous career as a Royal Artillery officer with a passion for hunting before he gave up the army to become a professional painter, in the late 1850s. The year of Edwin's birth, 1869, was the year of one of his best paintings, known as *Three Race-horses* — an alarmingly vivid, snorting, sneering close-up of a tight finish. The canvas is almost filled with the gleaming bodies of the horses at full stretch, with a crowd in the background, made up of about thirty figures who are recognizably the painter's family and clients. *Three Racehorses* was painted for Sir William Miller of Manderston in Berwickshire, and some three years earlier Charles Lutyens had painted the Miller children garlanding their St Bernard dog, 'Lion', with flowers for his birthday. 'Lion' himself was painted by the greatest animal artist of the time, Edwin Landseer.[5] This is the most certain connection between Landseer and Charles Lutyens, to support the family tradition that they were friends and that Landseer helped Charles Lutyens in his career. The evidence from the Landseer literature is that he wasn't given to warm friendships with other painters and hated taking pupils, but possibly Charles's introduction to Manderston and the value of Sir William's patronage was sufficient, along with the subsequent triumph of *Three Racehorses*, for Charles to name his new baby son for Landseer, who agreed to be his godfather.

There is another family story[6] that Landseer wanted to adopt his godson, but that his mother, Mary Lutyens, would not allow this. The great painter was already well into his decline, a mix of alcoholism and fits of despair that bordered upon insanity, which hastened him to his death before his godson was five. ('A merciful release', said Queen Victoria.[7]) Poor Landseer, lonely, and in a sentimental moment, may have seen the young life as a sign of hope (he had children, a son and daughter, by Georgiana, Duchess of Bedford, but they were unacknowledged at the time), and if the baby had been taken off to the care of the Misses Landseer, his sisters, perhaps he might well have inherited the painter's considerable fortune. But Edwin Landseer Lutyens stayed with his proper family, who always called him Ned, and even when he grew up he seemed consciously to avoid revealing his distinguished middle name. He never used it, and he only rarely used 'Edwin' in his signature and on his notepaper and drawings. No one actually called him 'Edwin' until they called him 'Sir Edwin', and he is often wrongly referred to as Edward – perhaps because, as Lady Diana Cooper thought of Edwin Montagu, Edwin is 'a difficult name'. And the 'Landseer' was hardly given a second's thought until people began to write books about him. It seems his first two names were largely dispensed with – for simplicity, because everyone had so much trouble with his surname, or because he wished to succeed on his own?

Mary Lutyens, his mother, having 'saved' her baby from Landseer, undoubtedly saved his life by nursing and praying him through childhood rheumatic fever. The illness cut short his schooling after about two years, and left him a weak and nervous child among an exuberant and athletic brood. Many years later Osbert Sitwell was to ask him if any other members of his family shared his genius. 'No . . .,' Lutyens replied, 'any talent I have was due to a long illness as a boy, which afforded me time to think, and to subsequent ill health, because I was not allowed to play games, and had to teach myself, for my enjoyment, to use my eyes instead of my feet.'[8]

The 'turning point' in this blighted young life was also brought about by his mother, who was instrumental in the family's move to the country. In the late 1870s, at about the time of Ned's eighth birthday, Mary Lutyens persuaded Charles to rent a rambling Georgian house in the centre of the small village of Thursley, among the sandy heather lands of deepest south-west Surrey. Charles Lutyens had recently painted Francis Scott, the Master of the Surrey Union Hunt, and this connection, and the prospect of some hunting for himself and the older boys, also played a part in the move.[9] The Lutyens home, known as The Cottage, had a small garden, a large yard of stables and barns, and was just across the road from the cricket green; most of the Lutyens boys would be found, at holiday times, around the stables or playing cricket – except for Ned, who was terrified of horses and never rode. In his secret heart, however, he loved cricket and longed to play; because of his weakness and in awe of his brothers' prowess, he rarely did. For most of the rest of his life he was easily led into a game on the lawn with a client's children, and ready with a present of a new cricket ball.

Edwin Lutyens's mother, Mary, in middle age. Charles Lutyens the painter, a self-portrait – or possibly by his son Frederick, also a professional painter.

The Thursley of Ned Lutyens's childhood was an isolated village. Just to the east the coaches on the London to Portsmouth road drove at full pelt across the bleak Hindhead Common, and out from the village, in every direction, stretched the sandy tracks across acres of heather and gorse. It was a good three miles to Elstead or Tilford, the old villages in the Wey valley, a little farther to Frensham in the west, and about the same eastwards to Witley and Milford, both with stations on the London & South Western Railway line to Guildford and London. In the 1820s William Cobbett frequently stopped at Thursley on his rides; it was a day's journey from Selborne in Hampshire and it took him another day travelling east to reach Reigate. Cobbett thought Thursley and its surroundings were pretty, and he noted the local people as 'happy as if all were young and all just going to be married' at the prospect of a visit from Mr Wyndham's foxhounds, which excited and absorbed them all.[10] In Ned Lutyens's youth, fifty years on, the railway may have been new, but little else had changed; Thursley life revolved around hunting and cricket.

Of his childhood years at Thursley, Lutyens's daughter Mary has written, 'I can believe that my father was a very happy child ... I have enough of him in me to know the joy of wandering by myself as a child through woods and along lanes for hours on end "imagining" and never being bored.'[11] As the son of a painter, it was only natural for Ned to draw; he watched his father set out, his long legs

4

dangling each side of his fat white pony, the clutter of easel, paints and stool about his shoulders. Ned, on his feet, but later on his bicycle, travelled lightly, with just a piece of clear glass and a pencil of sharpened soap for his sketching. His father portrayed his neighbours' horses and dogs, and increasingly the landscape; Ned drew buildings … for, as his daughter Mary has also observed, 'Surrey cottages were his first love, cottages that nestled and fitted the lives of those who lived in them and fitted also the English climate and landscape.'[12] This picturesqueness was already being turned into legend by professional artists like H. Birkett Foster and Helen Allingham, who both lived at Witley, but there was also much new building going on, simply because the artists made the countryside fashionable. On wet days, or when he tired of wandering, Ned Lutyens haunted the builders' and carpenters' yards and sites: 'He was intensely inquisitive about the few things that really interested him, and he had a remarkably quick eye and a phenomenal memory for detail.'[13] With all this, and some coaching in mathematics from his brother Fred, his future seemed inevitable: 'I believe,' writes his daughter Mary, 'that he *had* to become an architect – one cannot think of any other art at which he would have excelled.'[14]

Having formulated an idea of his future, the isolated prettiness of Thursley must have become claustrophobic. Idly observing 'the chop and rush of the trowel', the 'fat popping of the slaking lime', and the deft carpenter's plane giving out a 'long fragrant ribbon of shaving', relished by Gertrude Jekyll,[15] certainly instilled a feeling for materials in him, but brought him no nearer the profession of architecture. His family knew no architects, the London offices were remote, and there was little money to spare for the architectural papers. Ned seems to have had to make do with the architectural competitions in *Boys' Own Paper*.

An early hero was Randolph Caldecott, the Manchester bank clerk who had become the most famous children's illustrator, the 'Lord of the Nursery'. Caldecott was a well-known figure of Ned's childhood countryside, famous for his plum-coloured velvet coat, worn hunting with Mr Combe's harriers from Pierrepont or the Chiddingfold hounds. Caldecott often drew a peculiar round-ended building easily identified as the old Pierrepont Home Farm, and his 'Three Jovial Huntsmen' cavort across this countryside. The 'gruntin', grindin' grindlestone' (or was it 'an owd fossil cheese'?) bowled after them will find a place in Ned Lutyens's gardens for ever afterwards.

His first encounter with a real architect was when he was fourteen, in 1883, when J. W. Penfold came to Thursley to restore St Michael's church. Having spent a great deal of his time in church, forced through boredom to study the braces, ties and beams of the vast timbers that supported St Michael's roof, imprinting

They hunted, an' they hollo'd, an' the
   next thing they did find
Was a gruntin', grindin' grindlestone,
   an' that they left behind.
One said it was a grindlestone, another
   he said 'Nay,
It's nought but an owd fossil cheese,
   that somebody's roll't away.'

From Randolph Caldecott's *Picture
Book No. 1* – drawn from his
experience of hunting around
Frensham and Thursley. A 'gruntin',
'grindin' grindlestone', and often
more than one, found a place in
every Lutyens garden.

their dimensions on his memory, he naturally felt confident in drawing his own scheme.[16] Mr Penfold's reactions are not recorded.

Whenever Ned wandered or cycled out across the Thursley heath to the west there would loom on his horizon the chimneys of Pierrepont, the house Shaw had built for Richard Henry Combe, and it was little wonder that if the young Lutyens had a real architectural hero it was Richard Norman Shaw. Shaw, unwittingly, and Charles Lutyens, carelessly (for he seemed to have run out of sympathy with his children's dreams by the time it got down to Ned) were responsible for his escape from rural obscurity.

Besides the Combes at Pierrepont, Shaw had another long-standing client locally, a wealthy widow, Mrs Ellinor Guthrie, at Upper House, Shamley Green. He had enlarged Upper House twice for Mrs Guthrie and her family, the second time for her remarriage to an old flame, Forster Arbuthnot. In 1883 Charles Lutyens had painted one of her daughters with a pet dog for £25.[17] It was Arbuthnot who had 'discovered' Charles Lutyens, the picturesque 'old bohemian', probably at a meet of the local hounds; Arbuthnot was kindly and commissioned more paintings; it was on painting visits that Charles Lutyens mentioned his son's architectural obsession, and it was suggested that Ned be brought over to Upper House to meet Shaw.

The meeting was recorded by the nineteen-year-old Violet Guthrie, who was present. It was early in 1885; Ned, smartened up specially in largely borrowed clothes and boots, was presented to the great man, who 'looked askance' at the boy who had the temerity to suggest amendments to his drawings. Ned, consumed with nervousness, gabbled on about his experiments with wooden-framed buildings and heather-thatched roofs which harmonized with Nature – 'materials should be drawn from those obtainable in the area and foreign elements strictly eliminated'. 'Very interesting,' replied the kindly Shaw, 'but human beings demand something a little more in keeping with the age in which we live': the newly-rich, who were his own clients, demanded 'replicas of something they have seen in other countries they have visited'.[18] Shaw must have wondered where the confused but impudent youth had come from, he was so far removed from the polished and well-educated young men who were his pupils. The encounter had slipped his mind by the time he reached Guildford station.

The Arbuthnots continued to encourage Ned, and little wooden buildings with heather-thatched roofs found their way into the gardens of their friends; they still remain in the garden of Ellinor's cousin, Harry Mangles. They championed his cause and persuaded Charles Lutyens that his eccentric son should go to London for some formal education – they may even have paid his fees. Edwin Lutyens was sent to the South Kensington School of Art to study architecture in early 1885, just before his sixteenth birthday, soon after the meeting with Shaw.

Violet Guthrie added to her picture of him, remembering how, when the pent-up tensions of his interview with Shaw were over, Ned was released into a hilarious impersonation of Queen Victoria, as 'with puffed-out cheeks, a scrap of anti-macassar on his head, a slightly German accent', he mimicked risqué conversation with John Brown.[19] For such entertainments and for his undoubted talents they forgave him his less attractive 'bumptiousness' and ingratiating manner when he was eliciting a job. These, mixed with a very real, though uncharacteristic, bitterness about his lack of an education, were the legacy of his near-suffocation in the crowded rusticity of his Thursley home, where he was so little understood. Once he had glimpsed the stimulating world he wished to reach – both through the company at Upper House and then at South Kensington – he recoiled from that chaos and withdrew from any closeness with his family, except his mother, long before he left them in reality. A letter to his mother, written just after he had started at South Kensington, reveals at great length (ten pages) his need to bolster his own self-confidence in his knowledge of buildings, and to assert this sphere as his own. His father, like so many fathers, gave his son little credit, and so Ned firmly and respectfully asserted proof of *his* being right and his father wrong over an argument about the terra cotta panels at Sutton Place.[20] He blamed his father a good deal for his bad start, and as he moved into his working life he gave many people, including the young Emily Lytton, the impression that he was an only child and that his mother was a widow.

In her *Memoir* Mary Lutyens writes that her father did not finish his course at South Kensington because he believed that they had nothing more to teach him.[21] Not surprisingly, he would have liked to have been a pupil in Shaw's office, but the waiting list was too long, so he went to Sir Ernest George, some time after his eighteenth birthday, and probably in the autumn of 1887. There, as Herbert Baker later recorded, he puzzled them at first, '. . . but we soon found that he seemed to know by intuition some great truths of our art which were not to be learned there'.[22]

Lutyens struck up a friendship with Herbert Baker, who was chief assistant and seven years his senior. In the autumn of 1888 they went sketching together – a rare and much-remembered trip for Lutyens, just another sketching trip for Baker, and the comparison between them is stark. Baker, like Lutyens, came from a large family, but he was nearer to the top than the bottom; he was brought up in gracious and orderly comfort in a lovely Jacobean house, Owletts, near Cobham in Kent, which his grandfather had inherited by marriage. His father, Thomas H. Baker JP, had constantly enlarged the house for his growing family. Herbert Baker was well educated – he was captain of cricket at Tonbridge and went on to Oxford, where he won a rowing blue. While Ned Lutyens was still cycling the Surrey lanes, Baker was articled to his uncle, A. H. Baker, a church architect based in London, and they spent much time working on a church in Caernarvon – both uncle and nephew were made honorary architects to the Cambrian Academy of Arts for their work.

Lutyens must have enjoyed George's office, because there were lots of jokes and impersonations, the expressions of his more relaxed self; but there was also the underlying iron determination to take what he could, and stay no longer. Margaret Richardson has observed that Lutyens actually learned a lot. There was George's personal style of perspective drawing, with a soft sepia pen-and-wash technique 'well suited to conveying natural textures . . . and above all, giving the effect of a building well rooted in the countryside'. George also angled his sketching viewpoint from low down, a stance which Lutyens immediately adopted, calling it 'a worm's eye view'. George had published designs for small houses and cottages, 'ready prototypes' which Lutyens adopted for his first small buildings.[23]

His first adaptation of a George design appeared in Thursley, for his first recorded paying client, a Mr Edmund Gray, for whom he converted a shop and cottage into The Corner, in the year he set up on his own, 1889. He added a large tile-hung wing to the back of the building, which bears a strong resemblance to a cottage at Harpenden in Hertfordshire by Ernest George, illustrated in *The Architect* of 1 June 1888 and exhibited in the Royal Academy that year.[24] Edmund Gray was the tenant of The Corner, with his sister, and the work was done at his expense by the owner of the property, W. Fosberry, a Thursley builder. It was probably Ned's 'ingratiating' to Fosberry, for the job, that Violet Guthrie so deplored.

Apart from this small job, he set up on his own in 1889 armed with a legacy from Miss Landseer of £100 (he later commented, 'I wonder if it is a good thing to give a boy a sum to start him – a fixed sum with no chance of more'[25] – it was something like £3,000 in our present understanding) and a commission, his first truly serious one, from Ellinor Arbuthnot's cousin Agnes and her husband Arthur Chapman, for a gentleman's cottage on land they had bought at Crooksbury Hill, between Elstead and Farnham.

It could almost be a motto for this book that it takes two to make a commission; as in other milestones of life, the voice that sows the seed of an idea usually needs support, before a reasoning human brain is confident enough to take action. However persuasive the architect, the building of a house, or any substantial building, is a major step in anyone's life. So Ned Lutyens needed support from a direction other than the kind but busy and sociable Arbuthnots, to forward his cause. She had, indeed, been present since his first wonderful year of achievement, 1885, the year he broke free, and she had been part of that wonderful year, probably introduced to him by Ellinor Arbuthnot. She was now to take her place as his guiding star – she had already asked the Arthur Chapmans, who were her friends too, to keep an eye on him while he was in London, she had had a hand in arranging for him to go to her friends the Stanleys at Wenlock Abbey on his sketching trip with Herbert Baker, and now that he needed jobs in Surrey she could do much more. This very important angel in Ned Lutyens's life needs a proper introduction.

BARBARA WEBB

A strange alchemy brought Barbara Webb into the young Lutyens's life. She arrived from far away, at the moment he needed her, and she was allowed to remain until just before his marriage to Emily Lytton. For just twelve years she was his patron saint; she loved him for all his irrepressibility and awful jokes, and for his talents, in the way of a woman who has no child of her own on which to fasten her hopes and second chances. She found him very like herself, and was determined that he

Left: Barbara Lyall: she was intelligent, outspoken and intolerant of pomposity. Under some pressure from her family, she married the widower Robert Webb of Milford in 1885 when she was forty. She died of cancer in July 1897.
Right: Edwin Lutyens about the time he started as an architect, *c.* 1891.

would win battles which she had lost. He was more than a little in love with her, he called her 'blessed Barbara', his baa-lamb. What was so strange, passing strange, was that she watched him fall in love with the child of the man that she had loved. There was a kind of reparation there, but not of her planning.

Barbara made her début as Mrs Robert Webb, wife of the foxhunting squire of Milford, immediately after the young Lutyens's meeting with Shaw at the Arbuthnots' home, and his celebrated performance as Queen Victoria with an antimacassar on his head. This was just the kind of thing she loved, and to hear of him must have lightened her dread of the stuffiness of the country society where she was now expected to preside. Robert Webb's first wife, Catherine, dearly loved at Milford, had died in 1883. He had married Barbara in the New Year of 1885; he was in his fifty-fourth year, she was forty. How she had come to Milford is the story of her life.

Barbara was born in 1845 at her father's rectory at Godmersham in Kent. She was the baby of the Lyall family; her three brothers were all to become distinguished Indian administrators, and her sisters were to make good marriages. Enchanting Godmersham, then little changed from Jane Austen's day, cast a nostalgic spell over her brothers and sisters, and Barbara's first deprivation was that she was born too late to spend much time there. Her upbringing was at less lovely Harbledown, just west of Canterbury, from where she watched her siblings leave for their dutiful and dedicated lives. Surrounded by elderly parents and so much earnestness, she grew up to be mischievous, noted for her spirited refusal to take things too seriously, seeing the funny side of serious situations, rejecting the intimidation of pompous people, of whom there were so many. She was highly intelligent and consequently bored; she was certainly always thought to be most like her cleverest and most brilliant brother, Alfred, whom she worshipped. She was sixteen when he came home on his first furlough from India, and they spent most of a glorious year in constant companionship – with the proviso that at the end of his leave Alfred returned to India accompanied by his new wife, Clara Cloete, a stalwartly capable foil for his sensitivities, and a complete opposite to both Barbara and himself.

Barbara's life can be glimpsed only through her brother's surviving letters, so it is fortunate that Alfred Lyall had a particularly strong need for close contacts with home to bolster his 'exile' in India. Their mother had fallen very short of his requirements, but now Barbara fulfilled them abundantly, perhaps too abundantly for her own good. She became a kind of feminine echo of Alfred's private self, she shared his poetic aspirations, fetched and carried to publishers and bookshops for him, learned the political and literary gossip of London so that she could relay it to him: in return, he filled her with stories of India, of the wonderful (and often dangerous) life that he loved, of the people and their easy friendships and genuine hospitality, so superior to the 'horribly frigid and formal' over-civilization of England which he scorned. Lyall was an attractive personality, and a brilliant Indian civil servant at every rank except Viceroy (his one disappointment), but it seems probable that his ability was vastly supported by Barbara's indulgence and understanding for his liberal and artistic tendencies, which would only have clouded his official judgements.[26]

After her father's death in 1865 Barbara was to be her mother's companion, and it was only after Mrs Lyall's death in 1878 that she was free to see India for herself. She had made several expeditions to Europe, especially to Italy and the haunts of her hero, Lord Byron's, last years at Venice, Ravenna and Pisa, but it was India which Alfred's letters and poems had woven into her dreams. She arrived in

Simla in the autumn of 1879, at a harsh moment, immediately after the massacre of Sir Louis Cavagnari and the Kabul garrison, for which both Alfred Lyall, the Foreign Secretary, and the Viceroy, Lord Lytton, suffered agonies of remorse. As the mood lightened over the following weeks, Barbara emerged with not only the deep gratitude of Alfred and Clara Lyall, but the affectionate friendship of Robert and Edith Lytton, shared by their daughters Betty, then aged thirteen, and Constance, eleven (though Emily was only six). Alfred Lyall gained 'much enjoyment and relief from the cares of office' from his sister's visit.[27] Lord Lytton was apparently susceptible to intelligent and lively female friendship, and he seemed to inspire Barbara's love. When the Lyttons left Simla, and India, under something of a cloud in July the following year, it was typically Barbara who broke the ranks of etiquette, racing after their carriage to say her farewells in private.

Once home, Robert Lytton wrote a series of letters to his 'friend in India' of which only fragments survive. Only one is among his collected letters, edited by his daughter Betty:[28] 'It is indeed,' he wrote from Knebworth House on 10 August 1880, 'like a dream to me that I should be writing to you this delicious afternoon, under an oak tree on the lawn of my grandmother's garden . . . the air bathed in the manifold scents of an English August, which pour back into my empty soul and frame, the times when I remember to have been joyful and free from blame.' He continues to describe how he felt on the journey home and upon arrival in England – but perhaps the above gives a flavour of the intimacy of the feelings that he knew were reciprocated. In another fragment which has survived, he wrote to Barbara, 'Cherish the poetry of your life while it lasts. The prose of life begins when we cease to ask questions that cannot be answered. But just as the poetry of life is not happiness, so the prose of life is not contentment – nor even wisdom.'[29]

For Barbara the poetry of her life must indeed have withered on the stony ground of provincial manners when she returned to England in the spring of 1881. Ladies were meant to go to India to find suitable husbands, and it seems that she had surely fallen in love with the perfectly well-married Viceroy. She was then thirty-six, and virtually homeless, for though she naturally returned to Harbledown Lodge, the home of her sister Sibylla Holland, she was clearly not welcome. In their resumed, twice-weekly correspondence, even Alfred scolded her with his beliefs that 'marriage was to a woman what a profession is to a man' and 'old maids are social anomalies'.[30]

The Hollands had a house in Surrey and knew many Surrey people; Sibylla was certainly determined to get Barbara 'settled' and off her hands (for Barbara's outspokenness often caused embarrassment at her sedate dinner-table), and immediately the lonely, widowed Bob Webb came into view, she must have pounced. That was in the summer of 1884. Bob Webb was kindly, a thoroughly good-natured, country-loving squire, and Barbara cheered him up immensely; he came to love her very much. Barbara was not so sure; she must have told Alfred about Bob in an autumn letter, and by the time Alfred wrote to her on 1 December he was anticipating news concerning Bob that would give him 'the greatest pleasure'. Barbara wavered up until the last minute, and on Christmas Eve, writing from Allahabad, Alfred expressed relief that her engagement was a *fait accompli*. He sent her £100 'to buy a really lovely ring'.[31] Barbara married Bob Webb in the New Year of 1885, and they arrived back at Milford House in the spring, after a wedding trip to Florence, Rome, Sicily and Naples.

The following July, in a letter to her son, Francis, Sibylla Holland reports on Barbara's new life: 'My visit to [Barbara] was very pleasant. She is serenely content with her lot, and I really think she has done very well with her life. After much variety, amusement, travel and freedom she finds herself exactly where other fortunate women of her own age are. I like Mr [Webb]. He has all the ease of a perfectly unpretending gentleman born in fairly good circumstances. There is much more interest in country life when the country is not treated as a toy, but where good or bad land, fair or foul weather, health or sickness among beasts, is a quite serious matter affecting the owner's pockets, and those of his poorer neighbours.'[32] This was probably Sibylla's way of saying that Bob Webb was a stalwart squire, and these worthy domestic interests were what governed his life: he was kind and jovial, but no poet.

Alfred too wrote to Barbara, on 11 July 1885, from a camp somewhere in the North-West Provinces (of which he was now Lieutenant-Governor): 'I am very glad indeed that you are so happily settled at Milford, better late than never. We have all to look back upon a certain number of mistakes, most of them irretrievable, which has not been your case, except possibly as to the heir of Milford.'[33]

So there she was, Mrs Webb of Milford, not really of Milford at all; the house stayed firmly as it was before she arrived, and does not appear to have had any of her personality stamped on it during her short tenancy. Sibylla Holland, needless to say, noticed everything: 'The house and grounds I like particularly,' she reported to Francis. 'No odd turns or surprises, or artful points of view within or without, but everything very comfortable and exactly what one expects. Lofty rooms, large high windows, thick walls, polished doors shutting off passages and staircases, an excellent temperature and solid, quiet, frightful ancestral portraits. A great yew hedge and long sunny wall enclosing a garden full of fruit and flowers; plenty of books, new and old. Witley steeple and Blackdown visible, so that you know whereabouts you are . . .'[34]

Outside, Milford House was architecturally distinguished, with five regular bays of soft pink brick banded and pedimented in cream stone; it had been built about 1730, or shortly after the death of Christopher Wren, and in his manner. It stood back from the road in the centre of Milford, with a gravel court in front. The house was high on flowery terraces above green water meadows stretching to the river Wey; there were sheep and a donkey, and a path winding through meadow flowers to a bridge over the river for the walk to Rake Manor or Enton Mill. All was beautifully kept, in well-accustomed hands, as it had been for many seasons since Philip Carteret Webb had married Mary Smith, heiress of Milford, in 1763, so starting the dynasty of which Robert Webb was almost the last.[35]

The inside of Milford House, particularly for the young Ned Lutyens, was a revelation of grace, which Barbara understood, and it was her pleasure. It has been

Milford House, the home of Robert and Barbara Webb: the hall had panelling and arches in the 'Queen Anne' style, which strongly influenced the young Lutyens (from a watercolour by Augusta Webb).

14

called 'pure early Wren',[36] but could not have been exactly that – it was English baroque, so very specifically an English exercise in architecture. It was exquisite – with a black and white marble chequered hall floor (ever to be Lutyens's ideal) and a panelled hall with classical columns, leading to a dark and handsome staircase with fluted, turned balusters and elegant polished treads. The ceiling of the hall leading to the back of the house, and on both floors, was a sequence of semicircular arches, panelled and rosetted, so that when Lutyens saw Wren's St Bride's or even their massive brethren in St Paul's, he would find them familiar, variations on a single theme in differing scales. Milford House, though Lutyens later outgrew it, was for him at sixteen the initiation of his pilgrimage to emulate Wren.

There were no children from Robert Webb's first marriage to inherit this lovely house, and now there never would be: when Barbara arrived the ménage was completed by Robert's bachelor brother, Godfrey, and when Bob and Godfrey were gone the estate would pass to their youngest brother, Francis, his wife Augusta and their daughters. There was presumably little incentive for changing things, and Barbara's talents were not for home-making. She needed a cause, she was impatient with domestic trivia and happily left the loyal Webb household to their regime, for which they came to love her. Though history only allows her to be seen as a pale reflection of her adored and distinguished brother Alfred, she was in reality a 'character', an adventuress, full of vigour and fun, a traveller in the realms of gold now voluntarily imprisoned, albeit in an architectural gem of a cell. Thus as soon as she met him, in the summer of 1885, Ned Lutyens became her cause, and he spent long, happy hours at Milford, indulging her in his stories and mimicry, which she loved; the peace and elegance of Barbara's house rescued him from the gypsy-like chaos of his Thursley home and gave him time to think and use his eyes. The chequered marble floor, the cool, spacious hall, the Wrennish arches, even Bob Webb's little panelled library, all lodged themselves in his visual memory, accurately measured to the very fraction by his extraordinary vision, ready to be filtered, rarefied into the finest new buildings, for Surrey gentlemen, then houses up and down the land, even for an Ambassador in Washington and a Viceroy in India, all of whom he had yet to meet.[37]

It seems likely that it was the Wren classicism of Milford, brewing in his brain, that led Herbert Baker to observe that Ned Lutyens seemed to know already things that could not be learned in Ernest George's office. But the George style of old English, he also quickly assessed, was the most suitable to the country gentlemen that Barbara Webb first gathered for him to meet. They were not patrons of architecture, but cautious, kindly squires who would give a young man a chance; thus he shamelessly 'adapted' George's designs for Squire Godman's little lodges,

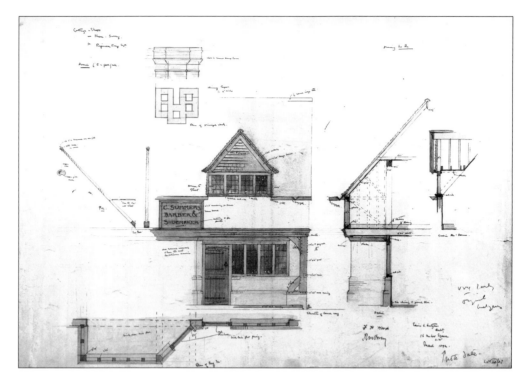

Lutyens's earliest buildings, built
for Surrey country gentry and
hunting squires. *Top:* shop in
Shere; *centre left*, East Lodge,
Shere Manor; *centre right*,
Lascombe, Puttenham; *bottom:*
Tilford Institute, Tilford.

right and left, at Hascombe, for Cowley Lambert's stables at Little Tangley on the Shalford to Wonersh road, Mr Summers's barber's shop and the Brays' new lodge at Shere, the Chapmans' small house at Crooksbury, Harry Mangles's gardener's cottage at Littleworth and Mrs Darnley Anderson's Tilford Institute. These little buildings, plus the cottages liberally sprinkled – at Frensham for the Combes, at Milford for Robert Webb, at Peper Harow and Shere – were the earliest efforts of one who would build palaces. The proof of his burgeoning talent was that they were not just copies from the worthy Ernest George, nor were they merely rebuilding the old cottages that were all around – they were Ned Lutyens's variations on these themes, a clever mix of the past traditions and present crafts, with more than a dash of Randolph Caldecott's fantasies brought to life from off the nursery page.

It now becomes abundantly clear that Barbara Webb, fearless as she was, cajoled and challenged everyone she met to let Ned build for them. She arrived in Milford and immediately took up the social pattern which Bob Webb, the house and the household were used to; if she hadn't been already aware of who exactly her neighbours were, one of those heavy, gilded volumes on the gentry of Surrey would have reminded her, and it is almost as if she used one of them as a guide, for so many of the moustachioed squires, for all their worthy doings, find their most vivid place in history as Ned's early patrons. Conversely, they were on the thick, gilt-edged pages because they were also the benefactors of the hunt balls, musical evenings, and summer-long tea and tennis parties and dancing afterwards that filtered annually through the lovely old gardens in the valley of the Wey, and slipped gradually eastwards to the Tillingbourne.

This magical land of Old West Surrey had a definite physical form that was an intrinsic part of the pattern of Lutyens's early patronage. To a great extent it was popular for ex-military men and would-be artists, as it was the Arcady already glimpsed from the confines of Aldershot and the open heaths north of the Hog's Back. The famous seven-mile-long chalk ridge is the northern bastion of Old West Surrey (Gertrude Jekyll said she never went north of it), and from this grandstand the whole of the lovely south country can be seen. It is dominated by the river Wey, which gathers its headwaters on the Hampshire borders in the west and flows to Frensham, where it lolls about among the sandy heaths, feeding the large and beautiful Frensham Ponds, and is bridged for the first time at Frensham Manor. Charles Lutyens painted this bridge. The Wey can be a quiet stream or a roaring torrent, and it has always been given respectful space through its water meadows south of Farnham; only the Cistercian brethren who built Waverley Abbey had some kind of symbiotic relationship with their river, which allowed them to find

17

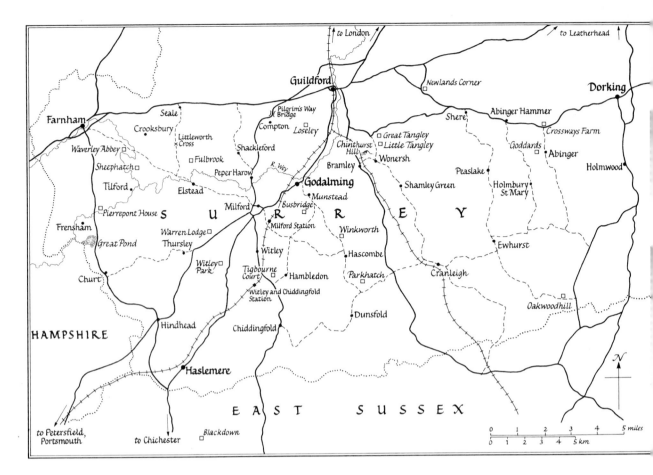

Old West Surrey, the world of Edwin Lutyens when he was young. The principal roads are shown but the main means of travelling was to take the network of firm sandy tracks across the heath-lands to the west and east of Thursley, his home village. The River Wey, with crossing places at Tilford, Elstead and Frensham, was a crucial part of the pattern. The London & South Western Railway brought him from Waterloo to Guildford, Godalming, Milford or Witley stations and became his main means of travel when he gave up cycling after his marriage. The only modern addition here is the diversion of the A3, London to Portsmouth Road, to the west of the town centres of Godalming and Guildford; this was done in the 1920s, and Lutyens designed the road bridge over the Pilgrims' Way at Compton.

the bridging places, at Tilford and Elstead, and their bridges have ruled the rights of passage for 700 years. (The timber construction of the Tilford bridges of his day was carefully observed and copied by Lutyens for Ashby St Ledgers, Lambay and for Edward Hudson at Sonning and at Plumpton Place.)

The Wey turns north through Godalming and Guildford, the undisputed capital of Old West Surrey, to foreign fields. Society bowled eastwards by landau and barouche, through Shalford, Chilworth, Albury and Shere, villages beside the tributary Tillingbourne, and southwards through the hollow lanes to Cranleigh

18

and Chiddingfold. Barbara Webb found herself to be part of a well-ordered and accustomed society; it was a mistake, as the architect and antiquary Ralph Nevill had pointed out at that time, to assume that there were no old families in Old West Surrey, for there were many who had held their lands since the time of James I – the Brays of Shere, the Mellershes, the Webbs themselves and the Evelyns of Wootton among them.[38] A tremendous stability extended across the acreages long held by many of Lutyens's earliest patrons, which was immediately accessible to Mrs Webb of Milford. Though she did not hunt, the great unifying factor was – it has to be remembered – the horse; for this reason society ran along the valley roads and hollow lanes in summer, and galloped hither and yon in winter. Hunting was the greatest force (it was a nice irony that a young architect who was terrified of horses gained most from a hunting society), and particularly the precise and mannered etiquette of those who galloped across each other's land and dined around each other's tables afterwards. It was not particularly fine hunting, there were none of the 'greatest gallops in the world', as in the Midland shires, for there were too many trees, too much heather, not enough good agriculture, not enough field hedges. Prettiness and good hunting do not go together and it was too pretty. But it suited the old hands, and sport and beauty made a congenial mix for the artists, like Lutyens's hero, Randolph Caldecott.

A perfect example of how this society worked, once Barbara Webb had introduced her young architect friend, is found with the Bray family at Shere. Shere

Witley Park boathouse: Lutyens's earliest classical work, was done for the maverick among the Surrey gentry, Whitaker Wright. Wright, a speculator, spent his fortune on the house and grounds at Witley, landscaping the lake and building an underwater room. Lutyens also built him a bathing pavilion, but these two little buildings were the end of Wright's spree. Whitaker Wright committed suicide in 1904 after being given a prison sentence for fraud.

and the Brays had been together since some time after the battle of Bosworth Field in 1485: by the 1890s they had settled in as the quintessential squirearchy, fair-minded, steady, wise and a little eccentric, ruling their little paradise in the lee of the North Downs. The reigning Bray, Reginald More, a barrister with a busy London practice, was appointed Recorder of Guildford in 1891 at the age of forty-nine; he was married to Lucy, daughter of the Barclay banking family at Bury Hill, Dorking, and sister of the novelist Florence Barclay. Their home was the rather spiky manor house on its knoll dominating Shere's village street; this had been built (*built*, rather than designed) by the family, out of the local stone from their own quarry, in the earlyish 1800s, and subsequently enlarged as necessary. They

William Edgar Horne (later Sir Edgar), MP for Guildford, represented 'Old West Surrey'; he was also a landowner, traveller and sportsman, a director of the Prudential Insurance Company, less enamoured of Lutyens than his fellows after troubles over the drainage at Tigbourne Court, Witley, which Lutyens built for Horne's daughter. Horne employed Henry Tanner Jnr, who was seven years younger than Lutyens (but his father Sir Henry Tanner was Chief Architect to the Office of Works) to build Aldro at Shackleford.

did not see any necessity for Lutyens to touch it. The Bray brood of bright young things was led by Reginald Arthur Bray, who was the same age as Ned Lutyens but a radical, socialist even, keen on education and progressive farming; a second son, Edward Neville, was an electrical engineer. In between them was Nellie, a great organizer, terrific tennis player, renowned for her 'good whip' and smart driving. Below these three were Marjorie, Lilian, Olive, Jocelyn and Francis, gradually emerging from the schoolroom.

Jocelyn Bray's acutely observed memoirs of his youth fill in the immutable routine of those palmy days when 'it was all a happy and carefree life and everybody always seemed to have plenty of money'.[39] Breakfast was at eight, unless their father had to catch the London train, when he started at 7.55; family prayers were at 8.30. There had been no morning tea, there were no elevenses, lunch was at one sharp, and then the house fell quiet while Mrs Bray rested until 2.30. Tea was served at 4.30, everyone was dressed for dinner by 7.45, into the drawing-room at nine, with tea and bread and butter as a nightcap at 9.45. Mrs Bray retired at ten, her husband at eleven: his powers of concentration were such that he had been reading his briefs through the drawing-room chatter.

Reginald Bray at home was still every inch the taciturn lawyer, and though he loved his estate dearly his family never heard much about it; everything ran on a well-oiled routine. The Brays did not hunt, but they kept a good shoot. Reginald Bray was also enlightened, keen for progress, and he encouraged his sons. Early in the 1890s a laundry was set up in one of the Upper Street cottages to give employment, and Edward Bray brought water-driven electric light to the village soon afterwards. To provide more employment, especially for a young carpenter named Bracher and his estate building team, Lutyens was asked to design first a village shop for George Summers, the barber (1892), then a new lodge and another pair of cottages (1894).

Lutyens was around enough in those early 1890s summers for the family, or at least its younger members, to imagine him in love with Nellie Bray.[40] The young Brays and their friends, with Nellie in the lead always, danced their summers away, constantly at garden parties, tennis teas and cricket matches, from one to another of the local gentry – the Vaughan Williamses on Leith Hill, the Lewins at Parkhatch, the Waterhouses at Feldemore, the Barnards at Burrows Lea, the Leaders at Burrows Cross – thence through the valley to the Thesigers at Bramley, the Cowley Lamberts at Little Tangley, the Fisher Rowes at Thorncombe Park and the Midletons at Peper Harow. Most of these families, or their connections, contributed to Lutyens's early career.

After her marriage this society governed Barbara Webb's days and seasons, but she had kept in just as close touch as ever with her beloved brother Alfred. Almost as soon as he thought her settled, Alfred began sharing with her his concerns about his own coming retirement and how he would fare in English society after such a long absence. For two years Barbara paved his way for him, and she also put in a word for Ned at the same time. She carefully constructed, out of her acquaintances, a circle of literary and artistic society which included the Tennysons at Aldworth on Blackdown (which could be seen from Milford House's windows and was often a journey's end), Jacques and Leonie Blumenthal, Margot Tennant and her sister, Laura (whose short life ended in 1886, less than a year after her marriage to Alfred Lyttelton), and their sister Charlotte Ribblesdale, Mrs Theresa Earle (Lady Lytton's sister), Herbert and Agnes Jekyll and Agnes's sister Frances Horner at Mells in Somerset.

Alfred Lyall came home in late 1887 and soon 'all the clever women in London were his devoted admirers'.[41] This was undoubtedly Barbara's work. His letters and diaries are filled with his society doings, among a continuing stream of Lutyens's future patrons; he stays with the Morrisons at Fonthill, the Stanleys at Wenlock Abbey, he goes to Ireland, to Augusta Gregory at Coole, and in the autumn of 1888 he writes to Barbara from the Blumenthals' Le Chalet, near Montreux, which was Gertrude Jekyll's favourite holiday haunt.

With Alfred happily lionizing and her young protégé Ned Lutyens building busily, Barbara resumed her own life. In the spring of 1890 she went to Paris to stay with the Lyttons – Robert Lytton was now the Ambassador. As usual, only fragments of Barbara's activities can be gathered from Alfred's letters and there is no mention of her going again, but the following year, 1891, was the year Lord Lytton died, suddenly, still in Paris. Whatever Barbara's own feelings might have been, they were subsumed in her sympathy with Edith Lytton and her family, who were now revealed to be rather poorly provided for; Barbara kept in close touch with them. They returned to England, to a rented house, The Danes, not far from their ancestral Knebworth, and Lady Lytton took a paying post as lady-in-waiting to Queen Victoria.

Alfred had written to Barbara from Le Chalet, where he had found time to ponder, that he understood her 'occasional longings for deeper draughts of life than can be had from the Surrey woods or the London water supply'; he concluded, in an effort to console her, that he believed we could have so little 'here below', and must be content.[42]

For whatever reason – the death of Robert Lytton, or that Alfred no longer needed her to be his poetic shadow – Barbara's habitual vigour was fading. In 1892 she went for an August rest at Le Chalet, and she had already been to Harrogate

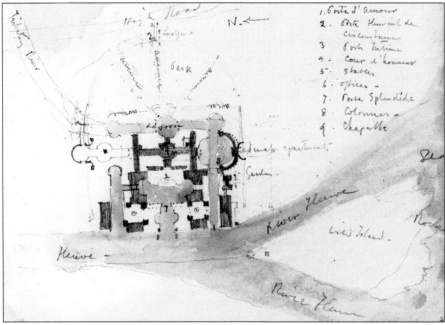

'Castle in the air' sketchbook: *Above:* with the sun smiling over Hindhead and a hammer pond, this sketch shows a room in Warren Lodge at Thursley which Lutyens was altering for the Webbs. *Below:* The plan of the 'castle in the air'. The sketchbook was made to amuse the ailing Barbara Webb, probably during the winter of 1894–5.

'for the waters', which was an unhappy sign. Through the next years she is sometimes well and sometimes not, and Alfred visits her frequently, so his letters are few. Only one, undated, letter in Barbara's large, round handwriting has been kept, perhaps because it was the last written with her characteristic vigour; she

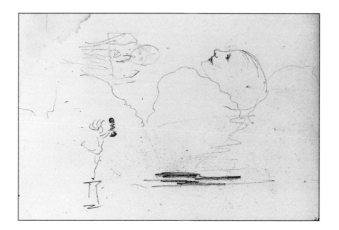

A 'secret' sketch of Barbara Webb
as she lay resting, from the 'castle
in the air' sketchbook.

curses 'the idiot post office' but continues writing of her 'great prostration and
lassitude' and her 'sensation of not being worth while to get out of bed and put on
horrid clothes and boots and face the world which is palpitating on the road
outside'.[43] She thought this was flu, but it was more likely her fatal cancer.

During her low times Ned Lutyens used to tell her stories and draw for her, a
dream palace on a Venetian lagoon, *Château d'Ease, en Air, sur Fleuve des Rêves*, her
castles in the air. This was a fantasy on Barbara's favourite Italian places, constructed from poring over her collected guidebooks. On better days she continued
to go out, often with Ned as escort, and in this way, in the spring of 1896, they
went to a musical party at the Blumenthals' house, 43 Hyde Park Gate, where he
met Emily Lytton for the first time.

They met again at summer dances, and Ned confessed his love for Emily to
Barbara; as a result Barbara invited Emily to Milford for a long stay at the end of
the summer, and Ned was able to see enough of her to declare his love. As he
struggled to win Emily, so Barbara's health failed. He wrote to Emily of how
pitiable it was not to be allowed to see her any more – he could only glimpse the
pages of her book turning through the window.

Barbara Webb died peacefully at Milford early in July 1897; she was fifty-two
years old. She is commemorated by a small bronze plaque on the chancel wall in
the church at Witley, the first of many memorials that Lutyens came to design.
Interestingly, after Barbara's death, Alfred Lyall put a great deal of his time and
influence in his remaining years into the cause of women's education.

II

ALLEGRO: JEKYLLIANA

The Lament of the Neglected

The Architect's wanted galore, galore,
The work's at a standstill for evermore;
The brick layers playing – they've nothing to do,
The carpenters smoking – they're idle too.
The plumbers carousing till all is blue.
Oh Plazzoh go hang, old Bumps is a bore
For Nedi's gone courting galore, galore!

(BUMPS POET GALOREATE)[1]

To Emily Lytton the young Lutyens characterized his first six years of practice as all work and cycling. Apart from Nellie Bray and her friends trying to inveigle him into dancing or tennis teas, he could quite honestly admit that the most constant companion of his young life was his Angelina, the sturdy, black iron-limbed steed of easy temper, with straight handlebars which he grasped as a bull by the horns when he was especially determined, which carried him through his early years. Angelina was pedalled furiously from Gray's Inn, where he had his first office, to Waterloo, thrown into the guard's van, retrieved at Godalming station, pedalled to the post office for his mail, then up the long hill to Munstead, forgotten for a while, then retrieved for the cross-country ride to Milford House and rest. The London & South Western railway, the Royal Mail (which often delivered his morning letters the same afternoon or evening) and the soft sandy lanes of Surrey made all this possible. If he had been born to a countryside of rutted clay he would never have got started.

Picture him then, his drawings in a tin roll across his handlebars, his T-square on his back, his city suit covered in dust, puffing up the hill to Littleworth Cross on a May afternoon in 1889. He was expecting a working meeting with Harry Mangles, but found a tea party in progress. The visitor-in-chief, come to inspect the rhododendron hybrid which Harry Mangles had named for her, was Miss Gertrude Jekyll from Munstead. She appeared to be a stiff, rather stout middle-aged lady, with beady eyes behind thick spectacles, in her 'Go-To-Meeting' dress and a hat with nodding feathers on the top. He later remembered how 'with one foot on the step of her pony cart and the reins in her hand, she invited him to Munstead Wood the very next Saturday'.[2]

Ned had undoubtedly heard about the Jekylls from Barbara Webb, who had probably relayed Miss Jekyll's eccentricities. She was unlike any other woman he had ever encountered; though she was old enough to be his mother (she was forty-five) and her figure was motherly with 'rotundities', which inspired his nickname of 'Aunt Bumps', she could not have been more unlike his adored mother; and whereas Barbara Webb had battled with the stifling conventions of her life, Gertrude Jekyll had triumphed over them. She came from a remarkably enlightened family.

She was born on 29 November 1843 in London, the fourth child of Edward and Julia Jekyll: their first-born, Caroline, had been followed by two sons, then Gertrude, who was followed by her favourite brother, Herbert, and finally Walter, born in 1849. Somewhere between Herbert and Walter the Jekylls moved their young family to the country, to the ugly but large and comfortable Bramley Park, just south of Guildford, which was surplus to the requirements of the Egremonts at Petworth. At Bramley Gertrude enjoyed an idyllic childhood, free from restraint, full of loving companions among her family and their neighbours, her talents admired and her abilities fostered with an excellent education. She was seriously short-sighted, and therefore earnest and studious, and her family knew she was something of an oddity, but they loved her for it; she may have been teased but she was never embittered, and she was encouraged in her aim to lead an independent, artistic life, a kind of celibate Pre-Raphaelitism, which owed much to her admiration of – and acquaintance with – John Ruskin.

Gertrude was sent to the South Kensington School of Art (twenty-four years before Ned Lutyens) and followed her two years there with an expedition to the Greek islands in the company of Charles and Mary Newton, he the keeper of Greek and Roman Antiquities at the British Museum, she the sister of Ruskin's friend, Arthur Severn. From then on Gertrude's life had been a kaleidoscope of beautiful and interesting places and wonderful works that had dropped from her hands – a tablecloth designed and embroidered for Lord Leighton, quilted curtains and mother-of-pearl inlaid panels of flowers for the Blumenthals' London home, a decorative scheme for the Duke of Westminster's Eaton Hall, shell pictures galore, silver dishes and caskets, jewellery, including an entwined 'LL' which Edward Burne-Jones gave to Laura Tennant on her marriage to Alfred Lyttelton in 1885, and a hundred other such treasures, all made with her painstaking labours and to her fastidiously high standards.[3]

All her achievements had taken their toll of her weak eyes, and in 1878 Gertrude

Gertrude Jekyll gardening at Munstead House, soon after it was finished in 1878. Her brother Edward is on the left, with Walter Jekyll in the centre.

was forced to settle down with her widowed mother at a new house built for Mrs Jekyll on Munstead Heath, south of Godalming and just up the hill from the childhood paradise of Bramley. Mrs Jekyll bought the eighteen-acre plot from the Thorncombe estate[4] and commissioned J. J. Stevenson, a new recruit to the Queen Anne style, architect of artists' houses in west London and a friend of Morris and Rossetti, who built for them the faintly Scottish baronial (in tribute to the heathland) Munstead House.[5] Here Gertrude's energies had gone into making a garden out of the heathland, and melding into it, much according to William Robinson's *The Wild Garden*, azaleas among the heather, an alpine garden 'of half-buried blocks of sandstone ... the setting for luxuriant clumps' of gentians, saxifrages, campanulas and thymes. The lawn 'faded into the wild heath' with 'stands of foxgloves and mullein growing in the bracken at the edge of the pine wood'.[6]

All these rather revolutionary wooings of nature were in addition to the usual Victorian garden establishment which fed the household and filled the rooms with flowers. Gertrude's naturalizing experiments were much admired, one commentator suggesting that it was the most lovely garden that could be made on such a site.[7] Thus challenged, she bought another in 1883, a plot of her own, across the road, which she called Munstead Wood. There she began organizing the natural woodland growth, cutting paths, making gardens, photographing everything she did and writing about it, settling into her new life as a gardener, with her habitual 'perfect method and completeness'.[8]

She had been working in her own garden for six years when she met Ned Lutyens. She was so secure in the divine rightness of her crusade, so completely lacking in pretension and perfectly capable of laughing at herself, and yet so *experienced*, that her interest in him was the nourishment his rather forced self-confidence required. He was naturally expecting to build for her, and when he heard that Stevenson had been her mother's architect (probably chosen by Herbert Jekyll), Ned might have assumed he would build in the Queen Anne style. We shall never know now if he was disappointed when he realized her passion was for the timber, stone and tile Surrey vernacular of her childhood countryside. For she viewed her Surrey through the rose tints of the returned exile: 'When I was a child all this tract of country was undiscovered,' she later wrote. 'Now, alas! it is overrun.' (She had personally been involved with building three houses on it.) In the preface to her book *Old West Surrey*[9] she continues: 'Formerly, within a mile or two of one's home, it was a rare thing to see a stranger, and people's lives ran leisurely ... London might have been at a distance of two hundred miles. Now one can never forget that it is a little more than an hour's journey.'

While others' reactions were to set about preserving chunks of the vanishing obscurity,[10] Gertrude's idea was a one-woman campaign of creative conservation, into which she led Ned Lutyens. In her smart pony cart, with 'G. Jekyll, Munstead' painted on the back, they toured the countryside, first to the villagers of Bramley she had known from childhood, then to their neighbours and further afield. She gained entrance to cottages and farms, she examined their pepper-pots, their bedlinen, lifted up and dusted off the best ornaments to carry them out, line them up on a table and photograph them. All this went into *Old West Surrey*, but when roof beams and window-catches, fireplaces and details of porches, walls and gateways were added, the expeditions were the preliminary to her new buildings. From about two years after their meeting Ned Lutyens was busy with a flurry of Munsteadiana – a timbered cottage for Miss Jekyll's Swiss head gardener, Alfred Zumbach, a substantial triple-gabled timbered house for Mr Heatley, a wine merchant, on the plot next door to Munstead Wood, Miss Jekyll's studio cottage, the Hut, in her garden, a small house for the family butler, and a little triangular pavilion on the wall at the end of the garden, her Thunder House, for watching the storms in the Wey valley.

Here a short pause, to mark the death of Mrs Julia Jekyll in 1895 and Ned Lutyens's first design for a tombstone. The occupants of Munstead House were now Herbert Jekyll and his wife, Agnes, and their family, Pamela, Barbara, and Francis, known as Timmy. They had just returned from a sociable spell in Dublin, where Colonel Jekyll had been Private Secretary to Lord Crewe. Herbert, too easily overshadowed by Gertrude's virtues, was hardly less clever; he had won the Sword of Honour at Woolwich Military Academy, and he was a talented wood-carver, a keen gardener, and a better musician than Gertrude, as an organist and founder member of the Bach Choir. Agnes Jekyll was the youngest of the eight children of William and Jane Graham, the patrons of the Pre-Raphaelites. She married Herbert in 1881, and around the table at their first dinner party were Robert Browning, John Ruskin and Edward Burne-Jones. But Agnes's talents were for more than cooking and entertaining (though she was the first person to supply recipes to *The Times*[11]), for if Gertrude was an artist-gardener, then Agnes was an artist-housekeeper. Lytton Strachey, not given to domestic compliments, said of her that 'whenever she appeared life was enhanced – intensified'.[12] The Herbert Jekylls, who were much more sociable and influential than the workaholic Gertrude (whom many people thought very odd), were to be very important to Ned Lutyens, far beyond the alterations at Munstead House that he did for them. They were, with Barbara Webb, his introduction to Agnes's sister, Frances Horner, at Mells.

Gertrude's money from her mother's legacy allowed her to begin on the chief task of her relationship with Ned Lutyens, the building of her own house, over which there had been endless discussions and disputations. She describes this great adventure in the first chapter of *Home and Garden* ... 'it is not exactly a new house ... I had been thinking about it for so many years, and the main block of it and the whole sentiment of it were so familiar to my mind's eye, that when it came to be a reality I felt as if I had already been living in it a good long time... It is designed and built in the thorough and honest spirit of the good work of old days' ... and she concluded, significantly, 'It has taken to itself the soul of a more ancient dwelling place.'[13] She rejoiced that she *knew* the oaks that held up her roof (they had been growing a mile and a half away fifteen years before) and that the Bargate stone was the sandstone 'that grows in our hills'. She is proud of her country builder (whom she does not name, but he was Mr Underwood of Dunsfold), and she preferred the 'vigorous vitality and individual interest' that marked the work of Underwood's men to the technical perfection of London firms.

Undoubtedly much of the perfection of Munstead Wood as a crafted building was the result of Gertrude's hawk-eyed (as only a myope can be) and pertinacious overseeing of the work. It must have been a lively building site. Her friends wondered why she hadn't designed her house as well, and she gives rather a nice explanation, that the work of an amateur 'will always lack the qualities that belong to the higher knowledge'. She continues with an analogy familiar to her, on how an amateur at needlework produces 'bungles and awkward places' and that any addition will look like 'a shame-faced patch boggled on to a garment'. But a good architect will make an addition like 'some Italian genius in needlework two hundred years ago ... glorified and ornamented and turned into some graceful arabesque of leaf and flower and tendril, enriched by cunning needlework of thread or cord or delicate golden purfling' ... into an enduring beauty and delight.[14] Like her builder, her 'good architect' was not named – but, as the most completely satisfied client, she always gave him the credit to everyone.

Inside Munstead Wood she had insisted on characteristics that became Lutyens's hallmarks: the low, broad treads and short flights of the stairs, the wide upstairs gallery, the deep cupboards, and the oak mullion flush with the outer face of the walls to give capacious sills for her ornaments and flowers – all such things were necessities, not luxuries, to her daily well-being. Her house was truly an expression of her personality, and as she could not tolerate pretension or affectation, so neither could her house. She rises to evangelical zeal in her contempt for 'fashionable devices of spurious antiquity', expounding her creed:

Internal fittings that are constantly seen and handled, such as window-fastenings, hinges, bolts and door-latches, are specially designed and specially made, so that they are in perfect proportion, for size, weight, and strength, to the wood and iron-work to which they are related. There are no random choosings from the iron-monger's pattern-book; no clashing of styles, no meretricious ornamentation, no impudence of cast-iron substitute for honest hand-work, no moral slothfulness in the providing of all these lesser finishings. It takes more time, more trouble; it may even take a good deal of time and trouble, but then it is just right, and to see and know that it is right is a daily reward and never-ending source of satisfaction.[15]

The unfinished house, helped by the spectacle of its portly chatelaine up a ladder giving instructions to a workman on the roof, brought Ned Lutyens his next great coup. The story is in the published *Letters*, but illumines delightfully the relationship between Miss Jekyll and Ned, and introduces important patrons, so is reproduced here.[16]

On 27 May 1897 Ned was in the train to Godalming, having been summoned by an urgent note from Gertrude: 'Something most amusing, highly flattering to Nedi and rather mysterious, want to see you about it as soon as possible.' He fantasizes in his note to Emily, 'Oh Love what can it mean?! Someone wants to give me an enormous job! Some rich body wants to adopt us and give us £40,000 a year.[17] The Duke of Westminster wants to give me some appointment?[18]

Sketch of Lutyens asleep drawn in 1897, after his marriage, possibly by Edwin's brother, Frederick Lutyens. There is a companion sketch of Lady Emily Lutyens.

G. Balfour?? Princess Louise wants to know if I would rebuild Windsor and should she give my name to her Mamma? Is it to do with Africa's Cathedral? Or is it a big church in England?'[19] Gertrude picks him up in Godalming High Street and drives up to Munstead, refusing to tell: at the house they find, first, Lady Constance Lytton, then Robert Webb, both needing guided tours, which Gertrude conducts while Ned speaks to the builders. When all is quiet they sit down in the garden. 'Well,' said Bumps, 'do you remember some time back I told you of Mr and Mrs Chance coming here with their architect Mr Ricardo?' He did.[20] 'Well,' Bumps apparently repeated, 'they came and were fearfully impressed . . . and they said all sorts of pretty complimentary things' about her house. After more visits, as Ned reported Miss Jekyll telling, 'they were even more enamoured of her house and confessed that though Mr Ricardo was an old friend and they normally loved his work, they liked Mr Lutyens's so much more'. Bumps was not easily swayed; and she was enjoying her long story. More visits, and even letters, had been exchanged; the Chances were sorry to have to disappoint their architect but, really, would Mr Lutyens *ever* consider designing a house for them? *No, no*, Miss Jekyll's young friend had scruples and professional dignity, he could *never* usurp another architect – until, finally, they broke down her reservations and 'she undertook to question Mr Lutyens as to his scruples'. 'Oh, Bumps has such a long story to tell . . .' writes Ned to Emily, 'and to make it short . . . the Chances have chucked Ricardo and I am to do the work – and I meet them on Wednesday on the site.'[21]

The site for William and Julia Chance's house was a mile or so up the lane towards Bramley from Munstead Wood; it was named for its acres of south-facing 'Orchards', but the house was to be at the western end of the site, with a glorious westwards view across the Thorncombe valley. William Chance was a successful QC, and in 1897 he was forty-four; his family money came from Chance & Company of Oldbury and Smethwick in the Midlands, who made lenses for lighthouses. Conscious of his own good fortune, most of his legal career was devoted to Poor Law and housing reform, and his desire to live in the country when he could, in a quiet, self-sufficient but gently philanthropic way, was equally deep-rooted. His wife was Julia Charlotte Strachey and they were married in 1884. She was the only child of Lieutenant-Colonel Henry Strachey, sometime Tibetan explorer; Lytton Strachey was her cousin, and she had more cousins at Newlands Corner.[22] She was a quietly talented sculptress and an Arts and Crafts believer.

The source of the Chances' unhappiness about Halsey Ricardo's design was not his architecture, but his failure to understand their site, which approached sacred ground in their feelings. They wanted a north light studio for Julia, a sunny aspect for William Chance's writing room, south-facing drawing- and dining-rooms

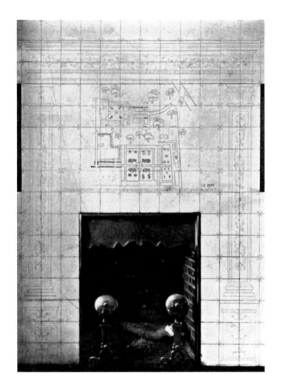

Above left: Orchards, Munstead, Surrey: the layout plan of house and garden painted on tiles above the study fireplace.

Above right: Orchards, the alcoves and basin designed by Lutyens at the end of the Dutch Garden; it is built of terracotta tiles with Portland stone trimmings and the lion mask is by Julia Chance.

Right: The Orchards Workbook: this was put together by Sir William Chance and included the names of all the workmen.

Earnest Redman Joiner Selborne Surrey
James Glue Labourer Dunsfold
James Boxer Bricklayer Wonersh
William Ede Labourer Loxwood
Edward Brown Carpenter Bramley
Sidney Holder Labourer Farncombe
William Fincham Carpenter Muswell Hill
Benjamin Anscombe Bricklayer Shamley Green
James Kingett Carpenter Rinfold Susser
Albert Holloway Carpenter Bramley
William Cobbett Stone Dresser Godalming
John Leyton Painter Crownpits Godalming
Charlie Bullock Carpenter Reigate Surrey
Murray Joy Bricklayer Farncombe
Samuel Norris Plasterer Godalming
Charles Goodchild Plasterer Shalford
Edward Blythman Labourer Wonersh
William Moon Bricklayer Bramley
Mark Strudwick Carpenter Guildford
George Salmon Labourer Alfold Surrey
Thomas Hamilton Painter Hascombe
John Alderton Bricklayer Ockford Road Godalming

The Orchards Workbook: some of the men who built the house posed in the courtyard. Mr Grinstead, the foreman, is seated second from the left with his pipe.

and their western view – and all, like Munstead Wood, of Bargate stone from their own quarry, rooted in their own earth, with croquet and tennis and walled vegetable and flower gardens – and still their view.

It was a tall order, but Lutyens's ingenuity and Miss Jekyll's wisdom worked it all out beautifully. The approach – a long wing of stables and an arched entrance (salvaged from Fulbrook) was on the north, with Julia Chance's studio beside the arch – with a huge north-light oriel. The eastern side of the square around a central court was a cloister, with William Chance's writing-room in the south-east corner; they could reach each other secretly, dry-shod, and the sculptress could, wiping the clay from her hands, appear in her own drawing-room as her guests were shown in from the front door. The best rooms looked south over a gravel terrace to rhododendrons, and the key, the pivot of the whole house, was the dining-room, on the south-west corner, where one stepped out on to the loggia terrace with the hallowed view spreading westward, and the garden terraced below eye level, at one's feet.

Because the Chances cared about such things, the Orchards Workbook was kept carefully, and for once the builders' names are known. Work on Orchards started in September 1897: the foreman, a burly pipe-smoker, was Thomas Grinstead. He is followed by sixty names, not all perhaps written by their owners, but there are many varied signatures – the large, carefully rounded letters of William Fincham of Muswell Hill (almost the only 'foreigner' on the job and presumably related to a Fincham working at Fulbrook), the untidy scrawl of the muscular hands of ironworker James Jackson of Bramley (whom Miss Jekyll acknowledges in *Old West Surrey*), the almost copybook script from William Cobbett, the stone-dresser from Godalming. Then come the hands of the labourers, those who dug and wheeled the barrows – James Glue, William Ede, Sidney Holder, Edmond Blitheman – and the bricklayers William Moon, John Alderton, Benjamin Anscombe and James Porter, the carpenters Charles Goodchild and Archie Walker, and William Brice the glazier. William Redman led the horse that carted the soil and stone. R. Alexander kept them all to time, and undoubtedly Mr Grinstead warned them when the architect or Mr Underwood was about.

The Chances were also happily satisfied with their house. Miss Jekyll wrote (anonymously) in *Country Life* that Orchards possessed 'that most precious quality' of restfulness. Cartloads of plants went from Munstead to Orchards, and under tuition, Julia Chance, who was 'not much of a practical gardener before', earned her friend's accolade for her aptitude for 'the ways and need of flowers' and for her quick assimilation of 'that fine sense' of what to plant in her garden.[23] The Chances were to live happily at Orchards for over twenty years, and Julia Chance quietly sculpted dolphins, sea-horses, turtles and other small ornaments for Lutyens's later gardens.

Lutyens's musings on the purpose of that summons to Munstead, which led to Orchards, were rooted in realities. Miss Jekyll and Barbara Webb had encouraged him to please HRH Princess Louise, for whom he did some work at Rosneath in Scotland. The Princess displayed rather royal caprice and dropped Lutyens for E. Baynes Badcock (who was more inclined to do what he was told), but she, being a princess, had considerable influence during her brief enthusiasm, as a well-polished brass plaque on the wall of Lloyds Bank in Guildford High Street still bears witness. The Princess, who had a mind for a time to live in Surrey, became involved with the Old Guildford Society's opposition to the Capital & Counties Bank's plan to replace their Georgian bank with a façade of Aberdeen granite. Her

Above: Julia Chance in the garden at Orchards.

Left: Orchards: photograph taken by Gertrude Jekyll of Julia Chance's niece, Dorothea Strachey, with Dinah the black kitten in the Dutch Garden.

Royal Highness made a private visit to pronounce against this folly, much reported, attended by Miss Jekyll and Mr Lutyens, and she 'prophesied a great future' for the latter. The wily Edward Baverstock Merriman, chairman of the bank, put his royal rap over the knuckles to good advantage, with the plaque explaining that 'at the special request' of the Princess he had preserved the façade (but nothing more) of the old building.[24]

Lutyens must have felt embarrassed, for he wanted nothing to do with this growing craze for conservation, and nor – more surprisingly – did Miss Jekyll. In the following year, 1900, there was a vigorous campaign to save Godalming town hall, with a petition signed by Philip Webb, Charles Voysey and Halsey Ricardo among a dozen prominent architects and by Mr Heatley, the Streatfeilds, Mellershes, Chapmans, Mangles and Robert Webb among Lutyens's patrons. Miss Jekyll's name is missing (so is Lutyens's) – a mark of her ironclad single-mindedness not to be diverted from her main purpose. She had also designed, though perhaps not worked, a suffragette banner for Godalming,[25] though her name is not linked with their cause. Great social campaigners – Octavia Hill, Barbara Bodichon, Emily Davies, Anne Jemima and Blanche Athena Clough, Mary Ann Ewart, Henry and Eleanor Sidgwick and of course Constance Lytton – were all well known to her, and some were her close friends, but she never appears in their lives except to speak of gardens, as if she was indeed seriously myopic as to their real endeavours. This single-mindedness now worked for Ned Lutyens in as much as he became part of her own career pattern; as Sally Festing has observed in her biography of Miss Jekyll, if she had died when she was fifty, before Munstead Wood was built, we would hardly have heard of her, for it was at that moment that her campaign began, her writing, photography, drawing her garden plans, leaving her legacy behind.[26]

The success of Orchards was cheering, and it was soon followed by another Jekyll coup: in the summer of 1898, via friends who were part of the Blumenthal circle, the Waterhouses at Feldemore, Holmbury St Mary, she was making an enormous hillside rock garden for their neighbours, Frederick and Margaret Mirrielees at Pasture Wood. The Mirrielees were newcomers to Surrey. They had been tempted by the feudal, and again faintly Scottish, charms of this heather- and birch-covered countryside on the long back slopes of Leith Hill to the west of Dorking. The parish of Abinger is long and fairly narrow, stretching from the North Downs through the Tillingbourne valley, passing Crossways Farm, the setting for Meredith's *Diana*, and southwards to the Sussex border. Much of the land had for centuries, since before the time of John Evelyn the diarist, been owned by his family; the present squire was the fearsome eccentric W. J. Evelyn, not at all as charming as the patriarchs already encountered by Ned Lutyens; he was known to have ploughed up his tennis lawns because Nellie Bray and her friends failed to arrive to play on the appointed afternoon. The Evelyn estate workers lived in hamlets of stone cottages tucked away in the woods, but their spiritual focus was the ancient church of St James on Abinger Common. In 1890, by a little local direct action, the glebe land around St James's was put up for sale as building lots, and the purchaser of Lot 1, a prime site of about thirteen acres, was Frederick Mirrielees. He subsequently exchanged this plot by a deal with Mr Evelyn for a larger woodland plot called Pasturewood, which looked west and south from the slopes of Leith Hill. Here the Scottish architect William Flockhart, who had just completed a London house for Mirrielees, 31 Hertford Street in Mayfair, built a large, rambling, timbered house, with Morris interiors, which was finished in 1893.

Frederick James Mirrielees was perhaps the kindest and most gentlemanly of all Lutyens's early patrons; his upbringing had been rather cosmopolitan, to train him to take his place in the family business, Muir & Mirrielees, with its department store near the Bolshoi Theatre in Moscow, an emporium which sustained the entire English community in Russia up until the Revolution. Frederick's connection did not last that long, though, for in 1873, when he was twenty-four and had just started to enjoy his work, he fell in love with Margaret Currie, one of three daughters of Donald Currie, the Perthshire MP, banker and owner of the Castle Steamship Company, with the monopoly of the mail run to South Africa. Currie would only agree to their marriage if the exceptional young Mirrielees came to work for *him*, and with some misgivings regarding his own family loyalties, that is what Frederick did.[27]

Donald Currie was a generous but possessive father and a loyal Scot. He was using the young Scottish architect James Maclaren, a graduate of J. J. Stevenson's office, to build an Arts and Crafts community on his Glenlyon estate at Fortingall; in 1889 he had brought McLaren south to build numbers 10 and 12 Palace Court, Bayswater, as the London houses of his other two daughters – Elizabeth, married to Percy Molteno, at number 10 and Maria, married to Captain Wisely, at number 12.[28] It was McLaren's death from tuberculosis in October 1890, aged only thirty-seven, which brought his patronage to a close, and introduced William Flockhart, another Currie protégé.

Gertrude Jekyll, bustling round to help Margaret Mirrielees with her rock garden at Pasture Wood, must have had yet another diplomatic challenge on her hands to win the Mirrielees' next building project for Ned Lutyens. But she was successful, and on a July afternoon in 1898 she and Ned went to view the seven-acre site at Abinger Common which the Mirrielees had bought for their philanthropic

Frederick James Mirrielees (1851–1914), who with his wife Margaret (née Currie) commissioned Goddards at Abinger as a holiday home for 'ladies of small means'.

exercise, a holiday home for 'ladies of small means', governesses and nurses who had to work long hours in London and would benefit from a month in the country. The site was a freehold smallholding with a stone cottage, known as Goddards since the early eighteenth century; it was mostly sloping pasture fields, with one significant beech tree almost in the centre, the point which they used as the focus of Lutyens's most symmetrical design to date. The idea, inspired by the Mirrielees, was for a large, timbered hall, known as the Common Room, with a 'cottage' on each end, each with a staircase leading up to three modest bedrooms for the ladies to occupy. The brilliant stroke was that the joint designers – for there was strong Jekyll influence here – 'read' the site well and placed the house facing west. From the east, entrance side, Goddards is severe and hints at a vernacular kinship with McLaren's Glenlyon buildings; it is whitewashed roughcast with brick mullions and soaring brick chimneys, with only the arched entrance as light relief. On the west, where the arms of the house are raked outwards to welcome the sun into the garden court, the building, low in the centre beneath heavy Horsham stone tiles, and soaring upwards at the sides, seems to bask like some gorgeous butterfly, settling in the sun among the flowers. This west face of Goddards, the deep eaves

39

Goddards, Abinger Common, Surrey: the Common Room as furnished in 1900 for the 'ladies of small means' with help from Gertrude Jekyll and in her 'Old West Surrey' style.
Above: Towards the fireplace – all the fire irons and fittings were made by the local blacksmith.
Below: The entrance from the hall and front door. The 'contraption' hanging from the ceiling is an antique bed-warmer, made of willow or hazel with an iron box for hot coals. From a miniature Christmas card.

shading the banded windows of the Common Room like heavy eyelashes, is the most seductive of Lutyens's garden façades and seems to express the very essence of its Surrey countryside.

This most delightful, essentially Surrey building was produced under the tension of both Frederick and Margaret Mirrielees' benevolent interest, with a Scottish accent. There was an overlay of sympathetic Arts and Crafts involvement, with lovely ornaments (ships in Delft tiles and engraved window glasses) bought for Goddards, and also the collection of Old West Surrey artefacts, horse bells, candle-snuffers and pewter. The style, much influenced by Miss Jekyll, was for simple country living with due regard to tradition. The furniture was old oak or new rush-seated ladder-back chairs, there was Surrey hand-made matting on the oak boards, plain distempered walls; all the ironwork, for fire-baskets and dogs,

The Courtyard at Goddards, sketch in 1906.

GODDARDS E·L·LUTYENS· TRANSLATED FROM A PHOTO
ARCHITECT·· BY·D·G·DRIVER· TFG delt·06

door and window catches and handles, was made by the local smith. For the garden there were cane chairs cushioned with pink paisley-patterned cotton, and in the skittle alley, built for recreation, there were reputedly Grinling Gibbons swags of fruit and flowers, which Frederick Mirrielees had picked up at a sale. Goddards was of intense interest to the locals; the builders were the Harrison brothers, who had themselves bought some of the glebe building lots, and had their 'yard' on one, just across the green from Goddards. There was a house-warming for everyone, and for ten years after its completion in 1900 Goddards sheltered a stream of overwrought but recuperating ladies of small means, and the Mirrielees family purred with pride in their enterprise. Though it was officially Margaret Mirrielees's project, Frederick was greatly influenced by his sister Maida and her

41

socialist husband, Harry Bernard. All the Pasture Wood house-parties were taken to see the ladies of Goddards, and the children especially looked forward to the skittle parties and teas. The young Donald Mirrielees and his cousin Ronald Cazalet, trying to prove their capacity, ate forty scones between them at one tea.[29]

In 1910 Lutyens added to Goddards, as a prospective country home for that same Donald Mirrielees and his American wife, Mary Pangbourne of Baltimore, who took one look and decided she wasn't going to be buried in the Surrey countryside in a spartan simplicity, even with electricity and gigantic fireplaces added. Lutyens, who couldn't help liking Mirrielees, also quite naturally had expectations of his connections, but nothing was to come of them. Sir Donald Currie had died in 1909, leaving his three daughters extremely wealthy and his son-in-law Frederick as the chairman of what was now the Union Castle Line. The following year the *Balmoral Castle*, in which Flockhart had prepared the royal suite, took the Duke of Connaught to open the first South African parliament in Cape Town. It was announced with some flourish that Margaret Mirrielees and her sisters had each donated £25,000 to the new university, and Frederick Mirrielees was consequently knighted. The Currie patronage had already gone to South Africa by direct line from McLaren's successors, Dunn & Watson, in Edinburgh, to Herbert Baker, who had overseen the Union Castle Building and Welgelegen, the house Rhodes had given to Currie.

Immediately after the great events in Cape Town, things began to go wrong for Mirrielees, and it seems likely that this highly-strung and essentially soft-hearted man began to succumb to big business stresses, which aggravated the old sense of guilt that he had betrayed his own family livelihood for the Currie empire, which now became difficult to handle. In 1912 the Union Castle Line was taken over, and though Sir Frederick and his fellow directors received an enormous cheque (for just over £5 million, the largest ever drawn on the Bank of England[30]) it was undoubted capitulation on their part. He retired to Pasture Wood, and though he and Lady Mirrielees sent out a charming 1912 Christmas card illustrating Lutyens's ingenious arched and pergola'd garden extension to their house, their building days were over. Sir Frederick's depression was aggravated by an accident, thought to have been an attempt at suicide, and he died in January 1914.[31] Lady Mirrielees let Goddards and eventually sold it; she died in 1925.

Knowing nothing then of what was to be this Abinger dead-end to his ambitions, the completion of Munstead Wood in 1897 was entirely a cause for celebration for Lutyens. His alliance with Miss Jekyll undoubtedly cheered his prospects and supported his capabilities, so that he won the hand of Emily Lytton early in the year and married her in August. His natural inclination to pursue

Pasturewood, Holmbury St Mary: a photograph from the Mirrielees' Christmas card of 1912 showing Lutyens's addition to their house (originally built by William Flockhart) and the small formal garden.

every job was now fired by his promise to look after Emily, and when she became pregnant, just before the end of the year, his job-hunting became frenetic. He must have momentarily cursed the broken reeds of Gertrude's aristocratic introductions, the reluctant Duke of Westminster, the capricious Princess Louise and Adeline, Duchess of Bedford, who had only wanted a garden walk[32] – and realized the truth of Shaw's prophecy that only new money people would build. Lutyens may even have wondered if his repeated appearances in the wake of an eccentric portly spinster in black bombazine would ever allow anyone to take him seriously and give him an important business commission. Munstead Wood was much admired, but everyone seemed aware of its idiosyncrasies, and of Gertrude's domination – interestingly commented upon at the time by Mary Watts, wife of the octogenarian painter George Frederic and busily engaged upon her own brilliantly eccentric mortuary chapel at Compton. The Wattses' own house, Limnerslease, had been built by Ernest George in 1890, so Ned Lutyens would have secretly enjoyed Mary Watts's envy. 'In the afternoon,' she wrote in her diary for 2 April 1898, 'we went up to see Miss Jekyll in her new house. It is wonderfully simple and good and gives one a conventual medieval feeling – *new* grey tinder coloured oak beams are my *envy*. Mr Lutyens explains that it is "English" oak. That is nonsense. "Wash it with lime and leave it lying about" that might explain it better. I wonder whether it [will] keep that *velvety grey*?'[33]

With Miss Jekyll settled with her velvety oak, it was now her brother Herbert's turn to progress the family patronage. The British participation in the Paris International Exhibition of 1900 was launched in early 1898 with the Queen's appointment of a Royal Commission a hundred strong: the Prince of Wales addressed the glitterati at Marlborough House, telling them that it bid 'fair to surpass any of its predecessors' as a magnificent display of every kind of art, industry and manufacture, that it would draw the eyes of the civilized world, and that a 'display not unworthy of the Empire' was their goal. Colonel Sir Herbert Jekyll had the mammoth task of welding the hundred dignitaries and their special interests into a unified whole at a particular place and time, and he appointed himself to the small but important committee on the Royal Pavilion. The members were Major-General Sir Arthur Ellis, chairman, Sir John Murray Scott, connoisseur and heir to a large part of Sir Richard Wallace's Collection, and Professor Aitchison, President of the RIBA and Professor of Architecture at the Royal Academy.

The brief for the Royal Pavilion was set out before the architect was chosen. Britain had naturally acquired the plum site on the Quai d'Orsay, twenty-five by twenty-eight and a half metres, for an attractive English house to be filled with the finest furniture and paintings. It was to be used by special visitors, most notably the Prince and Princess of Wales. The solution was plainly hatched up on a weekend at Mells, and in Frances Horner's presence the genial, elderly Aitchison, a long-time friend of Leighton and Burne-Jones, had no difficulty in agreeing that Mr Lutyens should be the architect. The ideal house was discovered at Bradford-upon-Avon, and flavours of Blickling and Knole were to be added. The whole Cartoon Gallery at Knole was actually added, in miniature, at the suggestion of Sir John Murray Scott, newly enamoured of the young chatelaine of that great Elizabethan house, the lovely Victoria Sackville-West. Lutyens must have encountered her for the first time when he visited Knole on this occasion, pre-sumably under Sir John's wing. As he was newly married, a new father after the birth of Barbara (for it was the late summer of 1898), this first meeting had no effect. Victoria, though, who was always loyal – '*Toujours loyal*' being her favourite phrase – might have noticed him, just for a moment.

The Paris commission was ideal for Lutyens, as it was pure art, uncluttered with the messiness of a real building. A snag was struck when the site revealed an old tunnel which would not bear the weight, but another old Jekyll family friend, the engineer Sir Benjamin Baker, came to the rescue with a steel platform to support the whole pavilion, which was also constructed of steel because of the fire precautions demanded for its precious contents. The outcome, a pastiche Elizabethan house of 'stone', was a great success. Doultons fitted out the bathroom, Elkington and Company copied Knole's silver light sconces, Waring & Son furnished the gallery, Gillow & Company the drawing-room – these best rooms were effectively panelled, hung with tapestries, and *real* Romneys, Hoppners, Gainsboroughs, Turners and Reynoldses lined the walls, hung by Sir William Agnew and insured for £240,000. One rather nice touch was that the real Jacobean oak tables were borrowed by Lutyens and Miss Jekyll from William Robinson's Gravetye Manor, and another that four Burne-Jones tapestries, belonging to Mr G. McCulloch of the Hall, Bradford-upon-Avon (the house that set the pattern for the pavilion), made the journey to be hung in the hall of the pavilion as a tribute to Sir Edward, who had died in 1898.

The architect played a vital but minute part in all this; he was awarded a Grand Prix, and paid a total of £839 19s. 2d. for his trouble. Enough has been said already to show how far-reaching the Paris affair would be, but it was also fateful in that it was there that he met, through his brother-in-law, Neville Lytton, the French banker Guillaume Mallet. There were to be three houses for the Mallets, two at Varengeville in Normandy and one near Grasse, in the south, but it was the Mallets' theosophical beliefs that were to distinguish them among clients.

III

MISS MAGGIE GUTHRIE AND THE HON. EMILY LAWLESS

A Retort

Stud all your shores with prosperous towns!
Blacken your hill-sides, mile on mile!
Redden with bricks your patient downs!
    And proudly smile.

A day will come before you guess,
A day when men of clearer sight
Will rue that deed beyond redress
    Will loathe the sight.

And, loathing, fly the hateful place,
And, shuddering, quit the hideous thing,
For where unblackened rivers race,
    And skylarks sing.

For where, remote from smoke and noise,
Old Leisure sits knee-deep in grass;
Where simple days bring simple joys
    And lovers pass.

I see an envied haunt of peace,
Calm and untouched, remote from roar,
Where wearied men may from their burdens cease
    On a still shore.

(EMILY LAWLESS)[1]

It is hard to imagine any other artist or architect who gained quite so much from the intricate networkings of his native society as Edwin Lutyens did from Old West Surrey. Quite apart from the family championship of the Jekylls, the connections of Barbara Webb and Ellinor Arbuthnot spread throughout his career; there was a certain irony in that he thought himself a London architect, and would

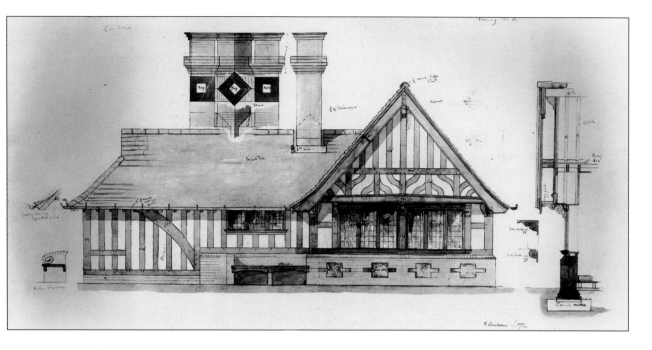

Gardener's Cottage for H. J. Mangles Esq., Littleworth Cross, Surrey: this is the commission that took Lutyens to Littleworth on the day he met Gertrude Jekyll in May 1889.

never have stooped to provincialisms, and yet sometimes it seemed that the very greensand of these Surrey hills and heaths sprouted adherents to his cause.

He had no particular liking for rhododendrons, but he had met Miss Jekyll at a rhododendron tea party, at the house of Ellinor Arbuthnot's cousin, the bachelor 'hen-peckable' and kindly Harry Mangles. There were endless small buildings and sketched ideas for Harry, and a delightful timbered cottage for his spinster sister Clara, which he later remembered from those 'happy and exciting days'. The Mangles were a rambling and distinguished family,[2] and, like the proverbial iceberg, their exact influence probably remains hidden, though the tip of it is traced here.

As well as being Ellinor Arbuthnot's cousins, James and Harry Mangles had been Haileybury contemporaries of Barbara Webb's brothers. James Mangles had spent only seven years as a district magistrate in Bengal before returning home because of ill health, marrying and settling at Valewood House, Haslemere, in 1860. He had discovered a passion for rhododendrons in India, and had been taught to hybridize them by Sir William Hooker of Kew; he has been posthumously dubbed 'high priest' of the rhododendron cult.[3]

The second Mangles, Harry, was accountant-general in Bengal during the late 1850s, and in 1863 was joined by another brother, Frank Mangles, who was to start

47

a coffee plantation in Coorg state. Harry returned home in 1872 having exchanged some land in Coorg for a plot of 'little worth', sandy heathland formerly part of the Hampton Lodge Estate at Seale. All that mattered was that it was good for rhododendrons, for Harry too was rhododendron-mad – his Littleworth acres were soon filled with young plants, and when poor James Mangles died, aged fifty-two, all his best plants came from Valewood to Littleworth. Harry enters horticultural history, with more than a little help from his sisters Clara and Alice, for the magnificent scented white flowers of the hybrid 'Glory of Littleworth'.

Another Mangles sister, Agnes, was married to Arthur Chapman, a director of Piggot, Chapman & Company, exporters, of Calcutta, and the Chapmans too had returned home. They lived in Hereford Square, South Kensington, to where, at Barbara Webb's request, they had invited the student Ned Lutyens when he was in Ernest George's office. Thus it was that the George 'Old English' found its way into a cottage at Crooksbury for the Chapmans that marked Lutyens's launching out on his own. Arthur Chapman wanted to retire from his business (which he did in 1902) and hunt and be a country gentleman: he became very politically involved as a champion of working-class Liberalism in perennially Conservative Farnham – which meant that Lutyens built Farnham's Liberal Club.[4]

The Arbuthnots at Upper House, Shamley Green, who had arranged the meeting with Shaw, never actually became Lutyens's clients. Ellinor was the daughter of Admiral Sir James and Lady Stirling (Ellen Mangles); she had nine children by her first husband, James Alexander Guthrie of Craigie, Dundee, whom she had married in 1856 when she was eighteen. These children came quickly: first Beatrice Mary ('Bea'), born in 1857, Amelia Margaret ('Maggie') in 1858, Agnes Dorothea in 1860, David Charles in 1861, Rose in 1863, Georgina Lilias ('Lily') in 1864 and Violet Hunter Guthrie (who wrote her memories of the young Ned) in 1866. Here a brief pause to note that the lovely Ellinor, slightly pregnant with Violet, and dressed in embroidered black silk, in mourning for her father, the Admiral and first Governor of Perth, Western Australia, who died in 1865, was the subject of a stunning swagger portrait by Frederick Leighton.[5] After Violet the Guthries had two more sons, James Stirling in 1867 and Walter Murray in 1869. All this persistent fathering and overwork caused the death of James Guthrie in 1873, aged fifty. Thus it was that Ellinor, a beautiful rich widow, brought her family to live in the country at Shamley Green, to be within reach of many of her Mangles relations.

In about 1879 Ellinor married again; her husband, who had been in love with her for years but had absented himself into the Indian Civil Service, was the forty-six-year-old Forster Fitzgerald Arbuthnot. He settled blissfully in Shamley Green (Shaw enlarged the house again), indulging his love of hunting, teaching the

Above: Mrs Ellinor Guthrie and her children, *c.* 1895. *Back row:* left to right, Beatrice (1857–1926), m. Capt. the Hon Henry Denison; Maggie (1858–1924) m. Ninian Elliot; Ellinor Guthrie, m. (2nd) Forster Arbuthnot; Agnes, m. Charles Anstruther; David (1861–1918), m. Mary Low of Savannah, Georgia and commissioned Lutyens to do their garden at East Haddon Hall, Northants. *Centre row:* left to right, Rose, m. Edward Bingham; Georgina Lilias, 'Tiger Lil', m. Sir James Rennell Rodd, who was Ambassador in Rome when Lutyens was building the British School at Rome – as Lord and Lady Rennell of Rodd they retired to Shamley Green; Violet, m. Edward Montagu Stuart Wortley, who inherited High-cliffe Castle, where Lutyens visited them. *Front row:* James Stirling (1867–1903), and Walter Murray Guthrie MP (1869–1911), m. Olive of Torosay Castle, Isle of Mull, where their descendants still live. *Below:* Emilia Margaret 'Maggie' Elliot in later life: after her marriage to Ninian Elliot she continued to practise as a doctor on Mull, where they apparently spent their summers, and in London. Maggie Elliot's name appears in the medical register until her death in 1924, at her home, Sandown, at Ascot.

younger Guthries to ride and bringing much happiness to Ellinor. Forster Arbuth-not, who seems to have had a ring of Fielding in *A Passage to India* about him, was a passionate orientalist, translating Eastern classics into English, and was an enthusiastic early Fabian.

When Lutyens returned, a fully-fledged architect in practice, it was to be Maggie Guthrie, Ellinor's second eldest daughter, who gave him his first really large commission. The story is fascinating and fraught with mysteries. Ellinor's eldest son, David Guthrie, had married Mary Low of Savannah, Georgia, in 1891 and been elected MP for Northamptonshire (South) the following year; they settled at East Haddon Hall, where Lutyens designed them a formal garden. Ellinor Arbuthnot had been a wealthy widow, and her children were all generously provided for. The Guthrie girls were rather good-looking, but Maggie was differ-ent. While her sisters dressed at the height of fashion, their hair piled beneath pert boaters, with frilled and flowered *décolletage* and leg-o'-mutton sleeves, Maggie dressed simply, with her hair, if not cut short, smoothed to appear so. She was smaller than the others, and had malformed hands, but she was no less good-looking and she had brains. The family marriages began with Maggie's sisters Bea (to Captain Denison) and Rose (to Cecil Bingham) in the 1880s. At the same time, when she was twenty-six, Maggie 'acquired' not a husband, but a building site, and the best in a large area, the south-facing slope of Chinthurst Hill, a dramatic outcrop across the Wey valley from Munstead, but with a superior and superb view across Sussex. 'Acquired' is the term, because although Maggie could well have afforded to pay for the site she does not appear to have done so.

The Chinthurst Hill land belonged to Lord Grantley, who had fallen upon hard times. He was selling a great deal, and sold sixty-eight acres of Chinthurst for £5,100 to 'a gentleman well known in the neighbourhood'. The property title begins with an indenture dated 24 November 1884 between Hugh, 4th Earl of Fortescue, and Maggie Guthrie: if Lord Fortescue was the well-known gentleman who bought the land, why did he give it to Maggie? Were they to be married? Was it a settlement for a broken engagement? Lord Fortescue married Emily Ormsby-Gore in 1886.

Right: Chinthurst Hill: the Lutyens office provided the plans for the sale catalogue when Maggie Elliot sold her house just two years after its completion. The plans show that Lutyens had given all the principal rooms a wide aspect over the southward view, negating what was supposed to be Maggie Elliot's dissatisfaction with her house. It seems most likely that the dissatisfaction was on the part of Maggie's new husband, who perhaps did not wish to have a house associated with his wife's life before he knew her. The poor architect suffered, never daring to return to this, his first major house, because of the unhappy outcome.

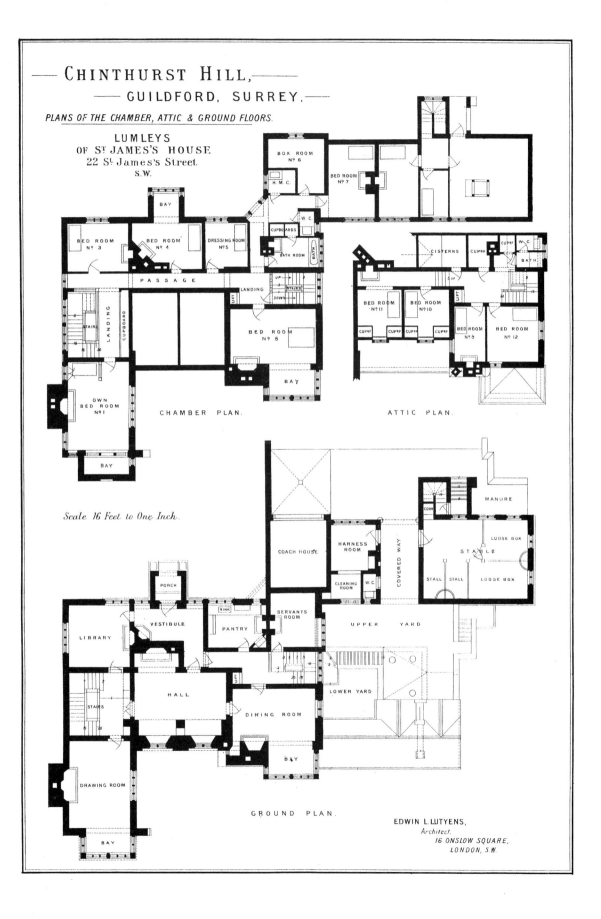

— CHINTHURST HILL, —
— GUILDFORD, SURREY. —

PLANS OF THE CHAMBER, ATTIC & GROUND FLOORS.

LUMLEYS
OF St JAMES'S HOUSE
22 St James's Street
S.W.

Chamber Plan:
BAY
BED ROOM No 3
BED ROOM No 4
DRESSING ROOM No 5
BOX ROOM No 6
H.M.C.
BED ROOM No 7
W.C.
CUPBOARDS
BATH ROOM
BATH
PASSAGE
LANDING
STAIRS
CUPBOARD
LANDING
UP
STAIRS
DOWN
LIFT
BED ROOM No 8
OWN BED ROOM No 1
BAY
BAY

CHAMBER PLAN.

Attic Plan:
CISTERNS
CUP.BD
CUP.BD
W.C.
BATH
UP
LIFT
BED ROOM No 11
BED ROOM No 10
CUP.BD
CUP.BD
CUP.BD
CUP.BD
BED ROOM No 9
BED ROOM No 12

ATTIC PLAN.

Scale 16 Feet to One Inch.

Ground Plan:
MANURE
CORN
COACH HOUSE
HARNESS ROOM
COVERED WAY
LOOSE BOX
STABLE
CLEANING ROOM
W.C.
STALL
STALL
LOOSE BOX
PORCH
SINK
SERVANTS ROOM
VESTIBULE
PANTRY
UPPER YARD
LIBRARY
LIFT
LOWER YARD
STAIRS
HALL
DINING ROOM
BAY
DRAWING ROOM
BAY

GROUND PLAN.

EDWIN L. LUTYENS,
Architect.
16 ONSLOW SQUARE,
LONDON, S.W.

In the midst of the Surrey Hills,

Half a mile from Bramley Station on the London, Brighton and South Coast Railway and three miles from Guildford on the London and South-Western Railway, and one mile from Shalford Station, South-Eastern Railway, whence there is an excellent service of trains, London being reached in forty minutes.

Illustrated Descriptive Particulars with Plans and Conditions of Sale

OF THE

CHINTHURST HILL

ESTATE

A BEAUTIFUL PROPERTY

OF

ABOUT 39 ACRES,

forming the surface of an elevation nearly **500 feet above the Sea**, with glorious views all round, together with

A Delightful Modern Mansion in the Domestic Gothic Style,

VERY SUPERIOR STABLING,

Terraced Gardens, Hill Walks, Kitchen Garden and all accessories for comfort and convenience.

THE PROPERTY IS FREEHOLD,

and will be Sold by Auction WITH POSSESSION by

Messrs. E. & H. LUMLEY

At the Mart, Tokenhouse Yard. E.C.

On TUESDAY, the 13th day of JULY, 1897,

At TWO o'Clock precisely (*unless previously disposed of*).

May be Viewed by Cards of the Auctioneers. Particulars of Sale may be obtained of Messrs. GASQUET and METCALFE, Solicitors, 92, Great Tower Street, E.C.; of WILLIAMSONS, Estate Agents and Upholsterers, High Street, Guildford; and of the

Messrs. LUMLEYS Land Agents and Auctioneers,

of "St. James's House." **22,** St. James's Street, London, S.W.

However Maggie came by her building site, she did nothing with it for nine years, until early 1893, when she appears to have asked Lutyens to design her a house. A further mystery arises in that she had also by this time started to study at the London School of Medicine for Women. She must have realized she would be absent a great deal while the house was being built, and what would a committed lady doctor want with an elaborate house on top of a remote Surrey hill?

As the mystery deepens, Lutyens was building a marvellous house, of carefully coursed Bargate stone, from its own quarry, with generous finishings to doors, windows and interiors of Bath stone, and a tiled roof. The interior was elaborately detailed: 'The flooring of the halls and reception rooms is of oak plain or in parqueterie, there is much solid oak panelling, beams and ceilings, while the fireplaces are of carved Bath stone with brick hearths and old Dutch tiles, linings and oaken fenders.' Each fireplace had a genuine sixteenth-century fireback, the lattice windows were paned in lead with 'fastenings and door furniture in hammered iron and other metal after original drawings' – by the architect – with Maggie's initials on principal door plates.

In character Chinthurst Hill feels like a cousin once removed from Philip Webb's Standen near East Grinstead, which was being built at the same time. (Lutyens's learning from Webb is more likely associated with Great Tangley, Wickham Flower's house adjacent to Chinthurst, where Lutyens saw Webb's work for the first time in 1891.) Chinthurst Hill's staircase is characteristically Lutyens, a tower of half-timbering, with low treads of limed oak; the drawing-room resembles Webb's lesser rooms at Clouds or Standen, long and lowish and beautifully proportioned, thrust forward into the huge south-facing bay window on a southern spur of the building with a view over Sussex. The best bedroom, above, had the same view and same bay, and below, cut into the hillside and giving directly on to the terrace, was the smoking-room. Chinthurst Hill was elaborately and expensively built – it must have cost almost as much as Munstead Wood, Miss Jekyll's own house, which came immediately afterwards, and it probably taught Miss Jekyll a great deal about what she did and did not want. She designed planting schemes for the garden, and she must have got to know Maggie Guthrie and like her, for there was a rare Jekyll touch, a mother-of-pearl inlaid plan of the house and garden, installed over the library fireplace.

Chinthurst was finished in 1895. Maggie Guthrie qualified as a doctor the same or the following year. According to her sister Violet's memoir (though it is difficult to believe) she came home to a house that horrified her. She thought it all back to

Left: Chinthurst Hill, Surrey, as illustrated in the sale particulars of 13 July 1897.

front, with too many rooms facing north (which the secondary bedrooms and staff rooms did), and she apparently paid off her architect. How did she imagine she could just go off and leave the house a-building for so long? How does Chinthurst have so many personal and special features – the mother-of-pearl inlay, the monogrammed doorplates – if she did not attend to those kind of details? And if she did that, how could she have so misunderstood the house in general? It seems more likely that it was not Maggie who so disliked her house, but her new fiancé, Ninian Elliot, whom she had met in Scotland and who came south with her for their marriage in 1896. Almost immediately they decided to forsake the south of England for a home on Mull, where in 1897 Maggie's brother Walter and his wife Olive inherited Torosay Castle.

Chinthurst Hill was bought by Lord Rendel of Hatchlands at Clandon, in July 1897, as a home for his widowed daughter, Rose Goodhart, and her son Harry. This observant ten-year-old boy found the house wonderful – 'an architectural symbol of life and adventure'.[6] He felt that its eccentricities were more than outweighed by his chances for escapades, he loved the complicated roof and the deep valley in it where he could hide, he was fascinated by the horn windows through which he could peer into the stairwell from a hidden passage, and happy in his allotted lair,

Engraving of Chinthurst Hill, 1897.

the Garden Room (originally the smoking-room) on the low level, 'made lower by most nonsensical large beams, with a brick floor, a great many leaky and draughty lead glazed casements on three sides of it, and a really enormous open fireplace'.[7] He also recalled that 'it was with something like fury that I watched my grandfather and mother's operations in altering its almost extravagant features, and decorating its interior so as to discord as little as possible with our furniture' which was mainly eighteenth-century.[8]

At least Harry Goodhart-Rendel's 'infatuation' with Chinthurst Hill came at an impressionable time in his life and was observed by his mother, who gave him a subscription to *The Studio*. Later in life, when he had become a distinguished architect himself and was the appreciative owner of Hatchlands with its serene Adam interiors, he always allowed that it was the 'adventure' of Lutyens's first house that had made him an architect.

The diary of Lord Rendel's coachman, William Philip Quicke,[9] provides a few further clues as to Chinthurst Hill's fate. Coachman Quicke was an assiduous diarist, recording the daily journeyings of the Rendel family and their friends. During the late summer and autumn of 1897 there were many trips to inspect Chinthurst Hill before Mrs Goodhart's furniture was finally settled in in early December. Rose's sisters, Maud (married to Herbert Gladstone) and Clarice (known as Clare) were much in evidence; Clare did a great deal of social work, and knew Maggie Guthrie through the London School of Medicine for Women. The Rendels' friends and companions also included the Misses Lyell, for whom Lutyens had enlarged a farmhouse at Okewood Hill, and Miss Mary Ann Ewart, who lived in her Webb-built Coneyhurst at Ewhurst. Perhaps, with Miss Jekyll also in attendance, it was the bevy of strong-minded women who intimidated the young Lutyens (he being totally absorbed in being in love and getting married that summer) and made him leave this particular house to its fate.

The questions remain, despite my considerable efforts to answer them: how did Maggie Guthrie acquire that wonderful site? Why did she commission a house of expensive stone and lavish craftsmanship and yet not keep her eye on its progress, *so* unlike Miss Jekyll? Was it possible – though she was eleven years older than Lutyens she looked younger – that her heart ruled her head? Whatever the true origins of this house, the fiasco did the young Lutyens a great deal of harm, not caused by Maggie herself but because the influential Lord Rendel, when he wanted work done at Hatchlands, let it be known that Lutyens had cost him enough already for the alterations made to Chinthurst Hill, and employed Reginald Blomfield.

The Guthries, however, continued to thread through Lutyens's life. Violet married Edward Stuart Wortley and they inherited Highcliffe Castle from Lady Waterford. Lutyens was invited for the weekend and arrived hot and bothered, but would not stop for even a fresh collar because he *must* see Christchurch Priory; Violet was rather hurt because the French Gothic Revival glories of Highcliffe went unappreciated! Violet remembered that she was one of the privileged friends he allowed to see the Doll's House before it was delivered to Queen Mary, after they had met at dinner at Agnes Guthrie's – who was married to Charles Anstruther. And Lily, who married Rennell Rodd, returns to this story later on.

EMILY LAWLESS

While Miss Jekyll at Munstead drew satisfaction from the clattering, swishing and chopping sounds of her builders at work, a few miles to the east Emily Lawless was hating every minute of her house being built. She hated the disruption to her birds and wild flowers: on a visit to the site in late May 1896 she registers the pain of 'stacks of raw planking' rising from the 'trampled briars and bluebells. . . The house stood roofed, but the inside was horrible. The reign of the Hammerer had spread to every creature with ears . . . the sound of it went far to extinguish the nightingales.'[10] Miss Lawless cared far more for her nightingales than she did for

The Hon. Emily Lawless (1845–1913): poet, novelist and Irish patriot, she lived out her self-imposed exile in the house Lutyens built for her and Lady Sarah Spencer, deep in a Surrey wood.

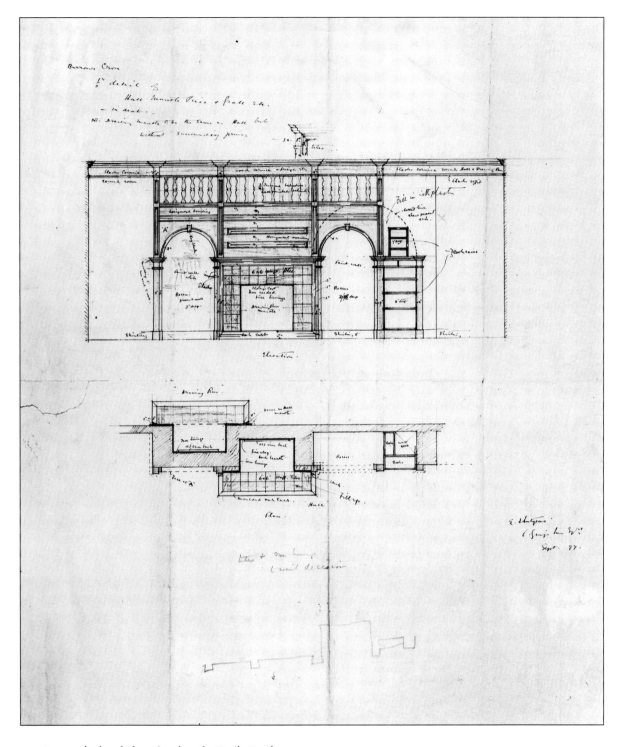

Lutyens's sketch for a fireplace for Emily Lawless.

Mr Lutyens (who only ever addressed her as Miss Lawless) or his or any architecture. She wanted her house as a peaceful retreat, as a shelter for dreaming her poet's dreams of other places; for her the North Downs that she could see in one direction were flushed in 'Irish indigo' and the heather-clad hills to the south supported her memories of the Burren of Clare. Emily Lawless was in exile from Ireland, from the troubles of the Land War, from her own past as a passionate lyricist of 'the wild Atlantic lands', but she chose to end her days 'in the least wild of all the shires of England'.[11] She lived quietly in the little house that Lutyens built for her and Lady Sarah Spencer for the last fifteen years of her life, and through her poet's eye and her writings, especially her *Garden Diary*, she left a vivid portrait of her world as she saw it.

The little Surrey house was named Hazlehatch, after the Lawless family home, Lyons House, Hazlehatch, in County Kildare. Miss Lawless was Lutyens's client, and she paid for the house, but it was a joint country retreat for her and Lady Sarah Spencer, and Lady Sarah's brother, the 5th Earl Spencer, paid for the plot of twenty acres.

It is just possible that Miss Lawless knew that her architect's mother had, like her own, come from Galway; her father was the 3rd Lord Cloncurry, and she and her brothers and sisters were brought up among the splendours of Lyons, a classical colonnaded pavilion filled with the treasures brought home from Italy by their grandfather.[12] Emily, 'born a rebel', with red-gold hair, tall, full of laughter and energy, rejected all the grander conventions for a love of wildlife and wild landscapes, for long walks, wanderings in Connemara and voluntary banishment to the Aran islands, living the simplest life. The sea was her natural element; she was a strong swimmer and fearless diver for treasures into the deep waters beyond the Atlantic waves. Augusta Gregory remembered her as a young woman with a 'hard, decided manner' – but this was when she was forced into polite society; she mercilessly cross-examined a young fellow guest on the economics of turf-cutting for an article she was writing 'On Bogs'. She later listed her recreations as dredging, mothing, gardening and geologizing.

To the considerable surprise of many who knew her, Emily Lawless began to publish novels when she was in her thirties: *Hurrish* was first, in 1886, *Grania*, perhaps the most famous, in 1892. Augusta Gregory thought that the streak in Emily's family 'that led to the suicide of her father and sister turned to genius in her',[13] and the particular repose of the genius was in Emily's poems and in her 'historical and imaginative study' *With Essex in Ireland* – which 'Gladstone, for one, had believed to be an authentic history written by its hero'.[14] In the slim volume *With the Wild Geese* she seems to assume her rightful guise and time with those seventeenth-century Irish exiles 'like the wild birds with their wailing cry' who left to fight for France and Spain. Of these few restrained and moving poems, perhaps the most poignant is 'Fontenoy 1745' – a song for the dead of Clare's Brigade, returning home after the battle:

> 'Mary mother, shield us! Say, what men are ye,
> Sweeping past us swiftly on this morning sea?'
> 'Without sails or rowlocks merrily we glide
> Home to Corca Bascinn on the brimming tide.'
>
> 'Jesus save you, gentry! Why are ye so white,
> Sitting all so straight and still in this misty light?'
> 'Nothing ails us, brother; joyous souls are we
> Sailing home together, on the morning sea.'[15]

'Fontenoy' and the rest of the *Wild Geese* poems lay, unpublished, among Emily Lawless's belongings when she moved into Hazlehatch in 1897. She had not written anything for several years, but she had many friends and was constantly visiting – she was well acquainted with George Meredith and even the reclusive Tennyson, the Batterseas, Webbs, Alfred Lyall, and she went to Dublin regularly (her architect's name was mentioned by her in many useful places). Daisy Fingall describes Emily at about this time: 'She gave one no idea of the passion and power within her. She was pale and flaccid, with half-closed, near-sighted eyes and limp white hands. Her speech was slow and she was very delicate and rather hypochondriachal and untidy in her dressing.'[16] She seems to have compromised with life in her settling down into her little world, which from now on had to make up for all the adventures she would never have. She wrote, as a response to feeling at home, 'the first sense of newness and desecration' of the building of Hazlehatch having wholly passed away, what she called her *Garden Diary*, which begins in September 1899. She opens it by confessing that her youthful dreams of being like Darwin or Stanley, Nansen or even Miss Kingsley, have gone and she has learned to 'grow down gracefully' as the sedums and pennyworts, and to set forth 'on the five hundred and first tour' around her little estate still 'brimming with expectation' and certain of new discoveries.[17]

Her diary jottings are discursive and sometimes perplexed – 'We have a habit of telling friends that we have "made" these gardens,' she admits, as she realizes that the 'admirable Cuttle', who came with the builders and stayed on, had cut the walks, made the beds, planted the shrubs and heather banks and done everything else. He seemed a law unto himself; she is sometimes asked whether Cuttle is their gardener 'and I am always rather at a loss what to answer', but Cuttle kept coming, and occasionally complying with requests, and stalking their holly-guarded boundaries with his 'satellite and shadow' – whether old or young, or a dog, they did not know. Such uncertainty is the lot of many a quiet country person and their 'gardener': perhaps it was that Hazlehatch's garden was not neat beds and rows of dahlias, but a naturalist's garden, of mown walks through birches and sweet chestnuts, with glades cut among the bracken and brambles. One of the diary entries is devoted to 'weeds' – which were hard to define for the naturalist in Miss Lawless, and she ends up admiring the energy and character of groundsels and creeping buttercup! On 27 October 1899 she closes the diary after a brief entry – 'poor little garden' . . . 'all quips and jests which in sunnier hours it gives rise to' are as nought, it has dwindled to an infinitesimal speck in the shadow of the beginnings of the Boer War. She leaves for London, only returning on Christmas Day, to stand staring out at the dead garden: 'Staring blankly out of the window, I feel myself for the moment a sort of embodiment of all the other vacant-eyed starers out of windows, up and down the face of the country this Christmas morning.' The only person she sees is Cuttle, with his 'homespun garment of British pride'. Emily, less well clothed, muses on England as 'Great Bully', 'Supreme Tyrant', walks out on Christmas afternoon to get more news and walks home 'feeling sorry, painfully fearful for the Bully now'. At 6 pm she writes:

> I had got as far as the grassy entrance to our copse when a sudden dazzling gleam of sunlight shot across it, sweeping over the fields beyond, and away up to the top of the downs . . . The yellow oak scrub . . . glowed with a sudden russet splendour. Upon the little garden wall the terra-cotta pots shone with a momentary reminiscence of that Italy where they were born and baked. The air seemed to tingle; the tall birches glistened, one sheen of feathery silver up to their tiniest towering twigs . . . Christmas 1899 will never seem quite so dark, never so absolutely despairing in the retrospect, as it would have done without that last benevolent gleam at eventide.

One entry especially reveals Miss Lawless in her times: it is for 12 February 1900:

> I had occasion to go to Guildford yesterday, and met in the train our eminent horticultural acquaintance, Mr R. P. On this occasion, seeing that he was coming from London, my first remark was not a horticultural one.
>
> 'Is there anything fresh?' I asked. 'News seems so often to come in just after the morning papers are out.'
>
> 'Fresh? Oh, you mean about the [Boer] war? No, I think not. Everybody seems to be pretty sick over the whole business. I saw Sir F. J. the day before yesterday and he was very much in the dumps about it. He says the Tommies out there don't like it one bit. That they must have got their tails regularly between their legs, and I'm sure I don't wonder.'

'How dare he! – I mean I don't believe a word of that!' I exclaimed. 'Anything else I am willing to believe but not that. We have got our tails between our legs here at home if you like; I am quite ready to admit that. But they! Never!'

'Well, I don't know. I only tell you what I hear. They have had a baddish time, you must remember. Of course it has been kept out of the papers. In the papers the Tommies always figure as heroes. Is Anemone Blanda in flower with you yet?' – this with a sudden rise of animation.

'Anemone Blanda?' I repeated, feeling slightly confused by the rapidity of the transition. 'Yes. At least no I think not – I haven't looked lately.'

'It is with me! Sixteen tufts in full flower – beauties! I shelter them a bit of course, but only to save them from getting knocked about. You never saw such a colour as they are! Yours were the pale blue ones, weren't they? I know there's a lot of that sort in the trade that are sold as Anemone Blanda, but they're not the right Blanda at all. Mine are as blue as, oh, as blue as – blue paint.'

'We have numbers of bulbs at present in flower,' I said severely. 'Scillas and chinodoxas, and daffodils, and tulips, and Iris Alata, and many others.'

'Ah, potted bulbs. They're poor sort of things generally, don't you think? Some people, I believe, like them though.'

'We have Cyclamen Coum in flower out of doors,' I added; garden vanity, or more probably deflected ill-humour, arousing in me a sudden spirit of violent horticultural rivalry.

'Oh, you have, have you?' – this in a tone of somewhat enhanced respect. 'Don't you shelter it at all?'

'Not in the least!' I replied contemptuously. 'We grow it out in the copse; on the stones; in all directions. It is a perfect weed with us. No weather seems to make the slightest difference.'

I am really surprised that I did not assert that we had Orchids and Bougainvilleas growing out of doors in the snow! It is probable that I should have done so in another five minutes, for irritation sometimes takes the oddest forms. Luckily for my veracity our roads just then diverged; my horticultural acquaintance getting out at the next station, and I continuing on my way to Guildford.

I don't think I have ever in my life felt more ruffled, more thoroughly exasperated than I was by that most uncalled-for remark about the Tommies. Had they been all individually my sons or my nephews I doubt if I could have felt more insulted! I adore my garden and yield to no one in my estimation of its supreme importance as a topic; still there are moments when even horticulture must learn to bow its head; when the reputation of one's flag rises to a higher place in one's estimation than even the reputation of one's flower-beds. 'Anemone Blanda!' I repeated several times to myself in the course of the afternoon and each time with a stronger feeling of exasperation. 'Anemone Blanda, indeed!'[18]

'Anemone Blanda' reveals Miss Lawless in her true light. She is far more a citizen of her world than a toiler in her Surrey backwood. Four days later, 'God be thanked!' for Kimberley has been relieved. She goes about her gardening as the weather lifts, making a wide grass walk, 'a walk of pride to people who have hitherto subsisted on two-foot tracks', up to her new northward view. But then she is shocked that Cuttle gives in his notice; fiercely defensive of her 'Tommies', she has not realized that he has been walking four miles each way, in all weathers, and digging, sawing and scrub-cutting all day in between. She was a true poet. She inhabited her little brick house that Lutyens had built in her Surrey wood, but it was merely a halting place, a stop-over, from the journeyings of her traveller's mind.

Miss Lawless takes the diary on to September of 1900, with less and less of gardening. She had yet to receive Mr Stopford Brooke, who, on his visit to Hazlehatch, came upon 'by accident' the poems that he arranged for publication in 1902 as *With the Wild Geese*. They brought Miss Lawless considerable notice; her biography of Maria Edgworth was published in 1904 and the following year she was given an Honorary Doctorate of Literature in Dublin. It was also the year that Lady Sarah Spencer died. Emily Lawless's last book, the *Book of Gilly*, was published in 1906, and she lived out her last years at Hazlehatch. She died in 1913 and is buried among the heathers, whortleberry, dog-roses and pines that make a wild garden of Peaslake's hillside cemetery. Her grave is marked with a tall Celtic cross. Her *Garden Diary* for 17 April 1900 had already described her last journey:

> The west wind this morning had a rolling sonorousness which sent my thoughts flying, swift as light, across all the little intervening ridges, over the plains, over the villages, across endless housetops, through multitudinous suburbs, over the big ugly, stately town; out again, over fresh sweeps of more or less encumbered green fields, hedgerows, lanes, roads; past meadows and orchards, redolent of centuries of care; past brickfields and coalfield, redolent only of defiling greed; over a fretful space of sea; across more fields, less enclosed, less cultivated, but certainly not less green. On and on breathlessly, until I stood – free of all encumbrances, free of any thought of luggage, conveyance, or the need of a roof to shelter under – upon a very familiar spot, close to the tumbling breast of the Atlantic.[19]

IV

THE IMPORTANCE OF BEING GERARD, MARK AND ERNEST

> There seems to be a view entertained by many architects and most building papers that houses are built in order to display the skill and taste of the architect. This is not the case. Houses are built for men to live in, and those who live in them are entitled to have them built to suit their fancy and convenience.
>
> (ERNEST MURRAY BLACKBURN to the *Building News*, 1902)[1]

Lutyens's happiest Surrey house – in human terms – is Fulbrook at Elstead, built in exciting days, impossibly crowded days and years, and almost unbelievably sandwiched between Munstead Wood and Orchards. But the story of Fulbrook begins at Pierrepont, Shaw's Pierrepont, the home of the Combes at Frensham. Richard Henry Combe came from a family whose City prosperity and brewing fortune dated from the early eighteenth century, so neither his money nor his manners were *nouveau*, but the coming of the railway made it possible for him to be a country gentleman. The Combes had bought the Pierrepont Lodge Estate at Frensham, where Shaw built a new house for them, with his favourite builder Frank Birch of Farnham[2] in 1876–8. Their house of sandstone with timbered upper storeys, enormous stone mullions and tall chimneys was wisely built on a knoll overlooking the water meadows of the temperamental Wey. Mrs Combe had determined taste and furnished her house to delight Shaw's heart; the huge, timbered hall, with its full-height window, was lightly hung with tapestries and sensibly scattered with Bokhara rugs, there were just a few huge, comfortable sofas covered in crewel work, and otherwise just masses of flowers and a few stately palms. The bedrooms were light, with plain walls, more comfortable chairs and sofas and crewel work, but essentially uncluttered; Esther Combe's style was more of country houses in the mid-twentieth century than the 1880s. In 1885, when she was twenty, their only daughter, Ida, married Gerard Dorrien Streatfeild from Chiddingstone in Kent. A daughter, Violet, was born the following year. Violet's first memories were of delicious summers at Chiddingstone Castle, eating sun-warmed apricots and sitting on top of a yew hedge so thick she could run along

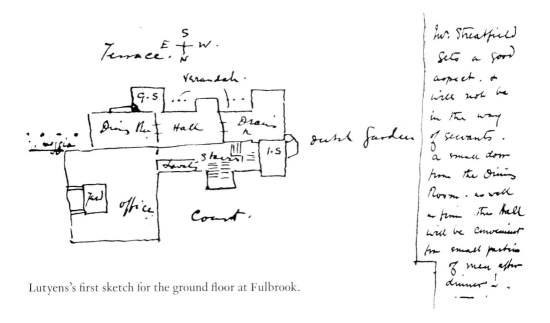

Lutyens's first sketch for the ground floor at Fulbrook.

Fulbrook, Elstead, Surrey: the house under construction, 1898.

the top, and of comfortable winters at Pierrepont, and of her grandmother, Esther Combe, with a lace cap and a perennial tache of old-fashioned white and double Parma violets.[3]

Violet's father, Gerard Streatfeild, was in his mid-thirties when he married, a gentleman of leisured interests in archaeology and ornithology, and when the time came, garden-making. He had a passion for cricket, had played for Eton Ramblers and I Zingari, was a member of the MCC, and once he encountered the famous Tilford village club he was a staunch and regular supporter for the rest of his life.[4] He had met Lutyens during the building of the Village Institute on Tilford's green by the River Wey – the cricket team had been temporarily banished to play at Pierrepont while an old chapel was demolished and the Institute – or village hall – was built, with double duty as a cricket pavilion. Having decided to build for themselves on an old farm named Fulbrook, on the southern slopes of Crooksbury Common, just north of Tilford and the river, the question of an architect arose, Violet remembered, and they said, 'Why not try young Ned Lutyens?' – so they did.

Gerard Streatfeild made the overtures at Lutyens's Gray's Inn office, but after that it was very much his wife's wishes that were carried out, with formidable assistance from Mrs Combe (with whom Ned Lutyens rather enjoyed verbal sparrings). Mrs Streatfeild was a remarkably modern woman, for all her frail beauty; she was passionately interested in motor cars, and her house was perhaps to illustrate a new Edwardian marriage. She wanted a bedroom each for her and her husband, with shared balconies over a verandah facing south. Other than that she needed three large, pale and airy rooms, not the panelled richness of Pierrepont – a hall, drawing-room and dining-room, the last to be next to the kitchen. And a sitting-room for herself, a smoking-room for Gerard, and perhaps nine or ten bedrooms altogether . . . and a lift for her boxes, and Men and Maids to be kept apart. Their architect sketched furiously: 'He made endless drawings and was chock full of ideas' for all these things – a lovely classical hall with round arches like those at beloved Milford House where blessed Barbara was dying (but which had so recently also held his adored Emily) – and then, inspired by walking the site which they called Romping Hangar, an entrance range of timbered lodges, with a gated arch, and a high wall along the drive sheltering a vast garden.

Eleven-year-old Violet Streatfeild always remembered her first 'visit' when she walked around with the water diviner, choosing the site for the well. The drive was cut, the site levelled, all was ready, but not the architect, whose drawings and quantities were not finished . . . and then on 3 February 1897, having missed his appointment with Gerard Streatfeild, he blurted out, 'Ned is going to marry

Fulbrook: Mrs Gerard Streatfeild and her daughter Violet in Mrs Streatfeild's Locomobile, outside the completed house, 1902.

Emily' – his long winter of uncertainty was over and all was well. After that, he settled down to build Fulbrook.

In retrospect the Streatfeilds were remarkable clients: there seemed to be no hurry, no cross words or loss of temper, they attended immediately to every question or decision and almost as promptly to every bill. While Fulbrook was building their lives kept an even tenor, but they also wished to be part of its creation and at some times their almost daily site visits exasperated their architect. Fulbrook may puzzle architects and architectural historians, but everyone who has come to know the house loved it – as the Streatfeilds did.[5]

The Streatfeilds were presented with the drawings for their house on a Saturday morning in late February 1897; there was much discussion of flues and stoves. They were adamant about their south-facing verandah with a deep overhang of roof, structurally puzzling but so that the bedroom balconies would be dry and shaded and curiously lit by the light reflected from the stone paving, especially when it was wet – the Old London paving with tooled edges was a luxury paid for by Mrs Combe. The roof over the verandah, supported by 'flimsy-looking' oak brackets, has precedents in Kentish Wealden houses, Roderick Gradidge has observed, which Lutyens intended for the sake of Gerard Streatfeild's home village of Chiddingstone.[6]

The twelfth of March 1897 brought Mrs Streatfeild an expenses slip (£28 5s. 9½d.) to be passed to her husband, who always dealt with the money; a week later on a site visit the architect found the road coming 'splendidly' and, the day after his twentieth birthday, i.e. 30 March, the estimate/tender of £6,840 was accepted, from a firm called Badcock and Maxey. E. Baynes Badcock was a surveyor/builder who actually joined Lutyens's office – perhaps Lutyens was less than shrewd about such business arrangements, but to the client he was confident – 'the builders are good so we ought to be congratulated' on a low tender – and impressive: 'you will require about 91,000 tiles.'[7]

On 5 April Mr Streatfeild received a request for £171, being $2\frac{1}{2}$ per cent of the contract sum, and a reminder about the expenses, which were paid immediately. Mrs Streatfeild had received an apology for the architect daring to ask for money, as no building had started, and she was given a warning, 'only remember do not order alterations and extras except through me'.[8] Three letters tumbled out of Lutyens's office that day, another to Mrs Streatfeild saying that a clerk of works had been found for 4 guineas a week which was an extra. She called at the office to say her mother would pay, and to protest her fears about a traction engine on the site getting stuck – Lutyens allays this with a comic sketch of the traction engine being pulled out of a hole by a horse, and distracts her with the design for the foundation stone, which Violet was to lay.

By mid-April Ida Streatfeild was laid up with flu, so her architect suggested she make one-eighth scale plans of her furniture to move round on the house plans. By the end of the month she was well enough to be on site inspecting with Lutyens – endless details of earth closets, manure pits and hay lofts surround elaborate discussions through May, about stables and garden walls, with a lovely scheme sketched for entrance lodges with an arch, a carriage house with a vast glass cover for car washing. The house itself approached ground-floor window level, and with a certificate for the builders' first instalment of £600, and the gloomy news that the entrance and stables dream would cost another £2,000, the Streatfeilds left for their holidays in the Haute Savoie and their architect went off to get married.

The builders, presumably without holidays, carried on; they were paid their second instalment, £400, and a third, £1,200, in December 1897, by which time the roof was on, and work was inside for the winter. The grand arched stable entrance was rejected (and immediately transferred to Orchards by the architect), and Gerard Streatfeild began planting the garden terraces, which he had had built up from the soil from the house site; he brought bulbs from Chiddingstone.

In January 1898 more questions arose. What kind of kitchen range? An Eagle? Slate shelves in the linen room? Some expensive fire-grates had been ordered, the terrace was being laid. In the spring, with Ida Streatfeild again indisposed, her

INVOICES AND STATEMENTS			
Date		Lutyens	Badcock & Maxey
		£ s d	£ s d
April 5 1897	Site Survey	180 4 6	
April 6 1897	Receipt of same		
July 31 1897	Certificate of Instalment 1	[33 8 0]	600 10 0
Oct 14 1897	Receipt of Instalment 2		400 0 0
Dec 3 1897	Invoice for Instalment 3	31 7 0	1200
			[1000]
May 31 1898	Certificate of Instalment 5	[53 0 5]	1000
Aug. 4 1898	Fee on Instalment 6		
Aug. 4 1898	Certificate of Instalment 6		
Aug 8 1898	Receipt of fee	40 0 0	
Aug 9 1898	Receipt from Badcock & Maxey		1500
Nov 12 1898	Fee on Instalment 7		
Nov 12 1898	Certificate of Instalment		
Nov 15 1898	Receipt from Lutyens	40 12 6	
Nov 18 1898	Receipt from Badcock & Maxey		1500
Dec 19 1898	Fee on Certificate 8	[38 0 0]	
Jan 10 1899	Receipt from Badcock & Maxey		1261 10 0
	Subtotal		£8461 10 0
Mar 24 1899	Statement from Lutyens		
Mar 29 1899	Receipt from Badcock & Maxey		638 10 0
Mar 29 1899	Lutyens receipt of settlement	[42 0 0]	
[Mar 29	Payment of £80 on Certificate 8 appears to have been made]		
	Total	£458 12 5	£9100 0 0
	To be paid on June 1st		150 0 0
	on Sept 1st		141 1 10
	Total paid to Builders		9391 1 10
	Total fees to Lutyens		458 12 5
			9849 14 3
	Cost of land purchase		2500 0 0
			£12349 14 3

This sum represents as near as possible the total cost of the house to the Streatfeilds

The final account of all costs incurred in the building of Fulbrook.

Below: Lutyens's own statement of costs on the building of Fulbrook.

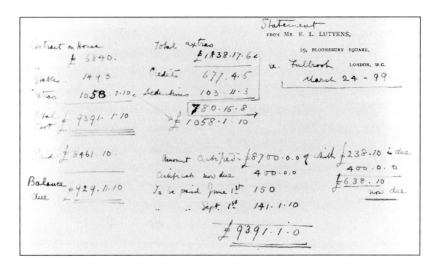

husband's firm hand takes over: he has missed – or rather his architect has missed – a meeting and is elusive – horrendous estimates from Merryweather's for fire hydrants have been received – Lutyens thinks 'hand grenades' are good enough with a staff fire brigade – how could Gerard Streatfeild remain cross when his architect sketched fire drill and asked to attend quarterly parades?

In early May 1898 the architect is granted permission to write to Mrs Streatfeild again about a gardener's cottage, a circular one? And an engine house for the generator? With this architect everything and everyone has a house. Andrew Chuter, a local builder whom Richard Combe had set up in business, tendered £624 for a rectangular cottage with sheds attached – a fair price.[9] After her illness Mrs Streatfeild visited her house, where the plasterers were at work, and wrote a long and appreciative letter to her architect. She had given his name to Lord Yarborough, whose Brocklesby Park in Lincolnshire had been partly burnt down (Reginald Blomfield got the job). During June they concentrated on the garden – Lutyens sketched a lawn sixty-six feet square with surrounding paths and flower beds and his special round-tile-topped wall. Mrs Streatfeild liked the wall but vetoed the engine shed as taking too much space where she wanted level lawn. She won.

In August there followed a flurry of problems, mostly marginal disputes between Chuter's working on the cottage and Badcock and Maxey still working on the house; but a delighted Mrs Streatfeild invited her architect to lunch, before she presumably went off on holiday again. On 8 August she was one of the very first to know of the birth of Emily's first daughter, Barbara, named for beloved Barbara Webb, whom Ned had lost.

During the autumn of 1898 the business of house building began to drag a little on the patient patrons. Their house was the scene of only fitful activity but many arguments – over the fire-grates, ludicrously expensive, the fitting-out details of cupboards, kitchen, pantry, scullery, lamp-room. Another Christmas at Pierrepont passed and Fulbrook remained cold, empty and unfinished. As 1899 gathered pace, finally things began to fall into place. The contractors had been paid £8,500 by the end of 1898, but were now quibbling and arguing, mostly with the architect, over the disputed extras; the case of Fulbrook was complicated by Lutyens's bad relationship with Badcock over other work, and in general one sympathizes with the Streatfeilds for having been caught up in this unhappy affair. Lutyens was not a good businessman, but he tried so hard, and his cavalier cheerfulness, and endless ability to turn a burgeoning row into a joke, only embittered the sharper practitioners, who shall be nameless, to determine to get the better of him. The final accounts show how badly he did from Fulbrook, for how hard he had worked.

Fulbrook: the Hall.

Most importantly, though, the Streatfeilds moved in in the spring of 1899; their house had been in their thoughts for three years and had taken two to build. Right at the start Lutyens had promised Ida Streatfeild a house she would love to live in, and his promise was fulfilled, with a happily-ever-after ending to this particular house and its owners. The Streatfeilds faded from Lutyens's life, except that Violet, when she grew up, remembered meeting him at dinner parties, where – as the great man he had become – he would infuriate or charm his hostess by drawing his latest scheme on her tablecloth. In 1907 Violet married Lieut.- Colonel Douglas Gordon, and they continued to live at Fulbrook after her parents' deaths. Violet, widowed in 1930, remained in her beloved house through changing times and fortunes until 1960, when she reluctantly sold it. She did not move far. She had written of their early days at Fulbrook when, at certain times of year, it was a kind of pilgrimage to go to the Mangles at Littleworth on Sunday afternoons: 'We either walked across the common or drove in the pony cart to see the rhodo- dendrons in bloom. It was a sort of ritual – I was frightfully bored . . . (especially

Lutyens's early sketch for the alcove in the Hall.

as I always had to get out and walk for the fat pony's sake) but I enjoyed the good tea with early strawberries and I daresay unconsciously absorbed a good deal of the gardening talk around me.'[10]

She must have done so, for she had grown up to be a keen gardener herself; and, as that young Violet, lolling in her chair while the rhododendron talk droned on, waiting for the appearance of tea and strawberries, she must have given a semblance of interest. For Harry Mangles named one of his hybrids for her, a pretty shell-pink 'Violet Streatfeild'. When she left Fulbrook, Violet Gordon rescued Harry Mangles's rhododendron and azalea woodland at Littleworth from the jungle it had become and she and her family have revived his lovely garden so that it blooms still. Annually the flowery ghosts of the world of the young Lutyens and his earliest patrons return, for Mangles's hybrid rhododendrons and azaleas were named for everyone he knew – 'Gertrude Jekyll', 'Alice Mangles', 'Clara Mangles', 'Hilda Spencer' (the wife of Colonel Spencer, for whom Lutyens built a small house at Lascombe nearby), 'Agnes Mangles', who married Arthur Chapman of Crooksbury, and their two sons, 'Paul Chapman' and 'Michael Chapman'. Michael married the lovely 'Lilian', known as Lily, the adopted daughter of George Frederic Watts and the subject of a portrait by him, in which she stands full face, holding a tray of enormous flowers.[11]

MARK FENWICK AND ABBOTSWOOD

The attention paid to the Paris Exhibition pavilion, especially in the illustrated papers and magazines, brought Lutyens's name before a wider public. At about the same time as he heard about his Grand Prix award, Lutyens also heard from Mark Fenwick that he had failed to buy Chadshunt in Warwickshire; that was in August 1900, and the following 22 April Lutyens journeyed north to meet the Fenwicks, who had now successfully found a house, Abbotswood at Lower or Nether Swell, just outside Stow-on-the-Wold in Gloucestershire.

The summons was to their rented house, Meldon Park near Morpeth, where he found the company playing croquet in the chill light of the evening. As far as his career was concerned, this hardy company was the introduction to what may be called his northern territory. There were two Fenwicks present, Mark and his distant cousin Bertie, and they were to lead to a string of Northumberland and Newcastle connections which Lutyens would serve to the end of his days, strongly

Mark and Molly Fenwick (née Clayton), newly married: they were two of Lutyens's favourite clients.

reinforced in the far-off 1920s when his daughter Ursula, as yet unborn, would marry Lord Ridley. The Fenwick cousins were a contrasting pair: Bertie was a playboy with a reputation, and had in tow at the croquet party a beautiful, over-dressed, red-haired American who aired her tastes for French literature and whom Lutyens thought was, but was not, his wife. When Lutyens eventually encountered Mrs Bertie Fenwick, he found her to be the beautiful, and very rich, former Miss Violet Perkins of Birtley, with a passion for houses and furnishing them. Mark Fenwick, just turned forty, slight, dapper, with pointed features, 'was very strict, but at the same time unpredictable'; he was moody and a perfectionist, and his reason for 'flitting' south was that he wanted to pursue his 'insatiable passion' for gardening. Mark Fenwick was extremely happily married to the former Molly Clayton, whom Lutyens rightly identified as 'delightful, quite simple, straight-forward, absolutely unaffected . . . very kind'.[12] Molly Fenwick was devoted to her sporty English countrywoman's life, which fortunately did not include gardening. She was the daughter of Nathaniel Clayton, the MP and amateur archaeologist for whom Richard Norman Shaw had enlarged Chesters, the Clayton home close to Hadrian's Wall. Molly's father had died in 1895, but the visit to her mother at Chesters was the highlight of Lutyens's trip to Meldon. As an architect to this Newcastle cabal, he was in many ways the apt successor to their great neo-classicist John Dobson, and to Shaw (who had also built Cragside for Sir William Armstrong).

The Fenwick money came from clan coal and mineral interests, and at that particular time the selling of Lambton's Bank in Newcastle, to Lloyd's. Mark Fenwick had worked in the bank since he was in his early twenties; the 'take-over' gave him the freedom to move south and garden, and provided, via his generous father, also a partner in the bank, the money for Abbotswood, with presumably a topping-up from Molly's Clayton money. When they acquired Abbotswood the Fenwicks had four daughters: Peggy was sixteen, Cecily and Hilda followed, and Audrey was seven. Constantia was born on 8 December 1905, when Mark was forty-seven and Molly was forty-four. Mark Fenwick's diary recorded 'an unwel-come little girl – we did so hope it would be a boy this time' . . . 'I walked up to Stow and sent a lot of telegrams and paid in my rent cheques.' Posterity has reason to be grateful for Constantia, for she recorded life at Abbotswood.[13]

Abbotswood had been built in 1860 for the Sartoris family. It was an ugly, 'far too ugly to be lived in as it was',[14] spiky stone house, with double-storey bay windows on its south garden front which looked semi-detached, and thin spindly chimneys. A conservatory, looking just like a modern advertisement for one, stuck out from the south-west. It was a model of propriety and dullness as a house, but

Mark Fenwick had bought it for its wonderful site. It was beautifully set in a gentle decline known as Swell Bowl, a generous green dip in the land flowing down from Nether Swell's little Norman church of St Mary's to the Dikler stream. Woods sheltered the house from the north, and a drive, half a mile long, connected it to the outside world – and, unfortunately, to the stables, kitchen garden and farm buildings.[15] Some of the older buildings were the remnants of Sir Thomas Atkyns's estate, though his house and garden, down by the stream, had disappeared.

When Lutyens saw the real Abbotswood and Mark Fenwick asked for his opinion, the reply came 'Blow it up, and start again!'[16] But his pencilled sketches on the old sepia photographs which the family kept show that he knew exactly how to deal with Abbotswood's particularly monstrous bits. The first photograph, of the entrance front, the inside of an L, facing north, had three painfully sharp gables – Lutyens's pencil has shocked the right-hand one out of its propriety, making its roof fall almost to ground level, a tiler's delight, and this dramatic gable now framed a classical doorcase, 'a pretty piece of scholarly design' flanked by gateless piers topped with stone pineapples. In photograph number two, away with the conservatory – it was replaced by a double height extension, to give a big room for parties, and outside the long, raised lily-pool terrace. Like so many Victorian houses built on terraces to accommodate the cellars, the builders of Abbotswood could think of nothing more than the usual surround of sterile grass banks, negotiable only by steps, of which there were two sets if one was lucky. Just as Lutyens would have nothing to do with conservatories, he would not allow sterile grass banks for breaking ankles. On the south front, where Mark Fenwick insisted the sunny bay windows were nice for living inside, Lutyens applied his talent for diversion – clothe them with plants, and then make such a lovely garden that no one would ever look at the house. Abbotswood's south front was turned into a walled garden, with wide grass walks around a sunken lawn, and the delicious little pavilion with a pointed cap of a roof on its circular platform in the corner.

Inside, Abbotswood became just one more exquisite echo of Milford House, at least in the first impression of the hall, with its fluted pilasters, round arches, and pedimented doorways, all in off-white. The Mark Fenwicks were not particularly interested in furniture or styles – theirs was country-house traditional – but their house was well lived-in. 'Get the house lived in,' Constantia remembered her father shouting when they returned from periodic absences in London or Northumberland. 'Put out some books, do the flowers . . . fill up the cigarette boxes – mind now, a box and ashtray on every table.'[17] Masses of flowers, Turkish cigarettes and tables littered with horticultural papers and magazines were Mark Fenwick's ideas of comforts.

Abbotswood: the house that Mark and Molly Fenwick bought in 1898.

Abbotswood: Lutyens's replacement for the conservatory – the unusual raised pool terrace.

Constantia was only two when her mother was paralysed after a hunting accident; though there were many attempts and long private agonies to find a miracle cure, none of this impinged on the 'Happy as Kings' life at Abbotswood. Molly Fenwick, in her wheelchair, 'managed to surmount it all and to remain the hub of the household – not grimly and stoically, but as though she were enjoying every minute'.[18]

Once settled, Mark Fenwick indulged his passion and persuaded Abbotswood's garden into ever fresher and flowery life: the lily tank on the terrace had only pale waterlilies and blue iris, with pots of blue hydrangeas or agapanthus and purple and white clematis on the walls. The south sunken lawn, used for tennis, was surrounded by low walls covered with aubrieta and arabis and the persistent giant verbascums which occasionally fell to a fast ball, and the raised paths around were accompanied by mixed borders – at which Mark Fenwick was a master – and roses on poles and iron hoops. To the east of the house was a Lutyens pergola, to mask a roof line he couldn't change, and a formal rose garden. Lawrence Weaver dubbed Mark Fenwick 'a master of all cultural mysteries', and though his formal garden was lovely, his *own* garden was on the well-watered slope behind the house. Audrey

Mark and Molly Fenwick in later life at Abbotswood.

Holland-Hibbert, his daughter, remembered it: 'a lovely garden, with small streams running down into ponds, planted with water plants and surrounded with trees and shrubs on a grassy slope. One of the features . . . was the Heather garden, sloping south and planted with every kind of heath and Japanese maple, so that there was colour from January, when *Erica carnea* started to bloom, until the flaming maples lost their leaves. Father had a passion for autumn colour . . . he always had a Westonbirt party on his birthday, 24 October, which he said was the peak time there for colour.'[19]

As the years went by Mark Fenwick and his garden became ever more admired and respected in gardening circles. Sometimes the Fenwicks mentioned selling Abbotswood and starting all over again, but, one suspects, Mark Fenwick looked at his heathers, growing miraculously and so brilliantly on the peat and lime-free loam overlaying the Swell bowl clay, all such hard work and achievement, that he decided to stay. Stay he did, until he was in his eighties, in the early years of the Second World War, when he is remembered, like a figure from a lost world, examining the exhibits at the RHS Vincent Square shows, dressed immaculately in frock-coat and top hat. Mark Fenwick died in 1945 aged eighty-four. Abbotswood was sold to Harry Ferguson, who famously made tractors, and he and Mrs Ferguson altered little, but enlarged the garden and maintained it immaculately – they retained the Fenwicks' head gardener, Mr Fred Tustin, who had started to work there in 1908.[20]

THE IMPORTANCE OF BEING TOM (OR ERNEST)

Oddly, the two most spectacular houses that Lutyens ever built, the two that architects love most, were not built for Souls, or Liberal Members of Parliament, or any celebrated beautiful personage of his Edwardian coterie. Little Thakeham, the house that Lutyens called 'the best of the bunch', and Heathcote at Ilkley, were both built for unassuming gentlemen of a very different kind. Heathcote comes later, but here, among scholars and garden-makers, comes Little Thakeham.

It was built for Ernest Murray Blackburn, 'Ern' to his wife, 'Tom' to his children (and here), a man of many parts and talents, who easily took to his leisurely country life, dressed in old tweeds, moving swiftly and silently about his domain, secateurs or trowel ever in hand, master-minding his fruitful garden. He also had the leisure and inclination to leave a record of what he did.

Tom Blackburn had been born in Teignmouth in Devon in 1856. He was the eighth of ten children of Edward and Charlotte Blackburn, who had recently returned from living in New York, where Edward Blackburn had made a great deal of money importing Madeira wine. Tom was sent to Winchester, and to Corpus Christi at Oxford, where he obtained a BA in classics and modern languages in 1879 and an MA in 1882; he became a schoolmaster, assistant master at Westminster for just over four years, then headmaster at Park House Preparatory School, Southborough, near Tunbridge Wells, until 1887. That year his father died, and – because he had taken his mother's side in their separation (which must have been in the 1870s) – Tom was rather surprised to be left his share of the fortune, which was £80,000, like his brothers. On the strength of it he gave up headmastering, got married to Fanny Julia Reid in 1891, and gave some thought as to where they should settle – he having no particular allegiance but wishing to be in the country, she liking to be in London. As a compromise he chose 79 The Drive, Hove, then a rural place, with the Downs a short walk away.

Tom Blackburn had invested his inheritance and intended to do the things he liked for the rest of his life: his life in detail as far as we are concerned begins on 22 July 1901, when he bought just over twenty-six acres of land a mile and a half from the village of Thakeham, on the north side of the Downs, just north of Storrington and about twelve miles north-west of Hove. He was able to add woodland to a total of thirty-seven acres. He employed a water diviner, Mr Tompkins of Chippenham, to walk the field he had in mind for his house, with his willow twigs; Mr Tompkins 'found' at a point which meant that the necessary pump house would have to be built just where Tom Blackburn had imagined his lawn. The diviner, grumbling, was sent to try again, further south, beyond the garden limit, and they dug a brick-lined well down to 110 feet where it found water resting on a bed of clay. The cost of boring was charged at £205 but the architect felt this was too expensive, and it was reduced to £180; the builders, Norman & Burt of Burgess Hill, charged £129 for the brick-lined well.

The architect, at this outset, was F. Hatchard Smith of 41 Moorgate Station Buildings in London; Blackburn doesn't even mention anything about the designing, so it seems that Hatchard Smith was left largely to his own devices, and Norman & Burt returned estimates for the house and stables (house £6,108, stables £2,833), which, after a little debate, was settled at a total of £8,383 6s. 3d. including the drainage. This sum did not include a fourteen-foot wide, half-mile drive up Strawberry Lane, the levelling of the croquet and tennis lawns and lower terrace, and drainage. The terracing and garden drainage started just before Christmas 1901 and carried on into the January.

On 10 January, attending to his New Year accounts, Tom Blackburn paid his architect £200 on account – and then got on with the things that really interested him. Memo: to plant humps of mushroom spawn in the meadow grass in the summer. Memo: the drive might be planted with hedges of the blackberry tribe. Memo: nelumbiums are grown in a tub sunk into the ground, with a winter cover of straw and glass, in May remove the straw and leave the glass till the plant pushes it off!

At the end of January 1902 it becomes clear that Mr Blackburn has been to have a talk with his bank manager and that his substantial holding of debentures, bonds and consols is to bolster the building of his house, and the bank will put up the loan. He borrows £500 which he immediately pays, as their first payment, to his builders, Norman & Burt. This was to be the pattern for the next two years. It also becomes clear that he has planned very carefully, and the drainage and levelling of the garden furthest from the house allows him to begin a little planting: *Ceanothus* 'Gloire de Versailles', with *henryi* lilies beneath it against a retaining wall, and *Agave americana* at the south-east corner of the tennis lawn. In April he bought Greenhurst Farm, a sixty-acre holding of small fields and meadows, for just over £1,000, including £150 for the timber, and a few days later his estate was completed with another twenty-two acres, making just over 130 acres in all.

At this point, 29 April 1902, the diary entry reads: 'I disagree with Mr Hatchard Smith, and Mr E. L. Lutyens . . . came down to the site, and advised that the house should be pulled down, and that a house of Pulborough rock should be built on one side of it, keeping the old kitchen and scullery. The house was already built nearly up to the first floor and all the window frames were made. Messrs Norman and Burt agree to take back all the doors which had been made, and to try to sell the window frames.'[21]

Tom Blackburn, for all his careful planning, after four months of site work, found a house he didn't like rising before his eyes, 'a large blot on the beautiful landscape, I came to realize it was a villa fit for Wimbledon or Putney, rather than a country house'.[22] His first reaction was to make the most of it – 'hide the front of the house with creepers and paint the windows some dark colour', and he thought he would get someone whose work he liked to do the interior. It was on this latter basis that he approached Lutyens, and Lutyens agreed to come, perhaps prompted by current work at Monkton, not far away – he liked 'gaggles' of jobs that could make a journey worthwhile. Blackburn had undoubtedly aired his difficulties and also checked the professional niceties: he had agreed to pay Hatchard Smith $2\frac{1}{2}$ per cent – and 'a small sum' for supervision – of the contracted sum of about £8,500 and realized that this would have to be, but then his attitude hardened: it was *his* house and *his* money, surely as a client he had rights too. Tempted by Lutyens's response to the site, a quick sketch of an H-plan, with bays and an oriel window facing south over the garden already growing, he couldn't resist (why should he?) a house which he really liked. So the builders did their unwork, and started building the stone house – no mention of a new contract, revised sum or anything of that kind. For the summer the diary mentions little of this; the brush attachment to the Ransome's roller, and the ploughing and finishing of the games lawns and terraces, were more important, plus the arrival of a Shetland pony and four Jersey cows.

With his July accounts, and the first payment of just over £40 to Lutyens, Blackburn sent Mr Hatchard Smith his 'full settlement' of £350. That was a total of £550 for six months' work and was a generous settlement. Some time afterwards, according to Lutyens, writing to Emily on 9 August,[23] Hatchard Smith went to see what was going on and, finding his brick house pulled down, and the stone one rising, he furiously penned a letter to *Building News* about the affair, quoting even that Mr Blackburn had likened his house to a suburban villa, and that really architects should not go around 'pinching' each other's jobs. *Building News* weighed in with an editorial about clients who changed their minds, and that in such cases any 'second' architect should refuse to advise. Tom Blackburn may have been more interested in his agaves and plans for orchards of apples and cordon pears, but he raised the banner for his fellows: 'There seems to be a view entertained by many architects and most building papers that houses are built in order to display the skill and taste of the architect. This is not the case. Houses are built for men to live in, and those who live in them are entitled to have them built to suit their fancy and convenience.'[24]

One can almost hear the derisive groans of the readers of *Building News*, and the instinctive cheer that went up around England. Blackburn retold his version of the story, recorded that Mr Lutyens's position was 'too well assured' 'for your words to do him much harm or mine to do him much good', admitting that 'all the advances were made by him'. *Country Life* weighed in, rather picturesquely, on the side of the country gentleman client, saying that an architect, once selected, was not 'like an old man of the sea, to be carried about for ever'. *Building News*, stung, said that old men of the sea notwithstanding, a client had, having appointed an architect, the right to let him finish the job, or get rid of him, pay him and find another. Blackburn mentioned, for the first time, the £550 he had paid Mr Hatchard Smith for just that purpose – it was twice as much as Lutyens was to earn on the job, and represented half a year's respectable salary; rightly, the subject was dropped.[25]

There is no way of knowing whether Lutyens had made up his mind about the interior of Little Thakeham at the first instance, when he thought that would be all he was doing, and in response to Tom Blackburn's request for something classically calm. Lutyens, advised by the solicitor George Riddell, kept a low profile during the Hatchard Smith débâcle; he had to attend an RIBA arbitration session, in the persons of Sir Aston Webb and John Belcher, in early September 1902, but the outcome did not perturb him. What is certain is that the architect conceived a great respect for this particular client.

During the autumn into winter of 1902 Blackburn went on borrowing and paying his builder, and Lutyens his average monthly fees of £40. On 21 January 1903 he recorded the progress of his house: the stony shell of it was tall, up at second-floor window level, with dark holes for the windows, joists stuck out from the dining-room and drawing-room ceilings, the great tall oriel window in the centre of the garden front, in the hall, was just a hole, but through it could be glimpsed the almost completed pedimented doorway through the stony screen that carried the galleried landing to the stairs.

East-south-east of the lawns and terraces the kitchen garden walls were complete, and the chief task of the earliest spring days was the planting of dozens of apples and pears, which he had bought from the famous Bunyard nursery at Allington, near Maidstone. The names, such as 'Pitmaston Duchess', 'Clapp's Favourite' (pears) and 'D'Arcy Spice' and 'Allington's Pippin' (apples) obviously intrigued him.

The mid-March 1903 note of progress on the building gives an insight into the quirks of the building; the floor-to-ceiling oriel window in the hall was being used as workman's entrance and exit, while the walls and bay windows each side of it were up to eave height. It was the interior that was taking shape – the hall fireplace was tiled, the screen of the hall was nearly finished, the cisterns were up on the rafters of the east end, the 'warming' hot-water pipes were beneath the dining-room, the larders were being paved and plastered, and as the first coat of plaster was going on the east, service stairs, some of that part of the building must have been retained from the first attempt. In the early part of April the service wing was nearing completion, and the roof was boarded – it was far in advance of the west, Lutyens's end, where the Blackburns' bedrooms were – though on 21 April he reported that the scaffolding was going up for the main roof. In May and June the house was progressing so well that the main building work on the garden, the pergola, and the lily pools in the east court, was done. On 1 July some Chicago Burlington and Quincy bonds matured and Tom Blackburn was able to pay the bank £1,000, reducing his overdraft to £13,700. Through August and September it was pay, pay, pay, and he was now keeping careful account of the allocation of costs; on 16 October 1903 he set down that his house had cost him £10,029 11s. 4d. to date, the stables £538 15s., the garden £686 2s. 5d., the fitted furniture £115 1s. 2d.

Left: Little Thakeham: Barbara, Julian and Hermione Blackburn in the pool garden, July 1912.
Right: Little Thakeham: Tom Blackburn and his son Aubrey in the garden, July 1912.

Little Thakeham, Storrington, Sussex: the garden front of Tom Blackburn's house, *c.* 1910.

It was well-timed that the roof went on in late summer and it must all have been drying out nicely by the time the weather cooled. Tom Blackburn concentrated upon bulb planting and making borders, writing long and lovely lists of violets, anemones, spireas, escallonias, fuchsias, clematis, primroses and syringa. He devoured catalogues, and with his love for words – he later published *The Study of Words* – seemed to revel in the Latin names as he 'collected' them, and the adventure of growing them to find out what they looked like.[26]

By the end of January the overdraft was up to £20,000; he concentrated on a recipe of paraffin, sugar soap and tobacco juice as a wash for the cherry trees, and planting a filbert walk and masses of peonies and lilies. Then, on 19 February 1904, came those three longed-for little words: 'The workmen left.' The family – Tom, aged forty-seven, Fanny, now thirty-four, Aileen, eleven, Sylvia, seven, Barbara, five, Aubrey, three, and Julian the baby – took over their own home.

There followed a magical April; Tom Blackburn paid the last big bills on 30 March, a total of just over £10,500 to Norman & Burt for the house (but with the addition of the building work in the garden and the stables the grand total was just over £13,000). But on 4 April the first daffodil came out, the grape hyacinths following, then the special forget-me-not, the earliest tulips showed colour, the grass walk was sown, and on 14 April the cuckoo arrived. Tom particularly enjoyed his tulips, probably because of their wonderful names – 'La Belle Alliance', 'Vermilion Brilliant', 'Couleur Ponceau' – and discovered other virtues: 'Yellow Prince is sweet-scented, like a rose.' The catalogue of welcomes for the flowers continues through the summer, and on, in this surviving volume of the diary, through the seasons and the years until 1912. The last Blackburn child, Hermione, was born at Little Thakeham in 1907, making eight in the family in all. Barbara Blackburn remembered how the first peach, or pear, was ceremonially cut into eight parts, so that they all learned the excitement of producing their own bounty.

Lutyens remained good friends with the Blackburns, and was welcome to stay at Little Thakeham whenever he was in the area. The coolly classical interior exactly caught Tom Blackburn's serenity of character, which Lutyens had grasped immediately and remarkably well: he told Emily, 'Blackburn is very slow apparently, but is really an artist and he does little at a time but what he does is singularly good I think. He has made the pergola delightful – in a way quite his own – with hollyhocks – and to enjoy the effect he postpones planting the more permanent things . . . like leaving a picture unfinished to enjoy the initial stages.'[27]

V

EMILY'S FRIENDS AND RELATIONS

This is the house by Cromer town,
Its bricks are red though they look so brown,
It faces the sea on a wind-swept hill –
In winter it's empty, in summer it's chill:
Indeed it is one of Earth's windiest spots
As we know from the smashing of chimney pots,
In August I ask for an extra quilt –
This is the house that Jane built.

(FREDERICK LOCKER LAMPSON)[1]

It might be thought a good career move for a bright young architect to marry an earl's daughter, but any familiarity with this particular marriage forces another conclusion. The marriage of Edwin and Emily Lutyens is left with few secrets; only that of Harold Nicolson and Vita Sackville-West can vie with it as a private relationship known to all the world. The letters that Ned Lutyens and Emily wrote to each other across forty years are in a public collection and many of them have been published.[2] No reader can be unsympathetic towards young people who, having found each other and fallen in love, are forbidden to meet, let alone marry; one lurches from despair to euphoria when all becomes possible, only to descend rapidly into fearfulness after too short a 'honeymoon' and the pitiable spectacle of two people loving an idea of each other, but being stubbornly blind to any reality. Ned Lutyens persistently sketches Emily with wings and an aura – oddly prophetic considering her later turn to theosophy – he places her on a pedestal and mounts his charger as her champion, only his visor keeps blinding him, slipping over his eyes. But it is quite possible that if he had been happy and fulfilled in marriage, we would never have heard his name.

Emily Lytton was twenty-two when she married him in August 1897; she was tall, fair, with intense blue eyes, rather plump but very pretty, well-read and clever in a vaguely intellectual way. Life had made her rebellious and a fighter:[3] she had come to consciousness treated like a princess as the child of the Viceroy in India,

1. Edward Burne-Jones, *The Golden Stairs*, 1880. Commissioned by Cyril Flower, later Lord Battersea, it symbolizes Burne-Jones's muse Frances Graham's entry into society via his paintbrush: Frances, who later married Sir John Horner, is at the foot of the stairs, leading her bevy of contemporaries who include May Morris (facing front, half-way down), with Laura Tennant (m. Alfred Lyttelton) in profile behind her, and Margot Tennant (m. H. H. Asquith) bending down behind her.

2. Milford House, the home of the Webb family, one of a series of watercolours painted by Augusta Webb in the 1920s, but showing the house as Lutyens would have known it.

3. Milford House, the boudoir.

4. Milford House, the drawing room.

5. *A Bloomsbury Family* by William
Orpen was painted in 1907;
William Nicholson's friendship
with Edwin Lutyens dates from
this time, when the Nicholsons
were in Mecklenburgh Square
and the Lutyenses were at 29
Bloomsbury Square. Lutyens loved
'bergère' wickerwork and designed
newspaper baskets and chairs
using this mix of mahogany and
cane.

6. The 'castle in the air' that Lutyens drew to entertain Barbara Webb when she was ill.
For a full description and additional drawing see pp. 23–4.

7. Design for the drawing-room set for J. M. Barrie's *Quality Street*, produced at the Vaudeville
Theatre, 1902. This is one of two drawings; the other is for the backdrop of walls, fireplace,
panelling and windows of the room itself, all designed to Lutyens's own taste.

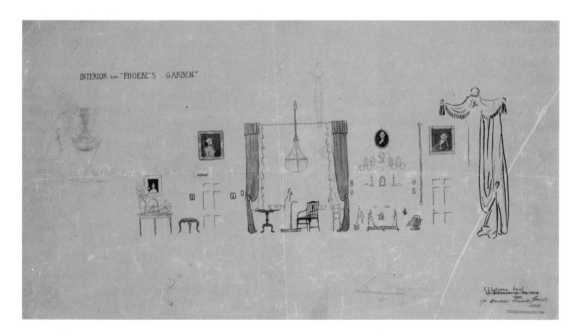

INTERIOR FOR "PHOEBE'S GARDEN."

8. Title page from the Orchards Workbook, 1897.
(*Below*) William and Julia Chance (née Strachey) soon after their marriage in 1884. Lutyens built their dream house, Orchards, at Munstead for them in the late 1890s.

ORCHARDS
The Property
of
WILLIAM CHANCE
in
the Parifh of
BRAMLEY SURREY

Building
begun feptember   1897
finifhed Iuly 1900
Edwin. L. Lutyens
of London
Architect
W & T. Underwood
Builders
of Dunsfold *near bye*

DEO NON FORTUNA

9. Munstead Wood: design for an entrance from Lutyens's sketch-book. Miss Jekyll insisted that the only way to approach her front door was on foot, so this was the main entrance to her garden and remained so until Munstead Wood was sold in the late 1940s.

10. Lutyens's sketches for Edward Horner's memorial in Mells church. The equestrian statue is the work of Sir Alfred Munnings, and dominates the small chapel (see p. 173).

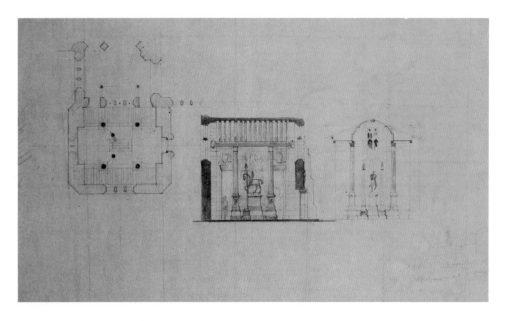

II. Reginald McKenna, as Chairman of the Midland Bank, by James Gunn.

12. Mrs Florence Phillips, the 'Queen of Johannesburg', by Jean Boldini.

Lady Emily Lutyens, taken in 1912 after she had become a theosophist.

and her young life continued so until Lord Lytton's sudden death in Paris, descending quickly into the comparative poverty of an undistinguished rented house and her mother's preoccupations at Court. Left vulnerable, she almost had an affair with her best friend's father, the devastatingly attractive Wilfred Scawen Blunt, from which she was rescued by her mentor, the elderly Revd Whitwell Elwin.[4] Elwin lived at, and Emily frequently visited, Booton, in the middle of a bleak tract of agricultural Norfolk, about ten miles north-west of Norwich. This was a rather nightmarish Gothic enclave of church, rectory and school which His Rev (as Emily called him) had built by supposedly Divine command, and where he and his family had lived for many years. His Rev thought of himself as 'God's builder' – which included being his own architect, a vocation discovered after a literary and well-travelled youth – and, if Booton's surviving atmosphere is anything to go by, one tinged with crankiness and more than a little strange. Elwin's influence over Emily was very strong, and if she picked up her notions of the sanctity of the architectural profession at Booton it was a bad omen.

She naturally found the reality a lot more fun and attractive to start; and if she was Elwin-influenced, then Ned Lutyens might have been equally following his beloved Barbara Webb's star. They met and fell in love under Mrs Webb's wing, and Ned Lutyens, more than a little susceptible to fate – 'As Fate Wills, Love Fulfils' is the motto he gave Emily – might well have sensed Emily entering his life by the door as Barbara was about to leave. In the first flush of happiness at Milford they make a delightful picture, wobbling with laughter as they pedal away to visit Compton's cool little Romanesque church, to where he is working on Warren Lodge by moonlight and to Munstead and a surprise dinner for 'Bumps', with chops and tipsy cake washed down with a great amount of Munstead's elderberry wine.

Miss Jekyll feared 'frivolous influences' on Lutyens's architecture, and on the progress of her house, long before 'The Lament of the Neglected'.[5] On Emily's side, her hard-pressed mother, the Countess of Lytton, coping with Queen Victoria's foibles, was horrified at the thought of an unknown and fortune-less architect to whom she 'had not even been introduced'[6] as a suitor for her daughter. He had to prove himself and his prospects to Emily's uncle, Lord Loch, and undertake an insurance out of his income for £10,000, before hopeless love turned to joy, and an engagement, and eventually marriage.

Emily's interest in both architecture and housekeeping were to prove short-lived, but in neither case was this entirely her fault. With the architecture she tried (her husband was proud of her ability to climb scaffolding), but she was a person of words, not vision, and she was both unobservant and visually insensitive. Early in their marriage she made a scrapbook of photographs she found in his office, titling her offering 'The Works of Edwin Landseer Lutyens' – but to his horror, and her shame, they were not, they were odds and ends, advertisements and 'Awful Warnings'.[7]

As far as the housekeeping was concerned, he set up standards and ideals (learned from the experts at Munstead) that were so demanding as to be almost cruel. He set his heart on an enormous house, 29 Bloomsbury Square, mostly because it was Shaw's old office and was being offered, at £60 annual ground rent

Letter from Ned Lutyens to Ida Streatfeild with news of his engagement to Emily Lytton, 1897.

Feb. 3 1897   6, Gray's Inn Square
                               London, W.C.,

My dear Mrs. Streatfeild,
I hope you are getting on all right.
I feel so awfully guilty about yesterday's appt. with Mr Streatfeild. I started — missed my train — got wet through and being so late and wet I didn't go on. The roads were wretched and I thought possibly he would understand it. I will go next Monday.
In the meantime I am pushing on the drawings full steam and I am having some rose-colored moirées dyed for you. Everything is Rose-colored now! For "Ned is going to marry Emily" Lytton. I was dying to tell you the other day but was not allowed as Lady Lytton said she had to tell the Queen at Osborne first. This part of it is too funny & a drefful bore —because you are not well I will draw you a picture but please *tear it up*.
Yours ever sincerely
E. L. Lutyens

and £200 for the lease as a 'special' rate for Emily, by Shaw's decorator, Aldham Heaton. For the house he designed every detail; he was a dictator of taste in menus, table flowers, tablecloths, as well as beds, furniture and lighting.

Emily, on the other hand, was a far better judge of people; she immediately saw through the 'pretty things' that Princess Louise whispered in Ned's ears, and offered further advice, culled from her sister Betty Balfour, who 'says that when Eustace goes to see the Duke of Westminster as an architect, he is never even offered a chair or expects it. And that is what men expect of you – to draw the line absolutely and distinctly between business and friendliness'.[8]

This was one line Lutyens never learned to draw. He was writing to Ida Streatfeild about rose-coloured moiré for Fulbrook when he burst out, 'Everything is Rose-colored [*sic*] now! For Ned is going to marry Emily'[9] . . . and on 4 March, a month later, 'May I see you on Sunday and might Emily come too?'[10] For Lutyens there was no division, his architecture was his life, and vice versa, but that made it no less easy for Emily.

It comes as little surprise to have to add that the sexual side of their relationship was equally misfitting. Ned's approach to love-making, enthusiastically puppy-like, might have been more easily forgiven had not Emily had the experience of Blunt's finesse. She was both physically and emotionally pained from their honeymoon, and a few months later, towards the end of 1897, with morning sickness upon her, and her struggles with household management both worrying her and boring her, Ned's dreams of pretty breakfasts, polishing maids and cheery cooks were a reality of arguments, walkings out and cold food. Emily soldiered on bravely, and accomplished one thing at least, early motherhood, with exceptional success. Barbara was born in August 1898, Robert in 1901, Ursula in 1904, Elizabeth in 1906 and Mary in 1908, a timetable that probably represents Emily's returns to Ned after periods of strain and parting, the former short, the latter long. He had to work, and knew nothing else, to keep his growing family, and he was in his office, at his drawing board, puffing at his interminable pipes (which made Emily feel sick, especially when she was pregnant) into the small hours. What they never said to each other face to face is in their letters, which tell the continuing adventure of their lives. This was why Lutyens worked, and why his clients, who were also, whatever the rules, his friends, were so important; how Emily solved her longings for 'ideal and soul-satisfying love' has been candidly revealed in her book, *Candles in the Sun*.[11]

Once their marriage was accomplished Emily's relatives did support Lutyens's career. His aunt-in-law, Elizabeth Loch, Edith Lytton's twin sister, was kind and encouraging: she thought Ned should do the South Kensington Museum – 'That would be a JOB'[12] (but it went to Aston Webb) – and it was the Lochs, just returned from South Africa, who raised the hope of 'Africa's Cathedral', of which Lutyens dreamed. All he actually got was Stoke College, their lovely country house at Stoke-by-Clare in Suffolk, where he added a kitchen and service wing, with bedrooms above, and a billiard room.

For his mother-in-law, who came to love him deeply once they had been introduced, he built a square little white house with hedges, flower beds, a croquet lawn and apple orchard at Knebworth.[13] Lady Constance, 'darling Con', who was five years older than Emily, lived with their mother. She was even more shy than Emily, and only tentatively emerging from the 'overmastering laziness and fatalistic submission to events' that she felt guided her existence',[14] edging her frailties into her courageous future and Suffragette martyrdom. She had been helping her aunt, Mrs Earle, with her *Pot Pourri* books, and had joined Aunt T. in

Lutyens's letter to his sister-in-law, Lady Constance Lytton, sketching her room in Homewood, the house he was designing for her and her mother, the Dowager Countess of Lytton. The letter reads:

'The room I proposed for you would look East Do you mind – or are you Aunt T. like loving West? With a biggish cupbd out of your room – you could keep room itself quite St. Ursulaish – & this is where I think would be nice for the cupbd' Beneath the sketch he continues: 'Cupbds under sink (hot & cold water) for dusters rags. In your room then you need have nothing but a bed – a chair & a table & a bookcase.'

Homewood: the garden front as it is today.

her strict vegetarianism.[15] Ned Lutyens was kindness itself to Constance, writing her notes to assure her of her place in the new house.

The Balfours, Gerald and Betty (Emily's eldest sister), also acquired a Lutyens house, Fisher's Hill on Hook Heath, near Woking, a deliciously romantic and secret house of brick and roughcast, with heavy oak doors and an outdoor, first-floor gallery overlooking the garden dell. Neville Lytton, artistic and slightly jealous of Ned Lutyens, rather unhappily married to Judith Blunt, describes to Constance a family tour of inspection of Fisher's Hill: 'The house, with certain reservation, I like very much … I think the windows are rather too small, though they look all right from outside. I think the shape of the gable is quaint and amusing, but not ideal. The chimneys are much better than any I have ever seen of his – inside I liked almost everything except the fireplaces …' (Green tiles were his abomination.) 'The whitewash in the kitchen is one of the most lovely wall surfaces I ever saw. Ned's aims are perfect, only in carrying out I think he wants thoroughness and chasteness.' He concluded that 'the delightful things are numberless' and that Betty and Gerald were very lucky to have such a nice house to live in.[16]

The Lytton family's wariness about matrimonial invaders outdistanced Ned's difficulties over marrying Emily, when, in the late summer of 1901, it became known that Victor, the eldest, was going to marry Pamela Plowden.[17] Pamela was

Knebworth House: the garden front, early 1900s.

far too lovely for any woman to say anything nice about her, and it might have seemed that only Ned Lutyens and George Meredith (though presumably Victor Lytton) were on her side. Meredith was her confidante; he pronounced the world 'too dull of wit to allow for circumstances and a young woman's battle with it' in defence of her 'flightyness'. Pamela's wedding to Victor, the following year, brought forth another Meredith gem . . . 'I should like to have seen the sweetest of unfolding wild-rose buds in her bridal happiness!'[18] he wrote from his seclusion in Flint Cottage at the foot of Box Hill. Ned Lutyens too was enchanted, and also lucky, for his new sister-in-law shared his tastes and loved his design ideas, she became a brilliant home-maker and hostess, and was forever finding him things to do, for her and for the important people whom she encountered. Their first task together was the garden at Knebworth House, which was too elaborate, a prey to the Lytton family eclecticism. They had cleared away the stucco ornaments and moth-eaten shrubs and replaced them with pollarded lime walks and a single, plain square pool in the lawn as the foil for Knebworth House's fantastic roofscape. Lutyens helped Pamela Lytton with a complete refurbishment of the interiors; they had a marvellous time, whitening dark and musty panelling, consigning embossed carpets and heavy curtains to the attics and replacing them with pale, plain carpets, and silks and chintzes. In the Long Gallery they had the oak pickled to pale it, and hung the walls with silk in folds, as the background for the pictures.

Neither of them needed lessons in appreciation of Knebworth's treasures, but everything was revealed in new beauty and interest by being carefully, and with restraint, replaced in its fresh, serene setting.

His marriage to Emily Lytton undoubtedly increased their weekend invitations, and naturally, to Ned Lutyens, the job prospects. Emily tried to be sociable for his sake, but her shyness made it agony for her, expressed in a letter to her mother from Hewell Grange in Worcestershire, the home of the Windsors, on an October weekend in 1899: 'All the misery of a country house visit is upon me. I got up to 9.30 breakfast – found Gay had breakfasted early with the children & all the other ladies in their rooms – & I was a solitary female at a table of shooting males. 1st misery – 2ndly agony of search for W.C. – but this safely accomplished. 3rd I don't know my way about this house – can only find the hall where there is no fire – & all the men pass – & I feel miserably conspicuous. I daren't try & find a drawing room lest I land in some men's quarter – so I am reduced to my bedroom. This is very uncomfortable & I have no book ... Everyone seems to disappear except me & I am always getting in the way & finding people who wish to remain hidden.'[19]

Poor Emily – this nightmare was played out in the most lavish and perfect temple of the Souls, and appeals to the hardest heart. She bemoaned her own shyness because Ned was shy too '& furious because I am'.[20] The Souls she generally scorned, calling them 'wooden', and soon after the Hewell Grange misery Emily gave up weekending with her husband. As she also hated to be shut up in London in the summers, she took the children to her friends or to rented houses. Jane Locker Lampson was a particular friend whom she had met at Crabbet Park with the Blunts, whose neighbours they were. Frederick Locker Lampson, tall, bearded, finely featured and poetical, may have reminded Emily of her father, but he died in 1895. (Lutyens was to work on the library at the Locker home, Rowfant, in Sussex, to hold a fine collection of books, folios and letters for Godfrey Locker Lampson in 1898.) After her marriage Emily went frequently to stay with Jane at Newhaven Court, 'the house by Cromer town' that Jane had built; that it was hideously ugly worried neither Jane nor Emily.

CYRIL FLOWER, LATER LORD BATTERSEA

Lutyens's Cromer connections were entangled with a man of real property of whom he had great expectations. Cyril Flower emerges 'all brinily radiant' from the

Above: Knebworth House: the White Drawing Room, as Lady Lytton found it.
Below: Knebworth House: the White Drawing Room after Lutyens and Lady Lytton had redecorated it.

Lutyens's sketch of Jane Locker Lampson in a letter to Constance Lytton.

Norfolk seaside, partly on the recommendation of his cousins, the Wickham Flowers at Great Tangley – where Gertrude Jekyll had taken Ned Lutyens prospecting, but where Philip Webb did all that was required. Cyril Flower's fortune had been made by his father, a wool merchant with Australian connections,[21] founder of P. W. Flower & Company in Moorgate. He had ventured successfully into property, encouraged by the architect James Knowles Jr, for whom he financed developments in Victoria Street, Pimlico and Battersea. In the classic Victorian working father–playboy son relationship, Cyril knew little of these labours: he was educated at Cheam, and then Harrow, where Dr Farrar reputedly portrayed him as Eric in *Little by Little*. Cyril came down from Cambridge in 1870 with a master's degree, moved into a flat in his father's Albert Mansions, which was decorated for him by Thomas Jeckyll, who was also his friend, read for the Bar and took up collecting. After their father's death in early 1872, Cyril and his brothers had to look to the business; Cyril much preferred country house parties to stuffy counting houses or even Battersea building sites – he 'could be tiresome, taking too much out of the estate, putting too little of it back', and vague – sending incomprehensible and hasty instructions into the office from wherever he was staying.[22] He had another solution, and left the business to run itself, in the hands of stalwart chief clerks and of Knowles, who was drawing enormous fees and was practically in sole charge. Cyril's undeniable beauty had long before pierced the heart of his Harrow schoolfriend's sister, Constance de Rothschild. At that time, in the mid 1860s, Constance could have had no hope of her beautiful Gentile, but in 1873 a remarkable thing had happened in the Rothschild enclave, when her sister married 'out' and still retained her Jewish faith.[23] So in 1877 Constance de Rothschild married Cyril Flower and they settled in more than comfortably with her mother at Aston Clinton, part of the family's Buckinghamshire fiefdom.

Cyril Flower's true ambitions were now revealed as political. Though Constance, richly idealistic, felt they should make their 'house beautiful' among his Battersea villas, Cyril more realistically bought Surrey House, at the corner of Edgware Road, with a view over Hyde Park. He entered the House of Commons as Liberal Member for Brecon in April 1880, and when the seat was de-franchised he stood successfully for South Bedfordshire; in 1885 Gladstone appointed him a junior minister at the Treasury. At this time Cyril took up photography – and (while Gertrude Jekyll was recording her growing garden at Munstead Wood) he was persuading the Aston Clinton house guests into the conservatory, where he had rigged up a romantic backdrop with pot plants and draperies for a series of portraits – the Gerald Balfours, Arthur Balfour, the Midletons from Peper Harow, the Rayleighs, the Bretts, Edward Grey, Eustace and Frances Balfour, the Desboroughs, H. H. Asquith and various Rothschilds and children.

Presumably tiring of this pastime, Cyril decided on a summer place; his mother's family had come from Norfolk and it was geographically convenient. In searching out the bracing Cromer air (Sheringham had been discounted after a rumour of typhoid), he discovered, a mile or so along the cliffs, Poppyland, or Overstrand as it has become. He bought two ugly villas on three acres of ground, and the sea frontage. Constance was not keen; Cyril adored the sea – and for the moment the villas at Overstrand were his private retreat. Because it was a quiet place, and because of his striking looks, Cyril immediately became a minor celebrity, immortalized by Mrs Alfred Berlyn's 'Vera in Poppyland' (she was Vera) which appeared in the *Lady's Pictorial*. Vera and her friends constantly and gushingly encounter Cyril 'in his startling white bath coat' along the strand, and are in awe of the smallness of his villa and his garden, where Princess Louise had recently been spotted.[24]

Cyril Flower, Lord Battersea, a self-portrait: thwarted in his public life, Lord Battersea, an otherwise generous and imaginative client, persisted with alterations that ruined Lutyens's design for the Pleasaunce at Overstrand.

The election of 1892 returned the Liberals to power and Cyril Flower to the House of Commons. Gladstone offered him not office, but a peerage, and as Baron Battersea he went to the House of Lords. The following year Lord Ripon called him in and requested him to go and govern New South Wales. For Cyril Flower, whose father had struggled to Sydney as the prelude to his wool trading fortune, it seemed a glorious justification: for Constance it was a disaster. She was not about to leave her Rothschild comforts for the other end of the world – and 'the idea of leaving my mother for so long . . . appeared to me like committing a sin,' she wrote. She thought that she understood Cyril: 'knowing Cyril's devotion to his mother-in-law and his oft-expressed determination of never leaving her for long, I thought, foolishly indeed, that he would agree with me on the advisability of refusing the offer.'[25] Cyril certainly did not wish to refuse, but of course he did.

Overstrand was to be his consolation; from now on his every whim beside the sea would be indulged. His appointed architect to build at Overstrand might have expected a future advantage from a man of property or the Rothschild connection; instead he found in Lord Battersea a thwarted, charming boy, determined to abandon the serious things of life for his building, his botany, his gardening, as playboy-in-chief in this playground by the sea. Soon the villas were swarming with bricklayers and carpenters to encase them in Lutyens's design. It is impossible to know exactly what he designed, for there were almost daily altercations as first his Lordship, and then her Ladyship (whose visits were far rarer), wanted to alter or undo building efforts. The Pleasaunce, as Lord Morley named it, has little documentary evidence and was subsequently regretted by the architect as a 'muddle'; it has some brilliantly characteristic Lutyensiana – a long brick cloister that recalls Webb's covered walk at Great Tangley, which Lady Battersea disliked while admitting that its value 'for bazaars and fetes is uncontestable', and a pert white watch-tower for the Lord of the Strand, which she also disliked.

In between sea bathing, botanizing and amassing more land for his private cricket pitch, Lord Battersea made his garden, immortalized as *The Garden of Dreams* by Lord Wolverhampton's daughter, the prolific novelist Ellen Thorneycroft Fowler, in *Ten Degrees Backward*:

The dream began on a velvety lawn, where the velvet was edged with gay flowers . . . then it turned into a formal garden, with paved paths between square grass-plots, and a large fountain in the middle lined with sky-blue tiles, as if a bit of sky had down fallen to earth, and had found earth so fascinating that it could not tear itself away again. Then the dream took a more serious turn, and led along sombre cloisters veiled with creepers. But it could not keep serious for long; it soon floated back into the sunlight and dipped into a sunk garden paved with coral and amethyst, as only pink and purple flowers were allowed to grow therein. Then it changed into a rosary . . . where roses . . . ran riot. Then the dream took quite another turn, and passed into a Japanese garden of streams and pagodas and strange bright flowers, till the dreamer felt as if he were living on a willow pattern plate. But he soon came back to England again, and found himself in an ideal fruit garden, where the pear trees and the apple trees were woven into walls and arches and architraves of green and gold. Then a wrought-iron gateway led him still nearer to the heart of England, for there lay a cricket-field surrounded by large trees; and beyond that again stretched the grassy alleys and shady paths of dreamland till they culminated in the very centre of the dream – a huge herbaceous border so glorious in its riot of colour that the dreamer's heart leaped up . . .[26]

Once the Pleasaunce was ready for use the Batterseas filled it with visitors every summer; a Norfolk contingent of Gurneys and Buxtons, then, led by the infirm but affectionate George Meredith (who dubbed Cyril Battersea 'the lusty morning plunger' . . . 'rising to the cliff from the embrace of his Nereids all brinily radiant'[27]), all the Asquiths, Betty and Gerald Balfour, Mrs Theresa Earle, the Garnet Wolseleys, the Rayleighs, Emily Lawless, Lornes and Lytteltons galore. Raymond Asquith, on the surface an arrogant Oxford undergraduate but underneath perceptive of the exact situation, portrays August at the Pleasaunce:

I expected to find a handsome athletic comfortable amusing weekend party of the ordinary kind . . . nothing of the sort; the house is reeking with the gross and human odours which ever cling about the skirts of philanthropy: one sits down to dinner with a rabble of small shopkeepers from Balham and Battersea: when I want to play tennis or bowls or croquet they are playing already: when I want to lie in the smoking room with a pipe and a novel it is already being subjected to the critical gaze of a retail tobacconist; when I want to look at the sea or the sky, some grocer or ironmonger has anticipated me and ruined the foreground irretrievably . . . They actually want me to play cricket with them tomorrow! I told my host I thought it was going rather too far: and he poor man agreed with me: he suffers terribly from his wife, who is full of philanthropy and temperance and all that sort of nonsense, and while she is entertaining the good templars and prison matrons and heavens knows what horrors down in Buckinghamshire, he has been deputed to arrange a cricket match between the serfs on the Overstrand estate and the tenants of his Battersea shops: also to entertain the visiting team for three days at his own table and in his own beds: and here they are eating and drinking and talking their curious dialect, and exhaling a poisonous atmosphere of retail religion through one of the most beautiful houses in Norfolkshire . . .'[28]

As a radiant god, Cyril Battersea continued to amuse himself at the Pleasaunce – and in London, where he indulged in the most fantastic Bugatti-designed bedroom, everything seemingly related to Viking shields and helmets[29] – for a dozen short years. The legend of the Overstrand generosity and kindnesses knew no bounds, but Lord Battersea, a diabetic, took his leave of it all in 1907, dying suddenly. He lies alone and in peace just outside the church door at Overstrand. One of his kindnesses was to Emily Lawless, for whom he had Lutyens build the little flint-walled room over the sea-gate to the gardens, where she could write: in return she left him 'A Valediction':

> Farewell again, truest, most helpful soul:
> This world is dearer to me for thy sake;
> No jot or tittle of its varying whole
> Is worth what love and loving friendship make.
> A broader summer track in life is thine,
> A narrower, more shade-infested, mine.
> Yet over both methinks, the same stars shine.[30]

What may be called the Poppyland connection brought a flurry of clients to Lutyens: there was Overstrand Hall for the 2nd Lord Hillingdon, whose wife was Alice Harbord, Lord Suffield's daughter – her father owned much of the land in the area. For a moment Lutyens had hopes of a connection with the Hillingdon family bank, Glyn Mills & Company, and Captain Algernon Mills had dreams of building grandly at Calcot Park, Reading, but all came to nothing. Lutyens designed houses at Overstrand for the gregarious solicitor Sir George Lewis, and for the actor-manager Sir George Alexander. Nothing happened to any of these schemes (the Lewises bought the wooden Danish Pavilion from the Paris Exhibition of 1900 and re-erected it on the cliff) – but Lady Lewis's godfather, Alexander Wedderburn QC, picked up the idea of brick and flint and pantiles by the eastern seaboard, and Lutyens built him the Hoo, at Willingdon in East Sussex.

The Batterseas' best contacts, as it turned out, came from what Raymond Asquith had called those odorous skirts of philanthropy, for the Barnetts, Canon Samuel and Henrietta, were Lady Battersea's friends and frequent visitors; through them and the good opinion of Alfred Lyttelton, Lutyens built the Hampstead Garden Suburb churches and Central Square.[31]

Emily Lutyens loved the sea and being beside the sea, no matter how cold or damp, so of all her husband's houses she favoured summer jaunts with the children to Lindisfarne and to the Barings on Lambay Island. Lutyens had first heard from Cecil Baring in July 1905, with a request to design a garden: Baring had seen Lutyens's work in *Country Life* and must have known of the design for Hestercombe, the grand garden for the Hon. Edward Portman and his wife, the Wenlocks' daughter Constance, which was being built.

MAUDE AND CECIL BARING

Cecil Baring was the second son of the 1st Lord Revelstoke, who had died in 1897. The Barings had had to sacrifice Membland, their beloved estate in Devon, and their other houses in the aftermath of the great Baring crash of 1890.[32] John Baring, 2nd Lord Revelstoke, was working furiously and successfully to restore the fortunes of the bank in London. Cecil had been dispatched to New York, where he eloped with the young wife of one of his partners, Maude Tailer, the daughter of Pierre Lorillard, whose wealth came from a family tobacco fortune. Cecil and Maude were eventually married in London in November 1902, when he was thirty-eight and she twenty-six. They spent a prolonged honeymoon in Europe, pursuing their mutual passion for music and Cecil's interest in classical Greece and Rome. Naturally this attractive couple's romance had caused gossip, so to save blushes at the recuperating bank in Bishopsgate, their absence was appreciated. After a year they found a house in London, but almost immediately their attention was caught by an advertisement in *The Field*, for an island for sale in the Irish Sea. It was called Lambay.

When Cecil Baring first set foot on Lambay he found a row of whitewashed cottages beside the little harbour and, just a little farther on, 'an almost, half-derelict, pebble-dashed, semi-fortified little stronghold with crow-step gables surmounting its splayed and battered walls'.[33] Growing around it were the remnants of its shelter, spindly and wind-shaped ash and sycamores: there were barns, stables and sheds, and a walled kitchen garden, and 'standing apart on a mound overlooking the channel, a small chapel'.[34] Behind this little enclave rose the peaks of the island, with a Norse burial cairn on the highest, called Knock-a-bane.[35] 'One thing is certain,' Cecil's daughter Daphne wrote, 'he fell immediately in love with it at first sight.'[36]

Cecil and Maude Baring paid £5,250 for their island, on 1 April 1904. Their daughter, Daphne, was two months old, so the three of them, plus Daphne's nurse-maid, moved into a hotel in Malahide, to supervise the work of making habitable their little stronghold, with its earth floors, leaky roof and outside stair. For £50 they refitted the island ferryboat, a thirty-foot-long brown-sailed lugger named *Shamrock*. Cecil had ousted the coastguard station and discouraged day trippers, for he was a passionate naturalist and ornithologist and had realized that ecologically the island was a time-capsule. Subsequent studies by experts from Dublin proved it to be so: they found five species new to science, three worms, a mite and a bristle-tail, twelve additions to the British fauna and masses of wild flowers.[37]

The Barings moved to their island in June 1905, and Lutyens arrived the following August in answer to a summons. Their meeting was a mutual delight: Mary Lutyens later wrote that her 'Father always seemed at his happiest with the

Lambay Island, Ireland: Lutyens and Maude Baring on the beach.

Barings.'[38] He imagined exactly how the little stronghold could be given added shelter and space, but for the moment repairs to the harbour had swallowed up all their funds, so he left, without a commission, but with new friends.

On Lambay, Cecil and Maude Baring were together renewing their childhood acquaintances with paradise, his in the Devon countryside by the sea, hers spent 'running wild' among the wooded hills of Tuxedo Park, her father's New York estate. They tended their animals, made their own butter (winning prizes at Dublin shows), studied their birds and kept weather records. Sometimes they were stormbound for weeks on end, but both were completely attuned to their island's temperament, tolerating the smoky fires, leaky roofs and endless nor'easter gales for the paradise of summer, picnics on the beaches or surrounded by wild flowers, and reading quietly together through the lamplit evenings. There was a constant trail of cooks and maids who found the isolation intolerable, but equally, there were staunchly loyal helpers who stayed for years. Maude Baring was not one to let standards lapse in paradise, and her daughters wore an all-white wardrobe – piqué dresses, lace-edged petticoats and drawers ordered from Paris – all cared for by the island's laundress and her daughter.[39]

For Lutyens, Maude Baring embodied much of his ideal of the 'peerless mistress' of home and honey and lavender's fresh presence, his dream of domestic bliss; he wrote to Emily of how 'strong and happy she was, thoroughly wholesome and beautiful' – though her American frankness shocked him when she told him that she had been so fat carrying their second daughter, Calypso, that she 'actually lay down and rolled down the hills'.[40]

In March 1908 the Barings gave the go-ahead for work on Lambay. The garden originally mentioned was made by constructing out of the island stone, a blue-green porphyry flecked with crystal, a circular wall, or enceinte, with a diameter of 700 feet. This enclosed and sheltered the old castle, the outbuildings, a new kitchen wing, and lawns and courts – and connected with the walls of the kitchen garden. It was possible to walk around on top of the wall, and cross over the entrance gate by a small timbered bridge.

The new building, with grey limestone from Skerries on the mainland for dressing, and grey pantiles shipped from Holland for its sweeping roof, was settled into its position across a small court from the old castle with such sensitivity that

Lambay Island, Ireland: an open day for the completed restoration of the castle. Maude Baring is standing in the centre, in a hat with her head turned, Cecil Baring is in a light suit, seated on the ground, second left, and their daughters, Daphne and Calypso, are in the centre foreground.

it knew its subordinate place, yet provided fresh kitchens, workrooms and new bedrooms. In the castle there were new stone fireplaces, and the Lutyens touch was given to the vaulted ceilings, the curving stair and 'an underground gallery in the new quadrangle which might have been conceived by Piranesi'.[41] No wonder the architect was at his happiest. He was allowed to employ his best builders, Parnells of Rugby, and together they nurtured the complex of ancient buildings into a new life. Lutyens prowled happily around, noting, sketching, measuring, contemplating, pulling on his pipe, amusing the Baring children and allowing himself to be photographed. It was a uniquely relaxing happiness; the romantic eccentricities of the Barings completely matched his own. There would never be another commission quite like Lambay.

However quietly the undercurrents ran, the realization of Lady Constance's being a Suffragette, and, all too soon afterwards, Emily's discovery of the equally radical theosophy, were worrying, and cast a shadow across those otherwise gloriously successful five years prior to August 1914. It was not just that the headlines announcing the doings of Lady Constance Lytton or Lady Emily Lutyens (their respective values to the militant Suffragettes and the theosophical movement lay in *who* they were more than anything else) would cause gruff murmurings in the partners' rooms at Barings or Farrers, along Whitehall corridors or in Pall Mall clubrooms; it was that Lutyens was perplexed in himself. He was supremely an artist, and not without his own 'Bohemian' sympathies, he had not a political nerve in his body and could not care for such causes, and his humanist and sympathetic soul told him that women, too, had talents, intelligence and a perfectly valid right to use them. He was liberally inclined. On the other hand he liked feminine talents to be used in the domestic arts – in decorating and furnishing, entertaining and theatre-party going: his ideals were Maude Baring, Frances Horner and Pamela Lytton.

For Emily, with her family of five completed by the birth of Mary at the end of July 1908, it was time to resume her quest for a soul-satisfying devotion. She tried sociology, the prostitutes' cause and 'venereal diseases' without satisfaction. Constance (who, like Emily, possessed an abundant candour) wrote in *Prisons and Prisoners* of how, searching for a role for herself, she 'stumbled on a piece of "social radium"' in the revival of folk song and dance, which sent her to Mary Neal and the Esperance Club in the East End. In the autumn of 1908 she accompanied a party from the club on a holiday to Littlehampton – to the Green Lady Hostel, an offshoot of the Canning Town Settlement, set up by Emmeline Pethwick-Lawrence and funded by Lord Swaythling and his daughters Lily and Marian Montagu.[42]

Constance met Annie Kenny and Mrs Pethwick-Lawrence, and, greatly attracted to the latter and finding they both admired the work of Olive Schreiner, Constance was persuaded to go to the office of the Women's Social and Political Union in Clement's Inn to offer her help. She was adamantly against militancy and said so, but it was agreed that she should use her influence to try to see Herbert Gladstone, the Home Secretary, to pave the way for a deputation. That was how Constance's journey to her martyrdom began: Edward Marsh wrote of her, 'If there was a fault in her character it was the extremity of her unselfishness.'[43] Within two years this tall nervous spinster, willowy 'to the point of frailty', with a lovely face and violet-blue eyes, would be reduced to a cadaverous invalid by her unselfishness: it might have been called great courage.

By a twist of fate the Pethwick-Lawrences were living in a Lutyens house when Constance first met them, and they loved it and were blessing his genius. Emmeline Pethwick had married Fred Lawrence, a lawyer who worked for the Canning Town Settlement, in 1901; they spent part of their honeymoon at the Abinger Hatch and visited Goddards, the 'home of rest for ladies of small means' which was just occupied – it seems that Goddards gave Emmeline the idea for the Green Lady Hostel. The countryside around inspired them too and they vowed to find a house. They recognized 'our house' advertised in the paper – it was the Dutch House at South Holmwood, which Lutyens had built for Wildman Cattley, a well-known City and Surrey personality, in 1897.[44] He did not like it. The Pethwick-Lawrences adored it; Emmeline particularly loved its 'three leaved clover design' and its setting, practically on the heathy common, with a wide path wide enough for a carriage 'bordered by a well-designed yew hedge which was part of the arch' leading to a circular and pillared porch.[45] This house by Lutyens was to be their refuge, and a place of recuperation for many Suffragettes, until after the war.

The rest of Constance Lytton's story is well known. Her attempted visit to the Home Secretary landed her in prison, and she was promptly released when it was realized who she was. So she defiantly set out as Miss Jane Warton, to get taken to prison without social cachet – which eventually resulted in the forced feeding which had such disastrous effects on her frail constitution. Emily supported her through all this; the final drama occurred on 15 January 1910, when Emily, at home in Bloomsbury Square, was contacted by the Press Association and asked if it were true that her sister was in Walton Gaol in Liverpool. Emily, naturally shocked, turned to her 'Chippy' – who was none other than Arthur Chapman, the client for Crooksbury, now widowed and her frequent companion and helper[46] – who spent half the night making all the necessary and desperate inquiries, ensuring Constance's release, and Emily took the train to Liverpool to collect her. Constance was tended at Bloomsbury Square where Mrs Pethwick-Lawrence and the Pank-hursts were naturally her visitors; Lutyens appeared to play no supporting role in all this, neither was he obviously absent. He was fully aware of Sir Arthur Chapman's adoration of Emily and condoned his presence as part of the family (he organized holidays, accompanied Emily to meetings and read aloud to her, all 'time-wasting' tasks) but it seems singularly odd that in such a family crisis he did not play his rightful part. Of course he would have hated it, and not acquitted himself well. But there is a hint that Emmeline Pethwick-Lawrence lost her admiration for him at this time: she later built a holiday home very near her own home, the Green Lady Hostel was extended (by Robert Weir Schultz), and the Pethwick-Lawrences built their retirement house on land between Shere and Peaslake after the war, but Lutyens was never involved. Not that they were great commissions, and the reason may well have been that he was too famous and too expensive: or was it that an artist cannot also be a hero?

It was a further twist of fate that he 'found' theosophy for Emily. His only connections from the Paris Exhibition had been the Mallet family, for whom he built Le Bois des Moutiers at Varengeville in 1898–1900. In 1909 they built a second house, Les Communes, and it was on his return from this that he mentioned the Mallets' theosophy. 'What does that mean?' asked Emily, but he did not know – he only knew that it meant a locked bookcase. Emily was determined to see for herself, and Madame Mallet explained all; for that Christmas she gave Emily Annie Besant's lecture volume, and Emily joined the London Theosophical Society in May 1910. Her daughter Mary wrote of this moment: 'Theosophy was to cause a break between my parents which widened as the years went by.' The following May (1911), Annie Besant returned from India with the two chosen boys, Nityananda and Krishnamurti, and Emily became enmeshed. As she told her husband, she 'wanted always to be at someone's feet . . . hero worship is the greatest joy of life';[47] in her youth it had been Christ, now it could be the new Messiah, her worship and love of Krishna would lead her to follow wherever he led. She did not abruptly leave home, but all her energies went into theosophy, lectures, travelling and meetings; she was away a great deal, and when she was home the house was filled with theosophical friends and prayer meetings; eventually she and the children became vegetarians, and her husband was to be banished from her bedroom.

Lutyens's reaction, as always, was to work harder than ever, and this time he told himself that it was more than ever necessary to keep his family financially well afloat, so that Emily could not have that excuse for actually leaving him. As far as it all was concerned, and not for the first time, he let his vizor slip over his eyes at the most hurtful and embarrassing moments.

Theosophy trailed a number of rich benefactors hitched to its star. Emily was particularly friendly with the American Miss Mary Dodge, who had many ideas for building which included a theatre, but which came to nothing. Mrs Besant, dumpy, white-haired, dressed all in white but with 'eyes like a tiger of a curious shade of brown', trailed Lutyens all over London looking for a site for the new London headquarters of the Theosophical Society. This was settled in Tavistock Square, and work was started on a building to cost £50,000. Dreadful conflicts arose, with Mrs Besant's dictums flying back from India (where she returned) insisting on all union labour, which Lutyens resisted, and Lady Emily in the middle, actually becoming her husband's client, as a member of the Executive Committee, complaining that it was difficult to find extra thousands of pounds as costs rose. It all ended in tears, with the partly completed building being sold and finished by other architects; the Burton Street wing by Lutyens that exists indicates that he was paying his tribute to Dance's Newgate Gaol.[48]

But theosophy was also instrumental in the making of a happy house, for through it Emily met a forceful and friendly German divorcée, Antonie Rosalie Schmiechen, who was a theosophist. Frau Schmiechen and her children had come to London with the German painter Hermann Schmiechen, who had been discovered by Madame Blavatsky to be responsive to her psychic powers; through this medium, Schmiechen had painted portraits of the Theosophical Masters, and also two portraits of Madame Blavatsky, but after this he seems to have returned to Germany. In 1910 Antonie Rosalie married a rich, elderly industrialist, Zackary Merton, and for his new family Merton bought Folly Farm at Sulhamstead in Berkshire, where Lutyens had already worked. It was for the Mertons that Folly Farm assumed its fabulous final guise; the Georgian farmhouse and the small 'doll's house' addition already done were extended to a large gabled wing for a dining-room, master bedroom and sleeping balcony. Miss Jekyll undid her first garden plan, for a simple shrub walk and tennis and croquet lawns, and Folly Farm was given its responsive garden, a sequence of courts, walks and flower-filled garden rooms. Because of the theosophical connection and her liking for Mrs Merton, to whom Lutyens also responded warmly (as she was Antonie Rosalie he called her 'mère-toni' or Mertoni), Folly Farm was to become a uniquely happy house, where Emily and Edwin Lutyens and their children were to have a rare chance of being a happy family.

THE GRACIOUS MISTS FROM MELLS

I suppose the summers were as inclement then as now, but looking
back on our summer holidays there, they seem to me a vision of
constant garden life, as if the sun always shone, and the wind never
blew – a vision of long days and moonlit evenings when we sat out,
and strolled amongst the scented borders, or slept out in the loggia
and watched the stars till darkness brought sleep and silence to us at
last.

(FRANCES HORNER, *Time Remembered*)[1]

Throughout Lutyens's career, especially at its most frantic and frustrating
periods, there seemed to be a leavening, soft and gracious, emanating as the
mists along the Mendip valleys, wreathing out from Mells. Mells is today one of
the places where the spirit of Lutyens's particular Englishness lingers, not so much
for what he built there as for its influence upon the pattern of his building, and
the people he encountered there. The chatelaine of Mells, Frances Horner, a
member of the Souls' circle, always understood him and brought forth the best in
him.

It is a scattered village, with tree-shaded lanes on different levels and gaggles
of Mendip stone buildings, of that 'holy greyness' Burne-Jones identified, amid
the headwaters of the River Frome, in a triangle between Frome, Radstock and
Shepton Mallet. The Horner family had been there since 1524, when the Dissolution
awarded them the monastic buildings and acres – the famous 'plum' in Little Jack
Horner's pie (a rumour strongly denied by the family).[2] Those sixteenth-century
Horners had built Mells Manor on the old foundations by the church and ridden
out across the deer park they enclosed. In 1724 a young Horner had married
Susannah Strangways, an heiress from Melbury in Dorset, and her fortune allowed
them to build in the park, a house of 'cleane stone work' in front though rubble
behind, for £210, designed by Nathaniel Ireson, a local man.[3]

Settled comfortably, the Horners took to a ruling passion, for their park and
its trees: Thomas Horner, grandson of Susannah Strangways, emulated his friends

Mells Manor House and the church, in Somerset.

at Stourhead and Painshill in an infinitely more rugged setting, cutting drives, controlling streams, planting and planting more and more, and planning follies, hermitages and pineapple houses, most of which were never to be built. It was the tree-planting urge that he passed to following generations, and during the nineteenth century the park had been constantly enlarged and glorified, with a particular Horner passion for conifers. They had done a little building also, adding new stables and a lovely arcaded courtyard, at the rear of the house, by Daniel Hague, a Bristol architect, in the 1760s. Sir John Soane had designed some interiors in the early nineteenth century. Then, for some thirty years, little happened but the daily country regime, and the trees a-growing; little wonder, when Edward Burne-Jones's heart was broken on hearing that his muse, Frances Graham, was to marry John Horner, he cried out against her giving herself to poverty and country isolation with the 'gardener'.[4]

Frances Graham and her sister Agnes, married to Herbert Jekyll, were the children of the good, rich William Graham of Glasgow and his wife, Jane. Graham, an India merchant, Liberal MP, strict Presbyterian and kindliest of patrons to living, struggling artists, had bravely taken his daughters to the lair of Dante Gabriel Rossetti and Edward Burne-Jones at a tender age. Burne-Jones, 'about forty and living a quiet life', was captivated by Frances, whom he had painted first when she was sixteen, as the young bride in *The King's Wedding* (1870). Painting her, drawing on linen or designing slippers for her to embroider, sending her letters full of amusing illustrations – 'many a patient design ... to adorning Frances and her ways'[5] – became a way of life. In return the Graham girls, dressed demurely in high-necked velveteens of sage green and autumn brown, who felt their own life dull and not full of balls and parties like other girls who were 'in society', and Frances in particular, amused him. There was a 'standing fiction between them that they would run away together'.[6] Frances entered society by way of Burne-Jones's paintbrush – she was his Eurydice, a nymph in one of the *Perseus* panels intended for Arthur Balfour's music room, the subject of endless pencilled profiles, and, when Cyril Flower commissioned *The Golden Stairs* in 1880, she became the first on the descending flight. Burne-Jones naturally wished that Frances would remain his unsullied muse forever, and she did remain so until she was twenty-nine, by which time perhaps she needed what she called (in *Time Remembered*) her 'coming to port after stormy seas'; and she knew herself well enough to settle in the country, the calm, consoling and companionable countryside of Mells which so exactly echoed her personality.

Frances found Mells Park rather short of furniture and in need of her needle-woman's skills. Soon after the birth of their first child, Cicely, she rather typically moved the family to a rented house in Guildford where, with Agnes, she cared for her father in his last months of life. Then Jane Graham, and presumably generous amounts of comfortable furniture and Burne-Jones paintings, moved back to Mells with them all. With such a sympathetic, contented mistress Mells Park was warmed back into a beautiful life which seemed to enchant everyone who came near: the family progressed, to Katharine and Edward and, lastly, Mark, born in 1891. Frances had 'serious discussions' with her husband about the age-racked and wind-damaged conifers and encouraged him to plant 'beeches and cedars and oaks and thorn everywhere' so that in spring, viewed from the house on its precipice, the park was pink with blossom. In 1895 John Horner was, by a rare appropriateness in public life, appointed as Commissioner of Forests and Woods; for this role the Horners felt they needed a London house, and they acquired 9 Buckingham Gate. Frances, who consulted Agnes Jekyll about all the important things in life, agreed that young Ned Lutyens might be just the person to help.

The summons to Mells in October 1896 was for Lutyens, like meeting Barbara Webb, and tea at Littleworth Cross with Miss Jekyll, one of the crucial encounters of his life. Mells Park House, with its unusual arcaded entrance court and Soane interiors, intrigued him, but the romantic Elizabethan manor house close to the church was more to his taste and enthusiasm. Inside the church was Frances Horner's memorial to her great friend Laura Tennant, who had died in childbirth a year after her marriage to Alfred Lyttelton. For Frances, Burne-Jones had designed a sombre bronze, with a peacock trailing its feathers across a bier. Laura and Margot Tennant had stood with Frances on *The Golden Stairs*. (Frances Horner would have had little difficulty in divining her young visitor's lovelorn state; she may have encouraged him. It was on the train home from Frome to Paddington that he wrote to Emily Lytton, declaring his love.)

At Mells Lutyens was always to find ease and an appreciation of his talents; when Frances Horner's mother, Mrs Graham, died in 1900, the Horner family decided to move from Mells Park into the more manageable Manor House, where Lutyens helped with alterations and the layout of the garden, for which Frances's friend Norah Lindsay did the planting.[7] The quality of society at Mells, which moved effortlessly from the Park to the Manor, was best captured by Raymond Asquith's diary record of his visit to Mells Park in the summer of 1899: 'The really best thing . . . the thing that almost compensated for a five mile walk around the Park which my host took me this evening to explain the various qualities and characteristics of his unique collection of pines was the bathing' . . . 'In front of the house is a terrace, beneath which after a steep fall of 100 feet runs a stream which has been dammed into a considerable lake about $\frac{1}{4}$ mile in length by 200 yards in breadth, covered with waterlilies and fringed with bulrushes, where they bathe.' He thought it beautiful, enhanced by the presence of the Horner girls, Katharine and Cicely, with their tall, lily-like slimness which contrasted so with the keenest member of the swimming party, his father's colleague Richard Haldane, QC, MP (Haldane would one day be a Lutyens client). The rest of the scene is irresistible:

> His immense but stately figure clad in a very scanty bathing dress and recklessly precipitating from dizzy altitudes into this green and flowery pond was really exquisite: the quiet slowness and dignity with which he put himself in the most ridiculous situations proved to me more conclusively than anything else could have done the real bigness of the man – to see this vast white mass with the brain of Socrates and the shape of Nero executing his absurd antics from a thin plank which bent double under his weight and sporting fantastically in the water with a divinely beautiful girl no whit abashed recalled the sunniest days of the Roman decline.

Minutes later they were all on the lawn for tea, where Haldane, in towel and Panama hat, was explaining Buddhism 'to a host of local spinsters who had flocked in for food and gossip'.[8]

The Hon. Alfred Lyttelton, photographed at Aston Clinton by Cyril Flower (Lord Battersea): Lyttelton employed Lutyens to build High Walls, his golfing holiday house at Gullane, and then to alter his London home and Wittersham House in Kent, and he was also a constant advocate on Lutyens's behalf, helping him to several major commissions.

ALFRED LYTTELTON AND GREY WALLS

Alfred Lyttelton was the first distinguished client of the Mells connection. He was the youngest of the 'Old Dozen' children of the 4th Lord Lyttelton of Hagley, by his first marriage to Mary Glynne. Alfred was 'the child who had cost his mother her life',[9] and was reared largely by his adoring sisters, Meriel, who became Mrs John Talbot, and Lucy, Lady Frederick Cavendish. His brothers were all fine sportsmen, but it was to be Alfred who outshone them all; it is impossible to write of his prowess without him sounding like a schoolboy hero, and he was the pattern for so many schoolboy heroes. At Eton he was brilliant in all sports and games, and studies, and left captain of almost everything, 'cloathed in unapproachable glory'. At Cambridge he was a cricket and tennis blue, a football international and still managed a brilliant degree. Perhaps his most heroic stamping ground was Lord's, where he played for the Gentlemen and Middlesex, as W. G. Grace so famously recalled, 'the champagne of cricket'. He met Laura Tennant in the summer of 1884 at dinner at Agnes Jekyll's and married her the following year: it was for that occasion that Gertrude had made Burne-Jones's silver entwined 'LL'. After Laura's death he absorbed himself in his barrister's practice, and spent time with his friends: he was found sitting for his portrait by Cyril Flower in the conservatory at Aston Clinton – what John Buchan affectionately described as 'the eager face, the judicial pent-house brows, beneath which twinkled his big boyish eyes'[10] – or at Mells, or with his family. Agnes Jekyll also kept an eye on him, and it was at her house that she introduced him to Edith 'DD' Balfour and subsequently, knowing that 'DD' was in love with him, engineered that they should walk together to a service at St Martha's church on the Pilgrims' Way near Guildford. There being no more romantic place, the ruse worked – and they were married eighteen months later.

Alfred Lyttelton was elected to the House of Commons in 1895, so they bought a division bell house, 16 Great College Street, which was to be their London home for the rest of his life. Lutyens did alterations for them there in 1900, but it was their 'cottage' – as it was first called – in Scotland that was really exciting. The passion for golf seems to have swept through the House of Commons in the 1890s like the measles; Lyttelton's long, loose athletic frame would adapt wonderfully well to golf and he needed the exercise – and the passion for golf seemed everyone's answer. He played at Rye with Arthur Balfour, and at Gosford with Hugo Charteris, and decided that for him golf could only be played in Scotland, on real links. He bought land at Muirfield, to build 'within a mashie niblick shot of the 18th green'. The design was put in hand in the summer of 1899; the Lytteltons wanted fifteen bedrooms but few other rooms, and Mrs Lyttelton wanted a fortress, to keep out the wind, but large windows as well! The architect's puzzlement was duly overcome and High Walls, as they called it, was completed for them to holiday there in August 1902: they loved it, and their architect later called it his favourite house.[11]

The Lytteltons spent five happy summers golfing at Muirfield. Alfred Lyttelton was colonial secretary in Balfour's Cabinet for two years, September 1903–5;

Grey Walls (originally called High Walls), Gullane, East Lothian: the entrance front, *c.* 1930.

he had missed most of one summer because of a trip to Newfoundland to sort out railway contracting problems, and – as so very much a younger son – he was never a rich man, and in the aftermath of office had to work harder than ever. 'D.D.' Lyttelton wrote that they felt 'the grey stone house at Gullane was too far away ... it was a wrench to sell the place, with its garden full of roses, the glorious stretch of sea, the fine air, but to keep up a large house for the sake of six weeks in the year seemed extravagant. In 1906 someone wanted to buy it and we made up our minds to accept the offer.'[12] The motivation for the parting was assuredly 'D.D.' Lyttelton's; she was becoming fearful of any separation from Alfred, or their children, Oliver and Mary (let alone the poodle Fisc), and the final push to their reluctance was a bad train crash at Grantham in September 1906, when she was trying the treatment at Ems on her doctor's advice and read of the accident in the paper, knowing that Alfred was travelling that night. He had taken a later train, but this only increased her fearful premonition. To make up for losing High Walls, she searched for and found a rectory, unwanted, at Wittersham in Kent, convenient enough for Alfred to play golf at Rye. It was 'a plain red-brick Georgian building – six sitting-rooms opening one out of the other ... the whole place in a great state of disrepair, without any modern comforts; some fine trees, the possibilities of a charming garden'.[13] Lutyens almost completely remodelled Wittersham, roofing it with pantiles (a tradition which he now honoured anywhere east of a line from Edinburgh to Brighton) and building a broad, pedimented, loggia-like entrance porch – thus turning one of the six sitting-rooms into a hall and allowing two separate rooms, each right and left. The garden, under the Lytteltons' care, became enchanting, enhanced by one of Lutyens's most unusual outdoor rooms – 'an open-air parlour', simply a patch of paving in front of an old wall, into which he built niches for statues, and four pilasters, each with a stone basket of fruit on top![14]

Alfred Lyttelton belies the legend of the extravagant and facile Lutyens client completely. He was neither rich nor extravagant, but something in him – his love of argument, his fund of good stories, his cheerfulness – found perfect response in the rooms that Lutyens made for him to live in. The Lytteltons doubled the size of their London house by buying 18 Great College Street next door, and Lutyens saw to the alterations for them; Alfred Lyttelton was instrumental in getting Lutyens the commissions for the churches at Hampstead Garden Suburb, and cast his benevolent influence through to the golfing developments that came later. He also encouraged Jack Tennant, brother of Laura and Màrgot, to let Lutyens build one of his largest houses, Great Maytham at Rolvenden, not far from Wittersham. He was, as John Buchan mourned him, 'of the tribe of the Sons of Consolation, always helping lame dogs over stiles, ever ready with advice and help, giving of his rich humanity to needy and shivering souls'.[15] His wife's growing premonitions came all too true: Alfred Lyttelton, the English hero *par excellence*, died at only fifty-six, after an operation for appendicitis that went awry, in the summer of 1913.

For Lutyens Mells was somewhere he felt totally at ease: Frances Horner described this best herself in *Time Remembered*, the Manor House filled with the good-natured crowding of the family and constant friends, with young ladies who didn't mind sharing rooms and young men content to be shunted out to cottages, and no one brought a maid or manservant: 'I suppose the summers were as inclement then as now, but looking back on our summer holidays there, they seemed to me a vision of constant garden life . . .'[16]

Frances Horner saw to it that though they couldn't afford great works, she found friends that could: on her admission she was no gardener, so it was rather fun to bring the excellent young garden-architect two exciting jobs. Lutyens had built a lych-gate at Kilmersdon for Lord Hylton, the Horners' neighbour at Ammerdown Park, but it was chiefly for Alice Hylton that Lutyens had his first chance to give a fine English house by James Wyatt a formal garden where once the deer had crept up to the windows to be fed! Deer ousted, Ammerdown acquired an Italianate 'star' sculpted out of yew, with paths radiating outwards, the principal one to the Wyatt orangery. Lady Alice Hylton loved all things Italian; she had been a student of Walter Sickert and was a fine embroideress – she was designing the Wells Cathedral embroideries. Was she talking about her garden with her head bent over her canvas one day, and overheard by 'the bazaar opener to the county', as Lutyens called Mrs Portman, and so came the commission for Hestercombe, which was particularly enjoyable because he could build his own version of a classical orangery? Hestercombe, an unquestionably ugly house, a 'self-satisfied, comfortable English sporting-squire of a house' with vast quantities of food and wine and endless talk of cattle and dog breeding, and Mrs Portman ever surrounded 'with refractory puppies that never behave or are let behave', was an alien atmosphere for Lutyens.[17] He would have punned mercilessly. It is only too clear that the Portmans subscribed to the beefy grandeur of Edwardian England, the jingoistic end of the scale of Englishry, so Lutyens played their game and gave them a garden that left neighbours and bazaar organizers gasping with astonishment. The same subtle game of conceal and reveal is heightened by the dullness of the approach, the grey-rendered mediocrity of the entrance porch, the stolid comfort of the entrance hall – so that nothing prepares the visitor for the staggering sight of the stony layers of garden, the extensive plot with criss-crossings of flowers and the long, long pergola cutting across the view.

The Portmans were typically people Lutyens didn't mind 'cultivating' because they had, or he thought they had, prospects. The prospects never materialized, however, and he did no further work for them, the Hon. Edward Portman pre-deceasing his father, the 2nd Viscount Portman, in 1911. Nothing could have been further from Hestercombe's flamboyance, though, than the help he gave at the same time to Montague Knight, the owner of Chawton House in Hampshire, the very essence of Jane Austen's England – where he gently and restrainedly 'tinkered' and added a tiny garden court, as Mr Knight's finances allowed.

The mists from Mells seem to wreathe so many of the happy, early clients into a new way of living. As Ida Streatfeild sits in her landaulette outside her door at Fulbrook, as Gertrude Jekyll and Julia Chance adjourn to their respective work-rooms, as Emily Lawless repeats '*Anemone Blanda*' at her latest exasperation, as the Goddards' home of rest receives its first lady of small means, as Lord Battersea emerges 'brinily radiant' from chilly waves, a particular new-century Englishness is born. William Lethaby defined it as 'Simple, well-off housekeeping in the country, with tea in the garden' (all easy to imagine exactly for the Jekylls, Streatfeilds, Mangles, Blackburns and Fenwicks), with 'boy scouting and tennis in flannels' added by Lethaby to make up the four best examples of the spirit in which housing the nation for the new century should be undertaken.[18] (Ignore, for the moment, that boy-scouting would breed a light-hearted chivalry that so deftly turned to self-sacrifice or that Miss Jekyll's tennis lawns repeat the symbolism of Drake's bowling green.) Eyes of hindsight must be closed, and only rose-tinted spectacles used; this Edwardian dream of Englishness – in which Lutyens's clients play such perfect parts – must be captured in words and pictures for all time.

The gentleman to do this had presented himself at Munstead Wood in the late summer of 1898, in search of an editor: he was Edward Hudson, a curious mixture of media man and monk. He was in the process of absorbing William Robinson's *Garden* magazine into his little printing empire and hoped Miss Jekyll would be a joint editor (with E. T. Cook). But he was always on the lookout for ideas for his most special enterprise, his magazine *Country Life*, which had first appeared in early January 1897. Among the pot-pourri-scented rooms and velvety oak of Munstead Wood he felt he had found an old tradition that might be called a new *style – Country Life* style.[19]

Hudson's monkishness came from his dreary, gaslit and Victorian upbringing, in a gloomy villa somewhere near Notting Hill, in a north country family which grew more prosperous from a successful printing business. His father had sent Edward into a solicitor's office when he was fifteen, but when he reached twenty-one he pleaded to be allowed to join the family firm, where he had become

Lindisfarne Castle: snapshots of
Edward Hudson with Madame
Suggia (left) and with Jack
Lilburn (right).

fascinated by the possibilities of illustration from half-tone blocks and had urged
the acquisition of the finest and most modern print machinery from America. In
1898 Hudson was forty-four; in printing brilliant photographs of beautiful objects
he had found an echo of the spotlit moments of his dull youth, moments when his
father had suddenly bought something of beauty, an inlaid table, a musical-box, a
portrait of a beautiful woman. Printing beautiful pictures was his passion.

Hudson was strange to behold: he had a large head and doleful eyes, a scrubby
moustache and an over-long upper lip, with rounded shoulders ending in long arms
that seemed to dangle, not quite sure of their purpose. Lutyens was to remark
that 'Huddy', as he became, 'was a brick' – but, after long experience of his kind
but clumsy good nature, added, 'He had no hands – in the horse-master's sense.'[20]
He still lived in the gloomy family home with its brilliant treasures, with his
spinster sisters and delicate brother, Henry, 'as fragile as porcelain', who was his
cross to bear. To please Henry he was taking an interest in architecture, especially
seventeenth-century English buildings; but he was 'married', devotedly, to his
new magazine, and on its behalf he pursued his acquisition of more beautiful
objects and brilliant people, for whom he had a collector's fine eye. Hudson's
idolatries were not always viewed sympathetically, and Lytton Strachey described
him cruelly, but accurately: 'a pathetically dreary figure ... a fish gliding underwater, and star-struck – looking up with his adoring eyes through his own dreadful
element ... A kind of bourgeois gentilhomme also ...'[21] Despite this opinion,
Strachey continued to be welcome at Hudson's lunches and musical evenings along
with many other celebrities who were viperish in their disdain; no wonder 'Huddy',
tetchy and impatient on the surface but lonely and vulnerable beneath, came to
admire 'without any reservation' and love sweet, non-poisonous Ned Lutyens.[22]

What is so interesting is that Hudson, as a patron, continued to act in his habitually proprietorial, magazine-owning (and editorial, interfering) manner; he 'collected' buildings, not for use, but because they gave him beautiful pictures, and he was to do so, erratically, for the rest of his life. The first example was the house he immediately decided to build, in an old orchard that he had found in the Thames-side village of Sonning in Berkshire. Lutyens, determined to do his best for this brightest of prospects, spent two days, 27 and 28 June 1899, surveying the site himself and discussing it with Gertrude Jekyll before he set out to design. In order to save as much of the orchard as possible for naturally 'wild' gardening, the house was kept close to the northern bounding wall, and was entered through a heavy oak door directly from the street. Amazingly, it was not a timbered hall one entered, but a vaulted courtyard, shaded and scented or wet and windy, according to the season. The vaults, banded in brick and white chalk, gave a Vermeer-like quality, in deference to Hudson's love of Dutch interiors; to the right was an enclosed court, filled with blue hydrangeas when fully dressed, to the left an arched entrance to the garden, and straight ahead another heavy door to the inner hall. This inner hall has become one of the most celebrated interior images of the

Deanery Garden, Sonning, Berkshire: the house Lutyens built for Edward Hudson, which Hudson really used as a promotional image for his magazine *Country Life*.

present century: it is double height, dominated by a west-facing oriel with forty-eight lead-light panels reaching to the ceiling, with a big, open fireplace *à la* Munstead Wood and unbelievably sinuous half-timbered 'arabesques' of oak for the upper walls. A small sitting-room on one side and dining-room on the other, both with south-facing windows on to the garden, made up the 'best' part of the house. Upstairs there were *two* principal bedrooms and *one* bathroom. Christopher Hussey wrote of Deanery Garden, as Hudson called it, as 'without overstatement a perfect architectural sonnet, compounded of brick and tile and timber forms, in which his [Lutyens's] handling of the masses and spaces serve as rhythm: its theme, a romantic bachelor's idyllic afternoons beside a Thames backwater'.[23]

Edward Hudson used Deanery Garden as an artistic image rather than a home. The lofty, timbered hall, photographed by the brilliant Charles Latham, who had just joined *Country Life*, pioneered the magazine's style in interiors; barely set with antique gate-legged tables, Jacobean chairs, a few expensive rugs, masses of freshly cut flowers in china bowls, a small Dutch picture or two on the wall, it presented Hudson's ideal image, much of which he had gathered from Munstead Wood.

The garden was no less a vehicle for the promotion of the partnership and Miss Jekyll's planting style. The exquisitely geometrical circular steps, the mock bridge and domed and cavernous pool beneath, the stone-edged iris rill across the lawn and the soft green paths immaculately projected across the orchard, all brought a perfect blend of order and charm. The roses, the vines on the pergola, the thrifts, pinks and lavender tumbling over stone walls and carpets of flowers beneath the orchard trees, all made a perfectly ordained and private little world. It seems all the more odd, therefore, that it was largely for public consumption.

Deanery Garden boosted Hudson's confidence in both Lutyens and Miss Jekyll. She became a fairly regular contributor to *Country Life*, and he, in partnership with George Newnes, published her books. Deanery Garden made a début in *Country Life* on 9 May 1903 and was in *English Homes* the following year. Millmead, the small house at Bramley designed and built by Lutyens and paid for by Miss Jekyll, as an intentional demonstration of good design in house and garden, was also featured. Hudson was a fixture in Lutyens's life, and he was regularly at Hudson's weekly lunches to meet prospective clients or hear new schemes (for the architect it must have been rather like having an agent). 'Huddy' became obsessed with opportunities – Ned should compete for the Victoria Memorial (the Mall approach done by Aston Webb), they should buy up the village of Burnmouth which he had discovered just north of Berwick and build a hotel; then the derelict Lindisfarne Castle came into view, which Lutyens converted into a romantic but damp and chilly holiday home, where Hudson dispensed lobsters and champagne. Again it

Lindisfarne Castle: Tom Blackburn with his sons, Julian and Aubrey, on a family visit in September 1911.

was all images, from the skinny, rather fey Barbara Lutyens, photographed by Latham in the likeness of a Dutch interior at Lindisfarne, to Hudson's own idolatry, fulfilled when Madame Suggia played for his guests the Stradivarius cello he had given her, and was subsequently painted doing so by Augustus John.[24]

Hudson sold Deanery Garden and kept Lindisfarne for August holidays, but he continued to forage for jobs for Ned Lutyens. There was a clock for George Newnes in Southampton Street, and as his first London building, the new home for *Country Life* in Tavistock Street in 1904, to be followed by 42 Kingsway for *The Garden* offices. Hudson himself moved into 15 Queen Anne's Gate, which Lutyens altered for him, and where several of his neighbours became clients.

There were to be many further useful introductions through Hudson or from *Country Life* readers, including Herbert Johnson, the stockbroker client for a large white house in Hampshire called Marsh Court, at Stockbridge. Johnson has melted into the anonymity of the years just as effectively as he suddenly emerged to his moment of fame as a Lutyens client, and there is little to be added to Hussey's note on him: he was fiftyish, the son of a clergyman, had made half a million on the Stock Exchange, loved fishing and so had bought a hilltop overlooking the valley of the River Test. Something in Herbert Johnson's 'adventurous traditionalism' and his love of fishing touched Ned Lutyens's soul, and possibly he never realized that Marsh Court was the reality, or nearest to it, of the white house that he had always intended to build for his own family. Apart from the introductions, there were Edward Hudson's never-ending speculations: Hun-tercombe in Buckinghamshire, Lympne Castle in Kent, Crossways Farm at Abinger, Heath House at Headley, near George Riddell's Walton Heath golf course (where the enthusiasm for golf momentarily struck him) and without doubt many other lovely houses were the subject of excited summonses.

Country Life reflected the growing craze, giving golf lavish coverage in the hands of the celebrated Horace Hutchinson. Soon so many of Lutyens's clients were taking to golf that it is worth asking what directions his career might have taken had he played. It held no fascination for him *at all*, however, but the networking of his clients who did play leads him on through these Edwardian years and it seems particularly appropriate that it is a *game* that should form the connection. It had begun, of course, with Alfred Lyttelton at Grey Walls, but the real business of golf clubs focuses farther south at Walton Heath. Walton Heath golf club was the pet project of George Riddell, a solicitor who was speedily turning into what today's parlance would call a media mogul. Riddell (1865–1934), a director of *Country Life* and a close colleague of Hudson and Newnes, having helped the Carr family to a successful ownership of the *News of the World*, was also managing director of that company. He was a supremely energetic, handsome, clubbable and manipulative man's man, with great passion for his newspaper, for Liberalism – a Welsh radical brand of it – as a cause, and for the career of David Lloyd George in particular, and for golf. With Walton Heath he found the perfect way of combining all three, largely because of his timely – perhaps canny – judgement.[25]

At the turn of the century golf was finding a wider and wider audience: the charismatic example of Alfred Lyttelton, mixed with the clearly professional advantages of playing with the right people, made it almost *de rigueur* in the House of Commons, and clearly the entrepreneur who could bring golf into easy reach of the division bell was likely to be a success. The Prince's Club on Mitcham Common was popular, but residentially and socially Mitcham was no man's land – the golf needed to be nearer a smart place to live. In 1902 a Prince's member, Henry Cosmo Orme Bonsor, who had been MP for Wimbledon until 1900 and was a director of the Bank of England and of Watney, Combe Reid, the brewers, overcame the legal restrictions on turning open heath into a golf course by acquiring, in the name of his son Malcolm Bonsor, the manorial rights to Walton Heath, adjacent to his home at Kingswood Warren. Cosmo Bonsor's brother-in-law, William Herbert Fowler, was a keen player and enthusiastic about designing a golf course – having learned from his annual pilgrimages to play at St Andrews. Herbert and Ethel Fowler moved to Walton; Herbert walked and rode the 600 acres – thick with heather and whins – which must have felt not unlike Scotland on the purply autumn days of 1902. A steam plough made the fairways and greens, gangs of women and boys picked stones, and the new course was seeded by Carters of Raynes Park (plus loads of manure from London stables) in late summer 1903. Walton Heath was open for play in the spring of 1904; the entrance fee was ten guineas with an annual subscription of five guineas for men, three guineas and two guineas respectively for ladies, and the first members' list had 265 men and fifty-two ladies. Though most of the course was east of the Dorking Road, because of its common land status any building had to be adjoining the village, on the west side; a prefabricated wooden clubhouse was hastily erected, a comfortable, rambling affair that could accommodate 500.

George Riddell's first formal connection with Walton Heath came in January 1904, when he witnessed the contract for the new club professional, James Braid, 1901 Open Champion, a young man who liked the heath as it reminded him of his native Scottish links. The glorious triumvirate of Braid, the current Open Champion Harry Vardon, and J. H. Taylor (three times Open Champion) played a great celebratory opening match; Vardon won – but the whole occasion has become one of golfing history's great moments.

As Walton Heath was clearly so successful, the wily Riddell (having negotiated for the development land around the clubhouse), with Hudson and Sir Alexander Kennedy, bought out the Bonsors and took over in November 1905 (on behalf of the *News of the World*). Hudson approached Lutyens in early 1906 to design a 'Dormie [*sic*] House', in the Scots tradition, which was built, with a Jekyll garden of roses, foxgloves and other homely summer flowers, and a path to a wicket gate leading to the neighbouring clubhouse. Hudson thought the Dormy House was superb; it had pantiles, pretty red brick quoins and stringcourses, whitewashed walls, green shutters, and big chimneys which could be seen from across the course. There were sixteen bedrooms and four bathrooms, a large sitting-room and a card room; members had subscribed separately from the main club, and bed and bath cost five shillings a night.[26]

On 25 April 1908 Lutyens spent a night in 'my Dormy House' with further plans under discussion. Herbert and Ethel Fowler had bought from Riddell a plot next door to the clubhouse, and there Lutyens built them their house Chussex, named for Chussex Plain, an area in the centre of the course where Fowler had carefully left untouched the considerable remains of a Roman villa. Christopher Hussey later wrote of Chussex, the Dormy House, Middlefield at Great Shelford and Knebworth Golf Club, which we have yet to reach, that they 'established the mode, almost by their own influence, of English domestic architecture for a

Dormy House, Walton Heath, from a painting remaining in the house.

Chussex, Walton Heath, Surrey: built for the course designer and first secretary of the Walton Heath Golf Club, W. H. Fowler, and his wife, Ethel.

generation. Their children have been as the sands of the sea – Council cottages after the 1918 Peace, rich men's mansions, by-pass semi-detached, petrol stations and road-houses.'[27]

Riddell also had more suggestions. He wanted a little house 'for a tenant' and 'then two small speculative houses'. It turns out that the tenant was none other than Lloyd George. Riddell had been wooing the Welsh Wizard, inquiring into his housing plans – he lived in a small villa on Wandsworth Common and was planning his new house at Criccieth. Riddell, a fresh-air fiend, would whisk him from the Commons in his open Rolls for golf, and he seemed to be on casual calling terms at 10 Downing Street. He seemed to be totally obsessed with Lloyd George, slightly drunk with this closeness to the seat of power – Riddell, as his diaries relate, would cultivate or dissimulate to please him, and his tempting lair was Walton Heath. Lutyens sketched the 'house for a tenant', but then Riddell stayed away, almost certainly because Lady Constance Lytton's name began to appear in the papers for her Suffragette activities – a matter on which Riddell, like all his friends, was highly sensitive. All Riddell's cultivations paid off when his knighthood was announced in January 1909: from now on his golfing guests included the Other Club, formed in early 1911 with Winston Churchill, F. E. Smith, the Marquis de Soveral, Lord Northcliffe, Max Aitken, William Nicholson, Lord Mottistone, Bonar Law and, of course, always Lloyd George. In November 1911 Riddell recorded that he had played golf with Churchill twice a week for a year – clearly far more of the business of Britain was done on Walton Heath than in the House of Commons. The Reginald McKennas were soon regulars, and Clementine Churchill played occasionally, as did the Asquiths and J. M. Barrie. Riddell went to Archerfield and the compliment was returned; James Braid went to Muirfield to play. Lutyens's house, now openly for Lloyd George, was built to additional designs by P. Morley Horder. Building began in late 1912. Riddell's fears proved well founded (though he couldn't blame his architect), and in the early hours of 13 February 1913 he was awoken by a telephone call saying that the new house had been damaged by a bomb. At a meeting in Cardiff that evening Mrs Pankhurst claimed success.[28]

The house was eventually finished and Lloyd George enjoyed using it. It is of blue and rosy brick, on a site across the road from Chussex, and was clearly inspired by Lutyens's original sketch, for a house of the same colour and texture as Folly Farm, though it is a dull and distant relative, a disappointing house which offers just gleams of the real thing. Lutyens's association with Walton Heath had come to an end, though the golfing conversations would go on, and his name must often have been mentioned, with so many clients past and future.

Grey Walls, Gullane: Mrs
William James with the baby
(centre) Edward on her lap, her
daughters (seated extreme right
and standing second from the
right), and visitors in the garden.

When the Lytteltons had reluctantly parted with Grey Walls, it was to a man who already owned one Lutyens house, the American William James, known as Willie (to distinguish him from his philosopher cousin). Willie James was staunchly unintellectual (scorned his other cousin, Henry), a devastatingly good shot and enormously rich, with a family fortune from railroads and intermarriage with the Phelps Dodge copper mining dynasty. Willie's first love had been big-game hunting, but after his brother was killed by an elephant he had taken refuge in English society and marriage. His bride was the exquisite Evelyn Forbes, and for her he bought West Dean Park on the Sussex Downs, with 10,000 acres, which included a lot of good shooting. With the help of Sir Ernest George he had converted West Dean into a plush baronial extravaganza of the Long Island style (the Jameses were lavish entertainers in the sporting manner) and Willie was actually a very good and interested landlord to his little world.

For the rather larger world the Jameses had an obsessive fascination, perhaps matched only by the Waleses today. Even Lutyens, when he was first summoned in March 1902, had his head buzzing with Belloc's ballad:

> And there it is that when the dryads ope
> Their young enchanted arms to grasp the Spring,
> There comes a coroneted envelope
> And Mrs James will entertain the King.[29]

Lutyens gleefully reported to Emily no untoward evidence of 'Royal favours'. And they were all wrong. For the rather poignant and most plausible truth, asserted shortly before his death by Edward James, is that the King's visits to West Dean were to see his daughter – Mrs Willie was Edward VII's child by Helen Forbes, the wife of Sir Charles Forbes of Allargue, the estate neighbouring Balmoral.[30]

Mrs Willie, of doll-like prettiness, exceedingly myopic, dressed by Worth, was lying on a sofa, enceinte, when Lutyens first saw her. She wished for a retreat on the Downs (for West Dean became stifling in summer – all that heavy embossed velvet and those furry hunting trophies), really a playhouse, where she and Willie could take the children. The result was Monkton House, high up, difficult to find, surrounded by beech and thorn, with a view out over Chichester to the English Channel. As Lutyens built it, Monkton had doll-like qualities; it was a simple rectangle, with a hipped roof, red bricks and red tiles surrounded by green trees. It had a secretive little entrance court at the side, and the rooms with the views had big arcaded windows, with large, white-balustraded sleeping balconies serving the four bedrooms above. Mrs Willie laid out the garden – her son Edward later thought her colour schemes were wonderful; Miss Jekyll had given her a little help at West Dean.

The Jameses had three daughters when they bought Grey Walls, and Edward was born there in 1907. He later recalled how he remembered in 'film-clips' from his unhappy childhood, and the first of these was of Grey Walls: he remembered the carriage horses clattering up to the front of the great grey-walled house . . . 'All around the poplars were in full leaf – it must have been the end of July or the beginning of August – and the dawn light was glittering through the leaves, which were all moving like aspens, and the mist was rising, being drawn up by the morning sun, by the dawn. Some of the poplars were still buried in grey mist as we came up the drive, and then, little by little, the swirls of mist were drawn away and the trees began to glitter in the early light.'[31]

VII

THE EDWARDIANS

> Few individuals are so brazen as to admit, even to themselves, that
> they buy art or build great architecture out of a straightforward
> desire to provide visible bulwarks to their social or political position.
> There is almost always . . . a more conscious and more positive motiv-
> ation, a desire to participate in, and contribute to, a cultural tradition
> learned through education and the experience and enjoyment of art.
> (CHARLES SAUMEREZ SMITH, *The Building of Castle Howard*)[1]

Throughout his career Lutyens's clients seem to crowd in around him to give
him the occasional especially wonderful year. One of these was 1897, then came
1901, his break into the new century and the world outside Surrey, and 1908 was
to be another, the beginning of his greatest vintage, and it and the years that
followed were the pinnacle of his whole professional practice. The glory lasted,
with anything from fifteen to twenty new commissions starting each year, and the
accumulation of works at different stages meaning forty or fifty jobs running in
his head, until the summer of 1914. The death of King Edward VII on 6 May 1910
shocked and saddened both the architect and his patrons, but it did not impede
their buildings; the Edwardianly expansive mood blinked away a tear, bowed to
King George V and Queen Mary, and carried on. For Lutyens there was a personal
significance too: his adored mother, Mary Lutyens, died at Thursley in 1906 and
he designed the cross for her grave. In many ways she released him. Emily's last
child, a daughter named (Edith Penelope) Mary, was born in the summer of 1908;
always to be the happiest of the Lutyens children, the baby Mary perhaps reflected
the mood of exuberance from her father's successes.

It is interesting to run through those tumbling commissions: 1908 opened with
the bad news of Lutyens's failure to win the competition for the new County Hall
in London. New Place at Shedfield was finished but he didn't like it, the major
alterations and additions for the Hon. Ivor Guest at Ashby St Ledgers were under
way, the garden at Hestercombe was nearing completion, the Gerald Balfours
were planning more at Fisher's Hill, there was steady work for Pamela Lytton at
Knebworth, and Lord Lytton was planning a new golf course development. Alfred
Lyttelton was installed in his new house at Wittersham, but encouraging the

The Earl and Countess of Lytton and their family at Knebworth House in the early 1920s: on the left, John and Hermione; on the right, Davina and Antony. Lord and Lady Lytton exerted a benevolent influence on Lutyens's career, and he was involved with the development of a golf course and village at Knebworth, which was largely curtailed by the First World War.

golfing enterprise at Knebworth and at Walton Heath; largely through his good offices, Lutyens began 1908 with the news of the approval for the buildings in Central Square and houses in North Square at Hampstead Garden Suburb. He had so longed for churches and now he had two, St Jude's and the Free Church, facing each other across the Central Square. He had also longed for 'a nice big house to do and heart to do it well',[2] and 1908 actually brought him two: Bertie Fenwick bought Temple Dinsley in Hertfordshire, an exquisite small Georgian house in a park which he, or rather his wife Violet, wished made into a big house with elaborate formal gardens, and Alfred Lyttelton again turned up trumps, bringing in H. J. 'Jack' Tennant, who had also bought an old house in a park, this time pulled down and replaced by Lutyens with one of his largest, most Edwardian houses, Great Maytham. Frances Hodgson Burnett had stayed in the old house and written *The Secret Garden* from her memories, so the old walled garden was saved.

Temple Dinsley, Hitchin, Hertfordshire: the transformation of a small Georgian house into a grand Edwardian mansion for Mrs Bertie Fenwick.

In the north, Heathcote at Ilkley was finishing, Whalton Manor was being converted from a street of cottages for a rich widow, Mrs Eustace Smith, a garden was being made at Angerton for the Strakers, and there was a first summons to Sir George Sitwell at Renishaw. In August 1908 Lutyens did a characteristic mad dash – to Ilkley, as he felt the Hemingways needed supervision ('Curtains, carpets, gardeners, electricians, door handles, carvers, and now I go to Leeds to see the furniture makers tomorrow'[3]), dashing home to see the newborn Mary, born 31 July, then to Marsh Court before 'Ireland and the Barings loom close'.[4] The same year of 1908 also meant Middlefield at Great Shelford near Cambridge for Dr Henry Bond of Trinity Hall. It was the summer of the Franco-British Exhibition at the White City, in which Lutyens played no part but where his visit must have instigated ideas (fibrous cement was used for the first time to simulate stone)

128

which would lead to Rome: in the department of omens, he had played house-party pranks at Renishaw with Miss Eve Fairfax, who had been sculpted by Rodin, and who would, or her likeness would, return in his future far away in South Africa. Miss Jekyll at Munstead was fervently hoping for her new outbuildings and potting sheds, as her nursery and garden designing were flourishing.

Through these frantic years of work, Lutyens always sketched everything himself. His pads were taken on to site, to first discussions (the back of an envelope or even a starched napkin would do), and a worm's eye view and a rough plan with special details resulted. Back in the office, late into the night, every night, he would stand at his drawing desk, always stand. And puff at his pipe, as he drew out, freehand, the house plan, elevations and perspectives, on squared paper, using his own peculiar 'modular' system, inspired by his chosen classical proportion, and working through 'the quantitative relationships of every part of the plan'.[5] The next morning his assistants had the task of translating these into exact measurements, sometimes the most extraordinary fractions, and producing the measured drawings for the contractors. Every drawing was submitted for approval, and Lutyens's kindness was 'that he never corrected their actual drawing, he would instead sketch the correction on a long roll of tracing paper placed over it'.[6] He was always specific about the work of the office: his sketchbooks, sometimes water-coloured, and later the beautiful perspectives professionally drawn by Cyril Fairey, were for charming clients. The real office output was the technical drawing that was 'merely a letter to a builder telling him precisely what is required of him'.[7]

From 1897 until August 1910 the office was the ground floor of 29 Bloomsbury Square: clients calling for their initial encounters with their architect occasionally tangled with Nanny Sleath and a large black pram, or a gaggle of small children, but on the whole strict decorum was observed and only Lutyens frequented both the office and the upstairs domestic world. The office was in the charge of A. J. Thomas, who had joined in 1902 (and was to remain until 1935). After early troubles, the affair of E. B. Badcock, and an early office secretarial assistant who absconded with the cash, it was Thomas, with E. E. Hall as assistant manager (1902–33) and S. H. Evans (*c.* 1900–1925), who typified the loyalty and devotion of the staff. These were the office stalwarts, holding the fort, placating clients, acting as reliable presences, between the enormously hard-working but peripatetic architect and a continual stream of pupils and assistants, who invariably stayed long enough to learn what they required to set up on their own. Some of the most successful were Oswald Partridge Milne, who built Coleton Fishacre in Devon, so often mistaken for a Lutyens house, Fred Harrild, Paul Phipps, Hubert Worthington, G. Alwyn – and later George Stewart and Basil Spence.[8]

The appearance of such an architect's office from the years before the Great War has slipped into the obscurity of history; only that of F. L. Olmsted, the great American landscape architect, at 99 Warren Street, Brookline, in the Boston suburbs, is preserved, though it must have been typical. The assistants all worked at large draughting tables. Perched on high stools, under green shaded lights, they were surrounded by filing cabinets, card index drawers and large plan chests, with narrow drawers to hold the large Imperial size sheets. The outer office held the manager's and assistant manager's desks, and one for the secretary. After the war Lutyens had a lady secretary, Miss Eleanor Webb, for many years.

The master was to be found in his back room, with comfortable armchairs and a coal fire for clients. He was gentlemanly but restrained about business meetings; these were short and to the point, and the point of introductory meetings was invariably a direct discussion of the client's requirements and means. It was impossible for Lutyens not to sketch as he talked, but he expected his clients to be familiar with his work, otherwise they would not have come. There was no question of a display of photographs (the office, unlike Olmsted's, did not deal in them), although Lutyens had to admit that Lawrence Weaver's monograph, published in 1913, was both flattering and useful. Each commission was specifically inspired by a mix of the client's dreams, his site or existing building, and his means. Lutyens tended to make his own assessments of the latter and act accordingly. The really creative work awaited a first site visit and, most importantly, Lutyens's inspection of the client's present living conditions – he judged a great deal from these, and made a point of seeing strangers 'at home' before agreeing to take the commission. Even from the early days, it was very much a matter of the architect vetting his patrons, rather than the other way around.

In August 1910 the office moved to 17 Queen Anne's Gate, a convivial enclave between St James's Park and Victoria Street. Here, with Edward Hudson at number 15, Lutyens was surrounded by friends, and a short step from Whitehall. Soon after the completion of 7 St James's Square for Gaspard and Henry Farrer, in 1912, their mews, the chauffeur's cottage they did not require, was opened as a separate Delhi office, an even shorter step from Pall Mall. These were truly the successful years.

In 1908 the second Jekyll generation took the stage with the marriage of Pamela Jekyll, Herbert's daughter, to Reginald McKenna, an event which was to have an immense effect on Lutyens's future career far into the 1930s. The marriage was a love-match, but as McKenna was in his mid-forties and Asquith's choice as his new First Lord of the Admiralty, and Pamela Jekyll was eighteen, they were a little shy of announcing their engagement. Margot Asquith illumined both of them when on 18 March 1908 she wrote to McKenna, 'I don't think you and Pamela will be able to keep it a secret; you both have too many friends. I hope you will be very happy and blest. It sounds so ordinary, this, but it means so much. As you know quite well, my affection and confidence in you are *very* great. Ever since I had the opportunity of knowing you I think you will agree Henry and I have been devoted to you.'[9] Margot knew Pamela little (she was just out of the schoolroom), but added, 'Her unselfishness to me and sweetness to the children have moved me deeply.'

McKenna, who his friends prophesied would grow younger with marriage to Pamela, joins the growing rank of Lutyens's best-beloved clients who have, as their defining characteristic, an innate, perhaps subconscious need for order, for a classical integrity in their lives, lives otherwise completely preoccupied with other than architectural notions. McKenna was fascinated by 'artistry' of all forms (Pamela Jekyll was an accomplished pianist) because his life thus far had been totally devoid of such things: the Mells and Munstead effects were to be the 'mellowing complement' to his austere, stoical exterior.

McKenna's background was Micawberish: his parents' modest but adequate means had crashed with the Overend Gurney & Company disaster of 1866, so Mrs McKenna and the younger children (Reggie was the youngest of eight) had had to resort to wandering in cheap continental lodgings, while William McKenna roamed America and Europe hoping for something to turn up. Reggie's patchy education, chiefly at St Malo and then at Ebersdorf, was set against much harsher lessons of life, while his elder brothers' incomes kept him and his mother afloat. He grew up with a strong sense of clan loyalty to his brothers, particularly the next eldest, the 'portly and indolent' Ernest, who looked after their mother, enabling Reggie to come to England on a mathematics scholarship to Trinity Hall in Cambridge in 1884. Once there, but without the traditional friendships of an English public school background, he worked so hard and became so serious, hounded by the uncertain nightmares of his past. His friends were chiefly older men who could help him, notably Sir Charles Dilke, under whose wing he was called to the Bar, and entered politics. He went to the House of Commons in 1895 as the Liberal for North Monmouthshire; he soon attracted attention because he was a stickler for details, assiduously picking up on points of order, seated and in a hat as Commons procedure allowed – 'but always in a borrowed hat of a neighbour with a far bigger or a far smaller head', and so he became a popular cartoonists' target. When Campbell-Bannerman formed his team in 1905, Reggie (as he was always known) became financial secretary to the Treasury, and in January 1907 he moved to become President of the Board of Education with a seat in the Cabinet. Lord Beaverbrook later summed Reggie up: 'His abilities are brilliant and his logic remorseless. He is angular, emphatic and positive. He likes to assert his own view, and if you run up against some projecting bump in his opinions you must merely nurse a bruise.'[10] One either begrudged the bruising, or put it down to experience: Cynthia Asquith hit what she called his being 'a monster of jealousy as well as of most other things' – though this was a second-hand bruising, and she soon learned to appreciate him and find him an amusing and consoling friend.[11]

Reggie McKenna married Pamela Jekyll in June 1908 and they moved into Admiralty House: he was in his element at the Admiralty, for he loved water in all forms and anything to do with the sea. Their first son, Michael, was born in January 1910 (his godparents were the Prime Minister, Asquith, and Sir John Fisher, the 1st Sea Lord). David followed just over a year later, and was christened by Archbishop Wilberforce in the crypt of the House of Commons.[12]

It almost seemed that the denizens of both Mells and Munstead must have felt strongly that Lutyens should build the McKennas a house, but they already had Admiralty House, and that Reggie McKenna must have said to Lutyens, 'Well, at the moment we don't need a house, but I know a man who does.' This was his great friend and supporter from his Cambridge days, Dr Henry Bond, for whom Lutyens built one of his most endearing and enchanting houses. Bond was a much-loved Cambridge figure, in his mid-fifties in 1908 but always seeming eternally young. He had been at McKenna's college, Trinity Hall, for almost all of his career, and was renowned for his expertise in Roman law. His other passion was rowing, and the Trinity Hall Boat Club: McKenna was in the Hall boat, and in 1887 he had rowed bow in the winning Cambridge boat. By 1908 Dr Bond and his wife wanted to move out of Cambridge, and they had bought some land at Great Shelford. Middlefield, as the house was called, for it was just that to start with, belies the idea that Lutyens could not build a perfectly delightful small house – a small house dominated by an enormous cap of a roof and tall chimneys, but with merely a study, drawing-room, dining-room ranged *enfilade* along the garden side, cosy rooms of small but beautiful proportions, with white painted woodwork, Lutyens's fireplaces and cupboards, barley sugar twists to put one in a good humour coming downstairs in the morning, and an open, airy landing, with characteristic low white panelled doors with small brass handles, opening into a modest five bedrooms. In the garden, in the middle of the field, with a distant view of the Gog Magog hills, Dr Bond's particular allegiance was carefully complimented – alone among Lutyens's gardens, Middlefield has a *patte d'oie* of radiating grass walks and big yew hedges – seemingly perhaps from Hadrian's Villa?

The building of Middlefield was a simple, undramatic affair, or at least there is nothing that says otherwise. On 17 September 1909 Lutyens noted that Dr Bond, 'who loves his house', had called; he, Lutyens, felt that 'he had got an extraordinary amount of dignity into it'.[13] He was to be congratulated; he was right.

In October 1911, because he was a man who accepted without grudge the buffetings of fate, McKenna gave way to Winston Churchill's impetuosity and accepted the Home Office so that Churchill could go to the Admiralty. The building of the McKennas' house, delayed by circumstances, though much discussed at Munstead, thus took place, but actually became *three* houses – 36 Smith Square for the McKennas, and 8 Little College Street and The Corner House, Cowley Street for Pamela's sister, Barbara, who married Francis McLaren MP, Lord Aberconway's son, and for Francis McLaren's sister, Lady Norman, married to Sir Henry Norman Bt.

In his gossipy but sharp chapter on Reggie McKenna in *Uncensored Celebrities*, Ernest Raymond mentions nothing of Lutyens but is amusing on McKenna and Smith Square: '... It seems inevitable – that having chosen Smith Square, he should live in no. 36. The house is so like him. It is solid, efficient, advantageously placed, built of the very best pressed bricks, irreproachably British, and a little forbidding in its aggressive freshness ... go inside and you will find every evidence of taste and education: ... there will be the due touch of old culture to correct the oiled smoothness of modern convenience: and yet – well, if you happen to be fanciful you will feel the grit just as you did outside ... For grit, in both senses, enters into the very being of Mr Reginald McKenna. He showed grit when he rowed bow for Cambridge in the famous victory of 1887 ... and in the years between 1895 and 1906 when he clung to the House of Commons, though the prospects were none too good for a highly practical and go-ahead young man.'[14]

In stark contrast to McKenna's knowingness and Dr Bond's dignity, one client, John Thomas Hemingway, seemed to inspire a less worthy architectural response. Hemingway was a victim of what Miss Jekyll called (and vowed *she* would never have), 'an exposition of architectonic inutility'.[15] Hemingway was more than an Englishman, he was a Yorkshireman, a race of which Lutyens had little experience. He had been born on 15 March 1857, of modest family, and started work at the usual early age for George Richardson & Company, one of the leading export wool houses of Bradford. By 1898, when he was forty, he had worked hard for a considerable fortune, which enabled him and his wife, Emma Jane (apparently a former mill girl), to live in wholly smart and desirable Ilkley with their son and daughter. Hemingway commuted daily by train into Bradford, along with many of his neighbours; Ilkley was virtually a spa town, with flourishing hydropathic hospitals and prosperous new churches, most notably St Margaret's, by Shaw, in the Byzantine style, finished in 1879 for £15,000.

The Hemingways lived in The Grove, one of the smartest roads, out to the west of the town, with a view to Ilkley Moor. They had a Victorian villa and a

HERE WE GO GATHERING TAXES TO PAY.

(The Chancellor of the Exchequer, accompanied by his wife and children and Financial Secretary, sets out to introduce his Budget).

Budget Day 1915: left to right, David McKenna, Edwin Montagu (First Secretary of the Treasury), Chancellor of the Exchequer Reginald McKenna, Pamela McKenna and Michael McKenna walk to the House of Commons from 36 Smith Square.

large garden, which stretched up the hill behind their house to front on to a new road, King's Road, which was being filled with grander villas. They were very quiet people; their names do not appear in the busily trivial networking of the social life of bazaars, operatics, local politics or even church doings, and one is forced to the conclusion that Ilkley society, which thought a great deal of itself, never quite accepted into its bosom the hard-working Hemingways, who probably spoke with the accents of their humble births. John Thomas was, however, proud of his success: he sent his children for continental educations, gave his wife all her heart desired, and decided that he would have a smart new house and that Edwin Lutyens should build it. He presented himself at Lutyens's office, discussed the matter, made it quite clear that he could afford it, and the deal was struck.

Lutyens found Ilkley dreadful, filled with suburban villas of many colours, built of 'a stone without a soul to call its own'. What follows does him no credit, but exhibits the growing pressures of his career, and that he had just returned from South Africa and was finding it difficult to get over the shock of Herbert Baker's success, or rather Baker's *chances* to build churches, cathedrals and the Pretoria government complex. He was 'in correspondence' with Baker, he had to prove that things were just as exciting in England, and poor John Thomas Hemingway came along just in time to become a vehicle both for impressing Baker and for taking another step along the golden road of Lutyens's pilgrimage to join Palladio and Christopher Wren. He had to prove that Pretoria could be built in England, even if it meant foisting off on an incomprehending and gentle man 'something persisting and dominating, with horizontal lines, to stratify the diarhetic [*sic*] conditions produced by the promiscuous villadom . . . To get domination I had to get a scale greater than the height of my rooms allowed, so unconsciously the San Michele invention repeated itself. That time-worn doric order – a lovely thing – I have the cheek to adopt. You can't copy it. To be right you have to take it and design it . . . It means hard labour and hard thinking, over every line in all three dimensions and in every joint; and no stone can be allowed to slide.'[16]

There is a strange sense here that the stones have indeed slipped, for this letter – so often quoted in search of Lutyens's highest classical motives – is not, it is best to be reminded, written concerning the British Pavilion for the Rome Exhibition nor even the Viceroy's house in New Delhi – for they are as yet unknown – but in the contemplation of a house for a man who wanted a home to express his success. The culprit, which at all costs had to be outdone, was Ilkley villadom – where, as Lutyens later admitted, a house like Little Thakeham would not have shone. Villadom demanded a spectacular come-uppance.

Heathcote, as it was called, rose above the Hemingways' own villa on the high part of their garden, facing south over the moor but accessible from King's Road on the north. It was a palazzo of grey-brown stone, sensitively wrought, looking more than anything like a hunting box for a Roman emperor on his way to the northernmost outpost of empire. The stonemasons must have thought they were building a cathedral. The neighbours must have looked on amazed. But, at the end of the day, Lutyens was merciless and cruel. He used the Hemingways to prove a theory of his own. Their house was so fantastic, too fantastic, and Ilkley and Ilkley society ostracized them even more. They shut themselves away, presumably content in the world they had wanted. Lutyens scorned their modest needs, that they hung their clothes over a chair when they went to bed, ate their supper in their slippers, but he spent their money inside too, giving them every kind of cupboard – his own glass-fronted cupboards and bookcases, the lovely peardrop glass panes in glass-fronted china cabinets, shelves with a drop-flap writing desk. The entrance hall/vestibule was long and low, a cross between Marsh Court and Little Thakeham, and painted 'a dull, indefinite blue'; the main hall was classical, like Marsh Court's dining-room, with columns of polished green Siberian marble. Heathcote was the house where Lutyens insisted on a staircase of black marble in spite of Hemingway's request for a wooden one. Lawrence Weaver commented that the client had 'the judgement to value the policy of the free hand' (it was after all what Philip Webb had merited). Only in this case the client didn't have any choice.

The Hemingways lived out their days in Heathcote. John Thomas died, aged sixty-nine, in 1926 and was buried in Ilkley's new all-denominational cemetery beside the river. Emma Jane lived on until 1937, when the local story is that she was found dead, alone – as she had been for many years – living entirely in one room of the monstrously beautiful house. Emma Jane had the last word, though; she had placed a Celtic cross, of the same stone as the house, over the grave for both of them, its shaft thickly carved with large bunches of grapes, and the inscription, from Matthew, chapter 20, verse 4: 'Go ye also into the vineyard.'

The extremes of wizardry with the orders and proportions of Heathcote emphasize Lutyens's aversion to the materials of Ilkley house-building. His theatrical response reveals patrons at the mercy of their architect, as much as the architect at the mercy of his materials. Lutyens's innate love of natural building materials, the stone and bricks that came from an area's soil over the centuries, was something he learned to exploit more positively, so that by these middle years of the Edwardian decade his buildings were having a strong influence on the way materials were used. His narrow, two-inch bricks were particularly in vogue.

The brickmaking passion had started with Walter Hoare, of the Fleet Street banking family, who lived in north Hampshire and had commissioned a house early in the new century. Hoare played cricket with the Eton Ramblers, as did Gerard Streatfeild of Fulbrook. Almost at the moment Fulbrook was finished, Lutyens had gone for a weekend with Hoare and his young family at their Georgian house in Basingstoke, and there was an immediate rapport. Hoare had bought 300 acres just north of the market town and, exploring, found out that the ridge was associated with a battle between Danes and Saxons, so they named it Daneshill. Having discovered this mutual archaeological interest, Hoare took Lutyens to the most notable ruin in the district, that of Basing House, the once fabulous home of the Paulets, royalists, which Oliver Cromwell had left in ruins after six months' siege in 1645. Basing was, and is, a store of treasures of early seventeenth-century building, but it was the bricks that fascinated Lutyens; they are a peculiarly rich orangey-red, from the local pockets of clay. There was a small diversion when Lutyens heard the story that Inigo Jones had been at Basing and had been held prisoner by Cromwell (the architect was thought to be working at the Vyne for Lord Sandys), so they went to The Vyne (now known to be the work of Jones's pupil John Webb). With its twisted brick chimneys, Webb portico (the earliest domestic portico in England, Palladio-inspired)[17] and delicious brick garden house, The Vyne must join the list of Lutyens's inspirational places. Thoroughly enchanted with the local bricks, he insisted they must look for clay at Daneshill, and when it was found, that the house must be built from it. A brickworks was set up and as many as twelve workmen made the bricks by hand on a row of hacks, semi-covered benches, and carried them to be fired in a kiln, which became the garage.

Having the house and cottages under way, Lutyens went on to encourage Walter Hoare to start a brickworks. The Daneshill Brick & Tile Company came into being and supplied the special bricks for Cubitts to build Marsh Court's twisted chimneys, for Parnells of Rugby to build New Place and Barton St Mary, for the Dormy House and Chussex at Walton Heath, for Hampstead Garden Suburb and the garden at Folly Farm, all for Lutyens, and for Ernest Newton's work on the Manor House at Upton Grey, for Charles Holme, editor of the *Studio*. Walter Hoare published an elaborate catalogue[18] which was printed by Hudson & Kearns. He was as enthusiastic as Lutyens, saying that it was perfectly possible to produce work as good as the late medieval and Tudor craftsmen – 'where cost will permit, thin bricks laid with a wide mortar joint are conducive to the happiest effect'. The 'Elizabethan' bricks sold at 60s. per 1,000, compared to stock bricks at 50s. per 1,000. The Daneshill Company also produced handmade quarries, garden bricks, copings and edgings, and semi-circular balustrading to Lutyens's designs at 3s. per foot run. Their speciality was fireplaces, Lutyens's designs for Daneshill House retailing at £4 for the billiard-room model, a double-arched grate for logs, with angled piers rising to meet the wooden cornice, and £1 10s. 0d. for a bedroom model. In 1905 Lutyens added a brick-works office, an exhibition building for all the firm's variety of bricks, and in 1909 he designed a temporary version for a building trades' exhibition at Olympia.

These late Edwardian years may be regarded as the height of Lutyens's passion for the craft of building in brick; he could never resist the lure of a client with a marvellous brick house, like the South African 'rand' baronet Sir George Farrar's Chichely Hall in Buckinghamshire, where some notable Lutyens brickwork was added to an eighteenth-century masterpiece. Lutyens and his clients for brick houses did a great deal for a pre-war revival of the craft industry.

The craft element of both house building and garden making brought Nathaniel Lloyd to Lutyens in 1910. Perhaps a little additional encouragement came from Edward Hudson (the Lloyds were in the colour printing business in London), with a dash of 'keeping up with' the neighbouring Frewens of Brickwall, Northiam, where Lutyens was making appearances (as will become clear in a moment).

Nathaniel Lloyd had largely relinquished daily labours in his family business to his brother, and he wished to live as a country gentleman, rather in the way of Tom Blackburn at Little Thakeham and Mark Fenwick at Abbotswood. Lloyd was a keen golfer, at Rye, and so he and his wife, the former Miss Daisy Field, looked for a house in the area where they could make a marvellous garden. At the other end of the village of Northiam from the Frewens' Brickwall, they were shown the ancient manor house of Dixter, which had been on the agent's books for ten years and was ramshackle and ruinous. Nathaniel and Daisy Lloyd took up the challenge, knowing that it was for them, and that it could be made to be truly marvellous. They consulted first Sir Ernest George, but without that initial empathy between client and architect; whether they then just stood on the rise of their grounds and looked across the Rother valley to where Great Maytham had risen (they probably actually saw it rising on their visits to their newly acquired steading) can only be surmised, as the two houses, Dixter and Great Maytham – though their families became firm friends – do represent the extremes of the Lutyens canon.

Lutyens came to Dixter, and rose equally to the challenge. The survey plan of the scattered farm buildings, with numerous ponds and relics of moats, the old orchard with medieval plough ridges, great barns and – overlooking all – the battered but beautiful manor house with a fourteenth-century pedigree – survives to show the pencil sketches of their conversations. Nathaniel Lloyd scoured the near countryside with his architect to find a suitable building to add to the Dixter manor house, and they bought a timber-framed house at Benenden which was about to be demolished, dismantled it carefully, setting the numbered timbers down in the orchard at Dixter, for melding into the original house. Lutyens's

Above: Great Dixter: Lutyens and the Lloyds searched the countryside and found a sixteenth-century hall house built at Benenden which was rebuilt as an addition to Dixter.
Right: Great Dixter, Northiam, Sussex: Nathaniel Lloyd, the client for whom Lutyens restored and transformed this ancient farmsteading.

creative conservation of Great Dixter (as it was named when the Lloyds added Little Dixter to their land) was so masterly that the innocent eye does not perceive it; the house is exquisite, but perhaps the organization of a scramble of stack yards and cow pens into the garden was the architect's greatest gift to his client. Nathaniel Lloyd took on the development, as he illustrated in his book, *Garden Craftsmanship in Yew and Box* of 1925, which showed the well-grown hedges and topiary yews with which he complemented the built framework of the garden around Great Dixter. Daisy Lloyd was the indefatigable flower gardener who filled the spaces with delights – and her enthusiasm and skills have passed to her youngest child, Christopher, who has made the garden a plantsman's paradise. But it is Nathaniel Lloyd who joins the ranks of Alfred Lyttelton, Tom Blackburn, Mark Fenwick and Cecil Baring – Edwardian gentlemen all, who knew exactly how they wanted to live, with countryish lives, lovely gardens and each his own particular interests; with Nathaniel Lloyd his experience of Great Dixter extended to the microclimate of houses and gardens, as well as their craft and structure. He also became an accomplished photographer and draughtsman – his classic book *A History of English Brickwork* has only very recently been superseded, and at Great Dixter there is his own water-colour design drawing for the formal sunk garden, dated November 1921.

With Great Dixter and Great Maytham facing each other across the Rother valley, it is time for Jennie Cornwallis-West, Clara Frewen of Brickwall's sister, Winston Churchill's mother, to join the list of clients. Lutyens enjoyed her vivacity and her slightly shocking American-ness, a little like Maude Baring's; Jennie, 'a committee in herself', was organizer-in-chief of the Shakespeare Ball, which took place at the Albert Hall on 20 June 1911, two days prior to George V's Coronation. Lutyens transformed the interior to the amazement of a glittering throng – H. Hamilton Fyfe, very much the commentator of the day, was greatly taken with the *realness* of the jewels, 'Glittering from the hair of fair possessors' and lower on their anatomies, and the reality of the velvet-knickerbockered noblemen, some the descendants of the characters they played. He also assumed the setting was an 'Italian' garden (all right for the Petruchios, Portias and Dukes of Milan but not so good for Anne Boleyn and Henry V), but it was of course a Lutyens garden: the boxes transformed into bowers in clipped yew, with 'quaintly-fashioned' birds on the top, the next layer pergola'd with vines, and the upper tiers balustraded – one set with supper as on a terrace, and over all a summer blue sky.

As soon as the Ball was over, Mrs Cornwallis-West turned Lutyens's attention to her next project – Shakespeare's England, Earls Court to be transformed into a sixteenth-century fantasy for the summer of 1912. Here, under another blue sky,

Lutyens had a field day constructing streets of dreams, a range from St John's College, Oxford, next to Exeter's Guildhall, snatches of his own Ashby St Ledgers and Great Dixter with Ledbury Market Hall, a court of the timbered Ford's Hospital at Coventry with a stone fountain from Trinity College, Cambridge, a Globe Theatre and a model harbour with a replica of Grenville's *Revenge*.

In between the Ball and the exhibition Jennie Cornwallis-West accompanied Lutyens to her sister Clara Frewen's home, Brede Place, between Rye and Battle. It was a place that was even more remarkable than any of the imitations: Brede, built in the fourteenth century from stone shipped from Caen, had belonged to the Frewens of Brickwall since the seventeenth century but had been almost discarded and was the home of an ancient gamekeeper when Clara Frewen

The Shakespeare Ball, 20 June 1911: the *Tatler* ran a long feature illustrating those present, including the Duchess of Sutherland and Mrs George Lambton (formerly Cicely Horner), shown here with Mr Louis Mallet (with hat) and Lord Charles Beresford. The Duchess and Mrs Lambton were among many of Lutyens's clients present in the Italian garden he had designed, which transformed the Albert Hall.

Shakespeare's England, Exhibition July 1912: sketch design for a Tudor building by Lutyens, a remnant of the work he did on this exhibition for Mrs Jennie Cornwallis-West and her committee.

discovered it on her visit to her husband's home in the 1880s. Clara had fallen in love with the place, but London and society called her more loudly and she let Brede to the American author Stephen Crane for the last years of his life, from 1898 to 1900.[19] When her husband Morton Frewen's switchback finances allowed (Frewen was *much* the most adventurous client, with his cattle ranching, bi-metallism and 'Electrozone' schemes),[20] Lutyens helped Clara Frewen with the house and garden. Brede was not a great commission, but the place, nestled in the folds of its own island hill, in the flat sealands that melt into the Channel, was the most romantic in his repertory of lovely places.

As a footnote to all his cipher Englishness, Lutyens built for one of the most English images of all, the Player's Navy Cut tobacco empire. The head of the famous Nottingham firm was W. G. Player, and Ednaston Manor, just outside Ashbourne in Derbyshire, was finished for him prior to the outbreak of war. Ednaston was not a happy house; Mrs Player refused to live in it and W. G. Player only ever used it as a fishing lodge – it is a large house with complete estate and farm buildings. Lutyens designed new offices for Player in Nottingham, but these were never built because of the war.

Also, his old clients were tremendously loyal. Mark Fenwick was cheerfully thinking of selling Abbotswood and giving Lutyens a free hand on a new house, as the excuse for a new garden for himself. His cousin, Bertie Fenwick, had paid up for Temple Dinsley, near Hitchin in Hertfordshire (which had been estimated at £10,300) – a large and enchanting Wrenaissance conversion of a small Queen Anne house. Lutyens achieved an assimilation of the original details, of walls, sash windows and chimneys – a re-statement which Hussey later likened to a variation on an old air 'apt in so far that the variations constitute a major work out of simple motifs'. Lutyens also added a brilliant brick-terraced, paved and walled garden.

The Fenwick northern connections had started an important sequence: a garden for a house by Dobson, Angerton Hall, for the Strakers, a noted Newcastle family, which now led to nearby Whalton and the conversion of two houses, Old Whalton Manor (late seventeenth- or early eighteenth-century, already linked by Lorimer to adjoining cottages) and Whalton Mansion to form an intriguing manor house, with an elliptical arched entrance and a classical interior, including a dining-room with a black and domed ceiling.[21] To plan this Lutyens had stayed at Lindisfarne and travelled to Morpeth to meet his client, Mrs Eustace Smith, 'a widow, 4 boys and a girl, *very* rich' . . . 'Colonel and Mrs Cookson, the owners of Meldon Park, where Mrs Smith now lives, came over to lunch, to meet me. They have come into a fortune and want me to build them new gates and lodges, which is good. Mrs Cookson seems a nice woman, her son married Harold Brassey's sister so it all hangs together.'[22]

It was possibly also the Fenwick coal-owning brotherhood that took Lutyens to Renishaw, where he met his match in Sir George Sitwell. He first went there on that same northern jaunt from Lindisfarne in September 1908 – finding Sir George courteous, like a character in a Disraeli novel, affecting all that is Italian, 'with a darling young wife', Lady Ida, a tall daughter of twenty-one, Edith, and two boys, Osbert, just gone to school and Sacheverell, about to go.[23] In no time Sir George's passion for altering things and making gardens had found its mark and was in full flow – they planned great rooms and water palaces and trips to Italy. The other joy of this visit was a trip to Hardwick – which Lutyens longed to get his hands on (but never did) – and also to Haddon Hall. His passion for the really great houses of England never abated – he *always* longed to match himself to the ghost of Inigo Jones, Vanbrugh or Gibbs and to work at Blenheim or Wilton. Precious little was achieved at Renishaw either, but there were repeated and enjoyable visits, both there and along the wilder shores of Sir George's dreams; Osbert later wrote that 'year after year, my father would regularly start a new hare to be coursed by the famous architect' – and then employ local men. Lutyens did decorate the Renishaw ballroom, and designed the adjacent Pillar Room; his work is evident in the lowest terrace of the garden and he designed a garden for The Green at Eckington, opposite Renishaw's gates, which Sir George built. Osbert Sitwell noted the tremendous energy that Lutyens exhibited in this, his prime – his 'expression of mischievous benevolence' as he sat 'with his bald, dome-like head lowered at a particular angle of reflection, as his very large, blue, reflective eyes contemplated a view, a work of art, or something peculiarly outrageous that he intended shortly to say'. 'His sense of irreverence, his spontaneity, his hatred of the pompous, made him a perfect foil to my father, whose admiration for him as an architect allowed a certain licence to the man and to his Jack-in-the-box forms of fun.' The 'bubbling flow of puns' *could* become tiring '... And so, though my father looked forward tremendously to his visits and would for weeks beforehand make plans ... being host did not prevent him from taking to his bed for longer and longer periods of the day when his guest arrived.'[24]

Osbert Sitwell, like so many other clients' children, adored Lutyens's entertaining visits, but the adults were often not so amused. Another lovely Sitwell quote comes from Sir George's agent, after – in 1911 – a valuable painting had been sold which meant Sir George had funds to spend: 'I am wishing Pierpont Morgan to Gehenna, for now all the wild schemes [of fifteen years] are to be carried out ...' Entrances were being moved, drives cut, a swimming-pool made under a waterfall, meaning the waterfall had to be raised, crowsfoot vistas and a terrace had to be pegged out, let alone a pavilion built in the lake – Lutyens suggested a stone ship![25]

If the laughter from those years of glorious buildings of before the war still rings, it is because Lutyens was beloved of so many of his clients' children, and they remember him still. He preferred their company to stuffy adult pastimes; the Fenwick girls, the Blackburn children, Violet Streatfeild, the Barings, Oliver Lyttelton, all, like Osbert Sitwell, found the architect their friend. Walter Hoare's children claim that Lutyens was not only good for a game of cricket, or a new cricket ball, but they started him on his only 'hobby', fishing; apparently he arrived at Basingstoke station on one of his visits, loaded down with all new fishing kit, demanding to be shown its use. They took him to a favourite place, a deep pool, one of the sources of the Loddon, just south of Basing House, where he caught three trout: and he was a devoted fisherman, perhaps more in his mind and fancy than actually with rod and line, for ever afterwards.

VIII

HUGH PERCY LANE

You that would judge me, do not judge alone
This book or that, come to this hallowed place
Where my friends' portraits hang and look thereon:
Ireland's history in their lineaments trace:
Think where one man's glory most begins and ends,
And say my glory was I had such friends.
(w. b. yeats, 'The Municipal Gallery Revisited')[1]

Cecil and Maude Baring might have sought and loved the seclusion of their island, but it was quite certain that they also held a place in Dublin society, and that Dublin society was both fascinated and knowledgeable regarding their doings. One person who missed little of importance in Dublin was Lieutenant Colonel William Hutcheson-Poë, of Heywood, Abbeleix. Heywood was his wife's inheritance – she was Mary Adelaide Domvile, they had been married in 1886 and had three children. Mary Adelaide was also related by marriage to the St Lawrences at Howth Castle; the lights of Howth were the welcome beacon on Lambay's horizon, and in return, a garden vista of high beech hedges in Howth's garden was focused on Lambay. The Hutcheson-Poës were also close neighbours of the de Vescis at Abbeyleix, and Constance Portman of Hestercombe was the mother of Ivo Richard Vesey (the son of her first marriage to Captain Eustace Vesey, who died in 1886), the heir to Abbeyleix estate. All this connecting would seem to be the double, if not treble, provenance that brought Lutyens his Irish commissions.

The Colonel's country home, Heywood, had definite similarities with Hestercombe: they were both elegant eighteenth-century houses encased in nineteenth-century bulky grandeur, with a substantial terrace buttressed above meadows, which gently drifted into a lovely landscape. Heywood was inherited from the Trench family. Its eighteenth-century core had been built by Michael Frederick Trench, a talented amateur architect, with some help from James Gandon, and it contained very lovely Adam-style rooms. Trench had also (like Copplestone Warre Bampfylde at Hestercombe) been interested in the landscape style, making a park filled with follies and a lake, but there was no formal garden.

Lutyens swept the path eastwards from the terrace, via a lime walk, to a large oval walled garden, made partly within existing walls. Inside the oval are tiers of flower-beds and walks around a central, oval pool, which was lightly attended by a gathering of baby turtles in bronze, sculpted by Julia Chance of Orchards. Lutyens's cleverest touch was to capture the small Tuscan arches that made eighteenth-century Heywood's entrance front so pretty, and put them into the small garden pavilion. The surrounding wall is regularly pierced with *œil de bœuf* ovals to give glimpses of the countryside – it was the first idea for a tiered circular garden that would eventually find a place in New Delhi.

Heywood was designed after Lutyens had visited Ireland for the second time in 1906 and slowly realized over the following years. It was the background to Colonel Poë's involvement with Lutyens's most notable commission in Ireland, for the Dublin Municipal Gallery; the Colonel was a great collector of paintings and furniture, well known in such circles in London and Dublin, and he was also a supporter of Lady Gregory's Abbey Theatre. But he was not the motivating force behind this story – that was another Irishman, Hugh Percy Lane.

HUGH PERCY LANE

After the publication of *With the Wild Geese* in 1902, Emily Lawless found that another name besides her own entered conversations about patriotism, heard in Dublin drawing-rooms. The gossip about Hugh Lane, a foppishly smart young art dealer, rediscovering his Irish roots and ingratiating himself at Dublin Castle by means of his London connections, was not complimentary. He was thought too charming, and his celebrated 'eye' for an Old Master languishing under layers of grime identified him as a rogue or an angel, according to one's experience.

Lane had been born in Ireland by accident; he was Augusta Gregory's nephew, the son of her sister, Frances Adelaide Persse, who was married to the Revd James William Lane. The Lanes had gone to Cork to take possession of a legacy, Ballybrack House, and Hugh Percy was born there on 9 November 1875. He was a sickly, nervous child, the baby in an already large family, and was brought up mostly in the ugly tin-mining town of Redruth in Cornwall, where his father was rector from 1877 to 1884. He was given little education, and his parents' marriage was a miserable affair of cruelty, recriminations and partings; compensating for all this gloom, he apparently clung to two boyhood memories of beauty – a visit to Paris with his father when he went to the Louvre, and the kindness of a picture restorer, who taught him the skills of her trade. At eighteen he left home; Lady Gregory found him an apprenticeship at Colnaghi's, where he was thought to be bumptious

Sir Hugh Lane by John Singer
Sargent: it was in order to be
drawn by Sargent that Lane went
to America in 1915, and was
drowned on his return journey
when the *Lusitania* was torpedoed.
If Lane had lived, he – like so many
others lost in the war – would
have made a great difference to
Lutyens's post-war career.

and loud, but he stayed for two years, then took himself off on a long study tour
of the Low Countries, making himself an expert on Dutch art. He cultivated his
own image: he was tall and naturally thin, but his thinness was emphasized because
necessity taught him never to spend money on serious food, and he made best
use of his large brown eyes in intense and persistent conversation. He dressed
fastidiously and he was always immaculate, scented and groomed, and rather
precious. His entire existence focused on artists, artists' studios, galleries and
salerooms, and he neither knew nor cared for anything else. On his first return
trip to Ireland in 1902, when he was asked to stay with his aunt Augusta Gregory
at Coole, and found himself in the company of W. B. Yeats, the composer O'Brien
Butler, Douglas Hyde of the Gaelic League, Edward Martyn and Sarah Purser, he
had nothing to say; he later scorned his aunt for losing her place in society by
entertaining such people.[2]

Lane's Emmaeus road conversion began the following year, when Sarah Purser
invited him to an exhibition in Dublin of paintings by Nathaniel Hone and Willie
Yeats's father, John B. Yeats. Lane admired their work and bought it; he conceived
his idea that Dublin must have a gallery to show the work of living artists, and he
began his campaign. His aunt Gregory noticed that he changed; his cloying per-
sistence became precision, he was less eager to please, less agreeable and extremely
unworldly. Hugh Lane had found his cause, and it was to pursue him to his end.

In Ireland he sought support for his Dublin gallery, furiously advocating and exhibiting the country's Old Master treasures, the virtues of the Royal Hibernian Academy and the new paintings of Hone, Walter Osborne, William Orpen, the Yeatses father and son, and John Lavery; a 1904 exhibition by Irish artists at the London Guildhall was spectacularly successful. Early the following year the committee of support for the Dublin gallery was formed; it included the Earls of Mayo and Drogheda and Colonel Poë from Heywood, the latter pledging £1,000 to the appeal, a sum matched only by the Prince of Wales.[3] Lane's heart was now irretrievably committed to the Irish Renaissance, and he was regularly in Dublin, persuading and pursuing anyone who would back his cause; perhaps his allegiance was most aptly proved by the vision of him, in impeccable white tie and tails, ushering out troublemakers from the Abbey Theatre during one of the early, rather riotous performances of J. M. Synge's *The Playboy of the Western World*.[4] That was in 1906; the following year the City Council approved the acquisition of Clonmell House, 17 Harcourt Street, as a temporary gallery for Dublin, and appointed Lane the director.

His gallery catalogue, published early in 1908, showed him to be a benefactor as well. Of the forty-three paintings by contemporary Irish artists, he had bought and given nineteen, including a landscape by Constance Gore-Booth (Countess Markievicz) and works by George Russell ('A. E.') and Frank O'Meara. Among the French Impressionists and Barbizon School were a Fantin-Latour and a Corot given by Colonel Poë, but these (over sixty) exhibits were chiefly the Monets, Manets, Renoir's *Les Parapluies*, paintings by Corot, Pissarro, Vuillard, Courbet, Puvis de Chavannes, the celebrated company of the Lane Collection. In addition there were three more rooms of drawings, etchings and watercolours, by David Cox, J. F. Millet, Augustus John, William Orpen, William Strang, Max Beerbohm, Lord Leighton, Hercules B. Brabazon, Charles Condor, Mark Fisher, Simeon Solomon, Will Rothenstein, Arthur Hughes, Sarah Cecilia Harrison and George Clausen. The finale was the small collection of sculpture, which included four pieces by Rodin, three from the Lane Collection and one, *The Age of Bronze*, which was Lane's gift. As he made clear in his introduction to this marvellous collection, the works that he had given *were given*, but the dazzling collection of mainly French Impressionists that belonged to the Lane Collection – it was his intention to present most of them 'provided that the promised permanent building is erected on a suitable site within the next few years'.[5] Lane was knighted in the Birthday Honours of 1909 for his services to art; perhaps it was hoped he would retire to live as an obscure gentleman?

Instead he took up another challenge, and he bought himself a house in London – this, his first real home after years of lodgings. The challenge was revealed when he was summoned by his friend Caroline Grosvenor, the Hon. Mrs Norman Grosvenor, to Tylney Hall at Winchfield, the English home of Lionel and Florence Phillips. Caroline Grosvenor, who was Florence Phillips's closest English friend, was to win the soubriquet of 'godmother' to the Johannesburg Art Gallery for her introduction of Hugh Lane to Florrie (as everyone called her); she was rather more involved because her daughter Susan was married to John Buchan, at that moment writing *Prester John*, which he dedicated to Lionel Phillips.

The Phillipses were setting out upon a glamorous English season for the coming-out of their daughter Edith, but it was also a farewell. Tylney was to be sold, and Herbert Baker was building their new Villa Arcadia, in the peaceful Woodbush in northern Transvaal, as their permanent home. From now on their energies would be totally involved in their new country, the Union of South Africa, which Lionel had worked so hard to bring about; Florrie was passionately interested in promoting the cultural history of her homeland, through arts and crafts, furniture-making and building restoration (she had one criticism of Herbert Baker, that he tended to 'over-restore'), but there were European arts, particularly paintings and sculpture, that she would miss – and naturally regarded as traditions which applied just as well in new South Africa as in old Europe. It was her dream to found a gallery for old masters in Johannesburg; money was no difficulty, she was well practised at touching the cultural consciences of her husband's mining colleagues, and the Wernhers, Beits and Ecksteins would see her point of view. She needed help to acquire the paintings, and this was where Hugh Lane was the perfect ally.

Lane answered the summons and hurried immediately to Tylney; in the course of the evening he persuaded her that old masters were too difficult to acquire, and surely contemporary art would be better value and more appropriate? He whisked her off to the Goupil Gallery, where an exhibition of Philip Wilson Steer was being set up, and he – persuasive as ever – bought three paintings on her behalf. That she had no funds ready did not matter, for she had on her finger a blue diamond ring, a present from Lionel, which launched the Johannesburg Art Gallery on its way.[6]

In November 1909 the Phillipses sailed home to South Africa. Florrie and Edie were kitted out with Paris clothes, for if their diamonds had sparkled beneath the chandeliers of a vintage English season, they were to sparkle just as brightly under South African sun in 1910, the year of the inauguration of the Union. Florrie had wheeled more than £20,000 towards her gallery from the mining millionaires, and Hugh Lane had spent £6,000 on works of art. Lionel Phillips also had a pet scheme for which funds had been promised, a memorial to the dead of the Rand Regiments, and it was in their minds that the gallery and memorial might be combined. All they needed was a site – and an architect.

With the Phillipses safely dispatched, Hugh Lane turned his energies towards his own home; he purchased 100 Cheyne Walk in Chelsea, known as Lindsey House. It had the date 1674 over its doorway, it had once been the home of Charles I's physician, and the legend was that Nell Gwynne had once performed in an opera there for the amusement of Charles II. Lane needed not a home, rather more a setting for his treasures (Lutyens, among others, later noted how he carried his own atmosphere with him, wherever he was). He was a great tryer-out – he was also exceptionally vain, and invariably tried out painters on likenesses of himself of which there are a string (by Orpen, Jack B. Yeats, Sargent, Mancini, etc.) – and he decided to try out Lutyens on 100 Cheyne Walk. There were small interior works at Lindsey House, but Lutyens's real contribution was the garden in the walled rectangle behind the house, which had an elderly, leaning mulberry tree just off centre. He tidied up the façade of the house with a pillared screen and designed simple, but brilliant, panels of grass and wide flagged paths, with flower borders at the margins, and a plain, circular central lily pool, over which the mulberry leaned. The vistas were closed at the end by pedimented niches, in which Lane placed, with no difficulty, perfect figures. He would not have cared that the pool had to be cleaned of leaves almost every day, for the elegance of the motif, and the annual crop of mulberries, were his delights. Lawrence Weaver noted that the side borders would be filled with arabis 'spreading its bloom and leafage over the paving'[7] and masses of carnations.

Lane's meanness over serious food, and the cost of letters and cabs, was legendary, but he loved, and happily spent money on, fruit, flowers and cakes; when he began entertaining at Lindsey House it was with tea parties, with elaborate cakes, taken around an octagonal Chippendale table, set with lattice-back chairs, a design which Lutyens later used. Besides having Colonel Poë in common, Lutyens had worked for the Rex Bensons at Buckhurst Park in Sussex; they were great friends of Lady Gregory's. Augusta Gregory told how Lane had delivered her to Buckhurst for a weekend with the Bensons, and upon leaving he found her on the terrace, which Lutyens had designed, with her arms full of roses. She presented the roses to his companion, who had mentioned that his children were having a flower service; afterwards Lane would remind her how much *he* would have loved to have had the roses.[8]

Lane and his architect got to know each other at Lindsey House, but it wasn't an easy relationship – 'they sparred and quarrelled and made friends again . . . and had their merry plans'.[9] One was that Lutyens would design a circular twelve-panelled room and Lane would commission twelve portraits of the wife he intended to have; another was that he would rescue Kirby Hall in Leicestershire and let

Lutyens restore it (the estimate was £200,000). It seems perfectly possible that they didn't actually like each other very much, but that each recognized the other's genius, and how it could be harnessed for his own ends. Lutyens threw away to Emily that Lane was 'a walking advertisement for me'[10] – Lane had suggested that Lutyens might do the Johannesburg Art Gallery – and then left for South Africa with the paintings that he and Florrie had bought as his luggage.

Lutyens left for Rome, to see how his pavilion for the 1911 Exhibition was progressing, and while he was there a telegram reached him with the formal request from Johannesburg. He hesitated apparently, because of pressure of work, the distance, and Baker, but was urged to go by Lord Curzon. Lutyens sailed for Cape Town in early November, leaving fifty-nine jobs behind and working on the sixtieth, Castle Drogo, on the voyage. He arrived in early December, in the excited and rather chaotic aftermath of the ceremonial visit of the Connaughts, who had opened the Union parliament and attended numberless pageants and parties (somewhat muted in mourning for King Edward) – but, more importantly in this present story, had laid the foundation stone of the Rand Regiments' memorial on an eminence in the Sachsenwald (on forty acres given by the Ecksteins) – and attended a gala exhibition of the Johannesburg Collection, staged by Lane. A site in Joubert Park had been promised for the gallery. Lane's artists for the Johannesburg Collection were a re-run of those he had bought for Dublin, with less of the Irish and additions of some (minor) Dutch old masters, which were naturally requested; he had presented five paintings himself and lent an Augustus John. The star of the exhibition was Rodin's *Miss Fairfax*, wreathed in romantic gossip about a noble, or even royal, donor (when Lionel Phillips had paid £800 to Eve Fairfax for her, a fact not revealed till much later).[11]

After the admiration and euphoria were over, Hugh Lane quickly became listless and bored; he lazed at the Villa Arcadia 'lying under mosquito curtains – a luxury of the imagination, for no mosquitoes came – smoking and reading news cuttings'.[12] The glories of the sunsets, which he vowed (to interviewers) would stay with him for ever, were taken for granted, and the mosquito net may have been a defence from the hero-worship of the young architect J. M. Solomon (who was finishing off Villa Arcadia for Baker) or the irksome attentions of Edith Phillips – who had been deputed by her mother to look after him and had now fallen in love with him. He was also feeling guilty: 'One cannot buy for two galleries (not the same sort of thing) and I want all the *bargains* for Dublin,' he confided, somewhat belatedly, to Thomas Bodkin in Dublin, after murmurs of jealousy from that quarter.[13] He really wanted to get away from this society which he 'openly despised' and home to Christie's and Cheyne Walk; the coming of Lutyens, who he feared would fray tempers even more, made him apprehensive.

Celebrations in Johannesburg at the Opening of the National Gallery Collection in its temporary home, the Transvaal University College. On the steps of the College are Florence Phillips (in white hat) and Hugh Lane (left); the Royal party, the Duke and Duchess of Connaught and Princess Patricia are already in their 'absurdly small' carriage. This splendid occasion, magnificently stage-managed by Lane and Mrs Phillips, was the *coup de grâce* of their campaign to build Lutyens's National Gallery.

Baker and Lutyens had not met since 1891. Baker had arrived in Cape Town in early 1892, ostensibly to help his brother who was fruit farming. He had met Cecil Rhodes, who was curious about 'that silent young man', which resulted in Baker's restoration of Groote Schurr, which Rhodes had recently bought.[14] Other houses followed, and as Diocesan architect Baker built three churches by 1900 before he started on St George's Cathedral, Cape Town. Though Rhodes had died in 1902, Baker was securely on his way – even at the moment Lutyens was building the tiny Goddards with Margaret Mirrielees's money, her father's and husband's Union Castle Line Building and the Mount Wilson Hotel in Cape Town were being supervised by Baker, among other large office buildings. Baker was involved with Pretoria railway station and Cathedral and Government House, before the commission for the government buildings was given to him in 1910. The irony of all this was that Lutyens imagined only tin sheds in South Africa, and that offering a partnership with Baker was a gracious act!

Lutyens arrived in Cape Town and was whisked by Baker to Groote Schuur and Prime Minister Botha, to Baker's own Rhodes memorial, the site for Cape Town Cathedral and lunch with General Smuts: they got on the train for Johannesburg, and then the beauty of the scenery, and the light, especially the light – 'the exquisite clear softness of the light over field and sky' – bombarded and enthralled Lutyens's senses: 'the silver greys and bright blues all clear as crystal and the purples are wonderful. Italy cannot touch it with all her mystery of the ages.'[15]

His sentimental heart grieved that such beauty had to be fought over, and by the time he had been received at the lovely Villa Arcadia by Florrie, in her best 'Queen of Johannesburg' mood, it all rather went to his head. There may have been an element of reaction – he had left London convinced that he was the busiest architect in the world, tossing off to Emily that he would graciously 'share' the gallery with Baker. The Johannesburg *Star* announced his arrival as rather implying the advent of the landscape-gardener: 'In his garden-designing Mr Lutyens stands unrivalled and the most distinguished feature of his buildings is the splendid setting in which he places his work.'[16] Discussions with the builders of nations and communion with the purple light seemed to make Lutyens euphoric, convinced of his divine architectural mission to provide the helpless soul of Africa (with no craft building tradition on 'which accidents can rely') with the 'best *thought* – the harder and purer the better' – and an almost manic classical absolutism. All this was to be done in one week.

His mission drawing office occupied a room in the Villa Arcadia – and designs poured out (he had his assistant E. Hall with him). He met the Rand Regiments' Memorial Committee and suggested they move the foundation stone, because his design was for an arch surrounded by elaborate gardens. They refused; the arch was subsequently built on its eminence, without gardens. Lutyens was paid £300, the memorial cost £18,000. For the gallery Baker had suggested a modest Dutch style – Lutyens designed a classical portico, based upon St Paul's, Covent Garden, for the gallery itself, with a sculpture courtyard behind, and four large corner pavilions with hipped roofs each rising to a tall rectangular chimney. The gallery was to hold the national collection, and the pavilions were to house an art library, a loan exhibition, a furnished old Dutch house and – the fourth – an energetic curator who also ran a school of art.[17] When the gallery committee came to dinner Lutyens chose to lecture them on town planning for Johannesburg, and he sketched layouts for the council, including a design for Joubert Park (with water gardens around the gallery), and then did the same – as Smuts had raised the matter of 'gardens' for Pretoria – around Baker's buildings. There was also considerable work on the planning of Cape Town University at Groote Schuur and the possibility of a magnificent church in Johannesburg.[18]

When Lutyens and Lane left for home after Christmas, poor Herbert Baker must have sighed with relief. Lutyens soon realized how impossibly he'd behaved and his true nature returned in an apology: 'I loved and do love the direct simplicity of your unwavering hospitality. Not a carping or ungenerous word, to me, who must by my very nature have tried you sorely ...'[19] But once he was home, he resumed his own affairs and his mission for South Africa was mostly forgotten. He designed a ballroom at Roehampton House for Hugh Lane's only private client, Arthur M. Grenfell. J. M. Solomon came to England, worked in Lutyens's office for a while, and stayed at Lindsey House; he was bewitched by Lane, and later wrote a vivid description of him, revealing the kind of Svengali that he appeared. In 'the quiet, rather sombre dignity of the long oak-panelled room, which over-looked the river, where the light of the barges, the warehouses, and the tall chimneys, becoming campinili in the night, reminded one irresistibly of Whistler's *Nocturnes*', Lane sat among his guests, 'nervously smoking his cigarette, perhaps a little melancholy at the turn the conversation had taken' (the recent death of J. M. Synge); 'by the dim light this pale, slender, dark-eyed knight, with his trim black beard, his slim hand, and his poised, nervous, elusive manner, presented an appearance similar to the figures in the paintings of that strange seer, El Greco.'[20]

The Dutch paintings, including the Rembrandt at Lindsey House, were for Johannesburg, awaiting dispatch and future wrangling. Lane was still buying for Lady Phillips, as she now was, but at the end of 1911 he resigned as director of the Johannesburg Gallery and was eventually succeeded by Robert Ross. Florrie was in England a great deal during 1911 and 1912; Edie was at the Slade (where her considerable talent was noted) and, having realized that Lane was not the marrying kind, worried her mother by devoting herself to her art and refusing all offers of marriage; she eventually married John Stuart Wortley at Tylney on 3 October 1912.

In Johannesburg it was Baker, in Florrie's absence, who was parrying the objections of the town council to the expense of the building and of the Transvaal Association of Architects to the nationality of the architect. Eventually, the foundation stone for the gallery was laid, in a thunderstorm, in a shrubbery in Joubert Park on 12 October 1911. The contractors could not start for lack of drawings; the architect was more concerned with other buildings, on other continents. When Florrie Phillips returned home in 1913 she was disgusted to find the stone lurking in the undergrowth, surrounded by a railing. Tenders for the gallery building were rushing to and fro. But 1913 was a bad year; there were serious riots in Johannesburg, the precious unity in the new Union was slipping away. During the year Florrie was seriously ill, near to death, after an operation for appendicitis, and in the December Lionel Phillips was badly injured in an attempt on his life. Despite all, Florrie extracted a promise from the new Labour government in early 1914 that they would go ahead with the gallery; it had become a symbol rather than merely a building, and even if it was built in brick it *must* be built, but they promised her it would be built in stone, as Lutyens intended.

In the autumn of 1912 Sir Hugh Lane had reminded the Lord Mayor of Dublin that he had promised their pictures for a 'few' years, but that five had passed. A meeting in January 1913 of the Dublin Council promised money as long as a site could be found. (It could be argued that a gallery director should have put his mind to this the day after the temporary gallery had opened, rather than take off half-way round the world and become another gallery's director.) The site suggested was on St Stephen's Green, which belonged to Lord Ardilaun, and on which he had made a garden. It might also be thought that having seen his architect ride roughshod over every sensibility in South Africa he would have been wary about Dublin. But no; Lane recorded joyously on 21 August 1912: 'Lutyens has promised me to architect the new Gallery and *garden* in exchange for an Old Master, so that now we only want the £25,000 and Stephen's Green.'[21] Both Lane and Lutyens were convinced that they could improve on Lord Ardilaun's garden and he would delightedly conform. Lutyens produced his first design, a low, classical pillared and porticoed pavilion, very restrained and rather elegant. Lord Ardilaun did not like it, was not prepared to sacrifice his garden, and they had to start all over again.

Half a dozen possible sites were suggested: Merrion Square (more sacred gardens), the old Turkish baths, a disused skating rink – the *Saturday Herald* cartoonist suggested it could be cantilevered on top of Nelson's Pillar. The jest was not so far from the reality when, with no site proving possible (Lane apparently, according to Augusta Gregory, fraught with premonitions of his own death), the bridge idea was born – the gallery should be on a bridge over the Liffey, poised between air and water. It was a little reminiscent of the king's new clothes – everyone, open-mouthed, seemed to think it a brilliant idea. Lutyens saw it 'as an idea so full of imagination and possibility that it is almost impossible to resist'[22] – and he sketched and William Walcot drew the twin pavilions joined by a classical bridge. The estimated cost was £45,000. The City Architect considered it would be 'a very great ornament', W. B. Yeats rhapsodized, '... beautiful. Two buildings

ART GALLERY SITE IN DUBLIN
---ANOTHER SUGGESTION.

MUNICIPAL
ART
GALLERY

ENTRANCE

Gordon. Brewster

In view of the recent controversy regarding the site for a Municipal Art Gallery, our artist ventures to suggest the top of Nelson's Pillar, where it could
not obstruct any view of the city.

Dublin Municipal Gallery: the
search for a site led to this
cartoon in the *Saturday Herald*,
12 April 1913.

joined by a row of columns, it is meant to show the sunset through columns, there
are to be statues on top.'[23]

The Corporation accepted the design and agreed, as they always had, to put
up half the money; the other half was to be subscribed. Lane, this time with some
excuse, for he was far from well, returned to London and left the scheme to its
fate. The money was slow. The rumblings of uncertainty came from the general
air of apprehension and focused on the gallery. Colonel Poë of Heywood had
promised £1,000 if others would match him; it would have taken so few matching
offers, but then there were few rich men left. Poë himself wrote to Lane in July
1913, after a Mansion House meeting at which the opposition had hardened: 'It is
simply disgusting . . . nobody could or would blame you if you decided to discuss
the matter no further. I feel quite sure you have the sympathy and the grateful

Dublin Municipal Gallery: Lutyens's design for the 'bridge' gallery across the Liffey.

good wishes of every right-thinking and decent person in Dublin . . . in what must we all know, be a bitter disappointment.'[24] What were 'disgusting' to Poë were the objections: that Dublin had poor to house, the gallery was a luxury, the river site impracticable, damp for the pictures and difficult to manage, and (the last straw) that Lutyens, despite his Irish mother, was an *English* architect. Lane was not in Ireland to fight his cause, he was in London suffering with neurasthenia. If either he, or perhaps Lutyens, had been there it would have been different. Poë's letter was probably the trigger, and Lane ordered his loan collection, most of the French Impressionists, to be moved from the Harcourt Street gallery; they were taken away piled on an open cart, to begin their long journey in a limbo of pain and recriminations.[25]

It was the end as far as Lutyens was concerned. His gallery was finally rejected by Dublin on 8 September 1913. Lane had paid him for Lindsey House with paintings, and he was scrupulously honest in this way, so more paintings, exquisite small and minor masters, followed for the abortive gallery attempts.

In early 1914, surprisingly, Lane was appointed director of the National Gallery of Ireland, amid a flurry of congratulatory notes – 'such a snub for Dublin (corporation)' from Robert Ross,[26] it will be a lovely gallery 'worthy of the Ireland of our dreams'[27] (Helen McNaghten) – all this, and his quarrel with the National Gallery in London, who had dared to submit his Impressionists to a hanging committee, occupied his failing energies. The war (and his generosity in helping out Arthur Grenfell who had been bankrupted in the summer of 1914)[28] put Lane in financial difficulties, otherwise he would never have agreed to go to New York on business despite the opportunity to be drawn by Sargent. He returned on the *Lusitania*, which was sunk by U-boats on 7 May 1915. Lane was last seen helping women and children aboard the lifeboats – he was among the more than 1,200 who died and his body was never found. Lutyens's last job for him was to design his memorial – at least, a note accompanying the wording by Sarah Cecilia Harrison confirms that was what happened.[29]

The news of Lane's loss on the *Lusitania* reached Florrie Phillips at the Villa Arcadia when she returned from yet another stormy meeting with the City Council, fighting for the building of her gallery. The portico and two wing pavilions were completed, and opened for use in the summer of that year, 1915, but with little ceremony because of the war. There were also anti-German riots, and the death of Sir George Farrar[30] to compound the despair of the war, and general hopelessness that anything creative would be achieved ever again. The city authorities steadfastly ignored Lutyens's layouts for the gardens around the city hall, let alone the completion of the gallery. J. M. Solomon, shattered by Lane's death, was now Lady Phillips's architectural protégé; he managed to secure permission to proceed on the university at Groote Schuur, leaving Herbert Baker hurt and disappointed – Baker had returned from New Delhi after quarrelling with Lutyens and would have loved to return to South Africa.

Lady Phillips never ceased to campaign for her gallery; on more than one occasion she 'dressed with customary care' and with Lutyens's designs and layout for the whole gallery and its gardens, 'and a bamboo pointer cut from a thicket at Arcadia' by the head gardener, taught her listeners a lesson.[31] It was more than a building, it was a symbol that paintings, sculptures, beautiful things, books and art education, for the people of Johannesburg, should all triumph over the beastly bickering, bitterness and hopelessness engendered by the war.

IX

NIMROD

One shall rise
Of proud ambitious heart, who not content
With fair equality, fraternal state,
Will arrogate dominion undeserved
Over his brethren, and quite dispossess
Concord and law of nature from the earth,
Hunting (and men not beasts shall be his game)
With war and hostile snare such as refuse
Subjection to his empire tyrannous.

(JOHN MILTON, Paradise Lost)[1]

Lutyens first went to Rome in the autumn of 1909. It was like a homecoming: 'There is so much here in little ways of things I thought I had invented.' It was for him what Hussey called 'a picnic in the Elysian fields' – and the most telling phrase in all Lutyens's euphoria was 'I do wish I could have come with Wren.'[2]

The trip was to plan for the building of the British Pavilion at the Rome Exhibition of 1911, which had come about partly from the success of Paris 1900 and partly by the consistent championship by Pamela Lytton to her husband, Victor, Lord Lytton, who was Chairman of the Royal Commission for Rome.

Wren was required because the idea was to adapt the upper tier of the west face of St Paul's for a classical pavilion, façade only, to front a steel framework of exhibition rooms for a collection of valuable paintings and sculpture.[3] Once again there was the 'Edwardian' duality, the determination to show off 'real' treasures of enormous price in a virtually fake building, and again, the steel framework was the most sensible for fire precautions. Also, once again, Lutyens had realized that he could not just 'lift' the façade, he had to re-work the proportions and details (the whole exercise might be thought suspect, as the chief glory of the west face of St Paul's is in the juxtaposition of the lower colonnade with the upper and with the dome above). The pediment was flattened slightly, the biblical sculpture in the tympanum replaced with the Royal Arms, and the columns reproportioned; the whole was placed on a platform atop a ceremonially monstrous flight of steps.

It was to stand once again on a plum site, at the north end of the terraced piazza which was the heart of the International site, gazing down past Germany, 'at' Austria, Serbia and France. The site was constructed around the Museo di Villa Giulia and was close to the Borghese Gardens; the Italian Exhibition, and the Vatican, were just across the Tiber.

Everyone voted the British Pavilion a great success, and it would possibly have been better if that had been the end of the story. What followed seemed to have origins in the personalities and popularity of the Ambassador in Rome, Sir Rennell Rodd, and the Mayor of Rome, Ernesto Nathan. Nathan visualized the Exhibition site as a new cultural suburb, and to this end offered the British site for a permanent building to house British educational interests in Rome. Ambassador Rodd was enchanted and flattered; what could be more gratifying than to turn the lovely temporary building, of fibrous plaster, into a stone imitation of part of St Paul's Cathedral in a Roman garden? The Rodds spent most of their time with this kind of fantasy, for they were famous for their marvellous parties and set pieces – Lady Rodd (none other than Lily Guthrie, daughter of Ellinor and sister of Maggie from Shamley Green, a 'prima donna' and so bossy they called her 'Tiger Lil') was habitually transforming the garden of the Villa Torlonia into 'a wood near Athens or a glade on the slopes of Mount Olympus' and 'blazing forth' to greet her guests attired as Juno or Titania, with her children and the Ambassador, who looked well in pale grey satin, in her train. Sir Rennell, wonderfully attractive, with a smooth handsome face, 'eyes that you knew were azure blue', a fluffy white moustache and eyebrows and a faint head covering of soft white hair, was, like the character he later inspired, Lord Montdore in *Love in a Cold Climate*,[4] deliciously ineffective, and though he looked so wonderful 'he might just as well have been made of wonderful old cardboard'. To have such a chance to turn a fantasy building into a real one must have seemed great fun. It is a pity that the architect did not suggest packing the whole ready-made gallery up and shipping it to Dublin.

The task in Rome, however, was to turn a façaded gallery into a school. The Commissioners of the 1851 Exhibition (Prince Albert's benevolent shadow had reached this far) put up £15,000 for the building, on behalf of the Rome Scholarships they were founding. These would be administered by an existing British School, already based at the Palazzo Odescalchi, a mainly archaeological institution headed by Dr Thomas Ashby. There was also the British Academy, the foundation of Emma's Sir William Hamilton, not to be left out of things. It can be imagined that all these interests and their representatives meant an unwieldy conglomeration of committees, of varying views. Lutyens estimated that the real building would cost £40,000; it could not just be a façade, it must have teaching

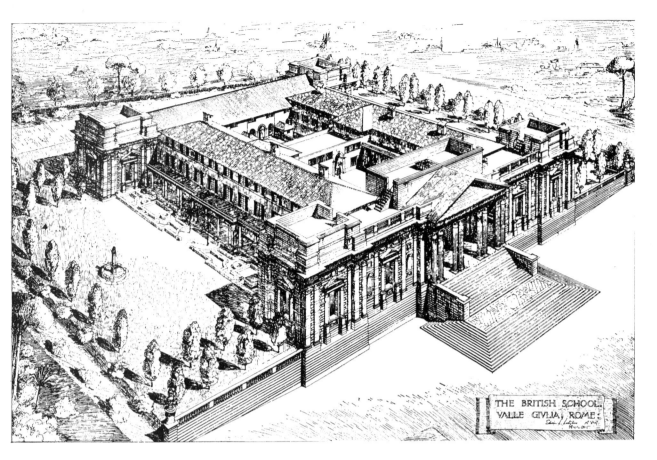

The British School at Rome: a perspective from Lutyens's office of his final scheme for the transformation of the British Pavilion from the Rome Exhibition of 1911 into a permanent academic building. The classical front, modelled on St Paul's Cathedral, is 'an assemblage of elements . . . each modified to give the overall composition a pleasing coherence'. The internal courts were for galleries and studios, with staff and student accommodation in the outer wings.

rooms and accommodation for twenty-five students and a director. He intended to do this by completing three sides of the square on the rear of the façade, three storeys, with pantiles and window shutters, to look like a villa. Humphreys of Knightsbridge, who had built the Exhibition building, were given the contract for rebuilding the façade, for £13,000; all materials were to be shipped from England. The building committee of Lord Esher, Reginald Blomfield, Aston Webb and Lutyens met in London in March 1912, immediately prior to Lutyens leaving on his first trip to India. The wily Esher was tetchy that Rome would not get enough of Lutyens's attention; Blomfield, as politically involved as ever and acting President of the RIBA (prior to election the same year), was nurturing jealousy. They decided to build the façade with Humphreys as contracted, and for the time being the students would have to make do with converted galleries as the 'school' and find their accommodation elsewhere.

Delhi then demanded Lutyens's almost complete attention; after total immersion in matters Indian – scenes, sights, smells, politics and buildings, the shrine- and tomb-ridden site for the new capital, Simla, the Taj Mahal, riding on elephants, talking of palaces and cathedrals with Viceroys and princes, from March until July – he returned to London in early August to plunge into the problems of the office (Hugh Lane, Ireland, Hampstead, the Provost of Clare College at Cambridge *and* to see the King). In mid October he got to Rome to stake out the site, and by mid November was *en route* to India again. In Rome, it comes as little surprise, things did not go well.

By the spring of 1913 the Commissioners of the 1851 Exhibition, whose money was being spent, were agitated that it was all façade building, with no educational benefits in view. Work had been stopped because the contractors encountered the Aqua Vergine, one of three sacred channels supplying Rome's drinking water. The law said that no building was to encroach within ten metres, and it required a great deal of Mayor Nathan's time and persuasiveness to overcome this – and expensive concrete casings had to be built around drainage pipes. Progress was then impossible because there were no detailed drawings on which to proceed, and in the summer of 1913 the building of the British School disintegrated into quarrelling, miserable site morale, and standstill. The site architect (though Lutyens thought of him only as clerk of works), Lord Esher's appointment, William Squire, expostulated, 'At the present rate of procedure the Grand Inaugurazione will take place in about twenty-five to thirty years time.'[5]

Unbelievably, everything then seemed to drift for two years. Lutyens made two more long expeditions to India, and eventually turned up in Rome again on 1 July 1915; 'War with three committees,' he complained to Emily, 'one in Rome and two in England make the British School so difficult and everyone seems X with me.'[6] Materials were, it seems, still being shipped from England, despite the war; Lord Esher actually decreed that if supplies were *held up*, the nearest Italian equivalents should be used. As if the gods were equally annoyed, it rained constantly in Rome and there was the shockwave from an earthquake. Lutyens waived his £350 fees for his July visit, to be used for fencing and to pay for a niche for a bust of Edwin Austin Abbey, the American artist domiciled in Fairford, whose legacy had paid for the accommodation wing. Sir Rennell Rodd, who had threatened to resign from having anything to do with what he had started if the School were not finished by the end of July 1915, extended his deadline until the October. Squire 'designed' a library of cheap panelling and temporary bookcases, with a concrete gallery – all as a desperate measure to be ready to use for students and for the books which had to be transferred from Palazzo Odescalchi, as the lease expired that summer. Dr Ashby, as the new director, finally took over his School on 30 April 1916.

In retrospect the fiasco in Rome was the illest of omens. Rarely can the timing in any architect's career have been so disastrous. Lutyens's divine mission to build for his world in the noble manner of Palladio and Wren came to fruition along a rocky road – via the (now vanished) classical court of Papillon Hall, Heathcote, Dublin's aborted gallery, Johannesburg's (much altered), and the Rome Pavilion *à la* St Paul's, gathering pace through the years from 1908, as if mounting to a mighty crescendo, only to be dropped into the 'huge black pit' of war. If it had been mere ambition, there would be no need to mourn; but for the essential sweetness and humanism of the man – 'this singular and delightful man' whose 'expression of mischievous benevolence' distinguished both himself and his work, this man 'of remarkable kindness and insight' who was made unhappy at the very sight of unhappiness in others[7] – for this man one demands some retribution, a hammering at the doors of fate.

If overweening ambition and vanity were the causes of these tragedies, they were less Edwin Lutyens's than those of his patrons and clients. The particular Englishness that he had expressed became a victim of the war as surely as the first casualties. Lutyens of the Englishness was appalled and bewildered by the war, *he* had no notions of patriotic fervour, or of jingoism – he knew from the onset that it meant the end of all he had been working for, even if he could not have foreseen that it would mean the actual decimation of his clients' sons. His whole nature abhorred such violence, and, in that moment of August 1914, the seeming relish of the violence. The young men in his office all volunteered; Sir George Sitwell, Herbert Johnson at Marsh Court and W. G. Player all stopped their building projects immediately; Lutyens fussed with little things, and sought comfort in the houses he loved best with Miss Jekyll, Lady Horner and the Lyttons.

And then, in November 1914, he set out on his fourth visit to India, and the war slipped half a world away.

Again in retrospect, the commission for Viceroy's House, New Delhi, coming when it did, has tainted Lutyens's reputation in the eyes of posterity. The anomalies and ironies are endless, and few belong here: perhaps architectural history seems preoccupied with the rise and fall of a hill, a length of road, the great quarrel between Lutyens and Herbert Baker as to whether the bulk of Viceroy's House, or only its dome, should show along the vista, while England was fighting for her life. Then, it was painful irony that this most sensitive of English architects, to some extent a pawn of his political masters, who played upon his ambition, was diverted to the great prize in India, for six interminable passages to India and back again, from 1 April 1912 until February 1917, with a break until November 1919, when the trips resumed. The whole idea of New Delhi seems to have been conceived for royal convenience: on an impulse left over from his father's wishes, King George V was reminded of the jewel in his crown. The visit and the Durbar (gathering of the princes) were fixed, but had no particular purpose; one had to be found, hence the idea of building a new capital, because it would make a suitably impressive royal announcement. It was strongly opposed in India, particularly by the British administrators, who were very happy in Calcutta, and were not consulted. It was Lord Crewe (who, as Secretary of State, accompanied the King and Queen on their month's stay, the rest of the time tiger-shooting) who was 'very really and very directly responsible'[8] for Lutyens's appointment. Crewe rejected an Indian architect, and another English one as 'too florid' (almost certainly Blomfield), preferring the 'simplicity of Lutyens's manner' and his 'purity of taste and contempt for mere ornamentation', though aware that 'some describe him as extravagant'. Crewe was confident: 'The extravagance of architects, however, is usually the fault of their employers.'[9]

It was intended that Viceroy's House should be completed in four years, which would have put it well within the term of a single Viceroy, Lord Hardinge – and all would have been perfectly well, for Lutyens and for India.

There were, however, enigmas in Charles Hardinge too, one serious. He had gone to India full in the pride of filial duty, in the steps of his grandfather, Sir Henry Hardinge, Governor General from 1844 to 1847. Hardinge was an experienced and worldly diplomat, seemingly the perfect Viceroy (he had served in Berlin, Washington, Bucharest and St Petersburg), *and* his wife, the former Winifred Sturt, was his devoted secretary and helpmeet, and a close friend of Queen Alexandra. Hardinge's father, Charles Stewart, the 2nd Viscount, had asserted his own artistic influence on his son,[10] but then it seems that artistry, and cricket, had been firmly quashed in favour of hard work and cramming (Charlie H. had actually been *forbidden* to get his blue for cricket at Cambridge), which had left Hardinge deeply conscientious and sensitive to propriety, rather stiff and forbidding, apt to discount artistic arguments. On principle, he was often not willing to see Lutyens's point of view; there were arguments, softened by Lady Hardinge, who was Lutyens's ally – she was also, more than anyone else, the inspiration of the Mogul gardens for Viceroy's House. Hardinge was badly injured by a bomb in December 1913 and rather lost his nerve; when Lady Hardinge was forced to return home in the spring of 1914, and died after an operation in the summer, he was a broken man. There was then the difficult and time-consuming task of changing Viceroys; the new one was Lord Chelmsford, who was less interested in building and more in the Chelmsford–Montagu Reforms, which took most of his time. There were to be two more changes before the building was finished – and it was to take seventeen years instead of four.

It was oddest of all that fate had provided Lutyens – who had a basic belief that war was anathema to architecture – with those long months in India, on another stage, to concentrate ostrich-like on architecture. Sooner, rather than later, he had to face reality, and it was perhaps the traumatic effect of the war on his semi-detached awareness that made him such an effective war memorial architect. Having arrived home in early May 1917 from his sixth visit to India, he was sent to France with Herbert Baker at the beginning of July.

Fabian Ware, who worked to establish the Imperial War Graves Commission in 1917, and who was largely responsible for the whole architectural style of commemoration of the Great War and the part that Lutyens played.

This all came about because of one man, Fabian Ware. Ware was the same age as Lutyens (both were forty-five in 1914), an energetic journalist and educational reformer, with the emphasis on the *reforming* spirit – which was strong in him. He had been with Milner in South Africa (where he must have met Baker) and had been editor of the *Morning Post* in London when the war started; too old to fight, he had volunteered for the Red Cross and taken his unit to France for the specific purpose of bringing in the wounded and burying the dead. At the beginning of the war, the impression in England was still that it was a gentlemanly business; the realities of trench warfare had not become apparent. It was soon clear to Ware that a particular task was awaiting him – the burial of the dead and the marking of their graves. The army had always proudly carried this out but the nature of the battle moving on, and the demands of the fighting, now made it impossible. Ware and his men moved through the fields of France, working out of his château headquarters of Lillers, with twelve vehicles, and four field units, searching out and burying, helped by local people and especially the children, searching out and retrieving and recording identifications, and marking the graves with those fragile wooden crosses. It was work that mattered to the troops in the field, who often, on the returning march or as the battle veered to and fro, passed that way again and found their former comrades carefully honoured. Tomorrow it would surely be their own turn. It was also important at home, too, where dying for one's country was a Christian, heroic thing, but a failure to find a proper grave was agony unbearable. The consequent anger and distress were bad for recruitment.

So Fabian Ware went about his noble if macabre task, with a growing military recognition. As he spoke fluent French he was able successfully to accomplish the negotiations with the French government in 1915 which allowed him to select sites for permanent cemeteries – those corners of foreign fields that would be 'forever England'. The headline news that the body of a British officer, a grandson of Gladstone, had been exhumed under fire to be taken home for burial in answer to 'pressure from a very high quarter' gave Fabian Ware his next problem. It was his diplomacy and dedication that brought about the commandments that no bodies, whosoever they were, would be taken home, and that any differences in life were overcome by comradeship in arms and in death. Men and officers would be buried as near to where they fell as possible, and be buried, as they had fallen, together.

The first meeting of the Prince of Wales's Committee to consider the question of permanent memorials took place on 27 March 1916. That summer Ware's Graves Registration Commission, as it was still called, was installed in a headquarters in Winchester House, St James's Square. The work had spread from France to the battlefields of Salonika, Egypt and Mesopotamia, and over 50,000 graves had been registered.

It is difficult to ignore our hindsight, and it has to be consciously remembered that, in London, in 1915, it was thought that the war abided by civilized rulings, and that it would be short. It was decided to start planting the cemeteries, and in early 1916 the assistant director of Kew, Arthur Hill, went on a three-week pilgrimage to see thirty-seven cemeteries, noting the soil and aspects and what plants would be suitable. The Red Cross agreed to pay for gardening, for the planting of annuals and grass, to 'cheer our men' who were 'constant visitors' and passed when on the march, wrote Mr Hill. He could not have known that Armageddon was at hand, and that the soils he tested would have to be gouged and blasted and drenched in blood before they could be planted again.

At home there were more squabbles. Ware's determination for his cause led to the announcement of the formation of the Imperial War Graves' Commission, of which Lord Derby was the chairman and Ware the vice-chairman, in early 1917. This Commission would have complete care of the cemeteries and, despite a competing claim from the Office of Works, Ware had the support of the Prince of Wales for his totally independent Commission and won the day. The IWGC came into existence on 21 May 1917.

Next came the questions of artistic taste. Ware's first task – after politely asking some of the great and the good of the galleries in London – was to send Lutyens, Baker and Charles Aitken, director of the Tate Gallery, to see for themselves. Lutyens's response was poured, almost incoherent with emotion, into a letter to Emily: 'It is all a sense of wonderment how can such things be' – the blurred trenches, the ruined tanks, 'the rough broken shell-hole pitted ground you assume was once a village', 'a ribbon of isolated graves like a milky way across miles of country, where men were tucked in where they fell'. 'For miles these graves occur, from single graves to close-packed areas of thousands – in some places so close one wonders how to arrange their names in decent order . . . The question is so big, so wide . . .'[11]

Once returned to the safety of London, the thoughts of the three men differed: Aitken voted for simple, modest cemeteries and most of the memorial money to be spent on a national university or some other useful memorial; Baker responded as a Christian gentleman – there should be crosses and in each cemetery a Great Cross of Sacrifice; Lutyens, by 'his own pantheism, coloured as it was by Theosophy',[12] imagined that in each British cemetery there should be 'one great fair stone of fine proportions, twelve feet in length, lying raised upon three steps, of which the first and third shall be twice the width of the second . . . This stone should be, wherever circumstances permit, on the east side of each cemetery, and the graves lie before it, facing east, as the Army faces now.'[13]

To resolve these differences Ware consulted Sir Frederick Kenyon, director of the British Museum, eminently tactful in arbitration between clashing tastes: his report, the Kenyon Report, was considered by the Commission in early 1918, and

Sir John Lavery: Étaples, 1919.

his recommendations set the now familiar style. Each cemetery was to be laid out in ranks of uniform headstones, in straight lines within a walled or hedged enclosure; each cemetery was to have a cross or altar-stone as a symbol; each would have a printed register of graves and a small building to shelter this and visiting mourners. Particular matters of taste, on lettering, inscriptions and symbols and the planting, were subject to further advisory committees. There were to be three Principal Architects to the IWGC, Herbert Baker, Reginald Blomfield and Edwin Lutyens,[14] they were to be paid £400 per annum; the work was to be divided between them and carried out on the ground by teams of Assistants.[15]

Lutyens supervised the design of 126 cemeteries. His 'great fair stone', usually inscribed with Kipling's words, 'Their Name Liveth for Evermore', was placed in all but the very smallest of them. His design of the stone, which was reminiscent of some heroic altar tomb, employed the system of optical correction or entasis used by the Greeks. This 'exquisite principle' meant that all its horizontal surfaces were parts of parallel spheres 1801 feet 8 inches in diameter, and all its verticals converge at a point 1801 feet 8 inches above the centre of those spheres.[16]

The Stone of Remembrance, as it came to be called, was designed in 1917, and it is the key to the sequence of events that followed; it might almost be said that its sublime and ghostly form will follow Lutyens through the years, to his own

Étaples Military Cemetery, the largest that Lutyens designed for the Imperial War Graves Commission, containing 10,761 British and 655 German graves. The cemetery was completed in 1924; the assistant architect was George Hartley Goldsmith.

grave. We may be thankful that it replaced his immediate emotional response to the battlefields, his 'only monument' – 'a solid ball of bronze'[17] – but the actual origin of its design lay beyond rational explanation. He may have found that Professor Hamblin's study of the mathematics of the Parthenon came to hand when he needed it; he was certainly determined that the symbolism of memorial had to be 'irrespective of creed or caste' (as he had written in regard to the All India Memorial)[18] and fervently against what he felt 'the inherent cruelty of the *forced* Cross'.[19] He always said that his creativity responded to internal and external pressures, and he was so convinced that *his* art, his mistress architecture, should produce the sincerity, the permanence, the healing symbolism that was required. Under these pressures, he was driven to the mathematical extremes that produced the Great Stone; its power, a mysterious vital force, carried events forward.

The stone was first used as part of the Great War Shrine, erected in Hyde Park to mark the fourth anniversary of the start of the war, in August 1918. The shrine, a temporary but necessary focus for a grieving and angry nation, was paid for by Mr S. J. Waring, of Waring & Gillow, a long-time supporter of Lutyens's exhibition

works, and this – and the popular press reaction to the endless queues of people filing past to lay their flowers, evoked the anger of Siegfried Sassoon. It was 'an outburst of national vulgarity', this 'gift of Waring & Gillow . . . erected at a cost of several hundred pounds' . . . 'one of our insults to the dead'.[20] Shell-shocked and justifiably bitter as he was, Sassoon was right. At least the experimental war shrine had identified the need for a national memorial, and that it had somehow to be 'beyond price'. Fortunately, the architect also had time to think again, for the Stone of Remembrance at the shrine had been flanked by two curious hollow pylons, each topped with a large fir-cone, which were never to be seen again.

The shrine had also assured Lutyens's position as the designer for a national memorial; he still had many friends in and around the wartime Coalition Cabinet, especially Edwin Montagu, who championed his work in India, Reggie McKenna, Augustine Birrell and Alfred Mond, Commissioner of Works; and Sir Frederick Kenyon and Ware at the IWGC were also for him. In early 1919 the Mayor of Southampton consulted Lutyens about the first of his civic memorials: Southampton's Cenotaph was his first working of a lofty, stepped catafalque, again employing entasis.

On 19 July 1919 the Prime Minister, Lloyd George, sent for Lutyens, to say that a 'catafalque' was required in Whitehall for the peace celebrations to be held at the end of the month. In an interview with Sir Frank Baines of the Office of Works, later the same day, Lutyens sketched the Cenotaph. That same evening he sketched it again for Lady Sackville and her daughter Vita Nicolson, with whom he was

Left: The temporary Cenotaph in Whitehall: the official dedication ceremony for Peace Celebrations on 29 July 1919.
Right: The temporary Cenotaph, with Lutyens walking away from the crowd around it after the ceremony. He was not invited to attend.

dining. The name 'cenotaph' came from his recollection of a monumental stone seat, named the Cenotaph of Sigismunda by one of Miss Jekyll's philological friends, which was in her garden at Munstead; he had written in his letter from the battlefield of 'the poppies and wild flowers that are as friendly to an unexploded shell as they are to the leg of a garden seat in Surrey'.[21] To Lutyens, the design of the Cenotaph was another mathematical pilgrimage in search of the sublime; his fair stone was elevated and merged into a catafalque, to suit its narrow site in the centre of Whitehall and the tall buildings that surround it. It is the synthesis of the Cenotaph and its setting, physically and emotionally in the heart of the government of the then Empire, now the nation, that makes it such a powerful monument. To see it, as a matter of course every day, standing serenely there, amid the herd of red buses, multi-coloured coaches and black taxis, ensures 'remembrance', a promise made and never to be broken.

The wood and plaster temporary Cenotaph was built in less than two weeks, and it was ready for the march past in Whitehall. Even in this form it was impressive; among the many letters which Lutyens received, and the tremendous press coverage, the most treasured note came from his old friend Sir James Barrie. Barrie had particular reason to mourn: he and Lutyens had encountered each other on the boat to France in July 1917, when Barrie was going to find the grave of George Llewellyn Davies.[22] The note was written from the fireplace alcove in his Adelphi eyrie, which Lutyens had designed for him, on 6 August 1919: 'The cenotaph grows in beauty as one strolls down alone o'nights to look at it, which becomes my habit. I stand cogitating why and how it is so noble a thing. It is how the war has moved you and lifted you above yourself. I think it was Milton who described poetry as "thoughts that voluntarily move harmonious numbers". This is a harmonious number and I feel proud of it and you.'[23]

The Portland stone Cenotaph was completed for the second anniversary of the Armistice, on 11 November 1920. Like the Stone of Remembrance, it has no verticals or horizontals: all the 'horizontals' are radials of circles, from a common centre at 900 feet below ground: the four corners of the Cenotaph, if produced upwards, would meet at a point one thousand feet above; the joints in the masonry are the thinnest possible, no more than one-sixteenth of an inch.[24]

On 11 November 1920, 'on the last stroke of eleven, the King pressed the knob on the top of a little pedestal ... and the two great Union Jacks that draped the Cenotaph fell to the ground'. After the two minutes silence[25] and 'O God, Our Help in Ages Past', the wreath layings began.[26] The double line of mourners were gently ushered past to lay their offerings – the line stretched up Whitehall, down Northumberland Avenue to Westminster; all around, from Parliament to Trafalgar Square, were patient, tired and weeping people. 'And all along the way the air was heavy with the pungent earthy odour of white chrysanthemums and the strong sweetness of the lilies ... the Cenotaph itself stood twelve feet deep in flowers.'[27]

Thus began what may be called Lutyens's term of ministry to the mourning nation: from the summer of the temporary war shrine, 1918, until well into 1924 there was a constant stream of memorials. Then, as though the habit was hard to break, or simply that Lutyens did it so well, the memorials of war slipped into tombs, his final work for so many clients and friends. Lady Horner summoned him, and he carried the tablet for Edward Horner's memorial down with him; arriving late and finding her alone, they slipped into the church together and there was 'no fuss'.[28] The family and the representatives of the village were to meet on Sunday afternoon to find a site for the war memorial. They walked round, 'a funny procession', but Lutyens had found the perfect site already on an early morning walk with Katharine Horner – 'which no one else found or thought of, and with a

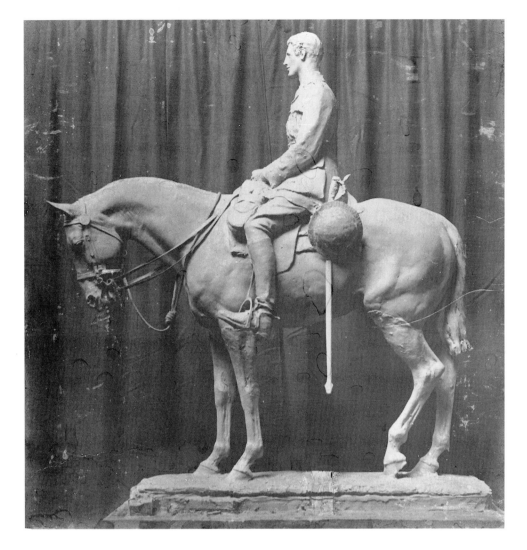

Sir Alfred Munnings's memorial to Edward Horner, the heir to Mells Manor, who was killed at the Battle of Cambrai, 21 November 1917.

little tact and patience it was carried by the villagers with acclamation'.[29] In the evening he was in the church, repainting the inscription for Raymond Asquith; 'my weekend was as a spring day, fun and tears. All their young men are killed.'[30]

In Surrey, in the churchyard of St James's at Abinger Common, the village stood in silence for the dedication of their war memorial, in the form of Lutyens's Great War Cross of 'specially selected best Portland stone', for which the bereaved Mrs T. H. Lewin of Parkhurst, next door to Lady Mirrielees, had paid £190. The Abinger cross was made by the stonemasons H. T. Jenkins & Sons of Torquay, who did many of Lutyens's memorials and were working on Castle Drogo before the war and afterwards.

Left: Mells: Lady Horner, her daughter Katharine Asquith and son-in-law Raymond Asquith outside the loggia Lutyens designed in the garden of the Manor House, *c.* 1910.
Right: Mells: Raymond Asquith and his daughter Helen in the Manor House garden, just before the First World War. The bench was designed by Lutyens for this garden.

Just a little farther west, another cross was the memorial for Busbridge in Miss Jekyll's churchyard of St John's. Barbara Jekyll's husband, Francis McLaren, had been killed in the Royal Flying Corps, and in 1922 she was quietly married to Colonel Bernard Freyberg VC, who had once commanded the Hood Battalion of the Royal Naval Division – it was through this connection that Lutyens designed the Royal Naval Division Memorial. The village of Wargrave, where the Edward Jekylls, Gertrude's parents, had lived in the 1870s, also has a Lutyens memorial.

In Hampshire, the Stockbridge memorial, another cross, stands at the end of the lane to Marsh Court, opposite the little cemetery where Lutyens designed the grave layout for Mrs Herbert Johnson. The next village, Kings Somborne, also acquired a memorial cross. In Gloucestershire, Mark Fenwick at Abbotswood paid for a little stone shelter and a memorial on the green near Lower Swell church. There was also a Lutyens memorial for Stow-on-the-Wold. Across in Hertfordshire, in the village of Ashwell, where Lutyens had enlarged Ashwell Bury for the Fordhams, he added a memorial, as he did in Rolvenden in Kent, the village close to the Tennants' Great Maytham.

The Norfolk connections now revolved around Breccles Hall, the home of Edwin and Venetia Montagu since their marriage in July 1915. Lutyens had altered the house for them, and frequently stayed there; it was a lively and lovely place to be, a respite for many of his old Liberal friends and patrons, and Edwin Montagu, Secretary of State for India from 1917 until 1922, was always ready to talk about Delhi's progress. Venetia Montagu was a marvellous hostess and she made her own enchanting garden at Breccles. It was just a short distance to G. E. Street's little church of St Ethelbert's among the fields at East Wretham, and Lutyens's wreaths of laurels in memory of Marc Andrew Noble, killed near Ypres in 1917.

Lutyens's knighthood and the Cenotaph brought many commissions for large civic memorials. Many of these are exceptionally beautiful, and easily recognizable as Lutyens's work. Rochdale in Lancashire, like Southampton, has a raised tomb on a cenotaph, with the Stone of Remembrance at its feet. The Manchester Cenotaph in St Peter's Square is flanked by stone obelisks on a platform with an upward and outward curving base; this upward and outward curve – also used for the bases of the obelisks flanking the Stone of Remembrance at Northampton – became the characteristic mark of Lutyens's gravestones. Some of these memorials, especially the civic ones, were a long time in the building, the outcome of painful differences of opinion; Manchester's was not unveiled until 12 July 1924 and Northampton's not completed until 1926. In many cases there is a long story to tell, rarely told; none of Lutyens's correspondence survives, but deep in local archives all over the country the evidence for this saddest chapter in any architect's work must lie.

On a slightly lighter note comes Osbert Sitwell's story of the Bradford memorial. They were on the train to London together and Lutyens struck up a conversation with a dark man in the corner. 'Where do you come from?' he asked.

'Bradford,' came the reply.

'I know a man who's just sold Bradford,' Lutyens remarked. 'He says it's the best bargain he ever made!'

'I'm the man who bought it.'

The answer brought even Ned to a standstill, and the dark stranger left the carriage and stood by the corridor window, beckoning Osbert Sitwell to him. 'Who is that man?' he asked, and, when 'Lutyens' came as the reply, 'The same man who designed the Cenotaph?'

Yes; the stranger returned to his seat and before the arrival in London Lutyens had the commission for Bradford's memorial too.[31]

Lutyens was always against the functional and practical memorial, because he believed these were contradictory terms; his elemental monuments were to griefs inexpressible in words. When the IWGC had completed the cemeteries there came the sombre realization that over half a million casualties were missing. As it was an IWGC principle that all names should be recorded on some memorial, it was decided to erect a series of monuments to the missing; the first planned was Sir Reginald Blomfield's Menin Gate at Ypres. It was intended that each of the Commission's principal architects should design one of these memorials, but such was the scale of the loss, that the French government became alarmed at the number and size of these proposals. Sir Edwin's first design for such a Memorial to the Missing was built at Faubourg d'Amiens at Arras – 'an extraordinary thin tall arch' – the commemoration of the missing of the Royal Flying Corps and Royal Air Force. His second design, for the memorial at St Quentin, was abandoned, and all his ideas, evolving around the theme of interlocking triumphal arches, of an unnerving hollowness and transparency, came to a conclusion in his last memorial, the Memorial to the Missing of the Somme at Thiepval, the Thiepval Arch, which was finally completed in 1932. The basic theme is that of a hierarchy of arches, of his favourite proportion of $2\frac{1}{2}$:1, with the height of the smallest arch being the level of the springing of the next arch, which is at right angles to the first, and so on up to the main arch whose springing is seventy feet up from ground level. 'At the same time the mass of the structure' composed of geometrical blocks of brick and stone 'recedes by a series of set backs . . . The result is a building whose form can only be appreciated visually' . . . 'on the main axis [it] seems to be a thin, open arch; on the diagonal it appears as a rugged, pyramidal mass. The penetration of the mass by the series of interlocking tunnels created a ground plan of sixteen rectangular piers . . . the initial governing purpose behind the design for this gave wall space enough to carve the names of 73,357 men who disappeared in the battles of the Somme.'[32]

X

INTERMEZZO: W.N. AND J.M.B.

Lutyens had two lifelong friends, with whom he formed an irresistible triumvirate of Edwardian wizardry: J. M. Barrie and William Nicholson. His first encounters with Barrie were in those long-ago summers around 1892, and the mutual attraction was cricket. Barrie, already friends with Archie Grove, then editor of the *New Review*, had been on a pilgrimage to George Meredith at Box Hill when he had rambled along the valley west of Dorking to discover Shere and a cricket match in progress on the Bray's field. From that moment his legendary team, the 'God Help Us' team, the Allhakabarries, resulted in years of midsummer madness.[1] They played at Shere – called 'Stoke-in-the-Ditch' by Barrie – and at several other pitches owned by Lutyens's early cricket-mad clients, at Tilford and Frensham with Gerard Streatfeild and at Shackleford with Edgar Horne. Lutyens never played with them but he certainly watched them; during the summer of 1892 Barrie rented Anchor Cottage in Shere with his sister Maggie, and that summer Lutyens was much in Shere working on the village shop for Reginald Bray.

Above: J. M. Barrie by William Nicholson.
Right: William Nicholson in the garden at The Grange, Rottingdean, *c.* 1910.

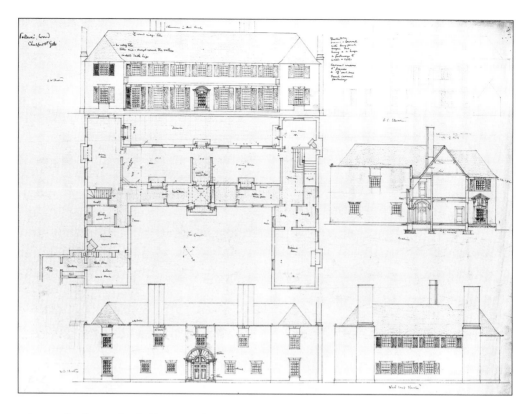

Above: Pollards Wood, Chalfont St Giles, as designed by Lutyens for Archie Grove, but never completed.

Barrie loved Surrey, like so many Scottish natives, and after his marriage to Mary Ansell they rented Black Lake Cottage, close to Tilford Green and the cricket, for many summers. The triumvirate came together for a notable event, the first production of *Peter Pan* (born at Black Lake Cottage),[2] which opened at the Duke of York's Theatre on 27 December 1904. William Nicholson designed the costumes for Gerald du Maurier's Captain Hook and his pirates, the Esquimaux and Indians, and, as Mary Lutyens remembers 'It was through our night-nursery window' that the Darling children flew.[3] Lutyens was certainly involved in the transformation of his own 29 Bloomsbury Square into a stage-set, but the programme credited Nicholson with the set design; Lutyens could not allow himself to break from the equilibrium of real buildings to the exaggeration of stage fantasy. Two years earlier, after the opening of Barrie's *Quality Street*, for which he had designed the set (and Emily Lutyens had inspired the character of Phoebe Throssal), Lutyens had written to Barrie of his conviction 'that the more real a scene is the better it must be in effect and that scenic conventions are a fraud'.[4]

Lutyens had a great respect for William Nicholson's paintings of buildings.

Above left: Thomas Newcomen Archibald 'Archie' Grove, one of the mystery men among Lutyens's clients: Archie Grove, journalist, politician and entrepreneur, always forwarding Lutyens's cause, commissioned two houses, Berrydowne Court near Basingstoke in the late 1890s and Pollards Wood, Nightingales Lane, Chalfont St Giles, in 1903. The fate of the latter is shrouded in mystery, and parts of it appear to survive in other houses; Grove was apparently bankrupted while Pollards Wood was being built and the builders used its components for other clients.

Above right: Sir George Lewis, Bart. (1868–1927), the fashionable lawyer who, with his wife Marie, was a loyal friend to Barrie, William Nicholson and Lutyens. Lutyens altered The Grange at Rottingdean for the Lewises and visited them there several times with Lady Sackville.

Their friendship was founded in the late summer of 1902, when Nicholson was embarking on his series of watercolours of Oxford colleges and sought Lutyens's advice; the night before Edward VII's Coronation, after supper at Bloomsbury Square, they had explored together, walking to view Dance's doomed Newgate Gaol which Lutyens urged Nicholson to paint.

The vortex of friendship, of paintings and commissions to alter buildings became part of the pattern of both their lives, probably far more than can be picked up by the clues remaining now. Nicholson had discovered the Sussex village of Rottingdean as a result of a commission from W. E. Henley (who had taken over the *New Review* from Grove) to draw Rudyard Kipling. The Kiplings had been living there briefly (it was 1894) and on his visit Nicholson had also met Frances Horner, who was visiting Kipling's uncle by marriage, the aged Burne-Jones.[5] In 1906 the Nicholson family rented the Old Vicarage, which they re-named The

Grange, at Rottingdean, and Lutyens's long association with that building began. It was typical of the little things that he loved to do (and did not despise) that he sketched for Mabel Pryde Nicholson a little thatched cube of a wooden studio that she had built in the garden of The Grange, with the proceeds of the sale of one of her own paintings for £600.[6]

The Edwardian years were years of obsessive hard work for all three of the wizards. Barrie was undoubtedly the most successful, and the richest, but the price he paid was dreadful; in retrospect it was interesting that James and Mary Barrie were almost the only married couple with whom Emily Lutyens felt that she and her husband could both be friends. After Barrie's divorce, it was friends that he and Lutyens had in common, Elizabeth Lucas, the wife of E. V. Lucas, and Sir George and Lady Lewis, who found him his first flat in the Adelphi. After the death of Sylvia Llewellyn Davies in August 1910 and Barrie's 'adoption' of *his* boys, the Llewellyn Davies boys, he assumed a stoical 'bachelor' life of outward gaiety, lunches at the Savoy Grill Room and dinners at the Garrick Club, much in the company of the Marchioness of Dufferin, the Countess of Lytton, Lady Horner, the Lucases and the Lewises, all of Lutyens's friends, until the war. For Barrie, the war soon brought the death of George Llewellyn Davies at Ypres in March 1915. This blow left 'the poor little genius' prey to long, lonely, dire hours, pacing his room, smoking his endless pipes. The following year, in the late spring of 1916, he moved up to the top floor of the Adelphi, to a larger flat vacated by the artist Joseph Pennell, which had marvellous views of London up and down the river. This was the room which Lutyens designed for him, panelled with many cases for his books, and the enormous inglenook fireplace, which became his true home, his carapace, and where Cynthia Asquith found him when she went to work as his secretary the following year.[7]

William Nicholson's fortunes were a little low after the start of the war, so Lutyens took him to India, to paint the Viceroy, Lord Hardinge. On board ship they met Aubrey Herbert (*en route* to the Intelligence Bureau in Cairo), who liked them both enormously: 'Nicholson is a wonderful man,' he wrote to his wife Mary. 'I should like to get him to paint you.' Lutyens was 'a divine imp, sillier than anything I have ever dreamt of, quite futile and occasionally brilliant . . . his life on board is a simmering revel.'[8] Nicholson found India perplexing and the Viceroy unresponsive; the subscription for the portrait was £1,000 and Harding wrote that the artist stayed six months in Viceregal Lodge to paint it – doing two or three portraits which did not work and making the impatient Hardinge sit again and again – the result was said to be like him but in the sitter's opinion 'not good'.[9]

The summer of 1916 is remembered by Mary Lutyens, then aged eight, for a

13. Lindisfarne Castle, which Lutyens renovated for Edward Hudson, the proprietor of *Country Life* magazine. It is now owned by the National Trust, as is Lutyens's other castle, Castle Drogo in Devon.

14. Lindisfarne, the East Bedroom, illustrating the Old English *Country Life* style of interior which Hudson found at Miss Jekyll's Munstead Wood and perpetuated through his magazine illustrations.

15. Jonathan and David Fenwick, the children of Lutyens's clients Mr and Mrs Bertie Fenwick, in the rose garden at Temple Dinsley. Portrait by Annie Swynnerton.

16. (*Left*) Mrs Antonie Rosalie Merton, painted as a young woman by her first husband,
Hermann Schmiechen.
17. (*Right*) Zackary Merton, who bought Folly Farm for his marriage to Antonie Rosalie in 1911 and his adoption of her children, from a portrait by an unknown artist.

18. Folly Farm in recent years.

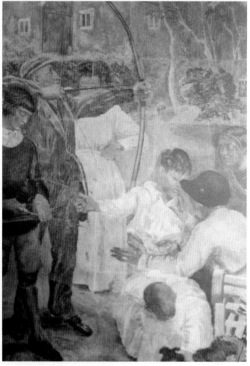

19.(*Above*) Ambrose McEvoy's painting of the Barings Senior Partners at No. 8 Bishopsgate, in the Partners' Room designed for them by Lutyens and subsequently transferred to the bank's new building. The four are, from left to right: John Baring, 2nd Lord Revelstoke (1863–1929), Cecil Baring, 3rd Lord Revelstoke (1864–1934), the client for Lambay Castle and many other houses altered or restored, and a large house in Cheyne Walk subsequently demolished; Gaspard Farrer (1860–1946), who with his brothers Henry and Frank, all three unmarried, commissioned 7 St James's Square and the Salutation at Sandwich in Kent, and Alfred Mildmay, for whom Lutyens added to Mothecombe House in Devon.

20. Archery at Lambay, detail from a fresco painted by Cecil and Maude Baring's daughter Daphne, showing the family at their island home, which Lutyens renovated and enlarged for them.

21. Alice, Viscountess
Wimborne, by Sir John
Lavery, in her music
room at Wimborne
House, Arlington Street,
London, 1937.

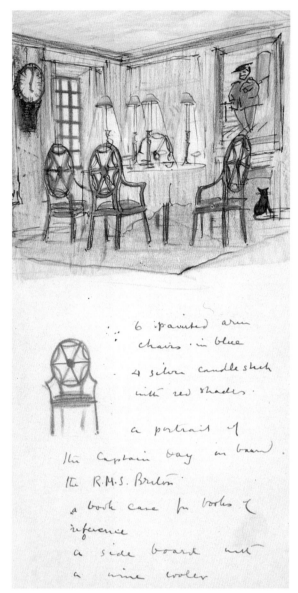

THE COMPANION
HALL   5.

Looking south over the
garden & the sea   see?
on either side of the Porch
is a bay   one for hers
& the other for Capt. Day
Happy days !

6 painted arm
chairs in blue
4 silver candle stick
with red shades.
a portrait of
the Captain Day on board
the R.M.S. Briton
a book case for books of
reference
a side board with
a wine cooler

22. Lutyens's designs for Captain Day's house, made as a diversion during the journey to Cape Town on the RMS *Briton* of the Union–Castle Line in the spring of 1919.

23. Memorial to William La Touche Congreve VC in the church at Stoke by Chartley, Staffordshire. In 1927, Lutyens added a companion memorial to William's father, Sir Walter Norris Congreve VC. William 'Billy' Congreve would have inherited Lindisfarne Castle had he lived.

24. Papillon Hall: all that remains of an elaborate 'butterfly' plan house, built for the Belleville family in Leicestershire and subsequently demolished to assuage a curse. The doorway was rescued by Lutyens's grandson, Viscount Ridley, and is at Blagdon Hall.

25. Marsh Court, Stockbridge, Hants: the farm buildings grouped beside the Stockbridge to King's Somborne road include this wonderful barn, a rare survivor of Lutyens's barns, many of which have been converted.

26. Ashby St Ledgers, Northants. Watercolour plan and elevation by Harold Stevens of Lutyens's cottages dated 1908 for the Hon. Ivor Guest, later Lord Wimborne.

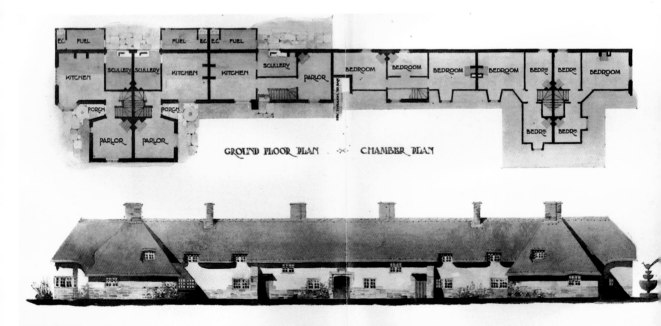

GROUND FLOOR PLAN ·×· CHAMBER PLAN

A ROW OF THATCHED COTTAGES.

FRONT ELEVATION

THE DRAWING BY HAROLD STEV

Edwin L. Lutyens, Architect.

Above: Folly Farm, Sulhamstead, Berkshire: Barbara Lutyens, the architect's eldest daughter, in the Tank Court at Folly Farm, during the summer of 1916 when she was on leave from the VAD.

Below: Folly Farm: Edward Knoblock, an unidentified lady, Lady Emily and Barbara Lutyens in the Rose Garden, 1916.

childhood happiness as it was the only time they spent in one of her father's own houses, and complete as a family. The Lutyenses – Edwin, Emily and the young Robert, Ursula, Elisabeth and Mary – were lent Folly Farm in the Kennet valley by the widowed Mrs Zackary Merton. Barbara Lutyens, a VAD, came for weekends with her friends, and other visitors abounded – even Gertrude Jekyll came on a brief visit and played Mrs Merton's pianola, and William Nicholson and Mabel Pryde were there a great deal of the time. Mary Lutyens remembered that sometimes they were fourteen for 'tremendous games' of crazy croquet, played 'on a very large, smooth lawn – the perfect game for all ages and any number . . .'[10] Folly Farm was a true farm (there were fat, black shiny pigs and piglets in 1916), as it had been for centuries; its most notable farmer, Robert Fenn, was awarded the Victoria Medal of Honour for improving potato varieties and was a churchwarden at Sulhamstead from 1882 until 1907, the year after he sold the farm to Lutyens's first client, Mr H. H. Cochrane. For Mr Cochrane Lutyens built the pretty 'doll's house' in William and Mary manner, with two shades of bricks, vermilion and

Folly Farm: the double-height hall, with black walls and red lacquer balconies, Lutyens's decorative scheme for the Mertons.

Left: William and Mabel 'Prydie' Nicholson with their son Tony, *c.* 1916. Prydie died in July 1918 and Tony Nicholson died of his war wounds three months later.
Right: The Owl, Number 2, October 1919, with Lutyens's name among the contributors.

slaty blue. The Mertons had bought it in 1912; they were rich and kind, and seemingly flamboyant, and Lutyens was allowed to build a spiky new west wing of the 'doll's house' and connect the two with an indulgence of a roof. And what a roof, subtly curved (his famous swept valleys) and balanced with little dormers, draping over the sleeping balcony of the master bedroom in the west wing and drooling round the tank court, supported on the 'bandy' buttresses of the cloister, doubling its magnificence by reflection in the pool. Steps led down into the pool (in fact a rainwater catchment tank) where the youngest Lutyenses fished for goldfish.

That is, apparently, when they were not rushing into the new dining-room, in the west wing, to alleviate William Nicholson's boredom and 'loneliness' while he painted the enchanting mural there for Mrs Merton – *trompe-l'œil* windows, decorated with trellis and birdcages, and all around on high a 'shadowy frieze' of decorative plates.

The year after the Folly Farm summer, Lutyens, whose Delhi office had been set up in the mews behind the Farrers' 7 St James's Square, was instrumental in Nicholson's acquiring his most famous studio, at 11 Apple Tree Yard, converted from a broken-down stable. It was to be Nicholson's studio and home for twenty-three years and became inseparable from his personality; down below, the stalls were kept for canvas storage, the saddle room became a tiny dining-room, with a black shiny ceiling to reflect candlelight (Lutyens again), and a steep stair led up to the whitewashed studio, lino squares in polished black and white, a pale blue washed brick fireplace, brass fender, white muslin curtains, 'soft sunlight reflected on every gleaming Chippendale surface, Empire mirrors and endless beautiful and fascinating ornaments' – paintbrushes were kept in a top hat and drums made side tables.[11]

Nicholson too had his tragedies: his wife, Mabel Pryde, died on 13 July 1918 and Tony Nicholson died of wounds on 5 October 1918. Nicholson, needing company, was in Lutyens's drawing office on Armistice night when the maroons went off – 'Another raid?' said Ned. 'No, by God!' said William, who had flung open the window, and caught the meaning of the shouting crowds who were surging past the end of the Yard . . . 'It's *peace*, my boy!' They joined the crowds together.[12]

The subject of the memorials and Cenotaph were constantly in debate in Apple Tree Yard gatherings; the Cenotaph sketch found its way into one of the three issues of Nicholson's *The Owl* anthologies, and into his painting *The Morning of the Peace Procession*, 1919. At this time, according to Robert Graves, married to Nancy Nicholson, his father-in-law considered a second trip to India, as Lutyens's assistant. That this did not happen probably had something to do with the fact that Nicholson married Edith Stuart Wortley. Edith, the daughter of Sir Lionel and Lady Phillips, had been widowed by the war. William Nicholson had known her for some time, had attended her wedding at Tylney Hall, and had painted both Phillipses in 1912, when everyone was immersed in the Johannesburg Art Gallery and Hugh Lane was around. The Phillipses gave the Manor House at Sutton Veny in Wiltshire to Edie (as she was always called) as a wedding present and the Nicholson cavalcade was less seen in Apple Tree Yard for a while. Nicholson called it 'our Tree'. Lutyens asked for a portrait of Gertrude Jekyll, but Miss Jekyll would not waste valuable daylight in sitting for him – which is why Nicholson resorted to painting her boots, inscribed 'For E. L. from W. N.' When she would sit, he placed a single lamp between her and himself, hence the direct spotlight on her hair, her half-profile and her beautiful, pondering – and perhaps impatient – hand.[13]

Another cheering project on which there was much collaboration – and some

Apple Tree Yard, St James's, 1922, a rare photograph of William Nicholson in his studio, standing in front of the large window Lutyens designed for him when they converted the former stable. Also in the picture, one of Lutyens's Napoleon chairs, perfect for Nicholson's long legs; one was intended to sit against the high arm, with a leg casually draped over the low arm.

William Nicholson (*right*) and his son Ben at Folly Farm, 1920.

disputation – was Queen Mary's Doll's House, for which Lutyens persuaded Nicholson to do decorations, some paintings and a scheme for its setting. The Doll's House, such a contrast of whimsical nonsense after real tragedies as to be almost exaggeratedly so, had a serious side in that it was for Lutyens's *most* important client, HM Queen Mary. It was the nation's tribute for all she was to them; Lutyens almost single-handedly at times (though there was a prestigious committee headed by Princess Marie-Louise) had to cajole and persuade all his friends, and others, to contribute. The toy theatre has the sets for *Peter Pan*; Nicholson painted *The Expulsion from Eden* for the landing and Queen Elizabeth I in ruffs and pearls over the library fireplace; the gardener was, of course, Miss Jekyll, but Lady Jekyll collected the miniature kitchen stores. In three years of labours, Lutyens was the 'presiding genius', and E. V. Lucas said that without him it would not have been done at all. Queen Mary was always interested in this model house of 1920 for a toy royalty six inches tall; 'Yesterday,' she wrote to the King in July 1923, 'I went to see the doll's house which is getting on very well, & is most beautiful & all the details quite perfect.'[14] For 22 January 1924 she recorded in her diary that she 'had arranged some of the rooms', as this was her task and wish before it went on display at the Wembley Exhibition.

One can only admire Lutyens at this time, rushing madly around the world, with no home to come home to – or at least no family – and the surreal contrasts

Mells Park: William Nicholson painting the portrait of Pamela McKenna and her sons David and Michael: the painting shows Pamela sitting on a rug in the foreground, David in a dinghy at the lake's edge behind her and Michael, in the distance, all arranged so that Nicholson could paint the waterfall below the stepping stones, which he most enjoyed.

in his work. On one trip to France in early July 1922 he stayed with the society decorator Elsie de Wolfe at her villa at Versailles, flirting delightfully with the pearl-dripping Anne Vanderbilt, saw the Russian ballet in Les Galeries des Glaces, explored Les Trianons with private keys, and watched Hugo Rumbold's *Marie Antoinette* – along with Elsa Maxwell – projected by the Armenian chauffeur in the ballroom where the sixty-year-old Miss de Wolfe usually did her physical jerks, which she demonstrated. All this sandwiched in between inspecting the stone-yard for Étaples and discussing the preliminary layout of Thiepval with the French government architect.[15]

Another whimsy (which may have played a part in the inspiration for the doll's house)[16] was inspired by Nicholson, when he asked Lutyens to take a young RFC veteran, Herbert Ward, to South Africa with him in early 1919, on the trip to Solomon to discuss the university at Cape Town. The passage home was on RMS *Briton*, the captain was Capt. Edward Day and Lutyens amused himself responding to the captain's idea of a retirement house. His delightful designs show a square villa, with a staircase (like the doll's house) rising centrally through the house with a balustrade of life-belts. There are sketches of myriad kitchen needs – a giant beer barrel, sieve, salt, mousetrap, and the cook, her feet up on the table absorbed in *Tit Bits*. A weekly drinking calendar shows 'Dry day Hum day Rum day Hock day', etc., to 'Champ any day', cutlery, glasses and eggcups, and a dining-room with six painted blue chairs of Lutyens's spider's web back design as used for *Country Life* in 1904. And, poignantly, in view of Lutyens's own missing marriage at the time, the Companion Hall with sitting bays on either side of the garden porch 'one for Mrs and the other for Capt. Day. Happy days.' The Days also rejoiced in a large inglenook fireplace, very Barrie-like.[17]

Michael and David McKenna in 1930, their Eton leaving portrait by William Nicholson. Both King's Scholars, Michael, *left*, was Captain of School, David Captain of Boats.

For poor Barrie, the last and worst blow came in May 1921, when Michael Llewellyn Davies was drowned in the Sandford Pool near Oxford. It was to Lutyens that he turned for Michael's tombstone in Hampstead churchyard, where he was laid along with the du Mauriers. Barrie, persuadable by Cynthia Asquith only into gentle society, retreated into his fireplace alcove; her abiding memory was of him there: 'For the rest of my life the scent of wood smoke will make me see that wide cavernous hearth and, on his knees beside it, Barrie – "most individual and bewildering ghost" – patiently, intently, fanning grey ashes into flame.'[18]

For Nicholson, though his marriage to Edie Stuart Wortley (their only child, Liza, whom he adored, was born in 1920) did not bring lasting happiness, the early 1920s were good. At Sutton Veny they were on tennis-playing terms with the McKennas and Asquiths at Mells, and from then through to the 1930s, Nicholson painted portraits of some of the people Lutyens loved most. At Mells, in the park, he painted Pamela McKenna and her sons, Michael and David, by the waterfall where Haldane had bathed, and a double portrait of Michael and David in a doorway for Eton College, as a leaving portrait. He painted Perdita Asquith, Katharine Horner's daughter, and beautiful studies of Mells Manor House and the Church, and the big elm and the church tower, for which sketches were used to illustrate Lady Horner's *Time Remembered*. He also portrayed the Revd James Hannay, rector of Mells, more widely known as the novelist George A. Birmingham. He had started to paint Ursula Lutyens at Folly Farm, and – in the way of Nicholson's lengthy working – he finally finished her at Blagdon in Northumberland, after her marriage to Lord Ridley in 1924; he also painted Euan Wallace MP, who married Barbara Lutyens, and the Ridleys' adopted daughter, Laura. By this time there was another painter-in-ordinary to the Lutyens family connections, the young Rex Whistler,[19] and the world moved on.

XI

LADY SACKVILLE

I like the splendour of this vast house, even if there are grammatical errors committed by Vanbrugh. The spirit of Sarah Jennings possesses me, and I should love McNed to build for me something very beautiful and very large.

(Lady Sackville's diary, 4 November 1917, on a visit to Blenheim)[1]

It was on a summer night, 24 June 1916, after a visit to Covent Garden, to Verdi's *Otello* – in Emerald Cunard's box in the company of Arthur Balfour and Ezra Pound – that Victoria Sackville whisked Edwin Lutyens home to Bedford Square, dropping him at the door, and recording afterwards in her diary that he was charming. Less than a week later, on the 29th, she was lunching at Bedford Square, to meet Emily – 'He is amusing, she is dull,' was her diary verdict – and with Emily's 'blessing' immediately achieved, Lutyens and his new friend went off to 34 Hill Street to see her 'Persian Room'.

For the next decade and a little more, Lady Sackville was Lutyens's client, companion, patroness and mistress. She was in turn exasperating, delightful, generous and pernickety, adoring, argumentative, indulgent and immensely kind. In 1916 she was eighteen years older than when he had first met her, as the chatelaine of Knole, the adored of Sir John Murray Scott, prior to the Paris Exhibition.[2] Sir John had died in 1912. The following year Lady Sackville had featured greatly in the salacious headlines of London newspapers when she successfully withstood the accusations of the Scott family, through their mouthpiece F. E. Smith, that she had influenced Sir John to make his will in her favour, leaving her an enormous sum of money (£150,000) and the fabulous contents, the residue of the Wallace Collection, of his Paris house. Lady Sackville deserves her place in legal history for her evasiveness and charm, which managed to exasperate both F. E. Smith *and* Sir Edward Carson, setting them squabbling and appealing to the Judge. The following year, 1913, on 1 October, her only child, Vita Sackville-West, had married Harold Nicolson, and her first grandchild, Benedict, had been born in August 1914. She had bought 182 Ebury Street in Belgravia as a London house for Vita and Harold, and had also helped them with the purchase of a country home, Long Barn at Sevenoaks Weald, in 1915.

From Lutyens's point of view, Lady Sackville was rich, beautiful, charming and persuasive: having introduced her to Emily right at the outset, she was also perfectly 'safe'. Emily was only too happy for her bothersome husband to have a playmate, one who shared his interests in every detail of décor and house alteration, who was safely married to a peer of the realm (Lord Sackville was serving in the war) and who would apparently add to the family resources rather than deplete them. For Lutyens himself, Victoria Sackville was not only attractive for all her desires to build, a subject she found as fascinating as he did, but she afforded him the chance to dissect one of the great houses of England, his perennial addiction. Their next outing was to Knole, at the end of July 1916, when he indulged, to his great delight, in the attics, roofs, perhaps not all 365 rooms and fifty-two staircases, but certainly the seven courts and all the state rooms of that great house. The excuse for his visit was that they were to go and look for a house by the sea at Hove which Lady Sackville felt would be nice for her grandchildren (Vita, having had a stillborn son in 1916, was now pregnant again), and – her frankness was part of her charm – she wanted a retreat from Knole, where her husband's return would only emphasize his long-standing relationship with his mistress, Olive Rubens.

In early August she visited the Lutyens family at Folly Farm, and confirmed her liking for him – 'I shall make him amenable to what I want,' she records in her diary. What she wanted was what she had been used to all her life – the affection and attention of a distinguished gentleman. This time he was a famous architect; her previous *amours* had included Auguste Rodin, William Waldorf Astor, and J. Pierpont Morgan – who all had, in common with her dear old Sir John Murray Scott, her 'Seery', a love of art and beautiful things. Dealing with fabulous furniture and pictures, about which she was immensely knowledgeable, was very lifeblood to her; the additional frisson of spending money, of which she was careless simply because she was rich, on building beautiful new rooms was a delightful challenge. She was in her early fifties and still had tremendous energy for life, and she not unnaturally wanted a companion. There was every sign that Lutyens was equally lively, he certainly shared her interests, and he seemed to be equally 'without' a partner.

In that first autumn of their friendship they set the fairly frantic pace that was to mark the years through until 1924. Lady Sackville paid £8,000 for some land at Hove and Lutyens was designing what they called the Grey House. He sketched joyfully, she eagerly accepted every sketch and promised to put them in a book. She visits Apple Tree Yard to inspect the Delhi drawings, they take a jaunt to Crowther's, the dealer in statues and ornaments, to browse together, and then to Hampton Court looking at stairs and chimneys, with lunch at the Mitre so that she can buy him meat, which Emily does not approve. On 18 October he goes again to Knole (she has bought him fillet of beef especially), and they go into Sevenoaks to discuss building restrictions at Hove with her solicitor; they walk back across the park in the dusk and she notes, 'He seems rather afraid of the dark.'[3]

The next morning Lutyens leaves Knole in the care of the 'rich vulgarian' as Lady Sackville called Mrs Rudd,[4] with whom he went to examine the site at East Grinstead, Felbridge, where he was designing the grandest of all his houses and gardens, had they ever been built. The Rudds, from South Africa, had commissioned, just after the start of the war, a classical house in Portland stone with a façade 300 feet long, a 128-foot-long formal canal and Italian garden built out from this front, and an integral domed swimming-pool. Lady Sackville undoubtedly felt she was being upstaged, but need not have feared ... though she felt a grander gesture on her part was necessary, so she went to Hove and rejected the Grey House site with the difficult planning restrictions, and found another, on the cliff, east of Brighton, next to Roedean's playing fields. She picked Lutyens up in her Rolls from Sibyl Colefax's at Buckhurst, where he had been left by Mrs Rudd – they looked in at Penshurst to see a fireplace and returned to Knole, to spend more time luxuriating in the details of stairs and fireplaces, to their mutual satisfaction. She vowed to win him, which meant expressing her intention to support him, and his cause, while he was gone to India. He uses Knole as a stopping off point *en route* to the boat on 1 November, presenting her with Lawrence Weaver's book, which touches her greatly, as a farewell – only to return for a night as the boat is delayed; she promises to persuade Lady Cunard to let him build her new opera house. Lutyens finally leaves for his sixth visit to India, via Spain, where, though there are more grand plans and sketches to be made, he continues to assure her that he sketches ideas for her house 'of the future' which is not forgotten.

Lady Sackville is added to his correspondence list; for her the big event of the New Year, 1917, is the birth of her second grandson, Nigel Nicolson, on 19 January. She was planning a little house in London to be built by MacNed (part of Lady Sackville's growing fantasy of herself and Lutyens was that *she* would do him as much good as Miss Jekyll had done, and as a result of this stream of thinking Lutyens had remarked that to be loved by a Jekyll one had to be named Mac-Something – Pamela and Barbara Jekyll having married Reginald McKenna and Francis McLaren respectively – so from now on they called themselves MacNed and MacSack (McNed and McSack), and will be called so here).

Lutyens returns from India at the end of May, to the comforts of Knole, luxuriating in visits to Mereworth, Cobham Hall, Chevening, Hever (where he 'held his head' in envy of F. L. Pearson's chances in rebuilding the whole village,

Edwin Lutyens's portrait of Lady Sackville and self-portrait, as MacSack and MacNed, 22 August 1920.

etc.), Groombridge Place and – a few days later – Lullingstone Castle. (This was the scene of their first love-making; she afterwards refers to his advances as 'Lullingstonisms'.) After all these magnificent houses it is little wonder that MacNed, after walking across Knole's park to look at Vita and Harold Nicolson's fourteenth-century cottage and added barn, asked proudly by Vita what he thought, expostulated, 'Sell it.'[5]

For the rest of the summer (they go to Munstead and she is approved) MacNed and MacSack are constantly together, constantly imagining, and he sketching, houses in London, gardens by the sea – for sites which have yet to be found, and delighting, rather like the two enthusiastic children they both are, in exploring castles and houses together. He stayed with her both before and after his harrowing visit to the battlefields of France in July 1917; he poured out all his ideas to her, and it seems that she was greatly necessary to him during this difficult time. She was also extremely patient and kind, for at this time, what to any other man would have been temptation and compromising circumstances, to the guilt-obsessed Lutyens were not. Driving home one evening she must have raised, delicately, the question of going to bed together, which brought his confession that he had never 'loved' another woman but Emily. For MacSack it was a matter of feminine pride;

193

she was very proud of her undeniable beauty, even in middle age, and of her desirability (she was very delighted that the menopause did not seem to touch her until she was well past her middle fifties) – and could it not have been sheer loneliness? It was public knowledge, and had been for years, that Lionel Sackville loved another; why should she not have love too? It was also very much a matter of what Harold and Vita thought – she wanted them to think she had a lover, and that it was MacNed. This caused Harold some embarrassment, and throws light on the Lutyens marriage, when he wrote to Vita on 19 October 1917: 'I was at a loose end last night, so I telephoned to MacNed thinking he was a widower too, but oh dear, oh dear, he wasn't, so he had to ask me to Bedford Square, and I'm sure it led to a row with Emmie ... a terrible Theosophist friend was there, and poor MacNed was such a darling. Emmie is a devil. She nags and jeers and sniffs and sighs at MacNed as if he was a naughty schoolgirl, and poor man is snubbed before that little swine of a Theosophist, who is not worthy to tie his bootlaces ... Poor, poor MacNed. She *is* a gloom. I do understand why B M [Bonne Maman, his name for his mother-in-law] cheers him up. Really, for once, there is a great deal in what B M says.'[6] It was not usual for Harold Nicolson to be appreciative of his mother-in-law.

By now the plans for MacSack's buildings had changed and changed again and again. Sites were being found and rejected at an alarming rate – a house to be built in Brook Street? Or was it to be Park Street or North Audley Street? Two Adam houses in Streatham were inspected. All the time MacNed sketches and sketches; MacSack does not realize that he is constitutionally bound to do this. Once an idea is mooted he *must* sketch, and she is constantly surprised and delighted when more and more delicious houses keep turning up – and equally alarmed that he must expect her to build so lavishly. The more she says, or has to say, no, the more hurt she feels and the more treats are lavished on the whole Lutyens family to make up for the hurts. If all the delights he drew for her on all those awkward Mayfair sites had been built then London would have been a charming city.

From the autumn of 1917 their relationship is at its closest (she was fifty-five on 30 September 1917); she is the recipient of all his troubles and fears, the diary is constantly noting that 'Ned is worried' – worried that the Archbishop of Canterbury insists upon a cross for war grave symbolism, worried about Baker and Delhi, worried about his finances and tax – all of which she listens to endlessly, equally patient in dispensing the comforts of her homes, the convenience of her chauffeur-driven Rolls (for which she acquires a gas bag when petrol runs short). She drives him to Kew to talk to Director Hill about the planting for the war cemeteries, she introduces him to everyone who might possibly help him – and

Edwin Lutyens, sketch for a dressing/bathroom – 'Long table for dressing-glass and wash-hand stand combined in one with flap table on left side and towel rail' – for Lady Sackville.

for him she is 'possessed by the spirit of Sarah Jennings at Blenheim', and reaffirms her intention to let him build something for her that will enhance his fame. All the time she is faced with this infuriating, inadequate lover, who plays endless games of patience and smokes continual pipes, behaves outrageously, telling the grimiest stories and endlessly punning at dinner tables they frequent together (she tries so hard to curtail the punning); and when he does end up in her bedroom, as undoubtedly happened during this autumn of 1917, it is to bemoan Emily's interests elsewhere or praise her saintliness, or to complain that MacSack is too mean to impoverish herself or mortgage her jewels to let him build. It is undoubtedly due to her skills if this was – momentarily, and on a few occasions – transformed into mutual comfort one of the other and love. For all this, she loved him: 'He wants me to be his best friend, and would eat the humblest of humble pies to remain in my good graces,' she wrote in her diary at the end of December 1917, immediately before Lutyens left for Spain, where his plans came to naught.

When he returned in mid January, straight to Knole, she is fearing she will never have enough money to build as he wants; she is delighted that Major Morrison is contemplating a village at Basildon and that Lady Lucas (Nan Herbert

195

had inherited her brother's title after he was killed in the war) was to build 'a big Library' at her Bell House, Dulwich, presumably in connection with her enmeshment with theosophy. By this time, Vita Sackville-West is involved in the MacNed campaign, smartening him up with new clothes, and mother and daughter visit Lord Leverhulme, to persuade him to carry out plans for Lutyens to build on Stornoway.

It was in the middle of March 1918 that Lady Sackville first took Lutyens to Brighton to see two houses in Sussex Square, numbers 39 and 40, which she thinks would make that seaside home she had originally intended; MacNed, who she thinks is unwell, is not impressed: 'We almost fought at his stupid remarks about the "grammar" . . . which is not enough *grand seigneur* for me.'[7] Nevertheless, she pursues the houses, and a third, 40a, which are bought separately. On 28 March she paid £2,850 for number 40, and, on 23 April, £1,300 for 40a; number 39 would be hers later in the summer for £3,500 – she was very trustful of the various elderly lady vendors, but it all turned out as planned. The houses, whitish stucco, on the east side of the square, really marked the boundary of Brighton, and there were then only sea breezes over the cliff-tops eastward towards Rottingdean. The houses were rather cliff-like, standing high, part of the early nineteenth-century Kemp Town development by Thomas Read Kemp (who lived at number 22 in the square) designed by the architects C. A. Busby and Amon Wild (father and son) in the style of Regent's Park, London, but of coarser detailing. Lutyens was quite right – they are big and imposing, but nothing of great quality.

Tunnels were part of the attraction – there is a tunnel from the Square garden to the beach, and number 40 had a tunnel behind, under what was the mews road, to a walled garden. Lady Sackville longed for Lutyens to design her a garden, chiefly so that she could have something of her own to match Vita's growing gardening enthusiasm at Long Barn.[8]

The summer of 1918 passed in MacNed's constant company (Emily is mostly with the children at Church Stretton in Shropshire, where the children were taken to be away from the war from February 1918 to July 1919), with MacSack constantly frustrated by his irrepressible behaviour when they are visiting together, his puns, and his undoubted lack of commitment, or finesse, in the bedroom. However, their mutual affection remains, despite arguments over what is to be done at Sussex Square, which are all part of the game, and her quickly alternating moods of flamboyant expenditure on furniture and rugs and other generosity, and despair of penury, when everything is halted – only to be started up again when MacNed is duly repentant. As she keeps telling her diary, she does care for him, she so wants to find opportunities for him and rejoices when they seem to come: Mrs

Charles Hunter of Hill Hall, Epping, might build? Gordon Selfridge is lunched to persuade him to use Lutyens instead of Philip Tilden (he didn't); perhaps she should buy 38 Sussex Square as well for the perfect opportunity! And all the while she fetches him and meets him, bids him farewell (equipped with vintage brandy and fur gloves for Paris), lets him work quietly, and gently supplies him with meals – all perfectly wifely activities which one cannot blame him for enjoying for once. Hardly surprisingly, he is captivated by her undoubted interest in his work and clients.

In *Pepita*, Vita Sackville-West remembers that she was with her parents in the library at Knole one evening in the spring of 1919, and all three were talking 'as people do talk after months and months of separation' – Lord Sackville having returned from the war. She felt they were all getting on together so well, and then, when her father quietly and casually said to her mother that it would be best to tell the bailiff in advance of work she wanted done so that the men's time could be planned, Victoria lost her temper, burst into tears and left the room.[9] In her diary MacSack notes that she had decided to leave her husband and her beloved Knole (by far the most difficult thing, for it had been her home before it was his) two days previously on 19 May 1919 – and she did so. For the rest of the summer she was busy retrieving her favourite things from Knole – without it showing that anything had been removed. She was living in one of the Sussex Square houses, which she had decorated with MacNed's help; her own bedroom had pale apricot marbled paper on the walls, with a darker shade of the same on the ceiling and a frieze of gilded stars. She slept in a small Empire bed which had carved feathers – a little like Prince of Wales's – at the head. She had a 'Chinese' bathroom. Vita's room was what her mother called 'a beautiful colour' – a kind of tomatoey-orange, washed out (Vita loved orange in any shade), with salmon and tomato-coloured lamps and cushions, and a green marble mantelpiece with six bright orange pots on it, and painted beads on the looking glass. The pictures – by Bakst, Rodin and George Plank (an American protégé of MacSack's) were framed in transparent ribbons. MacNed also had his own room in Sussex Square.

Lutyens has made lovely designs for the conversion of Sussex Square – three houses into one – but things are not running smoothly. He has left A. J. Thomas, his office manager, in charge, and though MacSack gets on well with Thomas – especially as she is inclined to pay her bills by handing him wads of banknotes, as much as £1,000 at a time – the office accounting of necessity gets out of kilter! MacNed is preoccupied with great things – the idea of Lucknow University (not built) spurs him to a great deal of designing, there is talk of a £1½ million National War Museum (not built) *and* he is in touch with Sir John Ramsden at Muncaster

Knole, Sevenoaks, Kent: the Colonnade Room, the focus of family life in the great house, a symbol of what Lady Sackville had given up – it was her own home before her marriage to Lionel Sackville-West in the summer of 1890.

Castle in Cumberland, who also owns Bulstrode Park in Buckinghamshire, who talks of spending £100,000. (No work for Sir John materialized, except his tomb.) MacSack fully understands that these people have to have his attention.

But, while Sussex Square blunders on, MacNed finds ever more comfort with what really became his new family. Harold Nicolson adored him – he was another of the select band of late-night droppers-in at Apple Tree Yard in the last months of the war. MacNed, as usual, had a special bond with children, revealed in his birthday letter to Ben Nicolson of 2 August 1919 (Ben was five): 'My dear Mick Ben – a Mickle is offspring of a Mack ... Ever so many happy returns ... I am in a train & cannot send you a present. I might say two trains – me travelling west at miles an hour (to Frome) and the other a train of thought of you – and what I can give you for your birthday? The train I had thought was to send you some

40 Sussex Square, Brighton: Lady Sackville's bedroom, with pale apricot marbled walls, gilded stars and some of the treasures she had retrieved from Knole.

Vita and Harold Nicolson, newly married, in Constantinople in 1914. Lutyens had the friendship and love not only of Lady Sackville, but of her daughter, son-in-law and grandchildren too.

Cadbury chocolate – but alas how can I? so I take the Bs before the Cs and send you a little Bradbury – by which means you can get chocolate – or what you will – tho' the world at large will never consider as means – will they? I have come to the conclusion that God must have been old and tired when he invented birthdays – for I am sure that if he had been just a few years younger he would have had shorter and quicker-to-come years – with their due course of birthdays. He would have ordained a year 4 times as short – we should have had 4 times as many birthdays and 4 times as much fun of a let-go-of things sort. The Psalmist would have numbered our days at 280 years. What more could one wish for? Oh Mick Ben I ask you? My venerations deeply veneered to your Macmother and Macgrannie – Bless you Mick Ben . . . your affectionate old MacNed.'[10]

The operatic warmth of MacSack's attentions propelled Lutyens through those traumatic post-war years of memorials, disappointment, frustrations in Delhi and fading finances. It is difficult to imagine how he could have managed without her. His notes to her, though few have survived – beginning 'My Velly MacSack . . .' – often continue in the same kind of openly loving and childish language he used to the children. He was naturally grateful for the constant flow of delicious dinners, the warmth and comforts of her beautiful house, the luxury of her chauffeured Rolls, and to have her constant interest in his work was perhaps

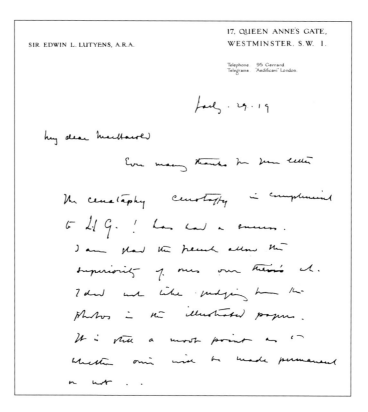

Part of Edwin Lutyens's letter to Harold Nicolson about the Cenotaph. The letter reads:

My dear MacHarold, Ever many thanks for your letter. The cenataphy cenotaffy in compliment to Ll G.! [Lloyd George] has had a success, I am glad the french allow the superiority of ours over theirs wh. I did not like judging from the photos in the illustrated papers. It is still a moot point as to whether ours will be made permanent or not ...

difficult to accept. But it does seem that, as a relationship, there was an instability, a mutual dissatisfaction that was caused by something other than Victoria's Spanish temperament and volatility *or* his annual winter absences in India. There was no doubt that he was forever in love with his wife, and never ceased to hope that she would 'return' to him; thus there was always *his* guilt and non-commitment to aggravate every turn of *her* temper. Poor man, he was just one of Barrie's 'lost Boys' – but poor MacSack too.

In the early spring of 1920, while he was in India (though sending her constant notes), she was overcome by a panic of poverty; on a visit to Sussex Square she flew into tantrums and stopped all building work. The mounting costs, then the 'cruel budget', forced her to decide to sell 34 Hill Street (which Lutyens had been carefully re-planning).

She found it difficult to face him when he returned in early May, *just* in time for Barbara Lutyens's marriage to Euan Wallace. As it turned out, he was so pleased to see her that he was not cross: 'I *am* his great friend,' she records in her diary. They go to Brighton together to sort things out; the lavish brilliance of their ideas is revealed: 'We are planning a plain panelled room of ebony and fireplaces sandwiched between two arches of *fleur de pèche* marble.'[11] William Nicholson agrees to paint a mural for the dining-room for £500, and they drive down to see Miss

Jekyll, who grumbles how poor she is, and how bad her 'seeds and plants' business is! Gertrude Jekyll's poverty seems catching; MacSack panics that her shares are down, A. J. Thomas wants £2,000 for the Sussex Square works (she has already paid him £5,500), Hill Street is unsold at £5,000, she has constant arguments with MacNed about 'his Grammar and his perfect measurements' for her rooms. Her solution is sell a Cartier bracelet for £11,000, which makes her feel better.

Thus the switchback of their affair settles down to its best aspects again. She listens to Lutyens's worries that real flags will 'get bedraggled and smear the Cenotaph' and takes him to Hampton Court for the comfort of exploring Wren's work. He feels that Wren was badly treated, too; it seemed the lot of architects. 34 Hill Street is to have its epitaph in the first issue of *House and Garden*. (The reason that Lady Sackville is not perhaps appreciated among her innovative contemporaries like Lady Colefax and Syrie Maugham is that she was so jealous of her own ideas, she hated anyone to see them; she forbade Lutyens to bring other decorators to her houses, feeling they would copy her ideas.)

At the end of the summer of 1920, the Lutyenses are installed in 34 Hill Street because 13 Mansfield Street is in builders' chaos. She is *the* most understanding client. Particularly as she has 'such a big row' with Thomas and the builders in Brighton that she tries to sell it as a hotel annexe; MacNed is so contrite as to offer to sell Mansfield Street, just bought, to help her pay for the work he has instigated! – 'Oh McNed, McNed! Where have you landed me?'[12] She cold-shoulders him, refuses him dinners – but then runs into him at a lunch party 'by bad luck', and so her heart and pride melt before his pleadings and all is forgiven. All this time Lutyens is working, harder than ever, and apparently drinking too much.

A fragment of a note, which maybe she did not send, dates from this time: 'Please, Nedi, don't let yourself be tempted by too many cocktails . . . You are too precious to die and I think you are shortening your life by drinking a *wee* bit too much and not going to bed earlier than you generally do. You are always sleepy in the evenings, poor dear, and I do want you to be strong and resist the temptation of cocktails and late hours.'[13] The ninth of November, two days before the Cenotaph unveiling, was his nadir: Barbara Wallace has had a miscarriage, Robert is going to Scotland to marry the Polish wife he does not approve of and Emily supports the marriage – he feels like leaving home.

At such moments MacSack's view of events is touching and loyal, compared to the self-derisory tone of his letters to his wife; the 'Great Day for Westminster Abbey' as the Dean called 11 November 1920, the day the Cenotaph was unveiled and the Unknown Warrior buried, was recorded by her with pride: 'A Great Day for MacNed', who had a special place among the bishops – she and Vita joined the party for lunch afterwards at the McKennas' house in Smith Square and later Lutyens walked them back to look at the Cenotaph and 'behaved as if he had never had anything to do with it. We remembered how he had designed it . . . alone with me . . . He asked to come home with me and rest in my "nice comfy chair", he was so tired, poor man . . .'[14] It was a winter of private terrors; Lutyens was, as usual, leaving for India in early December, until the following March. His only son, Robert, was making a marriage he did not approve of and he was threatening not to speak to Emily before he left if she went to the wedding. The moment he was leaving MacSack became ill and he was 'beside himself with fright'. He left, hoping that he would get the £1 million headquarters building for the Anglo-Persian Oil Company in Finsbury Circus.

The year of 1921 dawned in greater gloom. The Grosvenor Estates had made MacSack take down a porch MacNed had designed for 182 Ebury Street because Thomas had failed to ask their permission, Vita had gone to France in the midst of her affair with Violet Trefusis, leaving MacSack in chief charge of the little Nicolson boys, Olive Rubens was now officially mistress at Knole, and 15 February brought a depressed letter from India immediately after Lutyens's award of the RIBA Gold Medal, saying that the building would probably stop and Viceroy's House be finished in plaster.

Among all the extremes of great building projects and littlest human tragedies, Victoria Sackville was a patroness of heroic stance, for which perhaps it was she who should have been awarded a Gold Medal. It was she who gave lunches and pampered the people most useful to Lutyens, the influential Sir George Lewis, now living at The Grange in Rottingdean, which Lutyens had altered and enlarged for him, the Monds, he the Commissioner for Works; it was she who dug out Fabergé treasures for the Doll's House from her store – the 'smallest stone cat' Fabergé had ever made, and especially for her, tiny jewelled pots of roses and tulips, a miniature jade book mounted in gold, a diamond miniature to make into a looking glass, crystal bottles with enamel tops – one for the Queen's bathroom, one for whisky in the royal doll dining-room, Sèvres and Wedgwood plaques and an amber set of little bottles and miniature glasses.[15] It was she who scolded him, wisely, for spending more time on the Doll's House than on the Anglo-Persian Oil HQ; but she who fetched and carried him everywhere, to look at the Hove War Memorial (to his design), she who comforted him over his disappointment at not getting the Bank of England (it went to Herbert Baker), as he felt Lord Cunliffe, the former Chairman, had promised it to him. It is to her he moans in February 1922 when in India with the Prince of Wales, who is bored by Delhi – the only royal words were 'Good God', and to tell Herbert Baker that the whole thing should be stopped for costing too much money.[16] And then, when he returns on 14 April and she meets him at Victoria, they immediately start arguing over Sussex Square. But he spends the rest of the day designing the cover for V. Sackville-West's novel *The Heir*,[17] and it ends, in the diary: 'He wants me to lose all my personality and I won't. Never mind; he is a great darling, but I want to be more independent of him.'[18] She assures herself that she is a more original decorator than Lutyens, and this is perhaps corroborated by a press cutting she kept, describing 182 Ebury Street: 'If you are fortunate enough to know Lady Sackville, you get your Italy for nothing. You reach it through an old panelled hall full of such joys as dreams are made of – cabinets of tortoiseshell and ivory, *petit point* tapestries, treasures from the Wallace Collection arranged as only an artist can arrange them, glass of the most satisfying colours catching the sun through old windows round the frames of which ivy leaves and jasmine call you to the loveliest little garden in London.' This last would have pleased her, for *this* garden was nothing to do with Vita: 'ancient plane trees . . . and a grapevine, a deep flower border, and grass plots, and a great stone vase filled with growing blue'. Of course, it may have been even cleverer than it appeared, for MacSack had no patience with real plants, unless she sent out for them to be brought home from the florist's.[19]

The seventh of August 1922 was the Lutyenses' silver wedding, which they spent together; it seemed a peacemaking, and he gave Emily pearls, as MacSack duly noted in her diary. As soon as Emily left London he was happy to stay in Ebury Street; he admitted that he loved her comforts . . . but he was also guiltily shy 'and shook her scantily by the hand' as he left for an appointment with the King and Queen at Balmoral. For Christmas, though he was in India, he gave her six turquoise birds.[20]

Lutyens returned from India in mid January 1923, earlier than usual; though he is immediately at Brighton, and in 'good spirits', MacSack's diary explains: 'He and Emy were pleased with each other and Emy said she had never cared for him so much than since she had become a sister to him.' It does Lutyens no credit, for perhaps that something which failed in him over Lady Constance Lytton so long ago now failed again: he tells Lady Sackville 'how grateful he was for her friendship to them all, especially to him and how it had made all the difference to his life'. Perhaps he did not say that it was a harmless truce; Emily was leaving for Europe at the end of March 1923 – she went on to India and was away until April 1924.

MacSack decides that new ventures are required. She will sell the Sussex Square houses that have proved so big and expensive, and buy a seaside plot to the east of Brighton – 'The idea of a smallish house there smiles upon me.' Off they go again; after a joint site visit on 14 February MacNed makes fifteen drawings –

White Lodge-on-the-Cliff,
Roedean, Sussex: Lutyens's
sketch for Lady Sackville's last
house, with a spiral ramp down
from the road and the rooms
clustered around a big central
room with a fireplace at each end.
It was not actually built like this
and is now so much altered as to
be hardly recognizable as a
Lutyens house, but the diamond
motif, in tile and slate, still
survives in the clifftop garden.

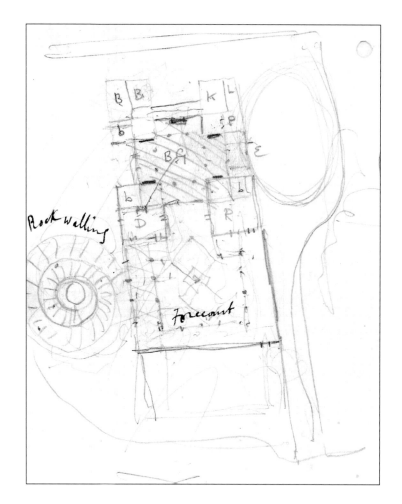

one scheme with a causeway (steep slope from road) leading to a barn, presumably existing, which would be used as the big central room, with a fireplace at each end, and her Persian tapestry hanging over one. The rest of the rooms would cluster around, with a big loggia and a big terrace and two herbaceous borders leading towards the end of the garden at the cliff's edge. On 12 March her offer of £5,000 for the seventeen acres is accepted. She decides to call it White Lodge-on-the-Cliff. MacNed's design, as usual, expands – the lodge is flanked by cottages, presenting a frontage of 200 feet to the road! Even he thinks it might be too big.

During the June of 1923 she was busy with the sale of the contents she had amassed at Sussex Square; here her true 'dealer's/collector's heart' was exposed, she loved the excitement of the sale and the new opportunities it presented. Unfortunately this sale was deeply disappointing; many of the beautiful things were treasures from the Wallace Collection which had come to her via Sir John Murray Scott – all twelve of the magnificent bronze Claude Balin vases from La

Bagatelle fetched only £1,200 – the first day's sale was only £4,500 in total and the second £1,400. For some people there were tremendous bargains, but for MacSack it was all a terrible misjudgement.

At this point her dream of building something 'very beautiful and very large' begins to recede slowly into the realm of the impossible. She is now concerned to make White Lodge pretty and comfortable but without great expense; from this moment real marble dreams are replaced by George Plank doing a great deal of *faux* marbling for her.

Through the late summer of 1923 MacNed is still regularly with her; she is much concerned with Vita, who, MacSack prophesies correctly, falls in love with Geoffrey Scott, the author of *The Architecture of Humanism*. On 23 September she is sixty-one; MacNed remembers, even though he is making 'himself pleasant' to Lord Curzon at Kedleston, who wants him to design a garden. His visit is delayed for a week, when he dines and sleeps at Ebury Street; the spectre of Millie, Countess of Sutherland, arises as she is talking of having MacNed build for her – MacNed protests 'that Millie would never be anything to him'. He is still writing a note to MacSack every day, when he doesn't see her, and pleads to show her the Doll's House – she refuses, repeatedly, hating to go to Mansfield Street, where the finished house occupies the front room, because Emily (returned from her travels) treats him 'shamefully' and 'humiliates and nags him' and the children also 'treat him with such levity'.

Though her own dreams are dying, MacSack's hard work and entertaining among her friends are now benefiting Lutyens's career as she had so hoped. The equally tempestuous Enid Bagnold was MacSack's close friend; she had met Sir Roderick Jones, the chairman and managing director of Reuters press agency at dinner in Ebury Street, and married him in 1920. Lutyens worked on their London house, 29 Hyde Park Gate – Sir Roderick was impatient, autocratic and indulgent of his new clever wife, and Lady Jones loved Lutyens's vision. The drawing-room emerged from a jumble of bits and pieces over the coach house 'as a sort of stage viewed from the dress circle. One looked down upon it over a low wall before descending the wide steps he built. All along the west side four french windows lead on to a terrace and into the garden. One peculiar pillar supports part of the ceiling. It is made of cement but appears panelled, and I remember Lutyens running his thumb down the still damp corners to blunt the sharpness – "Always do that," he said, "it adds a hundred years on." ' The dining-room, where Sir Roderick wanted to seat twenty-eight, was 'marvellous ... of a curious olive shade that Lutyens loved'. It was long, shady, stretching through the house from street to garden, lit at both ends by windows aflame with green; the tables, specially made, were marbled by Alan Walton in polished olive and charcoal, bound by a fine brass rim.[21]

After their town house, the Joneses were inveigled to Rottingdean by Sir George and Lady Lewis, their friends and MacSack's, and they bought the Burne-Joneses' North End House, other cottages and eventually The Elms, the house that Kipling had occupied. It was a buying spree around the green. 'If he could he would have bought the church,' wrote Enid Bagnold, and Sir Roderick also discovered the delights of his own planning and building. But when it was for his beloved Reuters only the best would do, and so in the early 1930s he commissioned Lutyens to build the new headquarters at 85 Fleet Street. It was to be Lutyens's last London building; he squeezed it in cleverly cheek by jowl with Wren's St Bride's, stepping back the upper storeys to protect the view lines to St Paul's.

In Lutyens's relationship with Lady Sackville, there were still moments of high farce: on 10 July 1924 they had driven to Munstead Wood, taking Miss Jekyll a chicken pie and twelve éclairs. MacSack noted, 'She had a horrid smelly beefsteak pie for McNed and me and did not offer us any of her chicken.'[22] At White Lodge there still seemed to be a lack of understanding between them: two weeks after the Munstead visit she arrived there, in Brighton, to find a pile of Portland stone at the door which MacNed thought 'would be for a beautiful Georgian entrance'. MacSack, determined not to spend money on such extravagances, when all she wanted was lovely rooms *inside* and her loggia and garden, sent the stone back. A week later, with no word about the stone, Lutyens arrived 'and put out his arms to give me a great welcome'; she wondered what was coming, but he was unconcerned, only telling her that 'he would always help me when I wanted his help' but he was a little sad that White Lodge was not now 'good enough'.

In 1925 Lady Sackville was diagnosed as diabetic, and she grew querulous and eccentric; her 1925 diary has not survived, but simply by force of circumstances Lutyens cannot have seen so much of her. He was in India until late March, then busily preparing for America to design the British Embassy in Washington, where he was for the whole of May. He was at White Lodge during the summer – it was now completed. MacSack particularly enjoyed her loggia, where she took most of her meals (even in winter, wrapped in furs), and her garden leading to the cliff edge, with an intricate sitting terrace paved with slates laid on edge (similar to the garden terrace at Gledstone Hall, the house he was building in Yorkshire for Amos Nelson). Her health was giving way, but there were still moments of flamboyant generosity; in the spring of 1926 she presented MacNed with a little grey drophead coupé Rolls Twenty, complete with chauffeur. (On 29 March, his fifty-seventh birthday, she gave him road maps as an encouragement.) MacNed went home from Brighton in it, and used it for a while just to give himself the pleasure of saying 'Home, James!' – but soon gave it up. Poor MacSack, who retreated into French when she was secretly hurt or ashamed, noted, 'Il a déjà commencé à me repayer pour le little car.' What is absolutely certain is that, great architect though he might have been, he was able neither to afford his own Rolls *nor* to accept her gift.

In many ways 1926, the year of the General Strike, is the most poignant year of their relationship. The cards are on the table. MacSack cannot build any more, indeed she has both Sussex Square and 182 Ebury Street (for which Ivor Novello offered a paltry £2,500 and was refused) on the market. MacNed, in ill-health himself, keeps up his daily note when he is away and is with her most weekends at White Lodge. With her he is a pathetic figure, with a chill, gastritis and worse, spending most of his weekends in bed, with puzzles and never-ending patience. She shares all his doubts and worries; life is the extremes of the Lewises and their bathroom at Rottingdean, and the Washington Embassy on the drawing boards and discussions with Reggie McKenna over the Midland Bank headquarters in Poultry. He loses Waterloo Bridge because it requires an 'experienced engineer' ('Alas for McNed' writes MacSack) – he gains a time-consuming commission from Lady Milner for Lord Milner's tomb at Salehurst in Sussex. He is at the beck and call of the War Graves' Commission about the Memorials for the Missing, which are still not resolved. On a June weekend he is 'exalt' about the claims of the Strikers, he talks radically, just like Emily, and proposes 'to give up everything for the good of the world'; she writes, 'If only they could agree again. I wish it for him.'[23] For most of August he is at White Lodge, apart from a visit to his sick sister Aileen at Thursley and to Lulworth in Dorset, where he is to build Weston House for the eminent doctor Sir Alfred Fripp.

In early September 1926 MacSack buys herself a new Phantom Rolls-Royce, though she hardly ever goes out; a terrible scene ensues because she remembers that A. J. Thomas 'owes' her some money from years before and she needs it to pay for the Rolls. Lutyens *has* to side with Thomas – on 16 October a long diary entry includes, 'I really intended to break off our friendship, but he lunched with McVita and said he really adored me and would do anything to get me back.' A week later, on 22 October, MacNed confesses he 'is terrified of getting blind and being a pauper when he is old and I am dead. He knows that his wife and children would forget him and neglect him . . . he is frightened of the future.'

Early in 1927, when her protégé George Plank returns from America, MacSack decides to build him a house; Lutyens designs it in the spring and hands the drawings to Plank. The house, Marvells at Five Ashes, was built, MacNed taking

Weston House, Lulworth: the newly built Weston House to the right of Lulworth Cove. It was built by Lutyens for Sir Alfred Fripp, the eminent surgeon, in 1927, and named in memory of Westonbirt in Gloucestershire, the home of Sir George Holford, who left Fripp a legacy with which he built his house. He had little time to enjoy it, for he died at Weston on 25 February 1930, leaving an endowment for an annual public lecture on 'Happiness'.

a constant interest in its progress, and MacSack paid for it. After that, her own health seems to deteriorate rapidly and she becomes increasingly distant, as her diary fades. There were, as ever, moments of returned enthusiasms, but longer and longer moments of despair.

One long, rather remarkable diary entry for 30 October 1927 is the epitaph to the MacNed and MacSack affair. She is sinking into the ills of querulous age and many allowances must be made for this: MacNed has been for the weekend, and she admits to her diary that she really has not liked his visit. All the festering incompatibilities of the preceding years come to her mind, in French and broken English. She does not want to put up with his 'naggings and scoldings'; she despairs that they cannot have a sensible conversation because he is always playing patience or doing puzzles, and when not doing these things, he draws. Many of the paper jokes she finds indecent (MacSack was fastidious in her proprieties) – 'Il me dit que ces dessins viennent de son "mond" et nullement de ses sens – Quelle curieuse mentalité!' What really hurts her is that though the jokes may be suggestive, he has no warmth for her in a physical sense – and MacNed returns to his games/patience. She feels she is required just to sit with him, in an overheated

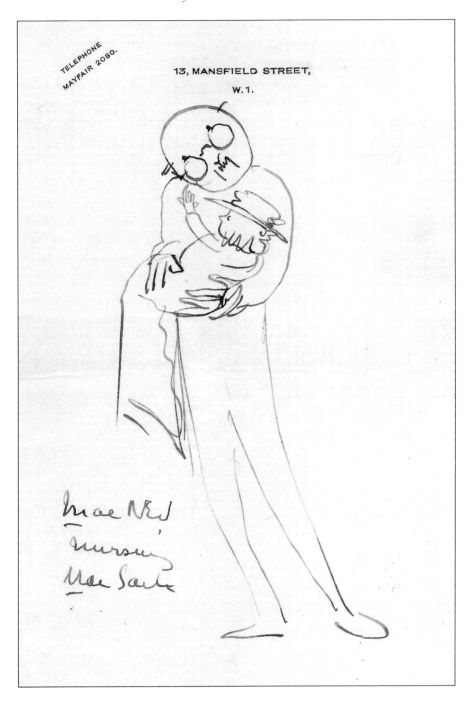

Edwin Lutyens, MacNed nursing MacSack.

room, windows shut, lights on, and tend to his incessant stream of pipes; when she complains, feels unwell, he panics – 'You *must* be well' or 'You must not give way to your nerves' – he has caught the idea of mind over matter from Emily, and MacSack duly resents that he screams at her just as Emily 'nags' Robert Lutyens. 'Alas! Alas! how long can my affection stand it.'

Poor MacSack: there was worse in store. In 1928 her husband, to whom she had consistently refused a divorce, died, and there was a tremendous and painful rift with Vita. Lutyens kept sending his habitual notes but visited less and less. What he had feared was not to be; his secret wish – and MacSack's – that Emily would return to him was granted. After a hiatus on the wires from California, where it was mooted that Mary Lutyens might marry Krishnamurti, the whole theosophical dream collapsed; Krishna dissolved the Order of the Star of the East and Emily Lutyens came home. She and her husband settled into a companionable last decade of his life. It was only poor MacSack that lived, and died, alone.[24]

XII

MORE THE DEAD THAN THE LIVING

We're here to be jolly, we're here to be fed,
But most for the honour and glory of Ned,
Who's sailing this week to the land of the ele-
phant, tiger, monsoon, Ranji, curry, and Delhi...

There are workers who have to be ready to start,
Who must be 'in the mood' for their science or art,
With every appliance at hand and utensil;
But all Neddy needs is six pipes and a pencil.

With these he is happy, provided for all,
With these inspiration is ever at call:
In the street, in the train, during soup, he'll begin it –
Your home or your tomb – and it's done in a minute.

He's always the same, as he draws or he chaffs,
And everyone likes him and everyone laughs,
From his fellow R.A.s and his ministrant Hindoos,
To the tortoise who died that his eyes might have windows.

(E. V. LUCAS, 5 December 1920[1])

Throughout the 1920s Sir Edwin Lutyens spent every winter in India; the verse quoted above was one[2] that marked the usual jolly mood of the annual farewell parties his friends gave. It interestingly reveals just the person who so infuriated Victoria Sackville for his inadequacies: the puns, jollity, pipes, patience, amusing enough to his clubbable friends at the Garrick, and to the dinner party hostesses who lionized him (seldom was a spare man so entertaining), were the heavy mask of the misery of that decade – for more than just the architect. But with Lutyens the paradox is simply demonstrated. Throughout the 1920s, while Delhi rumbled on every winter and in England Castle Drogo, started immediately before the war, slowly came together as a fragment of its intended self, out of 130 commissions, over half were for memorials and tombs. For the 1920s, Sir Edwin Lutyens's clients were more the dead than the living.

To Lady Sackville's unfinished projects were added over two dozen others, for which a great deal of drawing work was done before they were cancelled or directed elsewhere. It seemed that many Indian princes commissioned palaces which were never built, like the University of Lucknow, for which drawings were done. Big schemes – the University of London (done by Charles Holden), the rebuilding of Charing Cross Bridge and Euston Station – were hopes that were dashed. More critical failures were those associated with industry, which was surely where the new clients would be found? Immediately before the war the Directors of Vickers had commissioned Abbey House, a guest house for important visitors to their Barrow shipyards, and the names of industrial power brokers flit in and out of the list of clients. A London base for Armstrong Whitworth? The names of Sir Joseph Duveen and Sir Ernest Cassel hove into view, but faded; was there to be a hotel for Lord Leverhulme? Another hotel? The Midland Railway Hotel in Manchester? For all the signs of hope, of the new world, everything slipped into the realms of the 'unexecuted'. It was as if every new effort, every hopeful sign, slipped back into the abyss, and all that remained was another memorial or tomb.

The saddest personal loss was the death of Maude Baring. The family had managed to keep their summers at Lambay throughout the war. Just after the Armistice they had left Grange Court at Chigwell. Besides their house in Bryanston Square, Maude had a studio in Cheyne Row, where she painted in a 'highly detailed, delicate style of her own'.[3] She was taken ill with cancer in the autumn of 1921 and died on 2 April 1922. Cecil Baring and their children took her back to Lambay, into the 'kindly keeping of the island which she loved'.[4] Her coffin was covered with a crimson pall, the last offering of George Muntzer, who had helped her furnish all her houses, as he had helped Pamela Lytton, Pamela McKenna, Lutyens himself and so many of his other clients. Lutyens designed the Baring tomb among the ramparts of Lambay.

Cecil Baring, still working in the bank, also busied himself with finding jobs for Lutyens. He bought 18 Cheyne Row, which had two acres of garden stretching to the Thames Embankment, to be partly a home, partly a museum for his collection of china. Lutyens started designing 'a grey and red brick house ... well back from the river, surrounded by a garden ... an L shaped building', with a central Dutch gable over a classical portico. When Calypso Baring married Guy Liddell it was envisaged as their home, but, Daphne Baring remembered, 'Father and Lutyens had forged merrily ahead' and it was much too big and expensive for Calypso to run; she stood her ground and her father subsidized them to live in what was virtually a country house of great charm and a lovely garden – in the heart of Chelsea.

Cecil Baring had tried another house for the in-between-London-and-Lambay part of their lives; first a house called Birchville at Bushey Heath (which Lutyens does not seem to have altered) for a brief while, before he settled on Beechwood, in the centre of the then small country community of Slough, a convenient base now that Rupert Baring was at Eton. Lutyens did alter Beechwood. (In the winter of 1923 the Barings all went to India – after Christmas Day in Bethlehem – and stayed with Lutyens and Lady Emily at New Delhi.) Lutyens added to Mothe-combe House, in the Baring corner of Devon, for Cecil's cousin Alfred Mildmay, in 1923; Mothecombe, an exquisite Queen Anne house in its own beautiful estuary, was then thought to be by Inigo Jones, but is now known to be by the architect of Antony and Puslinch, both near by, a local man, nameless, but of great talent.

In 1929 the 2nd Lord Revelstoke died suddenly in Paris and Cecil Baring became the 3rd Lord Revelstoke. He never ceased to find work for his architect friend, though there were no more new ventures of his own. Lutyens altered 117 Eaton Square for his sister, Elizabeth Kenmare. The last war memorial, the Irish National Memorial at Islandbridge, Dublin, was undoubtedly connected with Lord Revelstoke and Lady Kenmare. In 1932, with eight grandchildren crowded into the little castle, came the last building, for Cecil's married daughters – the White House, called Babylon by Lutyens and built in the potato patch.[5]

It was thus the old faithful clients who warmed Lutyens's profession into life in the grim 1920s. Herbert Johnson added a large ballroom to Marsh Court at Stockbridge. And, in her diary for 3 April 1926 Lady Sackville had noted: 'McNed to Mells and Reginald McKenna. Very important.'[6]

The McKenna story is resumed with vigour in the irresistible personage of a great hero, Bernard Freyberg, VC, who entered into the lives of the Jekylls and McKennas at the end of the war. His amazing story winds the threadworking of Lutyens's clients a little more intently. Freyberg – a giant, over six foot, a champion swimmer, had left New Zealand in the spring of 1914 and after five months' adventuring, including a little fighting in Mexico, arrived in Liverpool three weeks after war had started. He had pursued his only contact, at the London office of the New Zealand press representative, who told him that another New Zealander, G. S. Richardson, whom he knew, had been newly appointed to the staff of the Royal Naval Division by the First Lord, Winston Churchill. Freyberg 'accosted' Churchill in Horse Guards and offered to serve. He was made an RNVR Lieutenant with command of the Hood Battalion, and after an abortive mission to Antwerp, the division set sail for Gallipoli. Freyberg found his fellow officers

Sir Herbert and Lady Jekyll's golden wedding, Munstead House, 1931: *seated*, Reggie McKenna, Pamela McKenna, Lady Jekyll, Sir Herbert and the young Paul Freyberg. *Standing from the left*, David McKenna, Francis 'Timmy' Jekyll, Lady Horner behind her sister's chair, and, in the checked suit, Barbara Freyberg, flanked by her McLaren sons, with Bernard Freyberg behind her. The others are friends and members of the household.

included Oc Asquith, Denis Browne, Rupert Brooke, Charles Lister and Patrick Shaw-Stewart (released from Barings to go to the war). He won his DSO for his heroic swim at Bulair, in April 1915, to lay the flares for the landing party, but he was also wounded, invalided home, and drawn into the social set of his brother officers, in particular by Violet and Cynthia Asquith.

This was how he met Violet's friend Barbara McLaren (Barbara Jekyll, married to Francis McLaren). Seriously wounded again at the Battle of the Ancre, where he won his VC, Freyberg recovered in Mrs Guest's nursing home in Park Lane; he asked to meet Lady Scott (Captain Scott was his hero, and E. W. Nelson, who had been on Scott's expedition, was in Hood Battalion), who in turn introduced him to Sir James Barrie. Barrie 'collected' Freyberg immediately into the heroic gathering of his adopted sons, and for six years they were immensely close.

Freyberg had a room kept for him in Barrie's eyrie in the Adelphi, and – he had a remarkable gentleness as the other side of his warrior's personality – he looked after Barrie when he was smitten low in 1921 after the death of Michael Llewellyn Davies. Lady Sackville's diary for 10 November 1921 noted 'McNed to Barrie after dinner' to arrange for Michael's tomb. The culmination of Barrie's love for Freyberg was the long-remembered eulogy on *Courage*, his famous Rectorial address to St Andrew's University. There was also, as she has told in her diary, the flirtation with Cynthia Asquith, Barrie's 'secretary' at this time ... which gave way to Freyberg's more serious friendship with Barbara McLaren (after Francis McLaren was killed flying in August 1917). Freyberg had another dose of war at Passchendaele, where he was again badly wounded (for the fourth time), and he married Barbara in a quiet wedding on 14 June 1922, at the little church of St Martha's near Guildford. Lutyens made them a dining-room lined with mirrors at 7 Clarendon Place, their London home; their son Paul was born in 1923, joining Barbara's sons, Martin and Guy McLaren, to make a complete family – doubled in completeness by the McKennas, Reggie, Pamela, Michael and David.[7]

Reggie McKenna gave up politics at the end of the war. He had entered the war as the Chancellor of the Exchequer and his ministerial career of eleven years ended with the fall of Asquith's Coalition; the distrust and suspicion that McKenna had for Lloyd George – kept so skilfully at a distance at Walton Heath golf course by Riddell – surfaced in the House of Commons wranglings of the war-torn Liberals. In December 1916 McKenna was fifty-four, he had filled four stormy Cabinet offices, but he was at the peak of his powers; he would not serve under Lloyd George, and in 1917 he accepted a place on the board of the London, City and Midland Bank and set out on his self-imposed apprenticeship to learn the banking business in the City. He still regarded himself as a politician, intending to keep his seat in the Commons, and as a minister-in-waiting should the call come; events chose differently, and hardly was the Peace known and his apprenticeship completed when Sir Edward Holden, his friend and the chairman at the Midland, died, on 23 July 1919, and McKenna became his successor. He was never a man for regrets, or even looking backwards, and he went firmly forward into a role 'of the kind most congenial to a man who needed to feel fully extended whether in an office or on a golf-course or at the bridge-table' with 'a superb organization to administer and a vast human service to control'. The chairmanship of the Midland, envisaged for ten years but in fact twenty-four, 'fulfilled every hope that he had entertained'.[8]

Sir Edward Holden had always been interested in the bank's buildings; he had said at his last chairman's address in 1919 that it was absolutely necessary to have good bank premises 'because a good bank with poor premises does not attract deposits in the same way as a bank with good premises'.[9] He had built over 500 new branches since 1890 with the bank's experienced architects, Whinney Son & Austen Hall of London and Gotch & Saunders of Kettering.[10] Expansion in the West End was in the air when McKenna became chairman, and the bank had acquired a prime site, the vestry hall of Wren's St James's Piccadilly; T. B. Whinney had designed a small stone building for the site and it was in the process of being approved. But chairman McKenna, instantly aware that to build *next* to Wren was the rightful job of only one man, asked Lutyens to design 196a Piccadilly as a 'test run' of what a good bank building should be. (There it stands still, ready to catch the eyes of the millions who might see it as they cross the Piccadilly pedestrian crossing – the sweetest little brick building in London, banded, quoined, swagged, pedimented, fully dressed in Portland stone, still fulfilling its banking purpose.)

The *contretemps* with Whinney was solved by Lutyens becoming the Midland Bank's designer of elevations and 'front of house', while the experienced banking architects took over for the working parts of the building. It was a role which suited Lutyens and his clients admirably, putting aside everyone's frustrations when he was gone to India, for long and regular periods throughout the twenties. The Piccadilly branch was quickly followed by the new headquarters for the Midland on the impressive Princes Street–Poultry site, next to the Bank of England, where Gotch & Saunders were the back of house and supervising architects. The system seemed to work well – Frederick Snow, a consulting engineer, remembered that Lutyens's drawings for the great façade, receding backwards and upwards from Poultry, were 'a dream to work to' . . . 'drawn more or less free-hand whilst lying on the floor, smoking his pipe' . . . 'calling things half equal, quarter equal or one-third equal until he reached the top of the building, the first example of modular co-ordination'.[11] All this, understandably, was in a purdah of concentration, guarded by an elderly office assistant. For the architectural assistants and engineers who followed, there was one overall dimension and 'one had to work out for oneself the remainder of the dimensions'. 'Even on the stonework it never quite fitted' – perhaps worked out to a 251st of an inch – but it was in this context of accuracy that the finest building standards were achieved.[12]

There was perhaps slightly more to it than accuracy and fine craftsmanship. In building for McKenna's bank Lutyens was enlarging on the tradition of building for McKenna himself. Is it fanciful to suggest that just as 36 Smith Square was unmistakably McKenna's house, so that integrity, that rugged probity and straightforwardness are also evident in the great Poultry building (which certainly out-banked the Bank of England!) and its (slightly) lesser relative in Manchester's Deansgate?

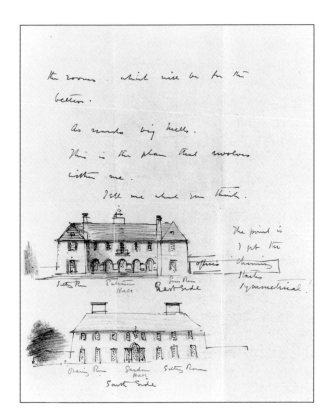

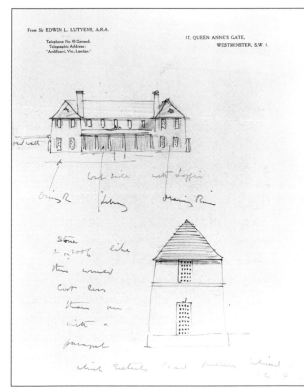

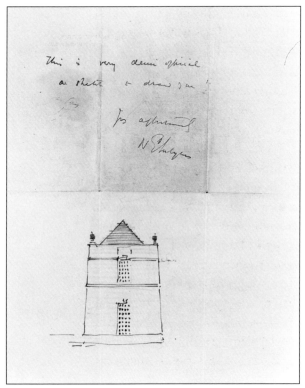

Mells Park: A letter from Sir Edwin to Lady Horner dated 6 January 1918 reveals that he tried to persuade them to rebuild after the fire of the previous year, despite Edward's death. The opening page of the letter speaks of a pair of cottages which he hoped Sir John Horner would build (he did not) and then continues:

As regards big Mells. This is the plan that revolves within me. Tell me what you think. A stone roof like this would cost less than one with a parapet which entails lead gutters behind it etc., P.T.O... This is very demi-official – a sketch to draw you! Yours affectionately, Ned Lutyens.

Mells Park, when rebuilt for the McKenna family, was to a totally different plan.

Mells Park House, Somerset, as rebuilt in 1924 for the McKenna family by Lutyens after the fire.

In April 1924 the McKenna family decided to make their country home at Mells; Reggie McKenna promised to take Mells Park from his brother-in-law, Sir John Horner, for a peppercorn, on the understanding that he would rebuild the house, badly damaged by a fire in 1917. All that was saveable was a lovely stone arcaded court at the back of the house, which had been added in the eighteenth century to make an entrance from the new stables. Lutyens's new Park House was built, almost four square, on to this court, exactly on the foundations of the old house. It is another McKenna building, spare, severe, grey stone, two storeys, hipped roof with pantiles, with only green shutters to lighten the mood. Reggie McKenna had, as usual, worked it all out on his squared paper. He liked consistency in his surroundings, and the pattern of his bedroom, bathroom and dressing-room in Smith Square was repeated at Mells Park. The enfilade of the reception rooms was also repeated, along the south-facing front, and at Mells this gave a large dining-room on the south-east corner, attached to the servery with the kitchen behind. Pamela McKenna felt that this was wasted on the dining-room, which was changed to the centre of the south front, so that meals were served across the central hall. In the new drawing-room there were big sofas around the fire, and at the south end two beautiful grand pianos; Pamela McKenna resumed her playing at Mells, and the house was filled with her music and her musical friends, including

219

Leon Goossens and Walter Elcot, the organist at Salisbury Cathedral. The McKenna boys, Michael and David, both schoolboys at Eton, had enthusiastically helped in the building; they were each presented with a silver trowel by their 'fellow builders' as a memento.

The whole rebuilding of Mells Park brought back the life and laughter. Reggie McKenna filled the house with his friends – the Neville Chamberlains, J. Maynard Keynes and his wife, Lydia Lopokova; Sir Herbert and Lady Jekyll were constantly over from Munstead (though not Gertrude, who rarely left home now), and Lutyens immediately discovered, as did Harold 'Bluey' Baker and Ozzie Dickinson, all close friends, that while the conversation was occasionally more sparkling at Lady Horner's, the food and accommodation were definitely better at the Park. The old park came into its own again; where Raymond Asquith had once been fascinated by the bulky Haldane sporting beneath the waterfall, his children joined the McKennas for sailing lessons from the chairman of the Midland Bank. The summer was for long expeditions, bathing, riding out through the generations of gardening Horners' trees to the 'steep green terraces and scented elder groves' of nearby Camelot, to the sanctuary of sheldrake and peregrine on Brean Down, to Glastonbury Tor and King Alfred's Tower. The grey village of Mells, to outward appearances 'a semblance of unbroken country peace' and tinged with the grief of its losses, was actually seething with activity: amateur dramatics, flower shows, folk-dancing, bell-ringing and always singing and music.[13]

For Lutyens the Manor House at Mells remained at least annually, and sometimes more frequently, a place of welcome and solace. Lady Horner regarded him as one of her oldest friends, for she had seen him rise from a nervous and lovelorn fledgling architect to his 1920s celebrity status. She, most of all his friends, seemed to have an intuitive understanding of the Lutyens that had designed the Cenotaph and paid such elemental elegant tribute to a grief beyond words – and yet had carried on, even jokingly, with life. Ottoline Morrell observed this in her diary – how 'with a certain amount of artistic and literary culture' Frances Horner could 'manage society, friends, a family, garden and household with ease and success' – while having 'few doubts; perhaps at times she has wondered what life comes to, but whatever the results of her questioning she has faced it bravely, and although she has had great losses ... she remains unsubdued and undaunted'.[14] In response to this assured stoicism, Lutyens was most at ease at Mells; Lady Horner never hesitated to call on him, and his unerring judgement was always appreciated.

In November 1925 Lutyens visited Katharine Asquith's close friend Mary Herbert to talk about a memorial for her husband, Aubrey, at the little church at Brushford, close to their home, Pixton Park, near Dulverton. Mary Herbert had

Sir Edwin Lutyens and Lady Horner, the oldest of friends, in the garden at Mells Manor, c. 1939. Lady Horner died in 1940; Sir Edwin died on New Year's Day 1944.

become a Roman Catholic after Aubrey's death. Katharine Asquith, strongly influenced by a friendship with Hilaire Belloc, had found consolation in Roman Catholicism and had also become converted (along with her son Julian, who became Lord Oxford and Asquith at the age of eleven, upon the death of his grandfather in 1928). Thus it is at Mells, and in the little church of Brushford, that the last great convolution of Lutyens's clients, the Roman Catholic connection, begins. It is a complex story.

Belloc, broken by the loss of so many friends in the war, became prey to a frenetic search for their salvation. He arranged for Masses to be said for Bron Herbert, Lord Lucas, even though Lord Lucas had not the slightest inclination to Rome when he was alive. It was the loss of this cousin, from which he never really recovered, that hovered over Aubrey Herbert, making him contemplate conversion, which never actually happened but played a part in Mary Herbert's turn to Rome soon after his death. Belloc also arranged for a memorial to Raymond Asquith in Amiens Cathedral, which Lutyens accompanied Lady Horner and Katharine Asquith to see,[15] and another to Edward Horner in Cambrai Cathedral.

Add to all this gentle persuasion Lutyens's experiences through the long night of all the memorials, and it is little wonder that he was, however much against his will, pondering on the devout. Something as intangible as that may have led him to the most remarkable encounter, in only too secular a setting, when he was approached by Archbishop Downey of Liverpool at the Garrick Club. Dr Downey – immensely rotund and jolly in appearance beneath his biretta, and with 'a voluminous sash' around his ample girth, had been appointed to the See of Liverpool in 1928 and was immediately concerned to get his cathedral built, to counter the Anglican cathedral by Sir Giles Gilbert Scott, which was then half-finished. Dr Downey rejected Gothicism naturally enough, but he wanted more than equal magnificence, and he wanted a dome, like St Peter's in Rome. The illustrations of Viceroy's House, now completed, would have indicated quite clearly who his architect should be (there was really no one else), and Lutyens was summoned to Liverpool. He arrived just before lunch, and was shown into a large dull-gloomed room, and waited, feeling nervous and rather shy, till in came His Grace, who held out a friendly hand; the first words he said were 'Will you have a cocktail?'[16] From that moment they were greatly in sympathy; Lutyens came away with the commission for a cathedral on Brownlow Hill. He started work immediately, picking up on the complex arches of Thiepval rather where he left off, drawing in an office set up in the racquet court behind 13 Mansfield Street, for the whole project to be kept a secret. The Cathedral of Christ the King was to be twice as large as St Paul's, second only in size to St Peter's, and the span of its dome would be larger than both. He began drawing in 1929 and the design was revealed for the first time in 1930. This was one of the happiest times of his life.

The world of Irish Catholic Liverpool was far away from the intellectual Catholicism in the air at Mells. Evelyn Waugh had been received into the Church on 29 September 1930 (he would marry Mary Herbert's daughter Laura in 1937). His teacher and confessor was a Jesuit, Father Martin D'Arcy. It is Father D'Arcy who becomes the charismatic key figure in the final act of the long-playing Mells connection to Lutyens's career.

Father D'Arcy was an embodiment of 'intellectual energy and passionate conviction'[17] who reminded those who knew him of the young Cardinal Newman. He was the youngest son of a barrister, educated at Stonyhurst, and had become a novice at eighteen. Full of 'proper ambition', he read Classics then Ancient History and Philosophy at Oxford and left in 1916 to return to teach at Stonyhurst – where he had a formidable influence:

> In mathematical classes,
> O, look after me,
> And especially in D'Arcy's, O Star of the Sea.[18]

D'Arcy was ordained in 1921. He was sent to Rome, where it was realized that the 'atmosphere' did not suit him, so he returned to Oxford and was eventually made Master of Campion Hall in 1933. It was the perfect setting for him, for he was essentially English, deeply traditional and nostalgic, with a real passion for the Stuart cause which pervaded his everyday life, down to his tastes in painting, furnishings and architecture. His additional 'cause célèbre' was the poetry of Gerard Manley Hopkins.

When D'Arcy came – or returned – to Campion Hall as Master, he replaced the unworldly, 'shy and anxious' Father Ernest Vignaux, who had conducted overtures towards a new building, to the extent of preliminary drawings by a Birmingham architect. Father D'Arcy was unsure about the plan (for a site off St Giles), but interestingly it was the practical aspects that worried him, not the aesthetic nor the theological. He consulted the manager of Claridges, Mr Gelardi (whose son/sons had been at Stonyhurst), on the 'hotel' aspects, and then, fortunately, Lady Horner, who he knew managed her house so well. Lady Horner's suggestion was 'Why not ask my friend, Ned Lutyens?'[19]

To find out how Father D'Arcy knew Lady Horner, we have to turn to Evelyn Waugh's *Life of the Right Reverend Ronald Knox*. Ronald Knox was at Summerfields school in Oxford with Edward Horner and the Grenfells, and went on with them to Eton and Balliol; from there, in January 1909, he had first visited Mells with Edward. Knox's spiritual journey took him into the Church – he was ordained an Anglican priest but received into the Roman Church in September 1917. He was deeply affected by the loss of so many of his closest friends in the war, and Edward Horner's death naturally took him back to Mells.[20] (He was also a close friend of Belloc.) He was appointed Chaplain to Oxford University after the war, and had met D'Arcy on his return from Rome.

With few prevarications, Lutyens's opinion of the proposed Campion Hall was 'low'. He agreed to help Father D'Arcy decide on the best of three further possible sites, which they walked. Lutyens's opinion was that the site of Micklem Hall, a lodging hall for Christ Church, in Brewer Street, next to the Cathedral Choir School, would be the best. It was also adjacent to the Old Palace building of the Roman Catholic Chaplaincy in Rose Lane, so Ronald Knox was a near neighbour. A new site gave Father D'Arcy the opportunity for a new architect, and he asked Lutyens to recommend a young man. He recalled that Lutyens answered, 'Why did I not ask him?' 'But you are far too expensive,' replied D'Arcy – but Lutyens, seeing perhaps his only chance for an important building in Oxford, said that he was so keen that he would charge only the minimum. D'Arcy was delighted, but kept to himself the thought that he was 'glad that I had Lady Horner to check extravagance. She had . . .

given him the chance as a young man, and so could control' him and 'watch that he did not land me into debt or too expensive ventures'.

Even in the early 1930s, Oxford did not accept new buildings easily. There were the ancient courtesies of neighbours, Pembroke College and St Peter's Hall, to be accomplished – Dr Chevasse of the latter coldly quoting Anglican–Catholic disputations over the cathedral site in Liverpool – which took time for Father D'Arcy to clarify. Physically, also, the site was restricted: they had to preserve Micklem Hall – D'Arcy had found a Tudor-style panelled room there which he coveted for a Common Room which had to be accounted for, and Micklem Hall also harboured death watch beetle and the whole structure had to be strengthened for its new life. Into the tight corner had to go the Hall of Residence for thirty students, library, refectory and chapels – the High Altar obviously had priority, but so did the prevention of the smell of food permeating the Library, and the organization of the feeding. Lutyens, at D'Arcy's insistence, designed special trolleys for the kitchen, and there could of course be no steps to intervene. A washing-up machine and water softener were a priority and discussed in the same breath as fittings for the Chapel. All these things were accomplished under the watchful, critical gaze of the City Engineer (let alone the archaeologists), as cellars, pipes, drains, electricity and telephone connections were inserted into the ancient surroundings. Lutyens, it must be said, was immersed in every detail – even to the design of toilet brushes.

The foundation stone of the new Campion Hall was laid on 24 November 1934 by Lady Horner's grandson, the young Lord Oxford. The contractors appointed were Messrs Benfield & Loxley of Oxford. To mark the building 'in a manner worthy of its distinction', Evelyn Waugh wrote his biography *Edmund Campion: Jesuit and Martyr*.[21] His dedication continued: 'to mark the joy of the occasion and my gratitude to the then Master to whom, under God, I owe my faith'.[22]

The building of Campion Hall, as building goes, was a joyful process. It was masterminded, with Father D'Arcy's passionate but intermittent interest, by the treasurer and Senior Tutor of Campion Hall, the Revd Father Leslie Ignatius Walker.[23] Walker was the opposite of the mercurial Master; he was of rugged, magnificent presence with 'the authority of a genial volcano'.[24] He was very interested in building and understood the intricacies of plans and levels, and he exerted a natural authority over everyone concerned, even, to some extent, the eminent architect, with whom he had an excellent relationship. 'As to the room,' Father Walker wrote to Lutyens on 5 December 1934, 'have you considered where the bed is to go? What with the doors and cupboards and washing basin, I don't quite know where the bed can be conveniently fitted in.'[25]

By March 1935 the roof was 'advancing rapidly'; the builders had presented their fourth certificate and about half of the eventual cost of £34,000 had been paid. Once the roof was on, the complex interior works began. For the architect there was a great deal of designing of fittings – the careful arrangement of drawers and chests for the sacristy, the pews for the chapel with their bright orange lintels to warn of tripping in the dim light, the wonderful cardinal's biretta chandeliers. In the dining room/refectory, where meals were taken in silence or with a reading, there are ingenious and unique napkin holders for the inmates.[26] There are four bells located around the building for meals, because a single bell would have had to have been so loud that the neighbouring choir school would have complained (the inmates of Campion Hall have learned to live with boisterous choristers let out to play!). There were necessarily altercations, changes of mind which infuriated someone, but the general tone of progress, which was speedy for a Lutyens building and entirely due to Father Walker, was suitably Christian in tone, with a continual offering of olive branches: one particular disagreement seemed to be over chairs. On 14 August 1935 Father Walker wrote to Sir Edwin personally – setting the following scene in 'a confessional in the Crypt of the new Liverpool Cathedral'. The Priest was invisible, the Penitent's feet were showing beneath the screen:

PEN: I accuse myself of being very angry with one of my clients.
PR: Did you use bad language?
PEN: So, so.
PR: For your penance go to the showroom of the firm from whom you are advising him to purchase furniture and gaze for ten minutes on the armchairs which are there displayed.

The chairs, from the firm of a Mr Worth in New Oxford Street, were 'about the size you would put in a doll's house!', according to Father Walker. He decided upon unilateral action and went to Amersham and High Wycombe manufacturers, Lutyens eventually accompanying him, and they found a chair they both approved.

The care over details at Campion Hall was endless: Lutyens designed the coat of arms for the silver, every mantelpiece had a design of its own as well as the clock above it (six clocks were designed, all different), 'the door handles were some distance from the side, so that a special instrument was needed to pierce the wood' – but, Father D'Arcy continued in his reminiscence of the building, 'though so individual in his detail', Lutyens was 'generous in admitting the work of others ... the diamond-written poem on the glass of the door leading into the garden' was by Laurence Whistler ... the murals in the ante-chapel were painted by Daphne and Arthur Pollen. Father Walker, when the builders had left, transformed the building yard into a garden 'with a pre-Raphaelite look'.

Campion Hall, Oxford, the platform party for the opening. *Back row*: Miss Robinson, Evelyn Waugh, Lady Horner, Katharine Asquith, Mary Herbert. *Front row*: the architect, Father Martin D'Arcy, the Duke of Berwick and Alba, the Vice-Chancellor and Revd Ronald Knox.

All the principals who had contributed to the new Campion Hall were present in the garden court for the dedication and opening on Friday, 26 June 1936 (featured in *Country Life* next day). Father D'Arcy had invited a descendant of James II, the Duke of Berwick and Alba, to perform the ceremony.

At Mells, Lutyens's other family, the McKennas, were coming to the end, by this time, of their fifteen-year lease on Mells Park. The death of the eldest McKenna boy, Michael, on 6 October 1931, aged only twenty-one, had saddened their lives; melancholy seemed pervasive at Mells. Sir John Horner died in 1937, and so it was agreed that the park and its trees tended by generations of his ancestors should be sold. Reggie McKenna also felt that he should be nearer London, so he found the site of an old castle, Halnaker in West Sussex, and commissioned Lutyens to build the third, and final, McKenna house, which descended in layout and personality from its predecessors.

Lady Horner died in 1940 and is buried in Mells churchyard; Lutyens had designed the tombstones for her and Sir John. He also designed the McKenna family grave. Reggie McKenna died in London on 6 September 1943, aged eighty,

Campion Hall, Oxford: a general view of the opening in the garden courtyard which shows the façade of Lutyens's only building in Oxford.

and Pamela McKenna died two months later. The Halnaker house was inherited by their son David, who reluctantly decided, amid the changes of the Second World War, that he could not keep it – he was approached by Mr Redmond McGrath, who was determined to have it, and did. There was a kind of justice: David McKenna, who remembered sailing summers of his youth when the McKennas had rented Menabilly at Fowey, had fallen in love with Cornwall; he and his wife Cela found a perfect house for themselves, and lived happily there ever after. As I write they are there still.

After her mother's death Katharine Asquith made a small Catholic chapel at Mells. Lady Horner had perfectly understood the conversion of Katharine and her son Julian, but the conversion of her daughter Lady Helen Asquith, received into the Church of Rome by Mgr Knox at about the time Campion Hall was finished, left her feeling 'deserted'. In 1947 Mgr Knox came to Mells to end his days; he is buried in the churchyard and nearby is Siegfried Sassoon who wished to be buried near him.

❧ XIII ❧
THE GREATEST CLIENTS OF ALL

> The pretentious buildings of the Viceroy's House and the Secretariat
> are of no known style. Made of tongue-coloured stone, which retains
> the dry heat of the day and throws it out angrily at dusk, they appear,
> at the far end of a processional drive, like a city built for an exhibition.
>
> (CECIL BEATON)[1]

In New Delhi the Viceroy, Lord Irwin, and his Court moved into Viceroy's House during 1930. The move was celebrated in January 1931, and after the formal dinner Lutyens quietly took his leave, pausing for a moment to kiss the wall of his House. In their architect's eyes the Irwins, Edward Wood and the former Lady Dorothy Onslow, were by far the best people for his building; he liked them tremendously and had stayed with them several times. The observant Robert Bernays noted that they were refreshingly unstuffy and allowed relaxation of the stiffly imperial etiquette – to the extent of lessening the number of ritual curtseys from seven to three – but if Lutyens liked them because they had the human touch, he also liked Lord Irwin because he was 'a charming, patient and *pukka* aristocrat'[2] and could get away with things. These qualities, wrote Andrew Roberts in *The Holy Fox*, saw him through those eighteen months when moving house was hardly high on his list of priorities; throughout 1930, the Viceroy was coping with the bombings, riots and mutinies of the Civil Disobedience Campaign of the Congress Party, and it was Lord Irwin's conciliatory charm which brought the wiry, semi-naked figure of Gandhi striding up the steps of the brand-new Viceroy's House. At the moment the Representative of the British Crown moved into his palace in India, India herself set out on the road to independence. The Irwins, at the end of their Viceregal term, left on 18 April 1931. Of their farewell ball, Robert Bernays had noted the warm night, the soft music, the fantastic setting of gardens and fountains and the lights of the new House, brilliant clothes – 'it seemed as if old Versailles had come to life' ... it was 'the kind of atmosphere that must have pervaded the closing years of the Second Empire'.[3] He was uneasy then as to how much longer the Indian Empire had, and in less time than it had taken to build Viceroy's House

228

Viceroy's House, New Delhi: the view from the Imperial portico of the Jaipur Column and Herbert Baker's Secretariat blocks, photographed by Cecil Beaton in 1944, awaiting the end of the Indian Empire.

it was all over. Cecil Beaton's impatience with the heat, the mirage-like qualities of it all, 'the distance of endless halls and marble enfilades', the 'long empty avenues and spacious vistas', was evoked by all the hard work of the late war years. In 1947 the Mountbattens, the last Viceroy and Vicereine, left Lutyens's great House for good.

Though the building of Viceroy's House occupied Lutyens for twenty years, and almost a quarter of that time was spent travelling or in India, it is a story that does not belong in a book on his clients.[4] Apart from Lord Hardinge's initial interest and Lord Irwin's final pleasure, the Viceroys as clients were passing through – Lords Reading and Chelmsford were far more interested in other things, Lady Willingdon (the Willingdons followed the Irwins) drove Lutyens to distraction with the changes she made – and also they were not paying. The British taxpayers were paying, something apparently in the order of £1,000,000, noted in 'a short statement' in the files in New Delhi as 14 million rupees (the architect commented that it was less than two battleships). Unlike the British School in Rome, with its labour and materials from England, at least it was built by Indians

229

with Indian materials. Lutyens called Hugh Keeling, the chief engineer, the 'veritable mother' of New Delhi, but 'the actual work of construction was parcelled out among many Indian contractors, Hindu, Muslim and Sikh. Some of them were already well established; others grew as the buildings went up. Most of the work on the main building was entrusted to Haroun-al-Rashid. The forecourt was done by Sujan Singh and his son Sobha Singh.'[5]

The building itself, stripped of its imperial symbolism but still profusely adorned with the lotus, cobra, elephants, sacred bulls and bells of the Delhi Order, the *chhajja* and the *chhatris* which Lutyens refined from Indian traditions, is now Rashtrapati Bhavan, the much loved home of the President of India. The only English ornament that remains is Sir William Reid Dick's bust of the architect which still stands in the Staircase Court; the architect too is much loved. Rashtrapati Bhavan, as an Indian house, a place where her 'distinguished sons and daughters are honoured', is now also much visited and the subject of a new guide for visitors. The author, H. Y. Sharada Prasad, ends his description:

> 'Architecture, more than any other art,' wrote Lutyens to the imperial apologist Valentine Chirol, 'represents the intellectual progress of those in authority.' Lutyens wanted to leave the stamp of British authority on India's brow. But India has managed to leave its stamp on the brow of the building he built. Rashtrapati Bhavan is a British building but one 'built in India for India'. It remains a shining addition to the long line of great buildings in India, some built by born Indians and others by those who came from outside.[6]

In the perspective of his other clients and patrons, the building of Viceroy's House elevated Lutyens to the status of an international architect, while it supplied neither the financial reward nor the supportive commissions to make him so. At home, as has already been mentioned, influential people were wary of giving him work because they felt it would suffer for Delhi – as the British School and Dublin and Johannesburg galleries undoubtedly did. In India there was a flurry of attention from every fabulously wealthy prince and maharajah – Bikanir, Jaipur, Baroda, Hyderabad, Kapurthala, Nawanagar, Kashmir. Many of them demanded houses too, but few other buildings were ever built. In fact, Lutyens gave to Delhi far, far more than he ever earned in return, in any way. He did not relish 'internationalism'; his other forays to prestige overseas, the British Embassy in Washington, work in Rome or Spain or France, did not catch his heart, and in Dublin and Johannesburg it was he who was conferring the favour. What was so special about Viceroy's House for Lutyens? For undoubtedly it took from him his prime, his vintage years. He becomes an architect of a brilliant beginning and an eminent end, but of very little in between.

That in between was occupied by the war, the memorials and Delhi. That time in his life, from the spring of 1912 and his first voyage to India to his farewell in January 1931, is curiously paralleled by Emily Lutyens's enmeshment in theosophy, and her spiritual pilgrimage towards the Star in the East. It was during the summer of 1911 that Emily conceived her worshipping love for the two Indian boys, the fifteen-year-old Krishnamurti and his younger brother Nityananda, whom Mrs Besant had brought to Europe. Krishnamurti was to be the 'vehicle for Christ', the World Teacher.[7] Emily's mysticism completely excluded her husband; they talked of divorce, but rather than that he let her have her own way, her freedom to devote her time and travelling to the cause. It has always seemed a peculiar coincidence that they both turned their eyes, separately, eastwards at the same time, but was it not more likely that Lutyens so welcomed the Delhi commission because it allowed him something in common with his wife? Emily embraced much of Indian philosophy, vegetarianism and politics, and her very connection with Mrs Besant and the movement for independence caused hurtful conflicts with her husband's role. His acceptance of the British Embassy in Washington seems tinged with the joy of having a job in America, where Emily was spending so much time. And in the late twenties, when Emily was much in India with the Star of the East Order, Lutyens 'courted' her again from a new perspective. So much so that she realized, after Krishna had publicly dissolved the Order and resigned from the Theosophical Society in the summer of 1929,[8] that she had sacrificed 'a very wonderful human love' to her theosophical absorption. They were together in India for that last visit, and Emily never visited any of her radical friends. Lutyens had created a great building for India, full of elemental beauty inspired by eastern thought and his own genius for a kind of universal humanism. Perhaps, in the final degree, he refined the astounding beauty of Viceroy's House out of his deep, illogical loyalty to his wife. In the end Viceroy's House is an offering of love, in return for twenty years of neglect and cruelty caused by Emily's infatuation. The idea that it should rank with the Taj Mahal would not have been lost on its architect.

At home, the building of Viceroy's House is almost exactly paralleled by the building of Castle Drogo, another dream dashed by the war which ended in inadequate compromise. The client for Drogo, Julius Drewe, must be Lutyens's most curious client, but in the end his too is a tragic tale that evokes only sympathy. In the golden days of 1910 Drewe had commissioned his brand new castle in Devon, to be built to medieval traditions. The idea of a castle perplexed and infuriated his architect – who wanted to build a nice, big house – but with a budget of £50,000 and another £10,000 for the garden, Mr Drewe was naturally irresistible.

Lutyens rose to the challenge; he cavorted with the Drewe family on a picnic planned to examine the site. They found a granite outcrop overlooking the valley of the River Teign which was just waiting for a castle atop it, and they plotted the course of the entrance road across a field of mangolds.

The castle was to be the monument to Julius Drewe's atavistic dreams, and they were curiously wrought. He – Julius Charles Drew (without the final *e*) was born in 1856, the son of a distinguished if pernickety cleric, the Revd George Smith Drew, Hulsean Lecturer at Cambridge, and his wife, Mary Peek. Both the Drews and the Peeks had prosperous grocerly connections (Meredith & Drew, and Peek, Frean & Company, come immediately to mind), and Julius Drew left school at seventeen to be apprenticed to his uncle Francis Drew's tea-importing company. The young Julius was sent to China to learn the tea trade, and soon, like his contemporaries Lipton and Sainsbury, realized that money was to be made by direct selling through a chain of his own shops. He opened his first shop in Liverpool in 1878, and five years later he and his partner, John Musker, moved to London, where their enterprise, the Home & Colonial Stores, prospered.

By 1889, when Drew was thirty-three, the stores were so successful that both partners could retire as country gentlemen, though keeping their substantial holdings. Unlike Lipton and Sainsbury, Drew did not wish to see his name on paper bags and packaging and known throughout the nation. He had contrived to make his fortune and keep his privacy, but the real reason was that Julius Drew was not happy with the name he had.

In 1890 the discreet and fortunate Julius married Frances Richardson, the daughter of a cotton manufacturer at Buxton in Derbyshire. They chose Culverden Castle in Tunbridge Wells, a battlemented former lookout tower in the grounds of Decimus Burton's Great Culverden, as their first home. Here three sons, Adrian, Basil and Cedric, were born, in 1891, 1894 and 1896 respectively.

Spurred on by the thought of his sons – and particularly the eldest, Adrian, whom he adored – having the inheritance of English gentlemen, Julius Drew began to take his ancestry more seriously, to the extent of commissioning a genealogist (with his brother William) to research on their behalf. Thus the link with the Drews or Drewes of Elizabethan Devon, namely one Edward Drew of Sharpham near Totnes, sometime Recorder of London and Sergeant at Law to Queen Elizabeth I, who had built Killerton House at Broad Clyst near Exeter, where he and his wife are commemorated. Edward Drew's eldest son was knighted – Sir Thomas – by Charles I, and he moved his family from Killerton to Broadhembury near Honiton. Here they stayed, at some time becoming Drewes with an extra *e*, until the late 1890s when, with beautiful timing, the last Drewe died, allowing Julius and William to buy the Broadhembury land in 1901 and dramatically enlarge a house in the village in a picturesque Tudorbethan style as William's residence. Julius and his family had now moved into Wadhurst Hall in East Sussex, a flamboyantly large 1870s hunting lodge, the former home of a Spanish banker, Adrian de Murietta, and his clan. Here two daughters, Frances and Mary, completed Julius's family, and his splendidly comfortable house and large and beautiful park allowed for an elegant country life, while the boys were sent to Eton.

There is an additional strangeness in Julius Drew's obsession with his background, for he was undoubtedly to all appearances a gentleman. He was stocky in build, not tall, with intense dark brown eyes and dark hair and a dark moustache contrasting with his pale, well-pampered skin. He loved his country life, he was a keen fisherman, passionately so, both interested in and efficient at managing his land (he planted thousands of trees in Wadhurst Park); he was a kindly employer, adoring father and appreciative husband. His entrepreneurial energies, however, were undoubtedly not sated by society and comfort, and these must have enforced his fastidious attention to details of his past and present. He was beautifully dressed in expensive tweed suits, *never* worn with a matching waistcoat, but always one of a rather dandy lighter shade, with a soft, knitted tie and diamond tie-pin and cream silk shirts. The days at Wadhurst were a leisured ritual – two-hour sittings for meals, interspersed with business, walks and dressing for dinner. Frances Drew was always beautifully dressed too; she was tall, slim and quiet with downcast eyes, Julius's constant shadow and companion. In 1910, when for a moment all three boys were in C. H. K. Marten's House at Eton, Julius quietly added the required *e* to Drewe, and Adrian, Basil and Cedric emerged as gentlemen of lineage, all grocerly connections expunged.

But Julius Drewe's obsession drove him on, even away from all the comforts of Wadhurst Park. The genealogist had taken his line far back to a possible connection with Drogo or Dru, one of William the Conqueror's henchmen, and a mythical Drogo de Teigne or Teynton, who had given his name to the village of Drewsteignton on the northerly edge of Dartmoor. Another coincidence, which Julius must have regarded as fateful, was that his wife's cousin, the Revd Richard Peek, had been the rector at Drewsteignton from 1895 to 1904, and through this contact the Drewes visited the area, loved its beauty and discovered land for sale. He was able to buy 450 acres south and west of the village, including 'The Rector's Twenty Acre Fir Plantation' which was to be the actual site for the castle he decided to build,[9] to amend the oversight of past generations who had failed to leave him one.

Lindisfarne and Lambay seem to have indicated to Drewe that there was only one architect for his castle. Cecil Baring was also involved, for he arranged for

Castle Drogo: perspective of the finished (but incomplete) castle by Cyril Farey, 1923.

Lutyens to make a tour of Flete, the home of his Mildmay cousins, and to see Cotehele while Lutyens was investigating the Duke of Bedford's plans for a new village near Endsleigh (which came to naught). Drewe would have liked the idea of employing the same architect as the Duke, Devon's premier landowner.

For Lutyens, starting a castle from a bare rocky outcrop was rather different from renovating the medieval models; from the start neither client nor architect seemed quite sure of what should be built or how far the proffered £60,000 would stretch. The first plans were for a castle on the Orchards plan of thirteen years before – around a square courtyard, entered on the north through a portcullis arch between the chapel and servants' hall – instead of an arch between Julia Chance's studio and the stables as at Orchards. The main rooms would be in the south-facing wing, entered through a long, low lobby, like Marsh Court and Heathcote, with dining- and drawing-room and great hall windows rising above the wooded gorge. In a second version the north wing was removed, leaving a U-shaped castle, each wing having a cruciform end, one for the chapel, the other for kitchens. The third manifestation of Drogo was an enlarged version in reverse of Goddards, the home of rest at Abinger of 1900, with the wings splayed each side of the north entrance courtyard. This last version, with a south range of principal rooms which bore a remarkable similarity to Philip Tilden's Bristol Central Library,[10] was more or less accepted – site clearance and pegging out started and Julius Drewe laid the foundation stone on his fifty-fifth birthday, 4 April 1911. Almost immediately he came to a stark realization of the enormous extent of his castle, and decreed it should be cut in half – only the eastern half of the splayed wing design should be built.

The hero of the building of Castle Drogo was Drewe's agent, John Walker. It seems certain that without Walker's exacting standards and experience, his stamina and determination and loyalty to his employer, there would have been no castle. He was a Yorkshireman, trained as a stonemason, and he had worked at Welbeck Abbey before moving to Devon. He lived in Drewsteignton, in a house called Hillside, with his wife and family, and drove to the site every day in his pony and trap. He had a site office built of rough timbers cut from the site and thatched, and from here he was the essential link with Drewe, to whom he wrote a weekly letter on progress, including the wages figures. He also dealt with Lutyens's office, most usually through A. J. Thomas, the office manager, with the builders, Lewis Bearne of Newton Abbot, and with other main contractors, especially the stone suppliers. Lewis Bearne had 100 men on site continually for the first four years, and another forty men were employed directly by Drewe's Estate in the site quarry, sand and gravel pits and roads.

Castle Drogo: Drewsteignton, Devon: Julius Drewe, Lutyens and John Walker on the site.

John Walker's story of the building of Castle Drogo is told in his eight letter books still at the castle; they each contain 1,000 faded, browning tissue copies of all his letters, from 10 May 1912 up to 10 September 1929.[11] Drewe was a kind employer, but he was an absentee one; the architect was not much present. Walker's letters are models of unfailing patience, attention to every detail, polite, taciturn commentary on events, progress and setbacks. Through that first winter of 1912–13 the conditions on this site, a bleak, exposed and lonely outpost, could have been little improvement on those in the granite quarries of Princeton Prison, where some of the stone came from. The masons and labourers worked all the hours light allowed, starting at seven in the morning: on 17 March 1913 Walker reported, 'Since Friday morning we have had some very heavy storms, and rough wet weather, but I keep the men on the walls whenever possible.' The men had two half-hour breaks for meals, lunch and high tea, taken in the rough log Luncheon House. Drewe also provided a Reading Room, and he encouraged a site football team – which the punctilious Walker vetoed, saying the money was needed to redecorate the Reading Room. Over 100 men must have lived on site; despite the amenities there were constant comings and goings, and it was especially difficult to keep skilled stone-cutters, who longed for jobs nearer their own homes.

Walker also had to contend with erratic supplies of drawings and information

236

from Lutyens's office – the architect was so often away in India. Juggling the supply of stone also kept him busy; he wrote endless lists specifying exact sizes and quantities – the rubble came from the site quarry, but the vast quantity of cut stone required was often difficult to locate. Three main suppliers were used, the Princeton United Stone Quarries, Eastons of Exeter and H. T. Jenkins of Torquay – the last company dealt in finest marbles and polished stones, and were to do many of the war memorial contracts for Lutyens.

Some idea of the size of this vast operation can be gauged from Walker's letter of 6 October 1913 to Drewe about the foundations for the buttressed walls of the forecourt – 'concrete spreading 5 feet on each side of the wall – which is itself 10 feet thick at the bottom, making a foundation 20 feet wide'. 'I shall expect to dig about 6 or 7 feet [down],' he added, 'and to get this out in sections, put in the concrete and fill up with rubble walling to ground level again to prevent the ground above from slipping into the trench, as we have tremendous weight above.'[12] Not surprisingly, when Lutyens was alerted to this immense labour everything was stopped while it was costed, and then considerably slimmed down.

For the labourers John Walker was paid weekly, submitting his account to Drewe on Fridays without fail. Lewis Bearne's 100 men cost between £120 and £140 per week; another £40 covered the forty or so estate labourers. Accidental injury pay – half pay – was paid for short periods. Walker's own payment varied from £38 to £45 per month.

The Drewes visited occasionally, but certainly not frequently. They were presumably occupied with their leisured life at Wadhurst Hall, with travelling, fishing in Scotland, and holidays in the south of France. Adrian was now at Cambridge; the two younger boys at Eton. Work on the castle was going so well that Julius Drewe imagined that he would occupy part of it in late 1914. During the summer of 1913, when Walker reported 100° F temperatures and no rain for three months, great efforts were put into a mock-up in wood of the curtain wall and entrance lodges – a barbican which Lutyens had designed. The Drewes took one look and decided not to build any of these features.

And then, of course, August 1914 changed the story of Castle Drogo as it did everywhere else. Much of the labour force thought that the army would be more interesting than the bleak, laborious building site, but soon the names inscribed in John Walker's account book were more permanently inscribed in the war graves registers. Work sputtered on, until the site was finally closed down on 17 January 1917. Walker moved his family to Wadhurst, where he concentrated on selling estate timber for the war effort. On 1 May 1917 he returned to the castle to see how things were – 'Today at Castle Drogo it is summer,' he wrote. There were traces of the hard winter, but inside it was warm and dry. A little work was done during the summer. And then the blow came. Adrian Drewe, serving as a Major in the Royal Artillery, was killed at Ypres on 12 July 1917. All his father's hopes and dreams had been raised on this handsome, clever son – and neither Julius nor Frances Drewe was ever able to recover from the blow of losing him. Shortly afterwards, Julius Drewe had a slight stroke and he was a partial invalid for the rest of his life.

When the war was over, building started up again. Basil Drewe, the second son, came home with a Military Cross and stepped into his brother's shoes, taking an interest in the castle's progress. The Drewes took a house in Torquay to be nearer things. Walker's letters show that wages alone for work from 1912 to May 1916 had cost them £42,000, to which has to be added the cost of the stone. Though costs were now so much greater, Drewe was still a rich man, and he was determined to carry on. Though so much of the heart had gone out of his great dream, he would see it through. On 22 December 1925 the last stone was placed and the giant crane that had always loomed over the castle was dismantled.[13] Two years afterwards the Drewes came to their ancestral home, but by that time Julius was a sick and broken man. He died at his house in Torquay, Kilmorie, four years later, on 10 November 1931. John Walker had died the same year.

Lutyens had no friendship with Julius Drewe as he had with so many other clients; the two men never really came to know one another. That they so often had different ideas is illustrated by the mystery of the garden at Castle Drogo. Lutyens introduced Drewe to Miss Jekyll in 1915, and their first triumph was the refinement and planting of the entrance drive. One idles through the Devon lanes and suddenly arrival is certain, into the embrace of the beech hedges; the drive extends an invitation by its direct rise through buttresses of dark green, and then comes the masterly, gradual unfolding of expectation around the curve – and lo! the southward fields and woods are at one's feet. It is a dramatic moment. One has glimpsed Drogo's Teign country, and now the drive rolls on to the castle entrance.

Lutyens, with £10,000 to spend on a garden (the whole of Fulbrook had been built for little more), could not imagine that even a castle owner would not want a garden outside his dining-room. He designed an elaborate sequence to be seen from the east-facing windows (not a desirable garden aspect but it was all the truncated castle allowed): he buttressed up great terraces, circular at the south end to hold his favourite Heywood- and Delhi-style tiered beds of flowers. A square garden was next to the circle and directly below the castle terraces, with a walk leading to a Fig Court of aerial hedges and classical pillars. Miss Jekyll, who did not apparently take to Drewe, had no part in this design, and the garden was never made.

After the war, Drewe's sadness led him to return to familiar people. Wallaces of Tunbridge Wells had worked satisfactorily for him at Wadhurst, so they, and their designer George Dillistone, took over at Drogo, taking the idea of Lutyens's garden but neither the site nor the geometrical finesse. The castle was given a garden series of rooms, sheltered by yew, a pleasant walk away.

It is perhaps very hard for comparatively ordinary life to outweigh great dreams and tragedies. After Julius Drewe's death his son Basil, a distinguished QC, looked upon the castle as his home, and lived there with his wife and family until his death, at the age of eighty, in 1974. His son Anthony and grandson Christopher then arranged for the castle to pass to the National Trust. It now receives 100,000 visitors during a summer season; but what do they find? On a brilliant blue day the sheer magnificence of the setting and the view, the gigantic Drewe lion and the portcullis at the entrance, the sunlight shafting down the endless corridors of pristine stone, through an ever-receding panoply of arches, and falling upon flowers and silver in the elegant rooms – all this brings a semblance of life, at least, of the measured life of long sittings at meals and quiet reveries over the port or the *Tatler* magazine. But those days are rare, and most in Devon are grey, with a hint of rain. Then, the overwhelming sadness takes over; there is a semblance of human comfort in the library and billiard room, which are most Lindisfarne-like in character, but the other main rooms are dull and drear, and even Lutyens's jokes – the naked granite frieze revealed above the dining-room panelling – fall dead. The pantries, with all their cupboards and fittings, Lutyens-designed and made by Dart & Francis, are appealing, but the dungeon-like kitchens, lit only by a corona, their chill vastness, the distant drip of water, have hardly more charm than their medieval counterparts. They strike horror into the modern heart. The source of the sadness is in the small room set aside in remembrance of Adrian Drewe. The fading mementoes of his young and vigorous life, his sporting prowess, his friends, the girl he would have married, all mock the tragedy of his death, his failing to come home to his inheritance. With all its perfection of stonework, its unbelievability, its propensity to look from a distance like a Hollywood mock-up of itself, Castle Drogo becomes one more war memorial.

By the 1930s, his seventh decade, Sir Edwin Lutyens was living the peaceful domestic life that had eluded him since the earliest days of his marriage. Lady Emily was at home, at their Adam house, 13 Mansfield Street, between Portland Place and Harley Street, and their children were out in the world and away, the situation he liked. In the racquet court, in the quiet mews behind Harley Street, he worked at his cathedral. He went to Rome in 1933 for Papal approval, and had the surety that his work was recorded in the Vatican annals; Archbishop Downey laid the foundation stone in Liverpool on 5 June 1933. It would seem that at last Lutyens had found the greatest client of all.

The others, among them his oldest friends, fell prey to mortality. Sir Herbert Jekyll died at Munstead House on 29 September 1932: at his funeral in St John's, Busbridge, his coffin was covered in crimson damask, flanked by Italian candlesticks and 'very Munsteady but dignified with his stars and orders'.[14] One who did not attend was the frail Aunt Bumps, who waited calmly for Death as 'a gentle and kindly bearer of tidings'[15] in the quiet of her room at Munstead Wood. She followed her adored brother to the family tomb a few days after her death on 8 December. Lady Jekyll died in 1937; Lutyens's tomb for all three of them has a hint of German Modernism that was very much of its day. Perhaps there was an unconscious association in his mind, for at the same time Sir Oswald Mosley, much in the headlines for launching his British Union of Fascists, commissioned the tomb at Denham for his wife, Lady Cynthia (Curzon), who died in May 1933. On a lighter note was the tomb in Melbourne for Dame Nellie Melba: they had famously met at lunch at Lady Colefax's Argyll House in the Kings Road, Chelsea, in the mid-twenties. Lutyens, faced with Melba's presence across the table, opened the conversation with 'And what do *you* do?' addressed as if to some shy nonentity. There was silence, the company waited, Madame Melba finished her fish, sipped at her glass, took a breath, and immediately hit her note – 'Mi chiamano Mimi ...' – '*That's* what I do.'[16] Lutyens had met his match; they left the luncheon party together and amused each other as friends whenever she was in London.

Old clients were tending to eccentricity or endearing whimsy. Herbert Johnson, though alone at Marsh Court, had added an enormous ballroom in 1927, and now installed a full-sized organ. Edward Hudson, having found his last home, Plumpton Place, nestling below the Sussex Downs between Ditchling Beacon and Mount Harry, was occupying his small, weatherboarded Mill House and dealing with the waterworks. The big house was a sixteenth-century moated manor but some insensitive resident had filled in part of the moat to make a causeway entrance. Hudson and Lutyens, the eternal romantics, cleared away the causeway, refilled the moat, and Lutyens designed one of his lovely timbered footbridges as the only way in, whether it was for logs or coal or dinner guests. Even more of the imagination was the 'green mansion' for Sir Saxton Noble, who lived at Batheaston and was a friend of Lady Horner's. This was a game, for Sir Saxton longed for a big house but had no money, so they planned a great hall, vestibule, portico, gallery, etc., all of yew, with a small Steward's House in the centre for Sir Saxton. To help with the garden Lady Horner introduced Lutyens to her friend Norah Lindsay, whose garden at Sutton Courtenay had made a prominent appearance in *Country Life* in May

1931[17] and perhaps he scented the idea of a new partnership? But nothing came of any of it. Two sobering thoughts arose: that the green forecourt was 'to be a monument to those who fell paying taxes' – which is how Sir Saxton felt – but also that here were two old gentlemen playing games with gardens, while the mighty Vickers-Armstrong and Armstrong-Whitworth firms, which Noble had once directed, and of which Lutyens had once had such hopes as clients, went on their way.

While the world moved on, Lutyens's eminence brought him endless consultations and a few plum projects. He was drawn into the great battle for a National Theatre and designed one for the Thurloe Place site in 1937 – and again for the South Bank site in 1942 for Edith and Oliver Lyttelton. The fountains and paving of Trafalgar Square, memorials to Admirals Jellicoe and Beatty, allowed him to 'join' his godfather Landseer's lions in that symbolic place. After a flight over London, and particularly Hampton Court, Lutyens's Hampton Court Bridge design paid his usual homage to Wren. After the death of King George V he designed the royal tomb in St George's Chapel, Windsor, and several other memorials to the King. Then came the scenery for the 1937 Coronation Ball, the Albert Hall transformed again, and the background for Gerald Kelly's portrait of the new King, George VI. With a frightening rapidity history seemed to repeat itself: the war started and the blitz destroyed London. Once again Lutyens's path crossed that of Wren, and he found himself helping to plan a new London. Sir Fabian Ware came to see him to prepare for the memorials to the dead of another war. In Liverpool, where building had stopped, the massively strong crypt, built to support the great cathedral, gave shelter from the bombing. Perhaps it was kinder that Lutyens should never know that the Liverpool blitz and the war meant that his great cathedral would never be built. He died, the drawings around his bed, on New Year's Day 1944. On the following Monday, 3 January, *The Times* noted the passing of Sir Edwin Lutyens, OM, KCIE, PRA, at the age of seventy-four. The funeral procession took his coffin past the Cenotaph on the way to Westminster Abbey on the following Thursday afternoon. The Abbey was crowded with representatives of the arts establishment, but there were many that he would not have known. Among his old clients there were Lady Chance, Sir Roderick Jones, Canon Hannay from Mells, Lady Colefax, the young Lord Wimborne, General Sir Fabian Ware, but no one else – there were none left to come. After cremation, Sir Edwin's ashes were taken to the crypt of St Paul's, and surely his adored Wren led the chorus of welcome to heaven.

In the 1930s Lutyens had had two particular clients who seemingly still inhabited the Edwardian age. One was the 9th Earl of Jersey, who married as his second wife

UNDER THE DIRECT PATRONAGE OF THEIR
MAJESTIES THE KING AND QUEEN

CORONATION
COSTUME BALL
WILL BE HELD AT THE

ROYAL ALBERT HALL
THURSDAY, 13th MAY, 1937
TO HELP TO PROVIDE A NATIONAL THEATRE

THE SETTING WILL BE "A MIDSUMMER NIGHT'S DREAM" DESIGNED BY SIR EDWIN LUTYENS, R.A. THERE WILL BE MANY SPECIAL FEATURES ✠ ✠ ✠

THEIR MAJESTIES HAVE RESERVED THE ROYAL BOX FOR THEIR ROYAL GUESTS ✠ ✠ ✠ ✠ ✠ ✠ ✠

COMMITTEE : Mrs. Kenneth Barnes   The Countess of Bessborough   Lady Bird   The Duchess of Buccleuch   Lady Colquhoun of Luss   The Lady Diana Cooper   Lady Craik   The Lady Desborough   Mrs. Walter Elliot   The Countess of Erne   Viscountess Esher   Mrs. Fordham Flower   Miss Elsie Fogerty, D.B.E.   Miss Beatrice Grosvenor   The Viscountess Halifax   The Marchioness of Hartington   The Lady Hillingdon   The Hon. Mrs. Alan Lascelles   The Countess of Lytton   The Lady Moira Lyttelton   The Lady Louis Mountbatten   Lady Beatrice Ormsby Gore   The Lady Muriel Paget, O.B.E.   The Duchess of Rutland   The Marchioness of Salisbury   The Lady Stanley of Alderley   The Marchioness of Titchfield   Mrs. Geoffrey Whitworth   The Marchioness of Willingdon

CHAIRMAN OF THE EXECUTIVE COMMITTEE THE RT. HON. THE EARL OF LYTTON, K.G., P.C., G.C.S.I., G.C.I.E. VICE-CHAIRMAN THE HON. MRS. ALFRED LYTTELTON, G.B.E.✠ ✠ ✠ ✠ ✠ ✠ ✠ ✠ ✠ ✠ ✠ ✠ ✠ ✠

THE NEXT ISSUE OF TICKETS WILL BE AT THREE GUINEAS AND WILL INCLUDE SUPPER ✠ ✠ ✠ ✠

BOXES MAY BE BOOKED BY ARRANGEMENT. VERY FEW ARE LEFT ✠ ✠ RESERVED SEATS TO VIEW FROM THE BALCONY ARE ONE GUINEA, INCLUDING TAX ✠ ✠ ✠ ✠ ✠ ✠ ✠ ✠ ✠ ✠ ✠ ✠

TICKETS MAY BE OBTAINED FROM THE ROYAL ALBERT HALL ✠ THE TICKET AGENCIES ✠ THE NATIONAL THEATRE COMMITTEE, 59, PALL MALL ✠ AND FROM G. SHERWOOD FOSTER, 19, UPPER GROSVENOR STREET, TO WHOM ALL CORRESPONDENCE SHOULD BE ADDRESSED ✠ TELEPHONE : MAYFAIR 2052 ✠ ✠ ✠ ✠ ✠ ✠ ✠ ✠ ✠ ✠ ✠

AMBROSE AND HIS ORCHESTRA ✠ THE MAYFAIR ORCHESTRA ✠ TRUMPETERS ✠ PIPERS ✠ DRUMMERS DOORS OPEN 9.30 ✠ ✠ ✠ ✠ DANCING 10 - 4 a.m.

The Coronation Ball at the Albert Hall, 13 May 1937, 'to help to provide a National Theatre', was Lutyens's last great set-piece decorative scheme. Lord Lytton was the Chairman, Mr Alfred Lyttelton the Vice-Chairman, and the committee was dominated by his friends and clients.

Virginia Cherrill from California in 1937, and for whom Lutyens, helped by his son Robert, built his last great house, Middleton Park near Bicester in Oxfordshire. Middleton was famous for Lady Jersey's bathroom, all marbles and gilt, and *very* 1930s. However, in the habit of the rich English of the time, the Jerseys soon left for sunnier climes.

The other clients who seemed always Edwardian were the Wimbornes. Lutyens worked for them for twenty years, doing something that he did better than any other architect – welding a scattered, ancient habitation into a workable and comfortable place to live. It is fitting to end with the Wimbornes and Ashby St Ledgers, for here Lutyens defined the genius of a place, healed it and launched it into the twentieth century for human benefit he could not have foreseen.

Ashby is at the heart of England, where Warwickshire, Leicestershire and Northamptonshire converge. It is named for Saint Leodegarius, Bishop of Autun, who was tortured and beheaded in AD 676. The gloom of history does not reveal how his name came to Ashby, but modern historians have lighted the journey of the Catesbys, so many of whom lie underneath the floor of Saint Leodegarius's church, and who have brought the very history of England to this little village. In 1375 one John Catesby married Emma de Cranford, the heiress to Ashby,[18] and from then on the generations of Catesbys fought – the battles of York and Lancaster and on Bosworth Field; they married – de Montforts, Spencers and Throck-mortons; they collected taxes and played courtiers – all to embellish their Ashby estate and to guard their Catholic faith. Ashby was lost, forfeit after Sir William Catesby's siding with Richard III on Bosworth Field, and reclaimed, until the final disgrace of Robert Catesby's part in the Gunpowder Plot to blow up King James and his Parliament, and his subsequent death resisting capture on 8 November 1605. Ashby's manor house had been largely built by Sir Richard Catesby, either in Queen Mary's or early in Queen Elizabeth's reign: it had sheltered the Jesuit Edmund Campion, for which Sir William Catesby was arraigned before the Star Chamber, fined and imprisoned. But after the Gunpowder Plot, Robert Catesby's mother, Sir William's widow, Anne Throckmorton, was allowed to stay; though as Robert's sons both died childless, it passed out of Catesby hands and into a quiet country life under hunting and farming squires – l'Ansons, Ashleys and Senhouses. In 1903 the estate had been bought by Ivor Churchill Guest, 3rd baronet and later 1st Viscount Wimborne. Guest, enormously rich because of his father's industrial successes in the family business, Guest, Keen & Nettlefolds, was Conservative MP for Plymouth in 1900 and served in the Boer War. Then in 1906, on instructions from his mother, Cornelia, the Duke of Marlborough's sister, he crossed the floor and became a Liberal, like his cousin Winston Churchill, who also had to bow to Cornelia.

When Ivor Guest returned from the Boer War he bought Ashby St Ledgers; he had married Alice Grosvenor, Lord Ebury's daughter, in 1902, and Ashby was to be their country home. For Lutyens, his own grandiose and splendid tendencies had found an ideal client; it was to be a stormy relationship, ever smoothed by Alice, and a long one, lasting until Lord Wimborne's death in 1939. In a sense Lutyens foresaw more than one client – he imagined the whole Churchill connection, in particular Blenheim, which he longed to get his hands on, so it was important to do well at Ashby.

Once, however, he started work on Ashby, any thoughts of time-serving were subsumed into his fascination with the place. The legacy of the Catesbys was a jumble of buildings of ochre-coloured stone, prone to flaking, the small manor house divided into a hall and common room, both running north to south, a block of staff quarters, various stables and lodges with the little timbered room over the gatehouse in which the Gunpowder Plot had been hatched. In the first period of building, 1904–11, the manor house – without serious structural alteration – was made to hold a long, south-facing music-room, with a study and a drawing-room at the north and south ends in large projecting bays. A double-height timbered hall was added at the north end, connecting to a reconstructed timbered house brought from Ipswich, and a whole new Lutyens wing extending westwards, to contain a dining-room, kitchens and still-rooms and larders, the necessary complement. The kitchen wing connected, via a delicious domed archway with circular steps, to the refurbished staff wing. The archway reflected the arch under the Gunpowder Room, and the master stroke was in welding the whole together with granite sett paving faultlessly patterned to indicate paths and boundaries, even the unspoken boundaries between the staff and family pathways. The Catesbys' Tudor manor house was revealed, enhanced, looking down its original westwards view, across its new forecourt, down a green avenue into the heart of the village. All was adorned with Lutyens's loveliest silver grey oakwork, for gates with a drooping curve, for wickets and window frames, and a curving footbridge in the garden. The gardens were elaborately formal, with Gertrude Jekyll in full consultation.

Other developments at Ashby included an exquisite if sober E-shaped house for Lord Wimborne's land agent, and a row of cottages in the village street, thatched and picturesque in the style of Capability Brown's Milton Abbas.

Of all Lutyens's clients, the Wimbornes lived in the greatest Edwardian plush style: Ashby was awash with tapestries and sensational rugs, fine antique Tudor and Jacobean furniture, all cushioned, fringed and polished. Alice Wimborne was a lady in the grand manner – when the Wimbornes were in Dublin during the war she was known as 'Queen Alice'. After the war their London home, Wimborne

House in Arlington Street, where Lutyens also worked for them, was a splendid setting for fashionable gatherings. Alice herself, of all London hostesses, was the only one intelligent enough to have had a political *salon*, had she so chosen – but she preferred the arts, and particularly music.

In the early 1930s the private concerts that Lady Wimborne arranged at Wimborne House were spectacular social and musical events: one was famously painted by Sir John Lavery. But Alice Wimborne was also genuinely interested in and knowledgeable about music, and the talk of London concerned the young William Walton, whose *Belshazzar's Feast*, first conducted by Sir Adrian Boult on 25 November 1931, had been such a success. Walton's First Symphony was awaited with anticipation: it was still unfinished, but was given a first performance on 3 December 1934, and afterwards there was a party at Wimborne House: it was described, agog, by Siegfried Sassoon as 'Rome before the Fall' with seventeen footmen serving thirty-five guests for supper, and afterwards 'we moved into the vast music-room, with its fantastically lovely crystal chandeliers lit by hundreds of candles'.[19] This seems to have been the first meeting between Alice Wimborne and William Walton. Alice, though she was in her mid-fifties, looked twenty years younger and was known to have a taste for younger men. Walton was at a low ebb – he was distraught after the break-up of his affair with Baroness Imma Doernberg, hurt by the Sitwells' fading allegiance and exhausted from trying to complete his symphony. Alice took him in hand, which was exactly what he needed. Discreetly, for the Wimbornes' marriage was a triumph of Edwardian tact and diplomacy, Alice was kind and comforting, and undoubtedly spoiling; she discouraged his bad habits and pooh-poohed the Sitwells' barbs – she was proud to have 'rescued' him from their influence. When he was taken to Ashby St Ledgers, where he worked at a grand piano in the long gallery above the dining-room, with its beautiful westward oriel bringing in the afternoon sun, he must have smiled to think how recently he had been 'banished to a stable' with a 'senile, disintegrating upright' at Weston Park, Towcester, near by – the home of Sacheverell and Georgia Sitwell.[20]

Crown Imperial, the march for George VI's Coronation, was mostly composed in the gallery at Ashby St Ledgers. In the same year, 1937, Walton was so enthusiastic when he heard the young Benjamin Britten's *Variations on a Theme of Frank Bridge* that he immediately arranged for another performance at Wimborne House in the autumn. At the end of 1937 Walton was again ill, and had an operation for hernia: afterwards Alice whisked him to Ashby and then to Ravello, where he had always wanted to live. Alice came home and called on Lutyens to discuss designing a little Italian house – which he did, though the building was stopped by the war. Lord Wimborne died in 1939 and discretion was no longer necessary. Alice's affectionate care of William was the inspiration of some of his best music; his Violin Concerto 'enshrined the soul of Alice'.[21] They went to America together for Jascha Heifetz to give the first performance, but because of the war they had to return before that took place, on 7 December 1939, in Cleveland. So in England, the first performance was to be given by the Danish violinist Henry Holst, with whom Walton worked for long hours at Ashby, in the gallery, which contained little more than his piano and some bookcases 'except for an array of pipe-racks, each holding six or eight pipes, hanging at intervals along the walls'.[22]

At almost the same time, Walton was working on a film score for Shaw's *Major Barbara* with Roy Douglas, who visited Ashby, where the house was freezing though meals were still taken in the dining-room, each occupant having an oil-stove by their chair. 'We can have butter with our muffins today, William,' said Alice, 'for Mr Douglas has brought his ration.'[23] But the freezing cold house, the myopic butler who was a former gardener and kept dropping the china, the neglected, overgrown gardens, the peace exuded by that age-old ochre-coloured stone, the solemn, dark little church that the Catesbys built and where they came to rest after battles of so long ago – all this, the essential soul of Ashby, contributed to Walton's output of music. The comedy overture *Scapino*, the ballets *The Quest* and *The Wise Virgins*, *Music for Children*, many other pieces, but most of all the film music for *The First of the Few* with its *Spitfire Prelude* and for Laurence Olivier's *Henry V*, were imbued by William Walton with the Englishness of Ashby St Ledgers, Edwin Lutyens's Englishness.

This book began with Osbert Sitwell's comparison of Lutyens's Edwardianism with Elgar's; it returns to this musical theme with the words of Ralph Vaughan Williams, who concludes his examination of Elgar as a great composer:

> The one question we have to ask is, has Elgar achieved beauty? This is the one thing that is vital . . . The best composer is surely he who has the most beautiful melodies, the finest harmony, the most vital rhythm, and the surest sense of form. There is no other criterion. Elgar has the one thing needful, and all his philosophical, literary and technical excellences fall into their proper place; they are a means to an end. But to say that he has beauty is only half the truth; he has that particular kind of beauty which gives us, his fellow countrymen, a sense of something familiar – the intimate and personal beauty of our own fields and lanes; not the aloof and unsympathetic beauty of glaciers and coral reefs and tropical forests.[24]

Here, by substituting the name of Edwin Lutyens and one other change, that of architect for composer, we have the essence of the legacy of two great Edwardians.

❦ XIV ❧
THE COMMON LEGACY

Just over six years after Sir Edwin Lutyens's death, *Country Life*, faithful far beyond the grave, published the great *Memorial* – three folio volumes of drawings and photographs of his buildings and Christopher Hussey's massive, romantic and sensitive *Life*. Reviewing these volumes in the *Architectural Review* under the title 'Building with Wit', Nikolaus Pevsner questioned,

> Was he a great architect? ... For the paradoxes remain – the paradox of the builder of follies who was at the same time the architect of the common man, the paradox of the eccentric who achieved such remarkable worldly success, the paradox of the revivalist in whose work geometry is more insistent than in that of any living architect bar Corbusier, the crowning paradox of the twentieth century architect of prodigious gifts who contributed nothing to the mainstream of development in twentieth century architecture.

Pevsner's *tour de force* of critical prose (the whole piece was in this vein) acted as a wicked godmother's spell on Lutyens's reputation, which went deeply to sleep during the 1950s and 1960s while the mainstream of Modernism was abroad. But with those intriguing words 'wit' and 'paradox' he had laid the threads by which the princes could find it again, for these were irresistible notions, especially to architects frustrated by the chaos of post-Modernism. There were several princes following the thread – Robert Venturi and Allan Greenberg in America and Roderick Gradidge and the historian Nicholas Taylor here; the redoubtable Ada Louise Huxtable of the *New York Times* spoke for them all: 'Lutyens is exactly the kind of architect to intrigue us ... Today's architects, lovers of learned paradox, find his work full of marvellous visual ambiguities and erudite references. He is an architect of flux and surprise, wit, anticlimax, ambiguity and sheer delight.' Mrs Huxtable's kiss of awakening launched a revivalist party, the Lutyens Exhibition, at the Hayward Gallery in the winter of 1981–2. It was an enormously popular and visually stunning exhibition, and from then on Lutyens's reputation has not retreated; it seems unlikely that it will ever sleep again, at least among inquiring architects and architectural historians.

But among all this appreciation in books, articles, on gallery walls and, by the greatest flattery, the creation of graven and metaphoric images, the influence of the people who paid Lutyens to build, and in most cases had to live in the results, has perhaps not been sufficiently regarded. Many of his 'erudite references' are to his clients. My thesis has been their essential role: that they influenced his works, for good or ill, to an extraordinary degree, and that they were, in time and thought, Edwardians. My final task is to assert the impression that those clients and their architect have left on our world.

It would be useless to suggest that Lutyens's buildings have survived well, for the twentieth century has had too many revolutions in fortunes, tastes and ways of living for that to be possible. As I started this book, the death of the 4th Lord Revelstoke, Cecil Baring's son, was announced – though he died in a hospital in Dublin, he was buried on Lambay, with his parents, and Lambay Castle is almost the only one of Lutyens's major houses that has remained 'dynastic'. As I am finishing my story, with an appalling irony of history, Barings has crashed again, just under 105 years after the 1890 catastrophe, which actually brought Lutyens over *forty* commissions, as family, relatives and friends sought to rebuild their lives.

In the largest sense, therefore, Lutyens's buildings responded to the forces of history. Amalgamations and absorptions – the recurring themes of twentieth-century business life – also brought him opportunities: Mark Fenwick was liberated to garden in the south by Lloyd's takeover of Lambton's Bank in Newcastle, Frederick Mirrielees perhaps hoped that turning to Lutyens would assert his independence within the Currie-Union Castle empire, Edward Hudson's amassing of printing and publishing interests provided work for his favourite architect, and the welding of the Vickers-Armstrong-Whitworth and Anglo-Persian Oil conglomerates proffered dreams that were ultimately shattered by the Second World War.

Most of his clients, as we have seen, were middle-class, meaning that they were rich either through earned or inherited wealth, but they were not tied to the land on which they built by ancestral ties (although Julius Drewe so painstakingly constructed such ties). There was nothing to detain them, nor were there traditions to inhibit change – there was not *time* to engender either traditions or ties – and so all Lutyens's buildings were launched almost immediately into the stormy seas of twentieth-century insecurities. This is most poignantly illustrated by Lutyens's daughter Ursula, Lady Ridley, who was very close to her father during the 1930s and to the end of his life. Just after the publication of the *Memorial Volumes* she made a tour, a pilgrimage, to see some of his houses, which became 'a voyage of disenchantment and disillusion'. She found the early houses 'so dated and so unfashionable' that she didn't wish to live in any of them: 'But then none are lived in as he meant them to be and his large kitchens and inadequate bathrooms have inevitably led to desecration and vandalism. Can you see Bumps in a *pink* bath and loo ... Of his small houses only the Deanery, Sonning, seemed to preserve his intentions. But all the others had been mucked about and inappropriately furnished so that I wish I had never seen them.'[1] Lady Ridley lived in ancestral Blagdon; the work that her father did in the garden in the 1930s remains beautifully cared for and largely unchanged, though not because it was his, but because that is the way things have always been at Blagdon. Perhaps in the end it is *all* about whom you are building for?

The Great War remains, however, the ultimate manipulator of Lutyens's career, taking its awful toll of his clients' sons and fortunes. The war also saddened and disillusioned them beyond measure – for, if building is the ultimate expression of faith in the future, it was just such faith that they had lost. Of the Lutyens clients that died while still owning their houses, only a very few enabled a second generation to carry on: Nathaniel Lloyd at Great Dixter, the Drewes at Castle Drogo and the Wimbornes at Ashby St Ledgers all carried on, but the Tennants at Great Maytham, the Fenwicks at Temple Dinsley and the Mark Fenwicks at Abbotswood – all were both the beginning and end of the line. Lady Battersea kept the Pleasaunce till her own death in 1931, and Lady Hillingdon lived on at Overstrand Hall until 1940; both houses were sold as 'institutions' and have served admirably since, but new upheavals are on the horizon. Similarly, Hestercombe, which the client, the Hon. Edward Portman, enjoyed for only three years (he died in 1911) though his widow stayed on till the 1950s, when Somerset County Council acquired house and garden; having restored the Lutyens–Jekyll garden so triumphantly over the last twenty years they now find the house may be beyond Council means. Walter Hoare's Daneshill house passed to his son, but found itself the site for Basingstoke's overspill expansion of the 1960s. Herbert Johnson's Marsh Court, the Fenwicks' Temple Dinsley, Sir William Bird's Eartham House near Chichester, Woolverstone in Suffolk, have all successfully been schools – though Marsh Court and Woolverstone have recently reverted to private houses.

Some of the houses – and undoubtedly those which began in happiness have fared best in this regard – have found a continuum of understanding ownership. It is easy to imagine that some of those first owners – Emily Lawless at Hazlehatch, Antonie Rosalie 'Mertoni' at Folly Farm or 'D. D.' Lyttelton as she left Grey Walls – whispered into their walls some rules on future owners, which the house has happily enforced. (Oddly, the one house where psychical research sessions were carried out, Fisher's Hill, where Eleanor Sidgwick lived out her days with Gerald and Betty Balfour, has fared rather badly.) Bathrooms, pink or otherwise, are a modern difficulty, but comforts the original clients would happily accept, and the principal rooms are of greater importance. Tom Blackburn sold Little Thakeham and spent his last years in a cottage at Henley-on-Thames – but his house has fared well and is now a hotel. He would find his favourite rooms furnished much as in his time if he could return, and Mrs Alfred Lyttelton would probably feel the same about the rooms at Grey Walls, which is also a hotel. The Grey Walls story is a particularly happy one. When the William Jameses bought it they had Robert Lorimer to enlarge it in 1911; Mrs James never lived in it after the war and the house was let, until it was sold in 1924 to Lt.-Colonel Sir James Horlick for £10,000 – fully and well furnished, just as the James Estate had let it to rather grand tenants. Sir James and his family used it as their holiday home up until the Second World War, when it was requisitioned as a rest house for pilots at Drem airfield; later it was let to the Polish forces, and later still became a maternity home (Folly Farm was also a wartime maternity home). At the end of the war, Sir James wished to live on Gigha, where he had made his famous garden, and gave Grey Walls to his daughter Ursula, who couldn't imagine that she could afford to live in it but was loath to sell it, knowing she would never find 'such a pretty house again'.[2] Ursula's husband, Colonel John Weaver, came home from the Burma campaign, wondering what he would do if he left the army. They thought of running a hotel and had begun to look for one for sale when suddenly Ursula Weaver thought of Grey Walls, sitting, waiting, in the care of a staunch family servant, William Walker, who had more faith in the future than she. So all ended happily; the Weavers and their three sons went to Grey Walls, sorted it out and opened it up on 1 April 1948. It was an instant success. Women were not allowed in the Muirfields clubhouse, and when the Open Championship was played there that summer all the wives stayed in the hotel. Then the Yehudi Menuhins discovered it and brought all their musical friends, and so – in those difficult days – Grey Walls had found its new life.

As the houses all approach their hundredth birthdays – as hotels (Abbey House at Barrow is also a hotel), in multi-ownership (Great Maytham and Middleton Park at Bicester are both communities within themselves), some with their gardens open to the public for charity, Castle Drogo and Lindisfarne Castle, owned by the National Trust, and Heywood, Colonel Poë's garden at Ballinakill, now owned by the Irish Board of Works, the legacy broadens. To a great extent, the 'institutional' phase of ownership, which seems to be coming to an end, prolonged the status quo. Now more of Lutyens's buildings, large and small, will come into the housing stock. The vanished army of gardeners and chauffeurs in cottages and flats gives way to a whole new company of Lutyens owners, many of them young, 'first-time' buyers. I cannot believe that modern bathrooms will concern the ghost of an essentially humanist genius, who looks down on well-roofed, jolly sitting-rooms, their lamps gleaming into the night, roses round their doors – his new army of satisfied (though sometimes grumbling) clients multiplied a hundredfold.

I have been looking at Lutyens's buildings for over twenty years. They have come to represent a large, eminently good-looking and cheerfully-spirited family who have features in common – large and quirky gables, references back in columns and pediments to Sir Christopher Wren, the fat boy with his goose on each end of Midland Bank in Poultry, the exquisite marble wreaths in tiny churches up and down the land, chimneys that reach to touch the sky – a universal perfection in stone geometry, be it Trafalgar Square or a quiet village street, the legacy of Sir Edwin Lutyens and his Edwardian friends and clients to us that follow after, enriches our everydays.

The common legacy (or at least some of it) follows, without reference to private houses that cannot be seen from a public road or path, unless they are open at least occasionally for charity. Buildings, etc., are grouped geographically (except that I have added a list of churches and chapels). This is essentially a 'starter kit' and further references should be made, especially to the county volumes of the *Buildings of England* series.

THE SOUTH-EAST

In south-west Surrey, THURSLEY, the village of Lutyens's childhood, would still be recognizable to him. He lived in the Georgian house in the centre of the village, west of the road junction: it was, unbelievably (for a family of fourteen), smaller in his day. THE CORNER, north of Thursley Street, was where he did his first additions for Mr Edmund Gray. Half-way down the lane southwards is the Institute he built for the Revd Gooch, the vicar and a family friend (now Prospect Cottage, etc.), and this lane leads to the church, St Michael's. In the churchyard are Lutyens's memorials to his mother (1906) and to Derek Lutyens (1918).

MILFORD HOUSE, the home of Robert and Barbara Webb, has remained a sad ruin, beside the road northwards out of the village towards Godalming, since the fire in 1981. There are constant schemes for restoration, but the Wren-like details that so inspired the young Lutyens are gone for ever. There are cottages by Lutyens to the west, in the centre of the village on the road to the church – which has some curious old Webb family tombs.

The small bronze tablet Lutyens designed in memory of Barbara Webb is on the chancel wall of All Saints, Witley, on the A283 south from Milford. The village school opposite is Lutyensesque – and note the White Hart as typical of the Surrey picturesque that inspired Helen Allingham, Randolph Caldecott and Ned Lutyens. Farther south on the A283, over the railway and east of the road, is WOOD END (1897), and farther on, at the turning to Hambledon, is TIGBOURNE COURT, the exciting and beautifully crafted house of 1899 built by Sir Edgar Horne MP for his daughter.

By travelling east from MILFORD to Milford Station (where Lutyens often travelled with 'Angelina' in the guard's van), following Station Lane east to Hyde-style crossroads and turning left and north into Hambledon Road, you will climb through a definitive Jekyll-style hollow lane, where she loved to drive her pony and trap, fast! At the top of the hill, on the right, are some of the cottages built for Jekyll family retainers, and a turn right, a little further on into Homefarm Road will bring you face to face with Gertrude Jekyll's HUT (1894), once secluded in the garden of Munstead Wood, but now right on the Brighton Road. Across the Brighton Road, Munstead Heath Road passes, on the right, Munstead House (private) built for Mrs Julia Jekyll by J. J. Stevenson and later the home of Sir Herbert and Lady Jekyll. On the left, glimpsed via Heath Lane, is MUNSTEAD WOOD (private), where the garden is open occasionally for the National Gardens Scheme. By walking down Heath Lane, Lutyens's THUNDER HOUSE on the wall, Miss Jekyll's former stables and gardener's cottage (Munstead Orchard), may be glimpsed. The lane meets the main road at ST JOHN'S CHURCH, BUSBRIDGE. The war memorial is a Lutyens Cross; in the church there is a beautiful chancel screen for the Mellersh and Graham families, friends of the Jekylls and Webbs, and immediately outside the east end of the church, the Jekyll family tomb and the Julia Jekyll and Francis McLaren graves.

In GODALMING High Street, the MUSEUM has Lutyens and Jekyll exhibits.

At COMPTON take Down Lane (leading to the Watts Gallery and Mortuary Chapel), and a footpath westwards follows the Pilgrim's Way (passing Limnerslease, Watts's house by Sir Ernest George) to Lutyens's Pilgrim's Way Bridge (1931) for the original Godalming bypass. In SHALFORD, off King's Road, the B2128, there is a car-park for the CHINTHURST HILL open space, where part of the land which Maggie Guthrie acquired so mysteriously now offers walkers her view, one of the finest views in this countryside of fine views. Her Lutyens house is in the trees on the south slope and private, but the lodges can be seen in Chinthurst Lane, Wonersh. Follow the Dorking road, the A248, eastwards through Chilworth and Albury, the Tillingbourne valley road that Lutyens so often travelled. In SHERE, where the Bray family are still lords of the manor, are Lutyens's cottages, last but one on the left before EAST LODGE with its prominent green gable. In the Street, Summers' Barber's Shop still has its sign (1894), and the lych gate at St James's church is well worth close examination.

Continue east along the A25 to ABINGER HAMMER, and turn right for ABINGER COMMON: here is another Lutyens War Cross and, to the west of the path, next to the wall, there are the tombs of Sir Frederick and Lady Mirrielees, the builders of Goddards. Directly outside the east end of the church are John Arthur and Emily Gibbs 'of Goddards'. The house itself is clearly visible on the west side of the green with the Victorian well on it, south of the church. In Pixham Lane, DORKING, is a marvellous small church by Lutyens of 1903, to serve the expanding community and paid for by Miss Mayo, who lived in Pixham Lane.

Back in west Surrey, at TILFORD the Institute or Village Hall cum cricket pavilion (1896) is on the green and still the backdrop for famous matches. It will be remembered that Gerard Streatfeild of Fulbrook was a supporter of the Tilford team for many years, and so was J. M. Barrie – whose Black Lake Cottage is just outside the village. David Rayner Allen's *Peter Pan and Cricket* is recommended reading. In FARNHAM's South Street, next to Sainsbury's car-park, is the Liberal Club (1894), built under the patronage of Arthur Chapman of Crooksbury by a local builder, Mr Patrick, who stood much of the cost himself. It originally included a library, reading-room, billiard-room (the best in town) and meeting-rooms.

Daneshill Brick and Tile Works, Basingstoke: the original brickworks office built by Lutyens for Walter Hoare, to display the variety of bricks made. Now restored, the building serves as the estate office for the Kingsland Business Park.

Hampshire

The BASING HOUSE RUINS are well signed and worth a visit. The bricks of this marvellous ruin, in which Inigo Jones was a prisoner of Cromwell's siege, are a peculiar rich orange. These details inspired Lutyens to build Daneshill House (*c.* 1903) for Walter Hoare – it can be seen prominent on its ridge to the north of Swing Swang Lane, all now in the town's industrial estate. At Daneshill Roundabout turn north to find the Daneshill Brick and Tile Works office by Lutyens, now restored as the estate office, in Bilton Road on the Kingsland Business Park.

Kent

Alfred Lyttelton's WITTERSHAM HOUSE, 'suavely neo-Georgian', with pantiles, can be seen in the village, the war memorial may be by Lutyens. At ROLVENDEN there are Tennant memorials in the church, and, down Rolvenden Layne, first on the right, white clapboard cottages (miniature of Goddards) for Great Maytham, which is further on the right – splendid gatehouse and avenue approach. Great Maytham's (Country Houses Association) garden is occasionally open, and house and garden may be seen upon written request. At NORTHIAM, Great Dixter and Christopher Lloyd's marvellous garden in its Lutyens and Nathaniel Lloyd framework are open every day except Mondays (but Bank Holiday Mondays) from April till October. Plaxtol churchyard extension has magnificent Dalison tombs at the end of the central path.

LONDON AND ENVIRONS

The London buildings are best appreciated on foot, and are grouped for convenient walks:

36 SMITH SQUARE, Reginald McKenna's London house, is beside St John's church, at the corner of Dean Trench Street; it has been completely altered inside. The houses by Lutyens for Francis McLaren and his sister Lady Norman are both in Great Peter Street, though they are actually the Corner House, Cowley Street and 8 Little College Street. In Tufton Street is the building which began as St John's Institute, built for Archdeacon Wilberforce through the McKenna connection; it is now partly the Church Union Faith House bookshop and partly Watts & Company. Further south, via Marsham Street, are the Page Street flats, famous for their chequerboard patterned walls. Also shop pavilions and entry details – built 1929–30 for Westminster Council, Lutyens's only public housing project.

From Westminster, walk up Whitehall, passing the CENOTAPH to TRAFALGAR SQUARE: the fountains, similar to those in New Delhi, and the paving, are the memorial to Admirals Jellicoe and Beatty. Their busts are by Sir William Reid Dick. (The lions are, of course, by Lutyens's godfather, Sir Edwin Landseer.) In PALL MALL no. 67–68 has a façade by Lutyens for Victor Behar (1928); there was originally a banking hall below with flats above – note that the windows of each floor are different. No. 120 was for Crane Bennett & Company. North, in St James's Square, no. 7, on the corner of Duke of York Street, was the town house of Gaspard and Henry Farrer. The mews behind, Apple Tree Yard, was where Lutyens had his Delhi office and William Nicholson his studio – nothing of either remains, all the character engulfed in soulless offices. Across Jermyn Street walk through St James's Church to get the feeling of Wren before Lutyens's Midland Bank, 196a Piccadilly, comes into view; the banking hall is well preserved. Farther west, in Park Lane, Lutyens did the façade of Grosvenor House Hotel (1926) and in Victoria of Terminal House (1927), Grosvenor Gardens.

Note: Almost all of Lutyens's London commissions of the 1920s and 30s were for exteriors only (often with entrance halls and directors' offices), but interiors, for banking or offices, were a specialized, cost-controlled job for bread-and-butter architects, and have usually been endlessly refurbished. Conversely, the private houses, many in Mayfair, where Lutyens worked show no signs of his attentions on their outsides.

A second clutch of London buildings will be found in the West Central area. Lord Cheylesmore's Memorial is in Embankment Gardens. Nos 2–10 Tavistock Street, Covent Garden, was the original *Country Life* office of 1904 for Edward Hudson; 42 Kingsway was for *The Garden* (1906) for Hudson and William Robinson. In Great Russell Street, the Bedford Square end, is Lutyens's YWCA building (1928) which has an interesting history, good stairways, Queen Mary Hall and small library surviving. Most of these rooms are let for various uses, and can most likely be seen upon inquiry. In Tavistock Square is the memorial to Dame Louisa Blake (the corner of Endsleigh Place), and via Tavistock Place and Cartwright Gardens is Lutyens's Burton Street façade of the original Theosophical Society building for Mrs Annie Besant (1911). The building was never finished for the TS, it was bought by the British Medical Association and completed by C. Wontner Smith.

A City group begins in Fleet Street, with Lutyens and Wren together again, with Reuters, 85 Fleet Street, for Sir Roderick Jones (1935), cheek by jowl with St Bride's Church. There was originally the Cogers public house (now the photographic library) for the journalists. In St Paul's, besides Robert Lutyens's plaque for his father in the crypt, is Lutyens's tomb for Admiral Beatty and the gold flagon, chalice and paten and silver-gilt vases as a memorial to Lord Stevenson of Hombury, who died in 1926. Outside, the west front lamp standards are by Lutyens.

The Midland Bank headquarters building has façades on Poultry and Princes Street, next to the Bank of England. The banking hall is in splendid Lutyens grand style. In Finsbury Circus is the large headquarters building for Anglo-Persian Oil, later BP and now back in the same company ownership after an interval as let offices and various refurbishments. Lutyens did the entrance hall, lifts and stairs to the directors' suite, as he did at the Midland Bank. Moorgate Station is by Lutyens, part of the office building development. Also the City branch of the Midland, 140–144 Leadenhall Street.

On Tower Hill is the Mercantile Marine Memorial, 1926–8, added to by Sir Edward Maufe after the Second World War.

At GREENWICH, in the Maritime Museum, is the Elliptical Room (1936) as a memorial to Sir James Caird. The Royal Naval Division Memorial is at the Royal Naval College.

To the WEST OF LONDON Hampton Court Bridge (1928) pays another tribute to Wren's Palace building; the corner pavilions were never built and the bridge was altered for traffic reasons after the Second World War. At Hampton Court Palace the Chapel Royal has the splendid large altar cross in brass designed for Charlotte Dalison (Beresford Peirse) in memory of her husband (see Dalison tombs, above).

At RUNNYMEDE the road (A308) layout and bridge over the Thames were designed in connection with the gift of Runnymede to the nation, but have been altered for traffic reasons (the M25 now uses the bridge). The memorial to Urban Hanlon Broughton (d. 1929) who gave Runnymede, consists of the kiosks, piers and lodges at the Windsor end. The Broughtons (Cara Broughton became Lady Fairhaven) lived at Park Close – opposite them Mrs Julia Clark lived at Parkwood – and Mrs Clark's tomb, and that of her parents, Lord and Lady Baillieu, are probably two of Lutyens's finest. They are in the churchyard of St John's, Windlesham.

In WINDSOR the Doll's House is at the Castle; Lutyens designed the tomb for King George V and Queen Mary in St George's Chapel, and his memorial to King George V is at the corner of Datchet Road. In ETON, beside the College playing fields, is the bridge erected in memory of Denys Finch-Hatton, killed in a flying accident in Africa in 1933 – his story is told by Karen Blixen in *Out of Africa*.

Berkshire

At WARGRAVE the war memorial and Hannen Columbarium are by Lutyens. Deanery Garden, the first house for Edward Hudson, is prominent in the centre of Sonning, with chauffeur's etc. cottages opposite. The white, cliff-like NASHDOM, for Princess Alexis Dolgorouki, is beside the Bourne End road from Taplow to Cliveden. FOLLY FARM, at Sulhamstead, opens the garden for charity (see National Gardens Scheme annual booklet).

MIDDLE ENGLAND

CAMPION HALL is in Brewer Street, Oxford. ASHBY ST LEDGERS near Daventry rewards a quiet walk-around: the Manor can be clearly seen from the village and from the churchyard of St Leodegarius and the Virgin Mary, which contains Lutyens's war memorial and the tomb of Lord and Lady Wimborne – here lies Alice. In the village is the long row of cottages, dated 1908, with Ivor Guest's initials, and, on the road to Long Buckby, the former lodge to the Ashby Lodge Estate, which Lutyens converted into a golf pavilion for Lord Wimborne. The adjoining golf course, made after the First World War, has reverted to farmland.

VICTORIA PARK, LEICESTER: the war memorial and gates.

The tomb of F. E. Smith, Lord Birkenhead in Charlton churchyard, Northants.

At STOWE BY CHARTLEY in Staffordshire, in the lovely Norman church of St John the Baptist, are Lutyens's tablets to General Sir Walter Congreve VC and his eldest son, William 'Billy' Congreve VC, who was killed in the Battle of the Somme. Edward Hudson had intended to leave Lindisfarne Castle to him.

THE NORTH

LIVERPOOL ROMAN CATHOLIC CATHEDRAL of Christ the King: the CRYPT was built to Lutyens's design before the Second World War and gives an overwhelming impression of what the whole might have been. If his cathedral had been built, neither his reputation nor his legacy would ever have been questioned.

BARROW-IN-FURNESS: Abbey House is now a prominent hotel on the road into town; it was built as a guest house for visitors to the Vickers shipyards, 1913.

ROSENEATH, Dumbartonshire: the Ferry Inn. All that remains of Lutyens's great hopes of the royal patronage of HRH Princess Louise, Marchioness of Lorne, are the truncated remains of his wings.

GULLANE, EAST LOTHIAN: Grey Walls, originally built for Alfred Lyttelton, then owned by William and Edward James, and then sold to Lt.-Col Sir James

Horlick and still owned by his family. After the Second World War, his daughter, Ursula Weaver, had the bright and necessary idea of using her inherited house as a hotel, and it remains marvellously so. In North Berwick church there is a very early Lutyens chancel screen which may be connected with his father's client Sir William Miller at Manderston near by.

WHALTON MANOR, near Newcastle, in the village street.

LINDISFARNE CASTLE, on Holy Island, belongs to the National Trust.

HEATHCOTE can be seen from Kings Road, Ilkley, and from below, in Grove Road. Head office of N. G. Bailey & Company, to whom requests to visit may be made.

EASTERN ENGLAND

KNEBWORTH HOUSE in Hertfordshire (open to the public): much of Lutyens's work for his sister-in-law, the Countess of Lytton, can be seen, in the entrance hall, picture gallery, library and white drawing-room; the formal layout of the garden was entirely done by Lutyens and the Countess (with at least one visit from Miss Jekyll). In the park, the old church overflows with the sense that, at the last, Lutyens ministered to the sad and untimely ends of his patrons – in the church are the memorials to the Lyttons' sons, John and Antony, the former killed at El Alamein in 1942, the latter killed flying in 1933. The churchyard, south side and south-east corners, has the distinctive Lutyens tombstones for the Lytton family, the Lafones (Pamela Lytton's sister Beryl), the Buchanans and the family nannies.

In new Knebworth is St Martin's church, pantiled and rather alarming, but with definite Lutyens style inside; it was completed by Professor Albert Richardson. In the old village there are many Lutyens cottages alongside the earlier building patronage of the Lyttons, and evidence, in Deards End Lane, of the houses and golf clubhouse, part of a development Lord Lytton planned with Alfred Lyttelton's help before the First World War. The holly hedges were part of Lutyens's plan.

EAST WRETHAM, off the Thetford–East Dereham road, just north of Thetford, has the beautiful memorial to Marc Noble in the little church set in an unchanged countryside remoteness.

BELTON HOUSE, Lincolnshire, has a curious cross on the outside wall of the east end, next to Lord Brownlow's tomb (an unidentified detail but similar to Aubrey Herbert's chapel at Brushford).

On the north Norfolk coast a walk around Overstrand (for which there is a leaflet to guide you) will reveal all the towers, gateways and quirks of Lord Battersea's building at the Pleasaunce, plus another curious Lutyens chapel, with pantiles and tiled decoration.

THE WEST OF ENGLAND

At MELLS a leaflet describes the interesting buildings – Lutyens's memorial to Mark Horner is opposite the village shop, the war memorial is up the hill, the church has the memorials to Edward Horner (Sir Alfred Munnings's equestrian statue) and Raymond Asquith and various gifts from Lady Horner, who was a skilled embroideress. The churchyard, on the south-east, has the Horner tombs (and, not by Lutyens, those of Mgr Ronald Knox and Siegfried Sassoon) and the McKenna graves; the yew avenue was Lutyens's idea and the manor can be seen from the churchyard.

Near Stroud, in Gloucestershire, MISARDEN PARK, Miserden, the garden where Lutyens worked for the Wills family, is open midweek throughout the summer (and also for the National Gardens Scheme). Farther north, at Stow-on-the-Wold, Nether Swell village green has the war memorial and bus shelter paid for by Mark Fenwick: Abbotswood garden is open for the National Gardens Scheme.

Back south. HESTERCOMBE near Taunton in Somerset is open every day from May to September. CASTLE DROGO, National Trust, is open as advertised by the Trust. In South Devon, the coastal footpath along the Erme estuary, approached via Mothecombe (the house Lutyens altered for the Mildmays), will not reveal any Lutyens work in detail but follows the former Barings' Membland estate road and explains why they loved this part of the world – the path westwards leads to Stoke Point (now a caravan site) and the church of St Peter the Poor Fisherman, on the beach, from which the Revelstoke title was taken. Mothecombe House garden is occasionally open (National Gardens Scheme).

REPUBLIC OF IRELAND

The gardens of Howth Castle are open to the public. The large and eminently sad Irish National War Memorial is next to the rowing club at Islandbridge, Dublin, on the other side of the river from Phoenix Park. Much more cheerful but not dissimilar in style is Heywood House garden, the Salesian Fathers' Community School at Ballinakill in Port Laoise, which is open to visitors under Irish government ownership.

FRANCE

LES BOIS DES MOUTIERS at Varengeville, Lutyens's house for the Mallet family, is open throughout the summer and makes a convenient prelude to the roads south to the war memorials. The major Lutyens works are:

Gezaincourt Communal Cemetery Extension, Pas-de-Calais, and Hersin Communal Cemetery Extension, Pas-de-Calais; also Berlin CCE and the memorial to the missing and cemetery, Faubourg d'Amiens, Arras; the memorial to the missing at St Quentin, Nord; Étaples Military Cemetery; the memorial to the missing of the Somme at Thiepval; the Villers-Bretonneux Military Cemetery, Somme; and the Australian National War Memorial.

USA

In WASHINGTON, DC, the British Embassy is in Massachusetts Avenue, just west of Dupont Circle.

INDIA

The President's House, Rashtrapati Bhavan, is not normally accessible to foreigners, but the garden is usually open to all in February and March.

NOTE ON CHURCHES

There is still a Betjemanesque legacy that favours architects who worked on churches. Edwin Lutyens longed to do churches to emulate Wren, but he was never associated with any church establishment. His churches came via private clients and are as follows:

The Cathedral of Christ the King, Brownlow Hill, Liverpool (crypt only built, but marvellously impressive). The Great Model for the Cathedral is in the Walker Art Gallery.

Hampstead Garden Suburb: St Jude's Church and the Free Church in Central Square, Hampstead.

St Martin's, Knebworth, Herts (completed by Sir Albert Richardson).

Church in Pixham Lane, Dorking, for St Martin's, Dorking, for Miss Mayo.

Campion Hall, Oxford, chapel.

Hon. Aubrey Herbert Memorial Chapel, Brushford, Somerset.

Methodist Chapel, Cliff Road, Overstrand, Norfolk.

Notes

FOREWORD

1. 'The Work of the Late Philip Webb', *Country Life*, 8 May 1915, p. 618.
2. Caroline Dakers, *Clouds: The Biography of a Country House*, Yale University Press, 1993, pp. 49 ff.
3. Edward Marsh, *A Number of People*, Heinemann/ Hamish Hamilton, 1939, pp. 178–9.
4. Jeanne MacKenzie, *The Children of the Souls: A Tragedy of the First World War*, Chatto, 1986, p. 255.
5. M. and S. Harries, *A Pilgrim Soul: Biography of Elisabeth Lutyens*, p. 30.
6. Osbert Sitwell, *Great Morning*, Macmillan, 1948, p. 19. The stories of Lutyens's supposed extravagances are legion and have mostly become garbled with age and repetition; the best comes from Oliver Hill, who visited Sissinghurst Castle garden annually on his birthday armed with champagne and to encourage Vita Sackville-West to talk. On one occasion he told Vita of a seance with Dame Louisa Aldrich Blake (for whom Lutyens designed a memorial in Tavistock Square); it was some time after Lutyens's death, so Hill inquired if he was with Dame Louisa in the hereafter – 'Oh yes, he's here,' came the reply. 'What is he doing?' . . . 'Oh, building . . .' Vita thought for a brief moment; then, in her deep voice, she said: 'God must be very rich.' 'An Architect's Debt to *Country Life*', *Country Life*, 12 January 1967, pp. 70–72.

To establish some firm values: the Retail Price Index indicates that figures from before the First World War must be *multiplied by 35* to give an equivalent present value. Lutyens built many of his 1890s Surrey houses for around £10,000 (£350,000) but preferred patrons who spent £15,000 (£500,000) or more. He was not unduly expensive compared to other architects. The cost of Webb's Clouds, for Percy and Madeleine Wyndham, £80,000 in 1889, was a staggering £2,800,000. In her book on Clouds, Caroline Dakers notes that Webb received £4,000 in fees (5 per cent of costs) over eight years, thus his net income was less than £320 a year, about the same as a master stonemason, or the wife of a retired naval officer who felt herself 'passing rich' on between £3–400 a year. Professionals – dons, solicitors, architects such as Lutyens – did well on £750–1,000 a year; they could afford £1 a week for maids and 9s. a week for a garden boy.

The economics of the building trade seem to have been stable during the last twenty years of the nineteenth century. In 1881 Webb felt that 4 guineas a week was affordable for a Clerk of Works of the highest calibre for Clouds; in 1897 the young Lutyens paid the same, for the same reason, for the Clerk of Works at Fulbrook. The builders' men worked long hours, eleven a day in summer, less in winter, for about 8d. an hour. The contractor on Castle Drogo was persistently employing 100 men for a weekly wage bill of about £120 from 1912 onwards, and on this remote Devon site the men were given two half-an-hour meal breaks, their meals, a Reading Room and somewhere to sleep. They were in the charge of John Walker, Julius Drewe's Clerk of Works and Man of Business, who was paid an average of £30 per month. A gallon of lubricating oil cost 3/6d. and a new sledgehammer shaft 10d. At the other end of the scale, Tom Blackburn, for whom Lutyens built Little Thakeham Court (as it was first called), inherited £80,000 (almost £3 million) which, properly invested, meant that he did not have to work for the rest of his life. He paid 46s. for whisky, 50s. for champagne, 5s. for lunch at the Savoy and 20s. for a gallon of pot pourri from Miss Jekyll's Munstead nursery – or 9d. for a lavender and 1s. for a rosemary.

CHAPTER I: DREAMS OF PALACES ETCETERA

1. Christopher Hussey, *The Life of Sir Edwin Lutyens*, Country Life, 1950, p. 14.
2. See Mark Girouard, *Sweetness and Light: The Queen Anne Movement 1860–1900*, Yale University Press, 1984, p. 25.
3. Mary Lutyens, *Edwin Lutyens, A Memoir by His Daughter Mary Lutyens*, Murray, 1980, pp. 8–10.
4. ibid., pp. 1–5.
5. Charles Lutyens's account book, owned by the present Charles Lutyens, notes under 1869: 'Mr Miller's Committee £75 Mr Lansdeer's [sic] Portrait £50' – see also catalogue to an exhibition of works by Charles Lutyens, Eastbourne Art Gallery 1971.
6. Mary Lutyens, *Edwin Lutyens, A Memoir*, p. 10.
7. Richard Ormond, *Sir Edwin Landseer*, catalogue for the exhibition, Philadelphia Museum of Art/Tate Gallery, London 1981, p. 22.
8. Osbert Sitwell, *The Scarlet Tree*, Macmillan, 1946, p. 224.

9. The Scott commission, for which a £200 fee was prepaid, is entered in Charles Lutyens's account book for 1876; possibly the money paid for the new rental and move? See also Mary Lutyens, *Edwin Lutyens, A Memoir*, p. 12.

10. William Cobbett, *Rural Rides*, Penguin, p. 249.

11. Mary Lutyens, *Edwin Lutyens, A Memoir*, p. 15.

12. ibid., p. 17.

13. ibid., p. 16.

14. ibid.

15. Gertrude Jekyll, *Home and Garden*, Longmans Green, 1900, pp. 36–7.

16. A small number of drawings from this period of juvenilia are in the RIBA Drawings Collection. See pp. 59–60 in the catalogue of the Arts Council Lutyens Exhibition, and essay by Margaret Richardson, p. 58, Arts Council of Great Britain, London, 1981.

17. Charles Lutyens's account book; he also records 'Mr Combe's hunting picture £60' in 1887.

18. Violet Stuart Wortley, *Grow Old Along with Me*, Secker & Warburg, 1952, pp. 30–33.

19. ibid., pp. 32–3.

20. Christopher Hussey, *Life of Lutyens*, p. 12: 'Read the following extract to father it is from the Surrey Archaeological Society's paper – Speaking of Sutton Place, "the whole house is built of brick and terra cotta" ... When I came home from my first excursion to Sutton I told father that it was built of terra cotta and brick which he flatly contradicted ... Not that I bring any accusation against father but only to show him, what a small amount of confidence I have, in the little that I know ... [and] how necessary it is for me to concentrate my whole attention, energy and time on possessing that confidence ...' Note: the use of terra cotta at Sutton Place was so early as to be a subject of debate long after – it is quoted as such by Nathaniel Lloyd in *A History of English Brickwork*.

21. Mary Lutyens, *Edwin Lutyens, A Memoir*, p. 19.

22. Herbert Baker, *Architecture and Personalities*, Country Life, 1944, p. 15.

23. Margaret Richardson, catalogue of the Arts Council Lutyens Exhibition, 1981, p. 61.

24. ibid, p. 65.

25. Edwin Lutyens to Lady Emily Lutyens, 11 January 1908, *The Letters of Edwin Lutyens to His Wife, Lady Emily*, ed. Clayre Percy and Jane Ridley, Collins, 1985, p. 145.

26. Sir Alfred Comyn Lyall, PC, KCB, GCIE (1835–1911). See Sir Mortimer Durand, *Life of the Rt. Hon. Sir Alfred Comyn Lyall*, Blackwood, 1913.

27. ibid., p. 227.

28. *The Letters of Lord Lytton*, ed. Lady Betty Balfour, Longmans Green, 1906, vol. 2, p. 233, 10 August 1880.

29. E. Neill Raymond, *Victorian Viceroy, A Life of Robert, 1st Earl of Lytton*, Regency Press, London and New York, 1980, quotes this extract and writes that Lady Emily Lytton destroyed her father's letters to his 'friend in India'.

30. Sir Alfred Lyall to Barbara Lyall, letter of 24 December 1884 replying to hers of 5 December, just received, Lyall Papers, India Office Library.

31. ibid.

32. 18 July 1885, *Letters of Mary Sibylla Holland*, ed. Bernard Holland, Edward Arnold, 1907, pp. 98–9.

33. Sir Alfred Lyall to Barbara Lyall, letter of 11 July 1885, Lyall Papers, India Office Library.

34. *Letters of Mary Sibylla Holland*, pp. 98–9.

35. The Smith–Webb family dynasty papers are in Surrey County Council Archives, Guildford Muniment Room, and show the descent from Anthony Smith of Milford, Rake & Witley, gentleman pensioner to Charles I and Charles II (d. 1669), to Robert Smith Webb, Lieut.-Col. of Milford, who married Harriet Currie of East Horsley Place, the parents of Robert William Webb (b. 1831), Godfrey (1832–95), Francis David (three daughters) and Louisa Gifford (two daughters).

36. *Buildings of England: Surrey*, Penguin, 1971, pp. 366–7.

37. After the death of Francis Webb Milford House was sold; in 1939 it was an antiques showroom, and in the 1960s it was an hotel. On the night of 24 October 1983 it was destroyed by a fire, only the roofless shell remaining. Covered to protect it from the weather, it remains roofless still, though at the time of writing (February 1995) there are plans to restore it to residential use. However, the interiors which so inspired Edwin Lutyens can never be seen again.

38. Notes on the architecture of Rake House, reprinted from Surrey Archaeological Society, Vol. XVIII, by Ralph Nevill FSA, p. 57 – 'strangers to Surrey, imagining the county to be a suburb of London, often suggest that there are, of course, no old families in it ...' The Mellershes were prominent bankers and solicitors in Godalming and well known to the Jekylls. Sir Reginald or Reynold Bray was given land at Shere by Henry VII.

39. Typed MS *Reminiscences of Sir Jocelyn Bray*, unpublished, 1959, p. 17.

40. Nellie Bray (1870–1957) announced her engagement to Charlie Lloyd, of the banking family – remember Nellie's mother was a Barclay. The Lloyds had rented a local house in the spring of 1896. Was this the cause or result of Lutyens's falling for Emily Lytton at the same time?

41. Sir Mortimer Durand, *Life of Lyall*, p. 322.

42. Letter from Sir Alfred Lyall to Barbara Webb, n.d., from Chalet Blumenthal, some time in 1888, Lyall Papers, India Office Library.

43. 'Dearest Kindred One', undated, from Milford House, Lyall Papers, India Office library.

Notes

CHAPTER II: ALLEGRO: JEKYLLIANA

1. Bumps Poet Galoreate from Lutyens, *Letters*, p. 26.
2. Jane Brown, *Gardens of a Golden Afternoon*, Allen Lane, 1982, p. 32.
3. See Sally Festing, *Gertrude Jekyll: A Biography*, Viking, 1991.
4. Surrey Record Office, Guildford Muniment Room, deed dated 7 May 1877.
5. For J. J. Stevenson see Mark Girouard, *Sweetness and Light*, pp. 38 ff. and 111–19.
6. Judith Tankard, 'The Garden before Munstead Wood', *Hortus*, 20, Winter 1991.
7. ibid.
8. Jane Brown, *Gardens of a Golden Afternoon*, p. 23.
9. Gertrude Jekyll, *Old West Surrey*, Newnes/Country Life, 1904, p. viii.
10. See Gillian Darley, *Octavia Hill*, Constable, 1990.
11. Lady Jekyll's book was published as *Kitchen Essays – with Recipes and Their Occasions*, 1922.
12. Quoted in *Ne Oublie*, a memoir of Lady Jekyll by her daughters Pamela McKenna and Barbara Freyberg, privately printed.
13. Gertrude Jekyll, *Home and Garden*, pp. 13–14.
14. ibid., p. 34.
15. ibid., pp. 13–14; see also essay on Munstead Wood interiors in Jane Brown, *Eminent Gardeners*, Viking, 1990.
16. Lutyens, *Letters*, pp. 47–9.
17. The 'rich body' he had in mind was William Robinson, who he thought was enormously rich (as he was), with no children, nor anyone to leave everything to, and perhaps would 'adopt' them. William Robinson lived until 1935, his ninety-seventh year, so presumably used up a great deal of his fortune. He left his estate largely to the nation, the Forestry Commission.
18. Miss Jekyll, who had given advice upon interiors at Eaton Hall for the Duke, had presumably canvassed for Lutyens; he did a little garden work at Eaton Hall.
19. Africa's cathedral was Cape Town Cathedral, St George's, done by Herbert Baker with Francis E. Masey, 1897–8.
20. Halsey Ricardo was also connected locally, to the Ricardos of Bramley Park, which had been Gertrude Jekyll's childhood home. Though he lost the Chances to Lutyens, Lutyens failed in his hopes of wresting Sir Ernest Debenham away from Ricardo. Ricardo remained friends with Miss Jekyll and she helped him with his own garden, at Woodside, Graffham, Sussex.
21. Lutyens, *Letters*, pp. 47–9.
22. See *All Stracheys Are Cousins* (Weidenfeld & Nicolson, 1983) by Amabel Williams-Ellis, who was brought up as Amabel Strachey at Newlands Corner.
23. 'Orchards', *Country Life*, 1901, Vol. X. p. 272.
24. The press cuttings describing this are in Guildford Library, with the minute book of the Old Guildford Society and related papers.
25. The banner is in Godalming Museum.
26. See Sally Festing, *Gertrude Jekyll*, but also Jane Brown, *Gardens of a Golden Afternoon*, for her approximately 120 commissions with Lutyens and approximately 250 others. Also Margaret A. Hastings's bibliography of all Jekyll writings in *Gertrude Jekyll: Symposium to mark the 50th Anniversary of her Death*, ed. M. Tooley, Michaelmas Books, Durham, 1992.
27. See Harvey Pitcher, *Muir and Mirrielees: The Scottish Partnership That Became a Household Name in Russia*, Swallow House Books, Cromer, 1994.
28. See *James Maclaren 1853–1890 Arts and Crafts Architect*: catalogue of an exhibition at the RIBAD Heinz Gallery, London, 1990, ed. Alan Calder.
29. From an unpublished memoir by Maida Bernard (née Mirrielees), Lutyens Trust.
30. Marischal Murray, *Union-Castle Chronicle 1853–1953*, Longmans Green, 1953, p. 158.
31. Sir Frederick and Lady Mirrielees are buried in Abinger Churchyard.
32. At Woodside, Chenies, Bucks. See Jane Brown, *Gardens of a Golden Afternoon*, p. 54.
33. Mary Watts's diary for 2 April 1898 is among the archives at the Watts Gallery, Compton.

CHAPTER III: MISS MAGGIE GUTHRIE AND THE HON. EMILY LAWLESS

1. From *The Poems of Emily Lawless*, ed. with introduction by Padraic Fallon, The Dolmen Press, Dublin, 1965, p. 33.
2. Some idea of how distinguished can be seen in a letter from Major Ross Mangles published in *Country Life*, 1 July 1976, p. 34.
3. James Mangles (1832–84), shortly before his death, became close friends with Alfred Tennyson during his reclusive years at Aldworth. See W. R. Trotter, *The Poet and the Plantsman: Tennyson's Conversations with James Henry Mangles*, West Sussex History, no. 26, September 1983. There is a memorial to Harry Mangles (1833–1908) in the parish church of St Laurence, Seale. Henry Albert Mangles had a brilliant record at Haileybury, winning Classics, Maths, Persian and Sanskrit prizes, and served in India 1853–77.
4. Paper on '101 Years of the Farnham Liberal Association' by Brian Sell, *c.* 1986, Farnham Local Collection, Farnham Museum.
5. *Mrs James Guthrie* by Frederick Leighton, Mellon Collection.
6. H. S. Goodhart Rendel (1887–1959), typed MS of autobiographical notes. In private collection, but there is a copy in the RIBA Library. RIBAD has material on his works, and the National Library of Wales has a Rendel Collection.

7. ibid.

8. ibid.

9. Surrey Record Office, Guildford Muniment Room, ref. 1468/1, January 1897–January 1899. This is the only surviving volume from ten or twelve that he kept.

10. All quotations come from Emily Lawless, *A Garden Diary, September 1899–September 1900*, Methuen, 1901.

11. Stopford A. Brooke, preface to Emily Lawless, *With the Wild Geese*, Isbister & Co., Covent Garden, 1902.

12. The 2nd Lord Cloncurry had been imprisoned in the Tower of London for his treasonable friendship with Lord Edward Fitzgerald and the United Irishmen, and put his subsequent exile to good use. See Mark Bence-Jones, *Burke's Guide to Country Houses, Vol. 1: Ireland*, Burke's Peerage, London 1978, pp. 196–7.

13. Augusta Gregory, *Lady Gregory's Journals, 1916–30*, ed. Lennox Robinson, Putnam, 1946, pp. 218–20.

14. Stopford A. Brooke, preface to *With the Wild Geese*.

15. 'Fontenay 1745' from *The Poems of Emily Lawless*.

16. *Seventy Years Young: Memories of Elizabeth, Countess of Fingall*, told to Pamela Hinkson, Collins, 1937 (reissued Dublin, 1991) p. 175.

17. All quotations are from Emily Lawless's *Garden Diary*.

18. ibid., pp. 104–7.

19. ibid., p. 169.

CHAPTER IV: THE IMPORTANCE OF BEING GERARD, MARK AND ERNEST

1. Barbara Blackburn, typed MS, *Growing Up at Little Thakeham*, p. 22.

2. Frank Birch, of Longbridge, Farnham, worked for Shaw on Upper House, Shamley Green, for Mrs Guthrie/Arbuthnot, Knights Bank in Farnham (subsequently demolished) and many other buildings. See Andrew Saint, *Richard Norman Shaw*, Yale University Press, 1976, with list of works on pp. 403–37. Harold Falkner (1875–1963) was apprenticed to Birch (at Lutyens's suggestion) and worked on Voysey's Lowicks; Falkner saved some of Birch's building records, which are in Farnham Museum.

3. MS memories of Mrs Violet Gordon (copy in author's possession).

4. L. T. Pope, *A Cup for Cricket: Fifty Years of the L'Anson Trophy*, E. W. Langham, Herald Press, Farnham, 1951, p. 74.

5. Further material published in *Fulbrook*, ed. Jane Brown, Libanus Press, Marlborough, 1992, limited edition, from Gordon family papers, in the possession of the Lutyens Trust.

6. See Roderick Gradidge, *Dream Houses*, Constable, 1980, pp. 141–5.

7. *Fulbrook*, p. 41.

8. ibid., p. 42.

9. ibid., p. 60.

10. MS memories of Mrs Violet Gordon.

11. The portrait is in the Watts Gallery at Compton. Michael Chapman MC was killed on 12 April 1918.

12. Letter describing Meldon Park meeting, 23 April 1901, Lutyens, *Letters*, p. 89.

13. Constantia Arnold, *Happy as Kings: The Story of the Fenwicks at Abbotswood 1915–45*, published by Wilton 65, Flat Top House, Bishop Wilton, York, 1994, © Lavinia Orde.

14. ibid., p. 1.

15. ibid., p. 9.

16. ibid., p. 1.

17. ibid., p. 52.

18. ibid., p. 26.

19. Audrey Holland-Hibbert (née Fenwick), 'My Gardening Life', *Hortus*, 16, Winter 1990.

20. See Peter Coats, *Great Gardens of Britain*, Hamlyn edn, 1970, pp. 158 ff.

21. Hilary Richardson, *A Blackburn Family History*, unpublished MS, and *The Book of Little Thakeham (Court)*, diary MS handwritten by Ernest Murray Blackburn.

22. Barbara Blackburn, *Growing Up at Little Thakeham*, p. 22.

23. 9 August 1902, Lutyens MS letters, RIBA library.

24. Barbara Blackburn, *Growing Up at Little Thakeham*, p. 23.

25. ibid.

26. *The Study of Words*, Longmans Green, 1911.

27. 24 July 1904, Lutyens, *Letters*, p. 112.

CHAPTER V: EMILY'S FRIENDS AND RELATIONS

1. Frederick Locker Lampson, *A Character Sketch, including Letters and Bibliographical Notes*, edited by his son-in-law, the Rt Hon. Augustine Birrell, Constable, 1920.

2. The letters (already noted) are in the library of the RIBA in Portland Place, London; they have been indexed by Dr Angela Mace. The published extracts, ed. Clayre Percy and Jane Ridley, are in *The Letters of Edwin Lutyens to His Wife, Lady Emily*, Collins, 1985.

3. Mary Lutyens, *Edwin Lutyens, A Memoir*, pp. 28 ff. and 39.

4. The much-travelled Revd Whitwell Elwin (1816–1900) had been editor of the *Quarterly Review* 1853–60, since when he had lived in his Norfolk isolation conducting a literary correspondence with Frederick Locker, Tennyson, Thackeray, Bulwer Lytton, and Meredith. Many of his letters to Emily Lytton are in *A Blessed Girl*, her story of her early life, subtitled *Memoirs of a Victorian Girlhood Chronicled in an Exchange of Letters 1887–1897*, Rupert Hart-Davis, 1958.

5. See page 25.

6. Emily Lytton, *A Blessed Girl*, p. 304.

7. Lutyens, *Letters*, p. 54.
8. ibid., p. 42.
9. *Fulbrook*, p. 37, 3 February 1897.
10. ibid., p. 39.
11. Lady Emily Lutyens, *Candles in the Sun*, Rupert Hart-Davis, 1957.
12. Lutyens, *Letters*, p. 26.
13. The layout plan for this house and garden is in the Knebworth House archives.
14. *Prisons and Prisoners, Some Personal Experiences by Constance Lytton and Jane Warton Spinster*, Heinemann, 1914, p. 2.
15. ibid.
16. Neville Lytton to Lady Constance Lytton, Knebworth House archives.
17. Pamela Chichele Plowden and her sister Beryl (who married Edgar Lafone) were brought up in India. Pamela came to England under the care of Violet, Duchess of Rutland, and everybody thought that she would marry Winston Churchill – but she didn't, which gave her something of a reputation for flightiness.
18. Letter to Violet Granby, *The Collected Letters of George Meredith*, ed. C. L. Cline, vol. 3, Oxford University Press, 1970, p. 1442.
19. Lady Emily Lutyens to her mother, 28 October 1899, Knebworth House archives.
20. ibid.
21. Priscilla Metcalf, *The Park Town Estate and the Battersea Tangle*, London Topographical Society publication no. 121, 1978.
22. See ibid., pp. 39–41, for Cyril Flower's attitude to business.
23. Lady Battersea, Constance de Rothschild, *Reminiscences*, Macmillan, 1922.
24. Mrs Alfred Berlyn ('Vera'), *Vera in Poppyland*, Jarrold, 1891.
25. Lady Battersea, *Reminiscences*, p. 325. Much of the correspondence is in the Battersea Papers, British Library MS Collection.
26. ibid., pp. 331–2.
27. Letter to Miss Katharine Lewis, 1 September 1898, *The Collected Letters of George Meredith*, no. 1851.
28. Letter to H. T. Baker from the Pleasaunce, 2 August 1898, *Raymond Asquith: Life and Letters*, ed. John Jolliffe, Collins, 1980, pp. 41–2.
29. Illustrated in Stephen Calloway, *Twentieth-Century Decoration*, Weidenfeld & Nicolson, 1988, pp. 78–9.
30. Lady Battersea, *Reminiscences*, p. 390.
31. See Mervyn Miller and A. Stuart Gray, *Hampstead Garden Suburb*, Phillimore, 1992, for the fully documented story of the Barnetts.
32. Membland, with the various buildings of the divided estate, can still be seen; for the emotive description of what it meant to the Barings, see Maurice Baring, *The*

Puppet Show of Memory, 1922, and also Paul Horgan, introduction to *Maurice Baring Restored*, Heinemann, 1970.
33. Daphne Pollen, *I Remember, I Remember*, privately published, 1983, p. 56.
34. ibid.
35. ibid.
36. ibid.
37. Philip Ziegler, *The Sixth Great Power, Barings 1762–1929*, Collins, 1988, p. 274.
38. Mary Lutyens, *Edwin Lutyens, A Memoir*, p. 67.
39. Daphne Pollen, *I Remember, I Remember*, p. 74.
40. Lutyens, *Letters*, p. 135.
41. Mark Bence-Jones, *Burke's Guide to Country Houses, Vol. I: Ireland*, Lambay entry.
42. Emmeline Pethwick-Lawrence, *My Part in a Changing World*, Gollancz, 1938, p. 120.
43. Edward Marsh, *A Number of People*, Heinemann/Hamish Hamilton, 1939, p. 138.
44. Wildman Cattley had taken Lutyens out to dinner at Grocer's Hall on 24 February 1897 to discuss the redecoration; Lutyens did not do this, but he did build the Dutch House, an excursion into the Cape Dutch style.
45. Emmeline Pethwick-Lawrence, *My Part in a Changing World*, p. 128.
46. Sir Arthur Chapman had not been happily married, and after his wife's death he devoted much of his time and money to Emily Lutyens and her children, paying for holidays and presents. The Chapman family are of the opinion that Sir Arthur was deeply in love with Lady Emily.
47. *Letters*, p. 221.
48. The building was never completed for the Theosophists and was taken over by the British Medical Association, completed by C. Wontner Smith.

CHAPTER VI: THE GRACIOUS MISTS FROM MELLS

1. Frances Horner, *Time Remembered*, Heinemann, 1933, p. 195.
2. Christopher Hollis, *Along the Road to Frome*, Harrap, 1958, p. 242.
3. Copyright *History of Mells Park* by Michael McGarvie FSA.
4. Penelope Fitzgerald, *Edward Burne-Jones*, Michael Joseph, 1975, p. 193.
5. ibid.
6. ibid., p. 153.
7. See essay on Norah Lindsay in Jane Brown, *Eminent Gardeners*.
8. *Raymond Asquith: Life and Letters*, p. 70.
9. Betty Askwith, *The Lytteltons*, Chatto & Windus, 1975, p. 159.
10. Quoted in Edith Lyttelton, *Alfred Lyttelton, An Account of His Life*, Longmans, 1917, p. 245.

11. Christopher Hussey, *The Work of Sir Robert Lorimer*, Country Life, 1931, p. 22.

12. Edith Lyttelton, *Alfred Lyttelton*, pp. 324–6.

13. ibid., pp. 236–8.

14. Gertrude Jekyll and Lawrence Weaver, *Gardens for Small Country Houses*, Newnes/Country Life, 1912, p. 237.

15. Quoted in Edith Lyttelton, *Alfred Lyttelton*, p. 245.

16. Frances Horner, *Time Remembered*, p. 195.

17. Letters from Edwin Lutyens to Lady Emily Lutyens, 23 April 1904, *Letters*, p. 110.

18. William Lethaby, quoted by David Watkin in *The Rise of Architectural History*, Architectural Press, paperback edn, 1983, p. 95: 'By 1900 a new religion had been invented – or, at least, a new version of an old religion: the worship of England.'

19. Pamela Maude, 'Portrait of a Perfectionist', *Country Life*, 12 January 1967, pp. 58–9; also Bernard Darwin's *Fifty Years of Country Life*, Country Life, 1947, and John Cornforth, 'Lutyens and *Country Life*: "81 not out"', in catalogue of the Arts Council exhibition, 1981, pp. 25 ff.

20. Pamela Maude, 'Portrait of a Perfectionist'.

21. Michael Holroyd, *Lytton Strachey*, Penguin edn, 1980, p. 744.

22. Pamela Maude, 'Portrait of a Perfectionist'.

23. Christopher Hussey, *Life of Lutyens*, p. 95.

24. *Madame Suggia* by Augustus John is in the National Portrait Gallery.

25. George Allardyce Riddell (1865–1934) published three volumes of his diary in the 1930s: *Intimate Diary of the Peace Conference and After, 1918–23*, *War Diary*, and *More Pages from My Diary 1908–14*, Country Life, 1934.

26. Bernard Darwin, 'Memories of Walton Heath', *Country Life*, 30 May 1957, and Walton Heath Golf Club archives, especially notes on the history of the club.

27. Christopher Hussey, *Life of Lutyens*, p. 136.

28. George Allardyce Riddell, diary, 19 February 1913.

29. Philip Magnus, *King Edward VII*, Penguin, 1967, p. 332.

30. See Edward James, *Swans Reflecting Elephants*, ed. George Melly, Weidenfeld & Nicolson, 1982, pp. 14–15.

31. ibid., pp. 16–17.

CHAPTER VII: THE EDWARDIANS

1. Charles Saumerez Smith, *The Building of Castle Howard*, Faber and Faber, 1990, p. 25.

2. Lutyens, *Letters*, p. 146.

3. 5 August 1908, Lutyens, *Letters*, p. 156.

4. ibid.

5. Margaret Richardson, catalogue of the Arts Council Lutyens Exhibition, 1981, pp. 185–6.

6. ibid.

7. ibid.

8. See Margaret Richardson, *Sketches by Edwin Lutyens*, RIBA Drawings Monographs No. 1, Academy Editions, 1994, pp. 104–5 for the first published list of pupils and assistants.

9. Margot Asquith, quoted in Stephen McKenna, *Reginald McKenna, A Memoir, 1863–1934*, Eyre & Spottiswoode, 1948, p. 47.

10. Lord Beaverbrook, *Politicians and the War*, 1928, quoted in Stephen McKenna, *Reginald McKenna*, p. 2. (Reginald McKenna died in 1943.)

11. Cynthia Asquith, in *Diaries 1915–18*, Hutchinson, 1968, makes frequent references to Reginald McKenna.

12. The connection with Archbishop Wilberforce which came via the Jekylls at Munstead House to Pamela McKenna was one of which Lutyens had hopes. He discussed the remodelling of St John's Smith Square, and he did build the Tufton Street Institute (now Faith House) for the Archbishop.

13. Lutyens, *Letters*, p. 180.

14. E. T. Raymond, *Uncensored Celebrities*, T. Fisher Unwin, 1918, pp. 89–95.

15. Gertrude Jekyll, *Home and Garden*, p. 35.

16. Lutyens, letter to Herbert Baker; Christopher Hussey, *Life of Lutyens*, p. 133.

17. *The Buildings of England: Hampshire*, Penguin, 1979 edn, p. 635.

18. The only known copy of the Hoare catalogue, 'Beautiful Brickwork', is in Basingstoke Public Library Collection.

19. Miranda Seymour, *A Ring of Conspirators: Henry James and His Literary Circle 1895–1915*, Houghton Mifflin, 1989, ch. 1.

20. Allen Andrews, *The Splendid Pauper*, Harrap, 1968, and Anita Leslie, *Mr Frewen of England*, Hutchinson, 1966.

21. *The Buildings of England: Northumberland*, Penguin, 1992 edn, p. 623.

22. Lutyens, *Letters*, p. 155.

23. ibid., p. 158.

24. Osbert Sitwell, *Great Morning*, pp. 19–20.

25. Osbert Sitwell, *Left Hand, Right Hand*, p. 25.

CHAPTER VIII: HUGH PERCY LANE

1. W. B. Yeats, 'The Municipal Gallery Revisited', *The Last Poems*, from *The Yeats Companion*, ed. Ulick O'Connor, Mandarin Paperbacks, 1990.

2. Augusta Gregory, *Hugh Lane's Life and Achievement*, Colin Smythe, Gerrards Cross, 1973, p. 43.

3. Barbara Dawson, *Images and Insights*, catalogue of the Hugh Lane Municipal Gallery of Modern Art, p. 20.

4. Mary Lou Kohfeldt, *Lady Gregory: The Woman Behind the Irish Renaissance*, André Deutsch, 1985, p. 194.

5. Barbara Dawson, *Images and Insights*, p. 23.

6. Thelma Gutsche, *No Ordinary Woman: The Life and*

Times of Florence Phillips, 1863–1940, Howard Timmins, Cape Town, 1966.

7. Gertrude Jekyll and Lawrence Weaver, *Gardens for Small Country Houses*, p. 63.

8. Augusta Gregory, *Hugh Lane's Life*, p. 131.

9. ibid., p. 113.

10. 14 August 1910, Lutyens, *Letters*.

11. Dr Marion Hare, *Rodin's Bust of Eve Fairfax*, Johannesburg Art Gallery, 1994.

12. Augusta Gregory, *Hugh Lane's Life*, p. 112.

13. Thelma Gutsche, *No Ordinary Woman*, p. 260.

14. Baker actually restored it twice, the second time after it had been damaged by fire; for Baker's account of his work in South Africa see his book *Cecil Rhodes as I Knew Him*.

15. Christopher Hussey, *Life of Lutyens*, p. 206.

16. Thelma Gutsche, *No Ordinary Woman*, p. 263.

17. ibid., p. 340.

18. Christopher Hussey, *Life of Lutyens*, p. 210.

19. ibid., p. 216.

20. Augusta Gregory, *Hugh Lane's Life*, p. 130.

21. ibid., p. 87.

22. ibid., p. 90.

23. Miscellaneous papers, Lane Collection, National Library of Ireland, Dublin.

24. Poë's letter to Lane, 23 July 1913, Lane Collection, National Library of Ireland, Dublin.

25. The literature on the saga of the Lane pictures is very complex and lengthy. The clearest factual account is in Barbara Dawson's essay at the beginning of the current catalogue of the Hugh Lane Municipal Gallery of Modern Art, *Images and Insights*. For the documents in the case the most available source is Colin Smythe's Coole Edition of Lady Gregory's *Hugh Lane's Life and Achievement* (Colin Smythe Ltd, Gerrards Cross, 1973), which is a collection of memories, letters and other papers and includes Lane's will, the disputed codicil, and the debates of the 1920s in press and parliaments both sides of the Irish Sea.

26. Miscellaneous papers, Lane Collection.

27. ibid.

28. Lutyens's ballroom at Roehampton House for Arthur Grenfell was completed, but the garden he designed was never made.

29. Miscellaneous papers, Lane Collection. The memorial is illustrated on p. 15 of the Coole Edition of Lady Gregory's *Hugh Lane's Life*.

30. Sir George Farrar's home in England was Chichely Hall in Buckinghamshire, a house of 1723 noted for its marvellous brickwork. Lutyens, ever anxious to set his work beside other work of fine quality, did minor alterations including some lovely classical garden alcoves in gauged brickwork.

31. Thelma Gutsche, *No Ordinary Woman*, p. 340.

CHAPTER IX: NIMROD

1. John Milton, *Paradise Lost*, XII, 24–32.

2. Christopher Hussey, *Life of Lutyens*, p. 198.

3. It was to be of fibrous plaster, the convincing imitation of stone which triumphed at the White City in 1908 (though it had been used as early as 1893 in Chicago).

4. Selina Hastings, *Nancy Mitford*, Hamish Hamilton, 1985, p. 80.

5. Hugh Petter, *Lutyens in Italy*, British School at Rome, 1992, p. 39.

6. 2 July 1915, Lutyens, *Letters*, p. 312.

7. Osbert Sitwell, *Great Morning*, p. 30.

8. James Pope-Hennessey, *Lord Crewe*, Constable, 1955, p. 102.

9. ibid., p. 103.

10. The 2nd Viscount was a talented amateur painter and a friend of Landseer. See Briton Cooper Busch, *Hardinge of Penshurst, A Study in the Old Diplomacy*, Indiana University/Archon Books, 1980.

11. Christopher Hussey, *Life of Lutyens*, p. 373.

12. ibid., p. 375.

13. ibid., p. 374.

14. Charles Holden and Robert Lorimer were subsequently appointed.

15. For notes on the architects employed by the IWGC, see Gavin Stamp, *Silent Cities*, catalogue of an exhibition of the Memorial and Cemetery Architecture of the Great War, RIBA, 1977.

16. Christopher Hussey, *Life of Lutyens*, p. 376.

17. ibid., p. 373.

18. ibid., p. 369.

19. ibid., p. 375.

20. *Siegfried Sassoon Diaries 1915–18*, ed. Rupert Hart-Davis, Faber and Faber, 1983, 4 August 1918, p. 278.

21. Letter to Emily Lutyens, 12 July 1917, *Letters*, p. 349.

22. The eldest of the children of Sylvia and Arthur Llewellyn Davies, adopted by Barrie after their parents' death. See Andrew Birkin, *J. M. Barrie and the Lost Boys*, Constable, 1979.

23. Christopher Hussey, *Life of Lutyens*, p. 393.

24. See ibid., p. 392. Lutyens spent hours of his time and sheets of paper on these calculations but none of the workings were kept. Some drawings, including designs for stone flags (which he wanted in preference to real flags) and the bronze barriers are in the RIBA Drawings Collection.

25. The idea of the silence came from South Africa, where it was observed at the Rand Regiments' Memorial.

26. See Ronald Blythe, *The Age of Illusion*, Oxford University Press, 1983 edn, Ch. 1.

27. Lyn Macdonald, *1914–1918: Voices and Images of the Great War*, Penguin, 1988, pp. 326–9.

28. Letter to Emily Lutyens, 4 August 1919, *Letters*, p. 371.

29. ibid., pp. 371–2.

30. Raymond Asquith was killed in the Guards Division attack on Lesboefs in September 1916. Besides Edward Horner, all the young men who had frequented Mells before the war – Patrick Shaw Stewart, Julian and Billy Grenfell, John Manners, Bron Herbert – were dead.

31. Osbert Sitwell, *Great Morning*, pp. 22–3.

32. Gavin Stamp, Lutyens Exhibition catalogue, pp. 148–55, and Geoff Dyer, *The Missing of the Somme*, Hamish Hamilton, 1994.

CHAPTER X: INTERMEZZO: W.N AND J.M.B.

1. David Rayner Allen, *Peter Pan and Cricket*, Constable, 1988.

2. Andrew Birkin, *J. M. Barrie and the Lost Boys*.

3. Mary Lutyens, *Edwin Lutyens, A Memoir*, p. 81.

4. Christopher Hussey, *Life of Lutyens*, p. 152. Lutyens made only one further attempt at a stage set, for E. V. Lucas's *The Same Star* in Leeds in 1925. The play was not a success.

5. Nicholson's drawing of Rudyard Kipling appeared in the *New Review*, October 1897. See Colin Campbell, *William Nicholson: The Graphic Work*, Barrie & Jenkins, 1992.

6. Letter from William Nicholson to his daughter, Nancy, *c*. September 1912, in Sir William Nicholson Trust Archive.

7. See Cynthia Asquith, *Portrait of Barrie*, James Barrie, 1954, p. 132.

8. Margaret Fitzherbert, *Aubrey Herbert: The Man Who Was Greenmantle*, Oxford University Press, 1985, p. 145.

9. Lord Hardinge of Penshurst, *My Indian Years*, John Murray, 1948, p. 129.

10. Mary Lutyens, *Edwin Lutyens, A Memoir*, p. 147.

11. See Marguerite Steen, *William Nicholson*, Collins, 1943, pp. 127–30.

12. ibid., p. 132.

13. William Nicholson's portrait of Miss Jekyll is in the National Portrait Gallery; her gardening boots are in the Tate Gallery.

14. James Pope-Hennessey, *Queen Mary*, George Allen & Unwin, 1959, p. 533.

15. Christopher Hussey, *Life of Lutyens*, pp. 452–3.

16. The idea of the doll's house was mooted at a dinner party with Princess Marie Louise, E. V. Lucas, Lutyens and Sir Herbert Morgan all present.

17. The designs for Capt. Day are published in Margaret Richardson, *Lutyens and the Sea Captain*, Scolar Press, 1981.

18. Cynthia Asquith, *Portrait of Barrie*, p. 224.

19. Whistler's work for the Ridleys is illustrated in Jenny Spencer-Smith, *Rex Whistler's War 1939–July 1944: Artist into Tank Commander*, catalogue to the Special Exhibition at the National Army Museum, London, 1994. See also *Laurence Whistler: The Laughter and the Urn*, Weidenfeld & Nicolson, 1985.

CHAPTER XI: LADY SACKVILLE

1. Lady Sackville's diary, 4 November 1917. All entries from Lady Sackville's diaries by kind permission of Nigel Nicolson.

2. V. Sackville-West, *Pepita* (the story of her mother's early life), Hogarth Press, 1937.

3. Lady Sackville, diary entry.

4. The layout plan for the Rudds' enormous house and garden near East Grinstead is in folder 127 of the Reef Point Collection of Gertrude Jekyll's Drawings at the University of California at Berkeley. Only small lodges and a farm were built.

5. Lutyens did help them with the garden, see Jane Brown, *Vita's Other World*, Viking, 1985, p. 223.

6. Letter from Harold Nicolson to V. Sackville West, *Letters*, ed. Nigel Nicolson, Weidenfeld & Nicolson, 1992, p. 59.

7. Lady Sackville, diary entry.

8. See Jane Brown, *Vita's Other World*, for her gardening at this time.

9. V. Sackville-West, *Pepita*, pp. 255–6.

10. Nigel Nicolson, Sissinghurst papers.

11. Lady Sackville, diary entry.

12. ibid.

13. Letter fragment, Nigel Nicolson. Emily did not allow him alcohol at home.

14. Lady Sackville, diary entry.

15. ibid.

16. ibid., 22 February 1922.

17. V. Sackville-West, *The Heir*, Hogarth Press, 1922.

18. Lady Sackville, diary entry, 15 April 1922.

19. See Susan Mary Alsop, *Lady Sackville*, Weidenfeld & Nicolson, 1978, p. 217, for Honey Harris's story that she was sent out to buy £30 worth of artificial flowers to stick into the garden when Vita came to lunch for the first time.

20. Lady Sackville, diary entry.

21. Enid Bagnold, *Autobiography*, Century, 1985, p. 151.

22. Lady Sackville, diary entry.

23. ibid., 18 June 1926.

24. She died at White Lodge in January 1936. Lutyens was remorseful to Vita, writing that they did not understand her nor appreciate her talents. White Lodge, her last, and only Lutyens house, was left to her grandson Nigel Nicolson but he never lived in it, and it was soon sold. In 1994 he visited it again for the first time since the day his grandmother's will was read in 1936; it now has Brighton Marina at the end of the garden and is almost unrecognizable as a Lutyens house.

CHAPTER XII: MORE THE DEAD THAN THE LIVING

1. E. V. Lucas rhyme from Christopher Hussey, *Life of Lutyens*, p. 441.
2. ibid. He became a Garrick member in 1916.
3. Daphne Pollen, *I Remember, I Remember*.
4. ibid., p. 158.
5. Cecil Baring, Lord Revelstoke, died on 26 January 1934 and is buried on Lambay. Lutyens's very last job for the family was for Daphne and Arthur Pollen, modest additions at the Old House, Pyrford, Surrey.
6. Lady Sackville, diary entry, 3 April 1926.
7. Paul Freyberg, *Bernard Freyberg VC, Soldier of Two Nations*, Hodder & Stoughton, 1991.
8. Stephen McKenna, *Reginald McKenna*, p. 325.
9. Edwin Green, *Building for Bankers, Sir Edwin Lutyens and the Midland Bank 1921–39*, Midland Bank, 1980.
10. ibid.
11. ibid.
12. ibid.
13. *Michael*, privately printed (in the care of the Nonesuch Press) memoir of Michael McKenna, pp. 169–70.
14. Robert Gathorne-Hardy, ed., *Ottoline, The Early Memoirs of Lady Ottoline Morrell*, Faber and Faber, 1963, p. 178.
15. In July 1933; letters 1.207, RIBA Library.
16. Lutyens exhibition catalogue, p. 157.
17. Obituary, 1976, Father Vincent Turner on Martin D'Arcy, Campion Hall Archives.
18. Christopher Hollis, *Along the Road to Frome*, p. 134.
19. Martin D'Arcy, *Notes on the Building of Campion Hall*, MS in Campion Hall Library.
20. Evelyn Waugh, *Life of the Right Reverend Ronald Knox*, Chapman & Hall, 1959.
21. E. Waugh, *Edmund Campion: Jesuit and Martyr*, Longmans, 1935, reprinted Oxford University Press, 1980.
22. ibid., Preface.
23. Walker, born 18 October 1877 of a non-Catholic Birmingham family, was received into the church at twenty-one, and joined the Jesuits the following year. He was a military chaplain through the war. He arrived at Campion Hall in 1919, and stayed for forty years. D'Arcy wrote of his 'Cromwellian kind of face and gruff manner' (*Notes*).
24. ibid.
25. Walker to Lutyens, Campion Hall Archives.
26. ibid.

CHAPTER XIII: THE GREATEST CLIENTS OF ALL

1. Cecil Beaton, *The Years Between, Diaries 1939–44*, Weidenfeld & Nicolson, 1965, p. 246.

2. Andrew Roberts, *The Holy Fox*, Papermac, 1992, p. 42.
3. Robert Bernays, *'Naked Fakir'*, Gollancz, 1931, p. 280.
4. It has also been told in Robert Grant Irving's *Indian Summer: The Making of New Delhi*, Yale University Press, 1981.
5. H. Y. Sharada Prasad, *Rashtrapati Bhavan, The Story of the President's House*, Publications Division of the Ministry of Information in association with the National Institute of Design for Rashtrapati Bhavan, New Delhi, 1992, p. 41.
6. ibid., p. 101.
7. Mary Lutyens, *Edwin Lutyens, A Memoir*, pp. 93–7.
8. ibid., p. 240.
9. Michael Trinick, Castle Drogo guide, National Trust, 1978, p. 6.
10. Peter Inskip, 'The Compromise of Castle Drogo', in *Architectural Review*, April 1979, p. 233.
11. Walker Letterbooks at Castle Drogo as: I, 10 May 1912 to 24 February 1913; II, 1 March 1913–19 December 1913; III, 22 December 1913–21 October 1914; IV, 24 October 1914–28 December 1915; V, 28 December 1915–20 March 1919; VI, 22 March 1919–10 August 1921; VII, 10 August 1921–20 August 1924; VIII 30 August 1924–10 September 1929.
12. ibid.
13. Hugh Meller, Castle Drogo guide, National Trust, 1994, p. 54.
14. Sally Festing, *Gertrude Jekyll*, p. 263.
15. ibid., p. 262.
16. C. Hussey, *Life of Lutyens*, p. 440.
17. Essay on Norah Lindsay in Jane Brown, *Eminent Gardeners*.
18. Professor J. S. Roskell, monograph on William Catesby, 1959, quoted by Robert Catesby in a talk for the Friends' Patronal Festival, 1 October 1994, St Leodegarius's church, Ashby St Ledgers.
19. Michael Kennedy, *Portrait of Walton*, Oxford University Press, 1990, p. 78.
20. ibid., p. 66.
21. ibid., p. 102.
22. ibid., p. 106.
23. ibid., p. 110.
24. Ralph Vaughan Williams, 'What We Have Learned from Elgar', *National Music and Other Essays*, Oxford University Press, 1987, p. 251.

CHAPTER XIV: THE COMMON LEGACY

1. John Cornforth, 'Lutyens and *Country Life*: "81 not out"', p. 31.
2. Mrs Ursula Weaver in conversation with the author.

Select Bibliography

Abdy, Jane, and Gere, Charlotte, *The Souls, An Élite in English Society 1885–1930*, Sidgwick & Jackson, 1984.

Alsop, Susan Mary, *Lady Sackville, A Biography*, Weidenfeld & Nicolson, 1978.

Amery, Colin, and Richardson, Margaret (eds.), catalogue of the Lutyens Exhibition, Arts Council of Great Britain, 1981.

Asquith, Cynthia, *Portrait of Barrie*, James Barrie, 1954.

Battersea, Lady (Constance), *Reminiscences*, Macmillan, 1922.

Brown, Jane, *Gardens of a Golden Afternoon*, Allen Lane, 1982.

Davey, John (ed.), *Nature and Tradition: Arts & Crafts Architecture in and around Guildford*, Guildford Borough Council, Guildford, 1993.

Dunbar, Janet, *J. M. Barrie, The Man Behind the Image*, Collins, 1970.

Dyer, Geoff, *The Missing of the Somme*, Hamish Hamilton, 1994.

Festing, Sally, *Gertrude Jekyll, A Biography*, Viking, 1991.

Freyberg, Paul, *Bernard Freyberg VC, Soldier of Two Nations*, Hodder & Stoughton, 1991.

Gradidge, Roderick, *The Surrey Style*, Surrey Historic Buildings Trust, Kingston upon Thames, 1991.

Gregory, Lady (Augusta), *Hugh Lane's Life and Achievement*, Coole Edition, Colin Smythe Ltd, Gerrards Cross, 1973.

Horner, Lady (Frances), *Time Remembered*, Heinemann, 1933.

Hussey, Christopher, *Life of Lutyens*, Country Life, 1950.

Irving, Robert Grant, *Indian Summer, The Making of New Delhi*, Yale University Press, New Haven and London, 1981.

Jekyll, Francis, *Gertrude Jekyll, A Memoir*, Jonathan Cape, 1934.

Jolliffe, John (ed.), *Raymond Asquith, Life and Letters*, Century, 1987.

Longworth, Philip, *The Unending Vigil, A History of the Commonwealth War Graves Commission, 1917–67*, Constable, 1968.

Lutyens, Mary, *Edwin Lutyens, A Memoir*, Murray, 1980.

Mackail, Denis, *The Story of J. M. B.*, Peter Davies, 1941.

Mackenzie, Jeanne, *The Children of the Souls, A Tragedy of the First World War*, Chatto & Windus, 1986.

Percy, Clayre, and Ridley, Jane (eds.), *The Letters of Edwin Lutyens to his wife, Lady Emily*, Collins, 1985.

Richardson, Margaret, *Lutyens and the Sea Captain*, Scolar Press, 1981.

Richardson, Margaret, *Sketches by Edwin Lutyens*, RIBA Drawings Monographs, No. 1, Academy Editions, 1994.

Sackville-West, Vita, *Pepita*, Hogarth Press, 1937; Virago, 1986.

Steen, Marguerite, *William Nicholson*, Collins, 1943.

Weaver, Lawrence, *Houses and Gardens by E. L. Lutyens*, Country Life, 1913; Antique Collectors' Club, Woodbridge, 1981.

Index

Note: numbers in *italic* refer to illustrations.

St Paul's Cathedral, 159, 163, 207, 241
Sassoon, Siegfried, 170, 227, 245
Scott, Sir John Murray, 44, 190, 191, 205
Shakespeare Ball, 140, *141*
Shakespeare's England, 140–41, *142*
Shaw, Richard Norman, 1, 6, 7, 8, 10, 48, 73, 86, 133
Shaw-Stewart, Patrick, xi, 215
Sitwell, Sir George, and family (Renishaw), 128, 143–4, 245
Sitwell, Osbert (quoted), xii, 143, 144, 175–6, 246
Smith, Mrs Eustace (Whalton Manor), 128, 143
Smith, F. E. (Lord Birkenhead), 123, 190
Smith, F. Hatchard (architect), 78, 79, 80, 81
Solomon, J. M. (architect), 151, 154, 158, 187
Spencer, Lady Sarah, 58, 62
Stevenson, J. J. (architect), 28, 38
Strachey, Julia Charlotte *see* Chance, William *and* Julia
Strachey, Lytton, 29, 116
Straker family (Angerton Hall), 128, 143
Streatfeild, Gerard *and* Ida (*née* Combe): at Fulbrook, 37, 63–71, 87, 115, 137
Streatfeild, Violet (later Gordon): 63, 65, 70–71, 144
Studio, The (ed. Charles Holme), 55, 137
Suggia, Madame, *116*, 119
Sutherland, Millie, Duchess of, *141*, 206

Temple Dinsley, Herts. (Fenwick), 127, *128*, 143
Tennant, H. J. (Great Maytham), 113, 127
Theosophical Society, 105, 106

Theosophy and clients, 105–6, 211, 231
Thomas, A. J. (in Lutyens's office): and Castle Drogo, 235 and Lady Sackville, 197, 202, 208

Vaughan Williams, Ralph: (quoted), 246 family, 21
Viceroy's House, New Delhi (Rashtrapati Bhavan), x, 135, 162, 163–5, 203–4, 228–31, *229*
Vickers-Armstrong, 213, 241
Victoria, Queen, 7, 10, 43, 86, *87*

Walker, John (Drewe's agent), 235–8, *236*
Walker, Revd Fr. Leslie, 224–5
Wallace, Euan (*m.* Barbara Lutyens, q.v.), 189, 201, 202
Wallace, Sir Richard's Collection, 44, 190, 204, 205–6
Walton Heath Golf Club, 120–23, 126–7
WAR MEMORIALS AND CEMETERIES: 165–76, 252–60
   at Abinger, 173
   all over England, etc., 174–5
   Cenotaph, 170–72, *170*, *171*, 184, 202–3
   Étaples Cemetery, *169*
   Irish National Memorial, 214
   at Mells, 172–3
   Memorial to the Missing, 176, 187
   Stone of Remembrance, 168–9
   Temporary War Shrine, 169–70
Ware, Sir Fabian, 165–70, *165*, 241
Waring of Waring & Gillow, 45, 169–70
Warren Lodge, Thursley (Webb), *23*, 86

Washington, British Embassy at, 207, 208, 231, 260
Waterhouse family, 1, 21, 37
Watts, G. F. *and* Mary, 43, 71
Waugh, Evelyn, 222, *226*
   Edmund Campion, 224
   Life of Ronald Knox, 223
Weaver, Lawrence (*Houses and Gardens by E. L. Lutyens*), xi, 76, 130, 136, 150, 192
Webb, Sir Aston, 81, 88, 118, 161
Webb, Barbara (*née* Lyall), 9–24, *10*, *24*, 29, 35, 46, 47, 48, 59, 65, 69, 86, 109
Webb, Philip, x, 1, 37, 53, 55, 94, 97, 136
Webb, Robert and family (Milford House), 10, 12, 13, 14, 15, 17, 32, 37, 39
Westminster, Duke of, 26, 31, 43, 86
Whistler, Laurence, 225
Whistler, Rex, 189
Wimborne, Lord *and* Lady (Alice), 126, 243–6, *col. pl. 22*
   Alice and William Walton, 245–6
Witley Park, Surrey (Whitaker Wright), *19*
Wittersham, Kent, 113, 126
Womens' Social and Political Union (WSPU): and Constance Lytton, 104–5 and Walton Heath, 123
Wortley, Edward Stuart (*m.* Violet Guthrie), 7, 9, *49*, 56
Wren, Christopher, 1, 14, 15, 135, 159, 163, 202, 207, 217, 241

Yeats, Jack B., 148, 150
Yeats, John B., 147, 148
Yeats, W. B., (quoted), 145, 147, 155–6